C++

Study Guide

By

Rogers Cadenhead

Jesse Liberty

BPB PUBLICATIONS

FIRST INDIAN EDITION 2017

ISBN : 978-81-8333-532-4

Reprinted in India under arrangement with Pearson Education Inc., USA
Authorized reprint from the English language edition, entitled SAMS TEACH YOURSELF C++ IN 24 HOURS , SIXTH Edition, by Rogers Cadenhead and Jesse Liberty , Published by Pearson Eduction, Inc., publishing as SAMS Publishing, Copyright © 2016 Pearson Education, Inc.

Distributors:

BPB PUBLICATIONS
20, Ansari Road, Darya
Ganj New Delhi-110002
Ph: 23254990/23254991

DECCAN AGENCIES
4-3-329, Bank Street,
Hyderabad-500195
Ph: 24756967/24756400

MICRO MEDIA
Shop No. 5, Mahendra Chambers,
150 DN Rd. Next to Capital Cinema,
V.T. (C.S.T.) Station, MUMBAI-400 001
Ph: 22078296/22078297

BPB BOOK CENTRE
376 Old Lajpat Rai Market,
Delhi-110006
Ph: 23861747

COMPUTER BOOK CENTRE
12, Shrungar Shopping Centre,
M.G.Road, BENGALURU–560001
Ph: 25587923/25584641

Published by Manish Jain for BPB Publications, 20, Ansari Road, Darya Ganj, New Delhi-110002 and
Printed at Akash Press, New Delhi

Contents at a Glance

Introduction 1

Part I: Beginning C++

HOUR 1 Writing Your First Program 5
2 Organizing the Parts of a Program 13
3 Creating Variables and Constants 27
4 Using Expressions, Statements, and Operators 43
5 Calling Functions 61
6 Controlling the Flow of a Program 79
7 Storing Information in Arrays and Strings 95

Part II: Classes

HOUR 8 Creating Basic Classes 109
9 Moving into Advanced Classes 123

Part III: Memory Management

HOUR 10 Creating Pointers 135
11 Developing Advanced Pointers 155
12 Creating References 167
13 Developing Advanced References and Pointers 183

Part IV: Advanced C++

HOUR 14 Calling Advanced Functions 199
15 Using Operator Overloading 213

Part V: Inheritance and Polymorphism

HOUR 16 Extending Classes with Inheritance 231
17 Using Polymorphism and Derived Classes 251
18 Making Use of Advanced Polymorphism 267

Part VI: Special Topics

HOUR 19 Storing Information in Linked Lists 287
20 Using Special Classes, Functions, and Pointers 301
21 Using New Features of C++14 331
22 Employing Object-Oriented Analysis and Design 343
23 Creating Templates 373
24 Dealing with Exceptions and Error Handling 391

Part VII: Appendixes

A Binary and Hexadecimal 411
B Glossary 419
C This Book's Website 427
D Using the MinGW C++ Compiler on Windows 429

Index 439

Table of Contents

Introduction 1

Part I: Beginning C++

HOUR 1: Writing Your First Program 5

- Using C++ 5
- Compiling and Linking the Source Code 6
- Creating Your First Program 7

HOUR 2: Organizing the Parts of a Program 13

- Reasons to Use C++ 13
- The Parts of a Program 17
- Comments 19
- Functions 20

HOUR 3: Creating Variables and Constants 27

- What Is a Variable? 27
- Defining a Variable 32
- Assigning Values to Variables 33
- Using Type Definitions 34
- Constants 36
- Auto-Typed Variables 38

HOUR 4: Using Expressions, Statements, and Operators 43

- Statements 43
- Expressions 44
- Operators 45
- `If-Else` Conditional Statements 52
- Logical Operators 56
- Tricky Expression Values 58

HOUR 5: **Calling Functions** 61

What Is a Function? 61
Declaring and Defining Functions 61
Using Variables with Functions 64
Function Parameters 67
Returning Values from Functions 68
Default Function Parameters 70
Overloading Functions 72
Auto-Typed Return Values 73

HOUR 6: **Controlling the Flow of a Program** 79

Looping 79
`while` Loops 79
`do-while` Loops 83
`for` Loops 84
`switch` Statements 89

HOUR 7: **Storing Information in Arrays and Strings** 95

What Is an Array? 95
Writing Past the End of Arrays 97
Initializing Arrays 98
Multidimensional Arrays 99
Character Arrays 102
Copying Strings 104
Reading Arrays with Foreach Loops 105

Part II: Classes

HOUR 8: **Creating Basic Classes** 109

What Is a Type? 109
Creating New Types 110
Classes and Members 110
Accessing Class Members 112
Private Versus Public Access 112
Implementing Member Functions 114
Creating and Deleting Objects 116

HOUR 9: Moving into Advanced Classes 123
`const` Member Functions 123
Interface Versus Implementation 124
Organizing Class Declarations and Function Definitions 124
Inline Implementation 124
Classes with Other Classes as Member Data 127

Part III: Memory Management

HOUR 10: Creating Pointers 135
Understanding Pointers and Their Usage 135
The Stack and the Heap 145
Null Pointer Constant 150

HOUR 11: Developing Advanced Pointers 155
Creating Objects on the Heap 155
Deleting Objects 155
Accessing Data Members Using Pointers 157
Member Data on the Heap 158
The `this` Pointer 160
Stray or Dangling Pointers 161
`const` Pointers 162
`const` Pointers and `const` Member Functions 163

HOUR 12: Creating References 167
What is a Reference? 167
Creating a Reference 167
Using the Address of Operator on References 169
What Can Be Referenced? 171
Null Pointers and Null References 172
Passing Function Arguments by Reference 172
Understanding Function Headers and Prototypes 177
Returning Multiple Values 177

HOUR 13: Developing Advanced References and Pointers 183
Passing by Reference for Efficiency 183
Passing a `const` Pointer 186

References as an Alternative to Pointers 189
When to Use References and When to Use Pointers 191
References to Objects Not in Scope 191
Returning a Reference to an Object on the Heap 192
Pointer, Pointer, Who Has the Pointer? 195

Part IV: Advanced C++

HOUR 14: Calling Advanced Functions **199**
Overloaded Member Functions 199
Using Default Values 201
Initializing Objects 203
The Copy Constructor 204
Compile-Time Constant Expressions 208

HOUR 15: Using Operator Overloading **213**
Operator Overloading 213
Conversion Operators 224

Part V: Inheritance and Polymorphism

HOUR 16: Extending Classes with Inheritance **231**
What Is Inheritance? 231
Private Versus Protected 234
Constructors and Destructors 236
Passing Arguments to Base Constructors 239
Overriding Functions 244

HOUR 17: Using Polymorphism and Derived Classes **251**
Polymorphism Implemented with Virtual Member Functions 251
How Virtual Member Functions Work 256

HOUR 18: Making Use of Advanced Polymorphism **267**
Problems with Single Inheritance 267
Abstract Data Types 271

Part VI: Special Topics

HOUR 19: Storing Information in Linked Lists 287

Linked Lists and Other Structures 287

Linked List Case Study 289

Linked Lists as Objects 298

HOUR 20: Using Special Classes, Functions, and Pointers 301

Static Member Data 301

Static Member Functions 303

Containment of Classes 305

Friend Classes and Functions 312

HOUR 21: Using New Features of C++14 331

The Newest Version of C++ 331

Using `auto` in Function Return Types 332

Improved Numeric Literals 334

The `constexpr` Keyword 335

Lambda Expressions 338

HOUR 22: Employing Object-Oriented Analysis and Design 343

The Development Cycle 343

Simulating an Alarm System 344

PostMaster: A Case Study 350

HOUR 23: Creating Templates 373

What Are Templates? 373

Instances of the Template 374

Template Definition 374

Using Template Items 381

HOUR 24: Dealing with Exceptions and Error Handling 391

Bugs, Errors, Mistakes, and Code Rot 391

Handling the Unexpected 392

Exceptions 393

Using `try` and `catch` Blocks 397

Writing Professional-Quality Code 403

Part VII: Appendixes

APPENDIX A: Binary and Hexadecimal 411

Other Bases 412

Around the Bases 412

Hexadecimal 416

APPENDIX B: Glossary 419

APPENDIX C: This Book's Website 427

APPENDIX D: Using the MinGW C++ Compiler on Windows 429

Downloading MinGW-w64 429

Setting the Path Environment Variable 431

Testing Your Installation 433

Index 439

About the Authors

Rogers Cadenhead is a writer, computer programmer, and web developer who has written more than 25 books on Internet-related topics, including *Sams Teach Yourself Java in 21 Days* and *Absolute Beginner's Guide to Minecraft Mods Programming*. He publishes the Drudge Retort and other websites that receive more than 22 million visits a year. This book's official website is at http://cplusplus.cadenhead.org.

Jesse Liberty is the author of numerous books on software development, including best-selling titles on C++ and .NET. He is the president of Liberty Associates, Inc. (www.libertyassociates.com), where he provides custom programming, consulting, and training.

We Want to Hear from You!

As the reader of this book, *you* are our most important critic and commentator. We value your opinion and want to know what we're doing right, what we could do better, what areas you'd like to see us publish in, and any other words of wisdom you're willing to pass our way.

We welcome your comments. You can email or write to let us know what you did or didn't like about this book—as well as what we can do to make our books better.

Please note that we cannot help you with technical problems related to the topic of this book.

When you write, please be sure to include this book's title and author as well as your name and email address. We will carefully review your comments and share them with the author and editors who worked on the book.

Email: sales@bpbonline.com

Reader Services

Visit our website and register this book at **informit.com/register** for convenient access to any updates, downloads, or errata that might be available for this book.

Congratulations! By reading this sentence, you are already 20 seconds closer to learning C++, one of the most important programming languages in the world.

If you continue for another 23 hours, 59 minutes, and 40 seconds, you will master the fundamentals of the C++ programming language. Twenty-four one-hour lessons cover important features such as managing I/O, creating loops and arrays, using object-oriented programming with templates, and creating C++ programs.

All of this has been organized into well-structured, easy-to-follow lessons. There are working projects that you create—complete with output and an analysis of the code—to illustrate the topics of the hour. Syntax examples are clearly marked for handy reference.

To help you become more proficient, each hour ends with a set of common questions and answers.

Who Should Read This Book?

You don't need any previous experience in programming to learn C++ with this book. It starts with the basics and teaches you both the language and the concepts involved with programming C++. Whether you are just beginning or already have some experience programming, you will find that this book makes learning C++ fast and easy.

Should I Learn C First?

No, you don't need to learn C first. C++ is a much more powerful and versatile language that was created by Bjarne Stroustrup as a successor to C. Learning C first can lead you into some programming habits that are more error-prone than what you'll do in C++. This book does not assume that readers are familiar with C.

Why Should I Learn C++?

You could be learning a lot of other languages, but C++ is valuable to learn because it has stood the test of time and continues to be a popular choice for modern programming.

Despite being created in 1979, C++ is still being used for professional software today because of the power and flexibility of the language. There's even a new version of the language, called C++14, that makes it even more useful.

Because other languages such as Java were inspired by C++, learning the language can provide you insight into them, as well. Mastering C++ gives you portable skills that you can use on just about any platform on the market today, from desktop computers to Linux servers, mobile devices, videogame consoles, and mainframes.

What If I Don't Want This Book?

I'm sorry you feel that way, but these things happen sometimes. Please reshelve this book with the front cover facing outward on an endcap with access to a lot of the store's foot traffic.

Conventions Used in This Book

This book contains special elements as described here.

NOTE

These boxes provide additional information to the material you just read.

CAUTION

These boxes focus your attention on problems or side effects that can occur in specific situations.

TIP

These boxes give you tips and highlight information that can make your C++ programming more efficient and effective.

When you see this symbol, you know that what you see next will show the output from a code listing/example.

This book uses various typefaces:

- To help you distinguish C++ code from regular English, actual C++ code is typeset in a special `monospace` font.
- Placeholders—words or characters temporarily used to represent the real words or characters you would type in code—are typeset in *`italic monospace`*.
- New or important terms are typeset in *italic*.
- In the listings in this book, each real code line is numbered. If you see an unnumbered line in a listing, you'll know that the unnumbered line is really a continuation of the preceding numbered code line (some code lines are too long for the width of the book). In this case, you should type the two lines as one; do not divide them.

HOUR 1

Writing Your First Program

What You'll Learn in This Hour:

- How and why C++ was invented
- How to find a C++ compiler
- How to create and compile your first program
- How to link and run the program

Using C++

In 1979, a Danish computer scientist at Bell Labs in the United States began work on an enhancement to the C programming language. Bjarne Stroustrop explained on his personal website that he wanted a language "in which I could write programs that were both efficient and elegant."

A lot of other people wanted that too.

Stroustrop's creation, which he dubbed C++, has held a spot among the world's top programming languages for decades. Many programming trends have come and gone over the years, but this language remains a contemporary and useful choice for software development on desktop computers, servers, embedded devices like phones, and many other computing environments.

C++ is a portable language that works equally well on Microsoft Windows, Apple Mac OS, Linux, and UNIX systems. The best way to learn the language is to write programs without regard to the operating system the program runs on.

Sams Teach Yourself C++ *in 24 Hours* offers a hands-on introduction to the language that makes absolutely no assumptions about your operating system. The book can achieve this because it covers standard C++ (also called ANSI/ISO C++), the internationally agreed-upon version of the language, which is portable to any platform and development environment.

The code presented throughout the book is standard ANSI/ISO C++ and should work with any development environment for C++ that's up-to-date.

New features that are introduced in C++14, the language's current version, also are covered. Popular C++ development environments support this version, which has 14 as part of its name because it was released in 2014.

C++ programs are developed by a set of tools that work together called the *compiler* and *linker*.

A compiler turns C++ programs into a form that can be run. The compiler translates a program from a human-readable form called *source code* into a machine-runnable form called *machine code*. The compiler produces an object file. From the object file, a *linker* builds an executable file that can be run.

There are several popular environments for C++ programming that you might have used before or know how to obtain. Some of these are GCC (the GNU Compiler Collection), Microsoft Visual Studio, NetBeans, and Embarcadero C++ Builder.

If you have an up-to-date C++ compiler on your system and know the basics of how to use it, you will have no trouble completing the programming projects in this book.

If you don't have a C++ compiler, don't know how to use a compiler, or don't know how to find one, relax. You can learn how to download and install an excellent free compiler, GCC, in Appendix D, "Using the MinGW C++ Compiler on Windows." Do that now if you need a compiler before you proceed in this book.

Microsoft Visual Studio also supports C++ programming, and a free version called Visual Studio Community is available from the website www.visualstudio.com. Some guidance is offered in this book for people learning C++ with Visual Studio.

Compiling and Linking the Source Code

Before you create your first C++ program later this hour, it's worthwhile to understand the process.

C++ programs begin as source code, which is just text typed into an editor such as Windows WordPad, Gedit, Emacs, or Vi. Although Microsoft Word and other word processors can save files as plain text, you should use a simpler editor for programming because you don't need all the formatting and presentation capabilities of a word processor. Source code consists of plain text with no special formatting.

NOTE

There's a free text editor for Windows called Notepad++ that provides excellent support for C++ programming. It includes features you'll come to appreciate as you get experience creating your own programs, such as code highlighting, which displays different elements of the language in different colors. You can download it from https://notepad-plus-plus.org.

The source code files you create for C++ can be given filenames ending with the extensions `.cpp`, `.cxx`, `.cp`, or `.c`. This book names all source code files with the `.cpp` extension, the most common choice for C++ programmers and the default for some compilers. Most C++ compilers don't care about the extension given to source code, but using `.cpp` consistently helps you identify source code files.

Source code is the human-readable form of a C++ program. It can't be run until it is compiled and linked.

After your source code is compiled, an object file is produced. This file is turned into an executable program by a linker.

C++ programs are created by linking together one or more object files with one or more libraries. A *library* is a collection of linkable files that provide useful functions and classes that you can rely on in your programs. A *function* is a block of code that performs a task, such as multiplying two numbers or displaying text. A *class* is the definition of a new type of data and related functions.

Here are the steps to create a C++ program:

1. Create a source code file with a text editor.
2. Use a compiler to convert the source code into an object file.
3. Use a linker to link the object file and any necessary libraries to produce an executable program.
4. Type the name of the executable to run it.

The GCC compiler can handle compiling and linking in a single step.

Creating Your First Program

Now that you've been introduced to the process, it's time to create your first C++ program and give the compiler a test drive.

Launch the text editor you're using to create programs and open a new file. The first program that you create will display text on the screen.

Type the text of Listing 1.1 into the editor. Ignore the numbers along the left side of the listing and the colons that follow them—these are there simply for reference purposes in this book.

As you type, make sure to enter the punctuation on each line properly, such as the :: and << characters on line 5.

When you've finished, save the file as `Motto.cpp`.

LISTING 1.1 The Full Text of `Motto.cpp`.

```
1: #include <iostream>
2:
3: int main()
4: {
5:     std::cout << "Solidum petit in profundis!\n";
6:     return 0;
7: }
```

The point of this project is to become familiar with the steps of creating a C++ program. If you are confused by what each line is doing, don't panic—you'll begin to discover what's going on here during Hour 2, "Organizing the Parts of a Program."

After you save the file, it needs to be compiled and linked. If you're using GCC, the following command accomplishes both tasks:

```
g++ Motto.cpp -o Motto.exe
```

This command tells the G++ compiler to compile the file named `Motto.cpp` and link it into an executable program named `Motto.exe`. If it compiles successfully, no message is displayed. The compiler says something only if there's a problem, displaying an error message and the line (or lines) where the error appeared.

If you get a compiler error, recheck the program line by line. Make sure that all the punctuation is included, particularly the semicolons at the end of lines 5 and 6.

After fixing any potential problems, try the compiler again. If you continue to experience problems and can't find the cause, you can download a copy of this program from the book's website at http://cplusplus.cadenhead.org. Go to the Hour 1 page.

When the program has been compiled properly, you can run `Motto.exe` like any other program on your computer: Type its name, `Motto.exe`, as a command and press Enter.

The Motto program displays the following output:

```
Solidum petit in profundis!
```

This is the motto of Aarhus University, a public school with 38,000 students in Aarhus, Denmark, and the kingdom's second-largest university. The motto is Latin for "Seek a firm footing in the depths."

Aarhus alumni include Danish Queen Margrethe II, Nobel laureate chemist Jens Christian Skou, Crown Prince Fredrik, and some guy named Bjarne Stroustrop.

Summary

Congratulations! You can now call yourself a C++ programmer, though if you quit at this point no one will call you an ambitious one.

The C++ language has been a popular choice for software development for more than three decades. The language has its idiosyncrasies, but when you become comfortable with how programs are structured, it is easy to build on your knowledge by creating more sophisticated programs.

Over the next few hours, you learn the basic building blocks of C++, creating several programs each hour that demonstrate new facets of the language and programming techniques.

Solidum petit in profundis!

Q&A

Q. What is the difference between a text editor and a word processor?

A. A text editor produces files with plain text in them—just letters, numbers, spaces, and punctuation. There are no formatting commands for things such as bold or italic text, justified lines, special margins, and so forth. You don't need any of that formatting in C++ source code, and using a word processor can save things in the file that the compiler won't understand. If you have trouble getting the Motto program to compile and you're using a word processor, try a simpler editor such as Notepad (or Notepad++) on Windows to see whether that solves the problem.

Q. My compiler has a built-in editor. Is that the right thing to use?

A. It sounds like you're using an integrated development environment (IDE), a graphical tool that speeds the process of writing, debugging, and testing programs. Sophisticated compilers such as Microsoft Visual Studio include a full IDE, enabling the programmer to access help files, edit, and compile the code in place, and also to resolve compile and link errors without ever leaving the environment. These offer a much better way to write C++ programs, but only if you know how to use the IDE already. Trying to learn C++ as you learn the ins and outs of an IDE at the same time is difficult. That's one reason this book recommends GCC, which is simple, powerful, and free.

Q. Can I ignore warning messages from my compiler?

A. Absolutely not. C++ uses the compiler to warn when you're doing something as a programmer that you might not intend. The best approach is to heed those warnings and do what is required to make them go away. Getting an error means that the compiler figure out how to convert what you wrote into machine language. A warning means can convert it but maybe not in the way you expected.

Q. Do you only answer questions related to C++?

A. Nope. Ask anything.

Q. Groovy. Why doesn't anyone sell grape-flavored ice cream?

A. Unlike other fruit flavors incorporated into ice cream, grapes get almost all their flavor from their skins rather than the interior of the fruit. Without the skins, they just taste sweet in an entirely non-distinct and generic way, so you wouldn't know you were eating grape ice cream unless somebody told you.

When the skins are included to get around this problem, ice cream makers say that the resulting texture of the finished product freaks people out. So grape ice cream is extremely rare and a bit gross even when it is available.

Fans of the flavor can still enjoy grape juice, grape jelly, and grape soda. But not Grape-Nuts. That 120-year-old breakfast cereal contains neither grapes nor nuts.

Workshop

Now that you've had the chance to enter, compile, link, and execute your first program, you can answer a few questions and complete a couple of exercises to firm up your knowledge about the compiler.

Quiz

1. What tool turns C++ source code into object code?

   A. A compiler

   B. A linker

   C. An integrated development environment

2. What filename extension is most common for source code files?

   A. `.cpp`

   B. `.c`

   C. `.h`

3. What tools can you use to edit your source code?

   A. A text editor

   B. A word processor

   C. Either one

Answers

1. **A.** The compiler takes a file of C++ source code and turns it into object code. The linker links that object file and any other necessary object files to create an executable program.
2. **A.** Compilers can handle any source code file regardless of extension, but `.cpp` is in wide use as the file extension for C++ code. Using this extension makes it easier later when you're looking around your computer's file folders for a program's source code.
3. **C.** You can use any tool that saves the code as plain text. You can use the simple editors that come with your operating system (such as Notepad, Vi, Gedit, or Emacs) or others that are available. Have I mentioned Notepad++?

Activities

1. Modify the Motto program to display the text "Saluton Mondo!," the greeting "Hello world!" in the artificial language Esperanto.
2. If you don't have a C++ IDE and you're not comfortable using the command line, take a look at Notepad++, NetBeans at http://netbeans.org or Code::Blocks at http://codeblocks.org. They're free IDEs that can be configured to work in conjunction with GCC. You might find them easier to use as you read this book.

To see solutions to these activities, visit this book's website at http://cplusplus.cadenhead.org.

HOUR 2

Organizing the Parts of a Program

What You'll Learn in This Hour:

- ▶ Why to use C++
- ▶ How C++ programs are organized
- ▶ How comments make programs easier to understand
- ▶ What functions can accomplish

Although it recently turned 37, the C++ programming language has aged a lot better than some other things that came out in the late 1970s. Unlike disco, oil embargoes, shag carpet, and avocado-colored refrigerators, C++ is still in vogue today. It remains a world-class programming language.

The reason for its surprising longevity is that C++ makes it possible to create fast executing programs with a small amount of code that can run on a variety of computing environments. Today's C++ programming tools enable the creation of complex and powerful applications in commercial, business, and open source development.

Reasons to Use C++

During the seven decades of the computing age, computer programming languages have undergone a dramatic evolution. C++ is considered to be an evolutional improvement of a language called C that was introduced in 1972.

The earliest programmers worked with the most primitive computer instructions: machine language. These instructions were represented by long strings of ones and zeroes. Assemblers were devised that could map machine instructions to human-readable and manageable commands such as ADD and MOV.

The instructions that make up a computer program are called its *source code*.

In time, higher-level languages were introduced such as BASIC and COBOL. These languages made it possible for programmers to begin to craft programs using language closer to actual words and sentences, such as `Let Average = .366`. These instructions were translated back into machine language by tools that were called either *interpreters* or *compilers*.

An interpreter-based language translates a program as it reads each line, acting on each instruction.

A compiler-based language translates a program into what is called *object code* through a process called *compiling*. This code is stored in an object file. Next, a linker transforms the object file into an executable program that can be run on an operating system.

Because interpreters read the code as it is written and execute the code on the fly, they're easy for programmers to work with. Compilers require the more inconvenient extra steps of compiling and linking programs. The benefit to this approach is that the programs run significantly faster than programs run by an interpreter.

For many years, the principal goal of programmers was to write short pieces of code that would execute quickly. Programs needed to be small because memory was expensive, and they needed to be fast because processing power also was expensive. As computers have become cheaper, faster, and more powerful and the cost and capacity of memory has fallen, these priorities diminished in importance.

Today, the greatest expense in programming is the cost of a programmer's time. Modern languages such as C++ make it faster to produce well-written, easy-to-maintain programs that can be extended and enhanced.

Styles of Programming

As programming languages have evolved, languages have been created to cater to different styles of programming.

In procedural programming, programs are conceived of as a series of actions performed on a set of data. Structured programming was introduced to provide a systematic approach to organizing these procedures and managing large amounts of data.

The principal idea behind structured programming is to divide and conquer. Take a task that needs to be accomplished in a program, and if it is too complex, break it down into a set of smaller component tasks. If any of those tasks is still too complicated, break it down into even smaller tasks. The end goal is tasks that are small and self-contained enough to be easily understood.

As an example, pretend you've been asked by this publisher to write a program that tracks the average income of its team of enormously talented and understatedly charismatic computer book authors. This job can be broken down into these subtasks:

1. Find out what each author earns.
2. Count how many authors the publisher has.

3. Total all their income.

4. Divide the total by the number of authors.

Totaling the income can be broken down into the following:

1. Get each author's personnel record.

2. Access the author's book advances and royalties.

3. Deduct the cost of morning coffee, corrective eyewear and chiropractic care.

4. Add the income to the running total.

5. Get the next author's record.

In turn, obtaining each author's record can be broken down into these subtasks:

1. Open the file folder of authors.

2. Go to the correct record.

3. Read the data from disk.

Although structured programming has been widely used, this approach has some drawbacks. The separation of data from the tasks that manipulate the data becomes harder to comprehend and maintain as the amount of data grows. The more things that must be done with data, the more confusing a program becomes.

Procedural programmers often find themselves reinventing new solutions to old problems instead of producing reusable programs. The idea behind reusability is to build program components that can be plugged into programs as needed. This approach is modeled after the physical world, where devices are built out of individual parts that each perform a specific task and have already been manufactured. A person designing a bicycle doesn't have to create a brake system from scratch. Instead, she can incorporate an existing brake into the design and take advantage of its existing functionality.

This component-based approach became available to computer programmers for the first time with the introduction of object-oriented programming.

C++ and Object-Oriented Programming

C++ helped popularize a revolutionary style of programming with a funny acronym: OOP.

The essence of object-oriented programming is to treat data and the procedures that act upon the data as a single object—a self-contained entity with an identity and characteristics of its own.

The C++ language fully supports object-oriented programming, including three concepts that have come to be known as the pillars of object-oriented development: encapsulation, inheritance, and polymorphism.

Encapsulation

When the aforementioned bike engineer creates a new bicycle, she connects together component pieces such as the frame, handlebars, wheels, and a headlight (baseball card in the spokes optional). Each component has certain properties and can accomplish certain behaviors. She can use the headlight without understanding the details of how it works, as long as she knows what it does.

To achieve this, the headlight must be self-contained. It must do one well-defined thing and it must do it completely. Accomplishing one thing completely is called *encapsulation*.

All the properties of the headlight are encapsulated in the headlight object. They are not spread out through the bicycle.

C++ supports the properties of encapsulation through the creation of user-defined types called *classes*. A well-defined class acts as a fully encapsulated entity that is used as an entire unit or not at all. The inner workings of the class should be hidden on the principle that the programs which use a well-defined class do not need to know how the class works. They only need to know is how to use it. You learn how to create classes in Hour 8, "Creating Basic Classes."

Inheritance and Reuse

Now we're starting to learn a little more about our bike engineer. Let's call her Penny Farthing. Penny needs her new bicycle to hit the market quickly—she has run up enormous gambling debts to people who are not known for their patience.

Because of the urgency, Penny starts with the design of an existing bicycle and enhances it with cool add-ons like a cup holder and mileage counter. Her new bicycle is conceived as a kind of bicycle with added features. She reused all the features of a regular bicycle while adding capabilities to extend its utility.

C++ supports the idea of reuse through inheritance. A new type can be declared that is an extension of an existing type. This new subclass is said to derive from the existing type. Penny's bicycle is derived from a plain old bicycle and thus inherits all its qualities but adds additional features as needed. Inheritance and its application in C++ are discussed in Hour 16, "Extending Classes with Inheritance."

Polymorphism

As its final new selling point, Penny Farthing's Amazo-Bicycle behaves differently when its horn is squeezed. Instead of honking like an anguished duck, it sounds like a car when lightly pressed and roars like a foghorn when strongly squashed. The horn does the right thing and makes the proper sound based on how it is used by the bicycle's rider.

C++ supports this idea that different objects do the right thing through a language feature called *function polymorphism* and *class polymorphism*. *Polymorphism* refers to the same thing taking many forms, and is discussed during Hour 17, "Using Polymorphism and Derived Classes."

You will learn the full scope of object-oriented programming by learning C++. These concepts will become familiar to you by the time you've completed this full 24-hour ride and begun to develop your own C++ programs.

Disclaimer: You won't learn how to design bicycles or get out of gambling debt.

The Parts of a Program

The program you created during the first hour, `Motto.cpp`, contains the basic framework of a C++ program. Listing 2.1 reproduces the source code of this program so that it can be explored in more detail.

When typing this program in to a programming editor such as NetBeans, remember not to include the line numbers in the listing. They are included solely for the purpose of referring to specific lines in this book.

LISTING 2.1 The Full Text of `Motto.cpp`

```
1:  #include <iostream>
2:
3:  int main()
4:  {
5:      std::cout << "Solidum petit in profundis!\n";
6:      return 0;
7:  }
```

This program produces a single line of output, the motto of Aarhus University:

```
Solidum petit in profundis!
```

On line 1 of Listing 2.1 a file named `iostream` is included in the source code. This line causes the compiler to act as if the entire contents of that file were typed at that place in `Motto.cpp`.

Preprocessor Directives

A C++ compiler's first action is to call another tool called the preprocessor that examines the source code. This happens automatically each time the compiler runs.

The first character in line 1 is the # symbol, which indicates that the line is a command to be handled by the preprocessor. These commands are called *preprocessor directives*. The preprocessor's job is to read source code looking for directives and modify the code according to the indicated directive. The modified code is fed to the compiler.

The preprocessor serves as an editor of code right before it is compiled. Each directive is a command telling that editor what to do.

The `#include` directive tells the preprocessor to include the entire contents of a designated filename at that spot in a program. As you learned in Hour 1, "Writing Your First Program," C++ includes a standard library of source code that can be used in your programs to perform useful functionality. The code in the `iostream` file supports input and output tasks such as displaying information onscreen and taking input from a user.

The < and > brackets around the filename `iostream` tell the preprocessor to look in a standard set of locations for the file. Because of the brackets, the preprocessor looks for the `iostream` file in the folder that holds header files for the compiler. These files also are called *include files* because they are included in a program's source code.

The full contents of `iostream` are included in place of line 1.

NOTE

Header files traditionally ended with the filename extension `.h` and also were called *h files*, so they used a directive of the form `include <iostream.h>`.
Modern compilers don't require that extension, but if you refer to files using it, the directive might still work for compatibility reasons. This book omits the extraneous .h in include files.

The contents of the file `iostream` are used by the `cout` command in line 5, which displays information to the screen.

There are no other directives in the source code, so the compiler handles the rest of `Motto.cpp`.

Source Code Line by Line

Line 3 begins the actual program by declaring a function named `main()`. *Functions* are blocks of code that perform one or more related actions. Functions do some work and then return to the spot in the program where they were called.

Every C++ program has a `main()` function. When a program starts, `main()` is called automatically.

All functions in C++ must return a value of some kind after their work is done. The `main()` function always returns an integer value. Integers are specified using the keyword `int`.

Functions, like other blocks of code in a C++ program, are grouped together using the brace marks { and }. All functions begin with an opening brace { and end with a closing brace }.

The braces for the `main()` function of `Motto.cpp` are on lines 4 and 7, respectively. Everything between the opening and closing braces is part of the function.

In line 5, the `cout` command is used to display a message on the screen. The object has the designation `std::` in front of it, which tells the compiler to use the standard C++ input/output library. The details of how this works are too complex for this early hour and likely will cause you to throw the book across the room if introduced here. For the safety of others in your vicinity, they are explained later. For now, treat `std::cout` as the name of the object that handles output in your programs and `std::cin` as the object that handles user input.

The reference to `std::cout` in line 5 is followed by `<<`, which is called the *output redirection operator*. *Operators* are characters in lines of code that perform an action in response to some kind of information. The `<<` operator displays the information that follows it on the line. In line 5, the text `"Solidum petit in profundis!\n"` is enclosed within double quotes. This displays a string of characters on the screen followed by a special character specified by `"\n"`, a newline character that advances the program's output to the beginning of the next line.

On line 6, the program returns the integer value 0. This value is received by the operating system after the program finishes running. Typically, a program returns the value 0 to indicate that it ran successfully. Any other number indicates a failure of some kind.

The closing braces on line 7 ends the `main()` function, which ends the program. All of your programs use the basic framework demonstrated by this program.

Comments

As you are writing your own programs for the first time, it will seem perfectly clear to you what each line of the source code does. But as time passes and you come back to the program to fix a bug or add a new feature, you may find yourself completely mystified by your own work.

To avoid this predicament and help others understand your program, you can document your source code with comments. *Comments* are lines of text that explain what a program is doing. The compiler ignores them, so they are strictly for benefit of humans reading the code.

There are two types of comments in C++. A single-line comment begins with two slash marks (//) and causes the compiler to ignore everything that follows the slashes on the same line. Here's an example:

```
// The next line is a kludge (ugh!)
```

A multiple-line comment begins with the slash and asterisk characters (/*) and ends with the same characters reversed (*/). Everything within the opening /* and the closing */ is a comment, even if it stretches over multiple lines. If a program contains a /* that is not followed by a */ somewhere, that's an error likely to be flagged by the compiler. Here's a multiline comment:

```
/* This part of the program doesn't work very well. Please remember to
   fix this before the code goes live -- or else find a scapegoat you can
   blame for the problem. The new guy Curtis would be a good choice. */
```

In the preceding comment, the text on the left margin is lined up to make it more readable. This is not required. Because the compiler ignores everything within the /* and */, anything can be put there—grocery lists, love poems, secrets you've never told anybody in your life, and so on.

CAUTION

An important thing to remember about multiline comments is that they do not nest inside each other. If you use one /* to start a comment and then use another /* a few lines later, the first */ mark encountered by the compiler will end all multiline comments. The second */ mark will result in a compiler error. Most C++ programming editors display comments in a different color to make clear where they begin and end.

The next project that you create includes both kinds of comments. Write lots of comments in your programs. The more time spent writing comments that explain what's going on in source code, the easier that code will be to work on weeks, months or even years later.

Functions

The `main()` function is unusual among C++ functions because it's called automatically when a program begins running.

A program is executed line by line in source code, beginning with the start of `main()`. When a function is called, the program branches off to execute the function. After the function has done its work, it returns control to the line where the function was called. Functions may or may not return a value, with the exception of `main()`, which always returns an integer.

Functions consist of a header and a body. The header consists of three things:

- The type of data the function returns
- The function's name
- The parameters received by the function

The *function name* is a short identifier that describes its purpose.

When a function does not return a value, it uses data type `void`, which means nothing. To clarify: `void` isn't meaningless. It means "nothing," like how stars in space are separated by a ginormous amount of nothing called "the void."

Arguments are data sent to the function that control what it does. These arguments are received by the function as *parameters*. A function can have zero, one, or more parameters. The next program that you create has a function called `add()` that adds two numbers together. Here's how it is declared:

```
int add(int x, int y)
{
    // body of function goes here
}
```

The parameters are organized within parentheses marks as a list separated by commas. In this function, the parameters are integers named `x` and `y`.

The name of a function, its parameters and the order of those parameters is called its *signature*. Like a person's signature, the function's signature uniquely identifies it.

A function with no parameters has an empty set of parentheses, as in this example:

```
int getServerStatus()
{
    // body of function here
}
```

Function names cannot contain spaces, so the `getServerStatus()` function capitalizes the first letter of each word after the first one. This naming convention is common among C++ programmers and adopted throughout this book.

The body of a function consists of an opening brace, zero or more statements, and a closing brace. A function that returns a value uses a `return` statement, as you've seen in the Motto program:

```
return 0;
```

The `return` statement causes a function to exit. If you don't include at least one `return` statement in a function, it automatically returns `void` at the end of the function's body. In that situation, `void` must be specified as the function's return type.

Using Arguments with Functions

The `Calculator.cpp` program in Listing 2.2 fleshes out the aforementioned `add()` function, using it to add a pair of numbers together and display the results. This program demonstrates how to create a function that takes two integer arguments and returns an integer value.

LISTING 2.2 The Full Text of `Calculator.cpp`

```
 1: #include <iostream>
 2:
 3: int add(int x, int y)
 4: {
 5:     // add the numbers x and y together and return the sum
 6:     std::cout << "Running calculator ...\n";
 7:     return (x+y);
 8: }
 9:
10: int main()
11: {
12:     /* this program calls an add() function to add two different
13:        sets of numbers together and display the results. The
14:        add() function doesn't do anything unless it is called by
15:        a line in the main() function. */
16:     std::cout << "What is 867 + 5309?\n";
17:     std::cout << "The sum is " << add(867, 5309) << "\n\n";
18:     std::cout << "What is 777 + 9311?\n";
19:     std::cout << "The sum is " << add(777, 9311) << "\n";
20:     return 0;
21: }
```

This program produces the following output:

```
What is 867 + 5309?
Running calculator ...
The sum is 6176

What is 777 + 9311?
Running calculator ...
The sum is 10088
```

The `Calculator` program includes a single-line comment on line 5 and a multi-line comment on lines 12–15. All comments are ignored by the compiler.

The `add()` function takes two integer parameters named `x` and `y` and adds them together in a `return` statement (lines 3–8).

The program's execution begins in the `main()` function. The first statement in line 16 uses the object `std::cout` and the redirection operator `<<` to display the text `"What is 867 + 5309?"` followed by a newline.

The next line displays the text `"The sum is"` and calls the `add()` function with the arguments `777` and `9311`. The execution of the program branches off to the `add()` function, as you can tell in the output by the text `"Running calculator...."`

The integer value returned by the function is displayed along with two more newlines.

The process repeats for a different set of numbers in lines 18–19.

The formula (x+y) is an expression. You learn how to create these mathematical workhorses in Hour 4, "Using Expressions, Statements, and Operators."

Summary

During this hour, you were shown how C++ evolved from other styles of computer languages and embraced a methodology called object-oriented programming. This methodology has been so successful in the world of computing that the language remains as contemporary today as it did when it was invented in 1979.

I wish the mullet haircut I sported in college had survived the test of time as well. Instead, it lives on in Facebook photos that friends share to shock and awe.

In the two programs that you developed during this hour, you made use of three parts of a C++ program: preprocessor directives, comments, and functions.

All the programs that you will create in C++ employ the same basic framework as the Motto and Calculator programs. They just become more sophisticated as they make use of more functions, whether you write them from scratch or call functions from header files included with the `#include` directive.

Q&A

Q. What does the # character do in a C++ program?

A. The # symbol signals that the line is a preprocessor directive, a command that is handled before the program is compiled. The `#include` directive includes the full text of a file at that position in the program. The compiler never sees the directive. Instead, it acts as if the contents of the file were typed in with the rest of the source code.

Q. What is the difference between `//` comments and `/*` style comments?

A. The comments that start with `//` are single-line comments that end with the end of the line on which they appear. The `/*` comments are multi-line comments that don't end until a `*/` is encountered. The end of a function won't even cause a multi-line comment to be ended. You must put in the closing `*/` mark or the compiler will fail with an error.

Q. What's the difference between function arguments and function parameters?

A. The terms are two sides of the same process when a function is called. Arguments are the information sent to the function. Parameters are the same information received by the function. You call a function with arguments. Within a function, those arguments are received as parameters.

Q. What is a kludge?

A. A kludge is an ugly solution to a problem that's intended to be replaced later with something better. The term was popularized by Navy technicians, computer programmers, and aerospace engineers and spread to other technical professions.

In a computer program a kludge is source code that works but would have been designed better if there had been more time. Kludges have a tendency to stick around a lot longer than expected.

The astronauts on the Apollo 13 mission created one of the greatest kludges of all time: a system cobbled together from duct tape and socks that filtered carbon dioxide from the air on the spacecraft and helped them make it back to Earth.

The first known usage of the term was in a 1962 article in *Datamation* magazine by Jackson W. Granholm, who gave it an elegant definition that has stood the test of time: "An ill-assorted collection of poorly matching parts, forming a distressing whole."

Workshop

Now that you've learned about some of the pieces of a C++ program, you can answer a couple of questions and complete a couple of exercises to firm up your knowledge.

Quiz

1. What data type does the `main` function return?

A. `void`

B. `int`

C. It does not return a type.

2. What do the braces do in a C++ program?

A. Indicate the start and end of a function

B. Indicate the start and end of a program

C. Straighten the program's teeth

3. What is not part of a function's signature?

A. Its name

B. Its arguments

C. Its return type

Answers

1. **B.** The `main` function returns an `int` (integer).
2. **A.** Braces mark the start and end of functions and other blocks of code you learn about in upcoming hours.
3. **C.** A function signature consists of its name, parameters, and the precise order of those parameters. It does not include its return type.

Activities

1. Rewrite the Motto program to display the Aarhus University motto in a function.
2. Rewrite the Calculator program to add a third integer called `z` in the `add()` function and call this function with two sets of three numbers.

To see solutions to these activities, visit this book's website at http://cplusplus.cadenhead.org.

HOUR 3

Creating Variables and Constants

What You'll Learn in This Hour:

- How to create variables and constants
- How to assign values to variables and change those values
- How to display the value of variables
- How to find out how much memory a variable requires

What Is a Variable?

A variable is a location in computer memory where you can store and retrieve a value. Your computer's memory can be thought of as a series of cubbyholes lined up in a long row. Each cubbyhole is numbered sequentially. The number of each cubbyhole is its memory address.

Variables have addresses and are given names that describe their purpose. In a game program, you could create a variable named `score` to hold the player's score and a variable named `zombies` for the number of zombies the player has defeated. A variable is a label on a cubbyhole so that it can be accessed without knowing the actual memory address.

Figure 3.1 shows seven cubbyholes with addresses ranging from 101 to 107. In address 104, the zombies variable holds the value 17. The other cubbyholes are empty.

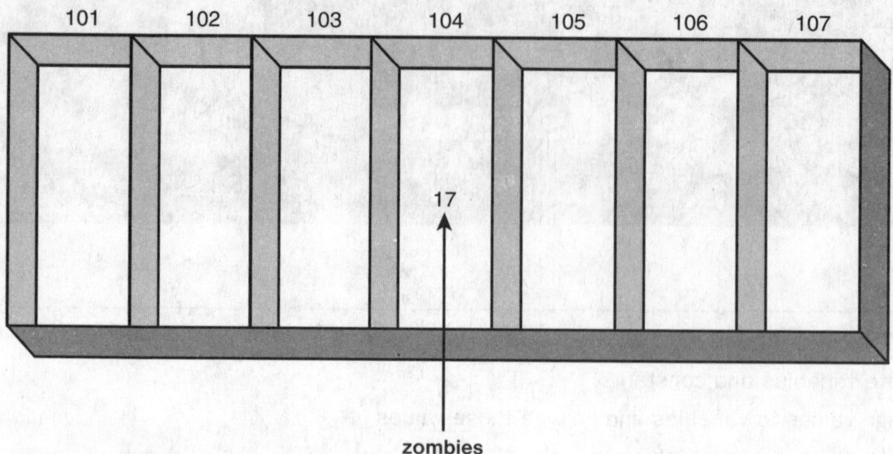

FIGURE 3.1
A visual representation of memory.

Storing Variables in Memory

When you create a variable in C++, you must tell the compiler the variable's name and what kind of information it will hold, such as an integer, character, or floating-point number. This is the variable's *type* (sometimes called *data type*). The type tells the compiler how much room to set aside in memory to hold the variable's value.

Each cubbyhole in memory can hold one byte. If a variable's type is two bytes in size, it needs two bytes of memory. Because computers use bytes to represent values, it is important that you familiarize yourself with this concept.

A short integer, represented by `short` in C++, is usually two bytes. A long integer (`long`) is four bytes, an integer (`int`) can be two or four bytes, and a `long long` integer is eight bytes.

Characters of text are represented by the `char` type in C++, which usually is one byte in size. In Figure 3.1, each cubbyhole holds one byte. A two-byte value such as a short integer could be stored in addresses 106 and 107.

True-false values are stored as the `bool` type (short for Boolean). The values `true` and `false` are the only values it can hold.

NOTE

Boolean variables are named for George Boole, an English mathematician who lived from 1815 to 1864. He created Boolean algebra, a branch in which values are limited to either true or false. His creation forms the basis of modern computing all the way down to the smallest digital circuits. He must have been good at true-false tests as a child.

The size of a `short` always is smaller than or the same as an `int`. The size of an `int` is always the same or smaller than a `long`. Floating-point numeric types are different and are discussed later this hour.

The usual type sizes described so far do not hold true on all systems. You can check the size a type holds in C++ using the `sizeof()` function. The parentheses that follow `sizeof` should be filled with the name of a type as an argument. Here's an example:

```
std:cout << sizeof(int) << "\n";
```

This statement displays the number of bytes required to store an integer variable. The `sizeof()` function is provided by the compiler and does not require an `include` directive. The Sizer program in Listing 3.1 relies on the `sizeof()` function to report the sizes of common C++ types on your computer.

LISTING 3.1 The Full Text of `Sizer.cpp`

```
#include <iostream>

int main()
{
    std::cout << "The size of an integer:\t\t";
    std::cout << sizeof(int) << " bytes\n";
    std::cout << "The size of a short integer:\t";
    std::cout << sizeof(short) << " bytes\n";
    std::cout << "The size of a long integer:\t";
    std::cout << sizeof(long) << " bytes\n";
    std::cout << "The size of a character:\t";
    std::cout << sizeof(char) << " bytes\n";
    std::cout << "The size of a boolean:\t\t";
    std::cout << sizeof(bool) << " bytes\n";
    std::cout << "The size of a float:\t\t";
    std::cout << sizeof(float) << " bytes\n";
    std::cout << "The size of a double float:\t";
    std::cout << sizeof(double) << " bytes\n";
    std::cout << "The size of a long long int:\t";
    std::cout << sizeof(long long int) << " bytes\n";

    return 0;
}
```

CAUTION

This program makes use of a relatively recent addition to the C++ language: the `long long int` data type, which holds extremely large integers. If your compiler fails with an error on `Sizer.cpp`, you probably are using a compiler that is out-of-date and does not support C++11, the version of the language prior to the current C++14. Delete lines 19–20 and try to compile the program again. If it works, that's the problem and you need to use a newer compiler.

After being compiled, this program produces the following output when run on either a Windows 10 or Linux Ubuntu 15.10 system:

```
The size of an integer:         4 bytes
The size of a short integer:    2 bytes
The size of a long integer:     4 bytes
The size of a character:        1 bytes
The size of a boolean:          1 bytes
The size of a float:            4 bytes
The size of a double float:     8 bytes
The size of a long long int:    8 bytes
```

Compare this output to how it runs on your computer. The `sizeof()` function returns the size of the specified object as its argument. For example, on line 16 the keyword `float` is passed to `sizeof()`. As you can see from the output, on the Windows or Ubuntu computers a `float` takes up two bytes of space and is equivalent in size to a `long` or an `int`.

Signed and Unsigned Variables

All the integer types come in two varieties specified using a keyword. They are declared with `unsigned` when they only hold positive values and `signed` when they hold positive or negative values. Here's a statement that creates a short `int` variable called `zombies` that does not hold negative numbers:

```
unsigned short zombies = 0;
```

The variable is assigned the initial value 0. Both signed and unsigned integers can equal 0.

Integers that do not specify either `signed` or `unsigned` are assumed to be signed.

Signed and unsigned integers are stored using the same number of bytes. For this reason, the largest number that can be stored in an unsigned integer is twice as big as the largest positive number that a signed integer can hold. An `unsigned short` can handle numbers from 0 to 65,535. Half the numbers represented by a `signed short` are negative, so a `signed short` represents numbers from –32,768 to 32,767. In both cases, the total number of possible values is 65,535.

Variable Types

In addition to integer variables, C++ types cover floating-point values and characters of text.

Floating-point variables have values that can be expressed as decimal values. Character variables hold a single byte representing 1 of the 256 characters and symbols in the standard ASCII character set.

Variable types supported by C++ programs are shown in Table 3.1, which lists the variable type, the most common memory size, and the possible values that it can hold. Compare this table to the output of the Sizer program when run on your computer, looking for size differences.

TABLE 3.1 Variable Types

Type	Size	Values
`unsigned short`	2 bytes	0 to 65,535
`short`	2 bytes	-32,768 to 32,767
`unsigned long`	4 bytes	0 to 4,294,967,295
`long`	4 bytes	-2,147,483,648 to 2,147,483,647
`int`	4 bytes	-2,147,483,648 to 2,147,483,647
`unsigned int`	4 bytes	0 to 4,294,967,295
`long long int`	8 bytes	-9.2 quintillion to 9.2 quintillion
`char`	1 byte	256 character values
`bool`	1 byte	true or false
`float`	4 bytes	1.2e-38 to 3.4e38
`double`	8 bytes	2.2e-308 to 1.8e308

The `short` and `long` variables also are called `short int` and `long int` in C++. Both forms are acceptable in your programs.

As shown in Table 3.1, `unsigned short` integers can hold a value only up to 65,535, while `signed short` integers can hold half that at maximum. Although `unsigned long long int` integers can hold more than 18.4 quintillion, that's still finite. If you need a larger number, you must use `float` or `double` at the cost of some numeric precision. Floats and doubles can hold extremely large numbers, but only the first 7 or 19 digits are significant on most computers. Additional digits are rounded off.

Although it's considered poor programming practice, a `char` variable can be used as a very small integer. Each character has a numeric value equal to its ASCII code in that character set. For example, the exclamation point character (!) has the value 33.

A special variable type called `auto` will be covered later this hour.

Defining a Variable

A variable is defined in C++ by stating its type, the variable name, and a semi-colon to end the statement, as in this example:

```
int highScore;
```

More than one variable can be defined in the same statement as long as they share the same type. The names of the variables should be separated by commas, as in these examples:

```
unsigned int highScore, playerScore;
long area, width, length;
```

The `highScore` and `playerScore` variables both are unsigned integers. The second statement creates three `long` integers: `area`, `width`, and `length`. Because these integers share the same type, they can be created in one statement.

A variable name can be any combination of uppercase and lowercase letters, numbers, and underscore characters (_) without any spaces. Legal variable names include `x`, `driver8`, and `playerScore`. C++ is case sensitive, so the `highScore` variable differs from ones named `highscore` or `HIGHSCORE`.

Using descriptive variable names makes it easier to understand a program for the humans reading it. (The compiler doesn't care one way or the other.) Take a look at the following two code examples to see which one is easier to figure out.

Example 1

```
main()
{
    unsigned short x;
    unsigned short y;
    unsigned int z;
    z = x * y;
}
```

Example 2

```
main ()
{
    unsigned short width;
    unsigned short length;
    unsigned short area;
    area = width * length;
}
```

Programmers differ in the conventions they adopt for variable names. Some prefer all lowercase letters for variable names with underscores separating words, such as `high_score`, `player_score`, and `new_world_record`. Others prefer lowercase letters except for the first letter of new words, such as `highScore`, `playerScore`, and `newWorldRecord`. (The latter naming convention has been dubbed CamelCase because the middle-of-word capitalizations look like a camel's humps.)

Programmers who learned in a Linux environment tend to use the first convention, whereas those in the Microsoft world use CamelCase. The compiler does not care.

The code in this book follows CamelCase.

With well-chosen variable names and plenty of comments, your C++ code will be much easier to figure out when you come back to it months or years later.

CAUTION

Some compilers allow you to turn case sensitivity of variable names off. Do not do this. If you do, your programs won't work with other compilers, and other C++ programmers will make fun of you behind your back.

Some words may not be used as variable names in C++ because they are keywords used by the language. Reserved keywords include `if`, `while`, `for`, and `main`. Generally, any reasonable name for a variable is almost certainly not a keyword.

Variables may contain a keyword as part of a name but not the entire name, so variables `mainFlag` and `forward` are permitted even though `main` and `for` are reserved.

Assigning Values to Variables

A variable is assigned a value using the = operator, which is called the *assignment* operator. The following statements show it in action to create an integer named `highScore` with the value 13,000:

```
unsigned int highScore;
highScore = 13000;
```

A variable can be assigned an initial value when it is created:

```
unsigned int highScore = 13000;
```

This is called *initializing the variable*. Initialization looks like assignment, but when you work later with constants, you'll see that some variables must be initialized because they cannot be assigned a value.

The Rectangle program in Listing 3.2 uses variables and assignments to compute the area of a rectangle and display the result.

LISTING 3.2 The Full Text of `Rectangle.cpp`

```
 1: #include <iostream>
 2:
 3: int main()
 4: {
 5:     // set up width and length
 6:     unsigned short width = 26, length;
 7:     length = 40;
 8:
 9:     // create an unsigned short initialized with the
10:     // result of multiplying width by length
11:     unsigned short area = width * length;
12:
13:     std::cout << "Width: " << width << "\n";
14:     std::cout << "Length: "  << length << "\n";
15:     std::cout << "Area: " << area << "\n";
16:     return 0;
17: }
```

This program produces the following output when run:

```
Width: 26
Length: 40
Area: 1040
```

Like the other programs you've written so far, Rectangle uses the `#include` directive to bring the standard `iostream` library into the program. This makes it possible to use `std::cout` to display information.

Within the program's `main()` block, on line 6 the variables `width` and `length` are created and `width` is given the initial value of 26. On line 7, the `length` variable is given the value 40 using the = assignment operator.

On line 11, an integer named `area` is defined. This variable is initialized with the value of the variable `width` multiplied by the value of `length`. The multiplication operator * multiplies one number by another.

On lines 13–15, the values of all three variables are displayed.

Using Type Definitions

When a C++ program contains a lot of variables, it can be repetitious to keep writing `unsigned short int` for each one. A shortcut for an existing type can be created with the keyword `typedef`, which stands for type definition.

A typedef requires typedef followed by the existing type and its new name. Here's an example:

```
typedef unsigned short USHORT
```

This statement creates a type definition named USHORT that can be used anywhere in a program in place of unsigned short. The NewRectangle program in Listing 3.3 is a rewrite of Rectangle that uses this type definition.

LISTING 3.3 The Full Text of NewRectangle.cpp

```
 1: #include <iostream>
 2:
 3: int main()
 4: {
 5:     // create a type definition
 6:     typedef unsigned short USHORT;
 7:
 8:     // set up width and length
 9:     USHORT width = 26;
10:     USHORT length = 40;
11:
12:     // create an unsigned short initialized with the
13:     // result of multiplying width by length
14:     USHORT area = width * length;
15:
16:     std::cout << "Width: " << width << "\n";
17:     std::cout << "Length: "  << length << "\n";
18:     std::cout << "Area: " << area << "\n";
19:     return 0;
20: }
```

This program has the same output as Rectangle: the values of width (26), length (40), and area (1040).

On line 6, the USHORT typedef is created as a shortcut for unsigned short. A type definition substitutes the underlying definition unsigned short wherever the shortcut USHORT is used.

During Hour 8, "Creating Basic Classes," you learn how to create new types in C++. This is a different from creating type definitions.

NOTE

Some compilers will warn that in the NewRectangle program a "conversion may lose significant digits." This occurs because the product of the two USHORTS on line 14 might be larger than an unsigned short integer can hold. For this program, you can safely ignore the warning.

Constants

A constant, like a variable, is a memory location where a value can be stored. Unlike variables, constants never change in value. You must initialize a constant when it is created. C++ has two types of constants: literal and symbolic.

A literal constant is a value typed directly into your program wherever it is needed. For example, consider the following statement:

```
long width = 19;
```

This statement assigns the integer variable `width` the value 19. The 19 in the statement is a literal constant. You can't assign a value to 19, and its value can't be changed.

The values `true` and `false`, which are stored in `bool` variables, also are literal constants.

A symbolic constant is a constant represented by a name, just like a variable. The `const` keyword precedes the type, name, and initialization. Here's a statement that sets the point reward for killing a zombie:

```
const int KILL_BONUS = 5000;
```

Whenever a zombie is dispatched, the player's score could be increased by the reward:

```
playerScore = playerScore + KILL_BONUS;
```

If you decide later to increase the reward to 10,000 points, you can change the constant `KILL_BONUS`, and it will be reflected throughout the program. If you were to use the literal constant 5000 instead, it would be more difficult to find all the places it is used and change the value. Using constants reduces the potential for error.

Well-named symbolic constants also make a program more understandable. Constants often are fully capitalized by programmers to make them distinct from variables. This is not required by C++, but the capitalization of a constant must be consistent in any statement where it appears because the language is case sensitive.

Defining Constants

There's another way to define constants that dates back to early versions of the C language, the precursor of C++. The preprocessor directive `#define` can create a constant by specifying its name and value, separated by spaces:

```
#define KILLBONUS 5000
```

The constant does not have a type such as `int` or `char`. The `#define` directive enables a simple text substitution that replaces every instance of `KILLBONUS` in the code with `5000`. The compiler sees only the end result.

Because these constants lack a type, the compiler cannot ensure that the constant has a proper value. Because these defined constants cannot be checked for type, it's better to use the standard constants and avoid using a directive just to set a constant.

Enumerated Constants

Enumerated constants create a set of constants with a single statement. They are defined with the keyword `enum` followed by a series of comma-separated names surrounded by braces, as in this example:

```
enum COLOR { RED, BLUE, GREEN, WHITE, BLACK };
```

This statement creates a set of enumerated constants named `COLOR` with five values named `RED`, `BLUE`, `GREEN`, `WHITE` and `BLACK`. The set of constants is called an *enumeration*.

Internally, enumerated constants hold integer values. The values begin with 0 for the first in the set and count upwards by 1. So `RED` equals 0, `BLUE` equals 1, `GREEN` equals 2, `WHITE` equals 3, and `BLACK` equals 4. All the values are integers.

Constants also can specify their values using an = assignment operator:

```
enum Color { RED=100, BLUE, GREEN=500, WHITE, BLACK=700 };
```

This statement sets `RED` to 100, `GREEN` to 500, and `BLACK` to 700. The members of the set without assigned values will be 1 higher than the previous member, so `BLUE` equals 101 and `WHITE` equals 501.

The advantage of this technique is that you get to use a symbolic name such as `BLACK` or `WHITE` rather than a possibly meaningless number such as 1 or 700.

The Compass program in Listing 3.4 uses enumerated constants for the eight compass directions, storing one such value in a variable named `heading`.

LISTING 3.4 The Full Text of `Compass.cpp`

```
#include <iostream>

int main()
{
    // set up enumeration
    enum Direction { North, Northeast, East, Southeast, South,
        Southwest, West, Northwest };

    // create a variable to hold it
    Direction heading;
    // initialize that variable
    heading = Southeast;
```

```
13:
14:     std::cout << "Moving " << heading << std::endl;
15:     return 0;
16: }
```

You may wonder what will be displayed when the value of the heading variable is sent over the output stream in line 14.

Compile and run the program to produce this output:

```
Moving 3
```

An enumeration is defined in lines 6–7. A variable is created to hold one of these eight enumerated constants and it is set to the value Southeast.

When this is displayed, the integer value of that constant is shown, not its name.

The Compass program has something unusual at the end of line 14: a reference to the object `std::endl`. Like `std::cout`, this is part of the C++ Standard Library. It displays the end-of-line character, just like using the `"\n"` character.

Auto-Typed Variables

As you have learned, a variable in C++ must have a type that indicates the kind of information it holds, such as `long` for long integers and `bool` for Boolean values. As a programmer you determine the type at the variable's creation:

```
int seconds = 86400;
```

The `auto` keyword in C++ enables a type to be inferred based on the value that's initially assigned to it. The compiler figures out a suitable data type.

Here are some examples:

```
auto index = 3;
auto multiple = 2.25F;
auto rate = 500 / 3.0;
```

These statements create an `index` variable that holds an `int` value, a `multiple` variable that holds a `float` and a `rate` variable that holds a `double`. The literal assigned to the variable at initialization determines the type.

In the `rate` statement, the expression `500 / 3.0` produces a `double` because one of the operands is a `double` value. (You learn more about expressions in Hour 4, "Using Expressions, Statements, and Operators.")

The compiler determines the type. In the preceding example, it's as if the following statements were encountered:

```
int index = 3;
float multiple = 2.25F;
double rate = 500 / 3.0;
```

When using auto, you must assign the variable a value at initialization.

Multiple variables can be assigned with an auto keyword as long as every one of the variables has the same data type.

```
auto a = 86, b = 75, c = 309;
```

For this hour's final project, the Combat program in Listing 3.5 calculates combat statistics such as those for a character in a videogame.

LISTING 3.5 The Full Text of `Combat.cpp`

```
#include <iostream>

int main()
{
    // define character values
    auto strength = 80;
    auto accuracy = 45.5;
    auto dexterity = 24.0;

    // define constants
    const auto MAXIMUM = 50;

    // calculate character combat stats
    auto attack = strength * (accuracy / MAXIMUM);
    auto damage = strength * (dexterity / MAXIMUM);

    std::cout << "\nAttack rating: " << attack << "\n";
    std::cout << "Damage rating: " << damage << "\n";
}
```

Because the auto keyword was added in a recent C++ version, you may need to compile `Combat.cpp` with a special command-line option. The -std=c++14 option causes the compiler to use the current version of C++. Here's an example command for the GCC compiler:

```
g++ -std=c++14 Combat.cpp -o Combat.exe
```

After its compiled successfully, the program displays the following output:

```
Attack rating: 72.8
Damage rating: 38.4
```

In lines 6–8, variables set the value of three attributes: the character's strength, accuracy, and dexterity. In lines 14–15, these are plugged in to formulas to calculate an attack rating and damage rating. If this code were part of a game, the values would be used when the character engages in combat.

All six variables in the program make use of the `auto` keyword, so if lines 6–8 are initialized with integers they are treated as `int` variables. If they are floating-point values, they're treated as `double`.

Make changes to the literal constants in those lines, then compile and run the program. Use different types of values to see how the output changes.

CAUTION

Older versions of C++ had an `auto` keyword that was supposed to be used to indicate that a variable was local to the part of the program it was defined in—a concept called *scope*. The developers of C++ inspected millions of lines of code and found only a handful of uses, most in test suites. They decided the keyword was redundant and replaced it with this new functionality. Any code that relies on the old meaning of `auto` will not work in C++14.

Summary

This hour covered how to work with simple kinds of information in C++ such as integers, floating-point values, and characters. Variables are used to store values that can change as a program runs. Constants store values that stay the same—in other words, they are not variable.

The biggest challenge when using variables is choosing the proper type. If you're working with signed integers that might go higher than 65,000, you should store them in a `long` rather than a `short`. If they might go higher than 2.1 billion, they're too big for a `long`. If a numeric value contains decimal values, it must be either `float` or `double`, the two floating-point types in the C++ language.

The `auto` keyword takes some of the work out of using variables, because it makes the compiler determine the type.

One thing to keep in mind when working with variables is the number of bytes they occupy, which can vary on different systems. The `sizeof()` function provided by the compiler returns the number of bytes any variable type requires.

Q&A

Q. If a `short` integer can run out of room, why not always use `long` integers?

A. Both `short` integers and `long` integers will run out of room, but a `long` integer will do so with a much larger number. On most computers, a `long` integer takes up twice as much memory, which has become less of a concern because of the memory available on modern PCs.

Q. What happens if I assign a number with a decimal to an integer rather than a float or double? Consider the following line of code:

```
int rating = 5.4;
```

A. Some compilers issue a warning, but the assignment of a decimal value to an integer type is permitted in C++. The number is truncated into an integer, so the statement assigns the `rating` integer the value 5. The more precise information is lost in the assignment, so if you tried later to assign `rating` to a `float` variable, it would still equal 5.

Q. Why should I bother using symbolic constants?

A. When a constant is used in several places in a program, a symbolic constant enables all the values to change simply by changing the constant's initialization. Symbolic constants also serve an explanatory purpose like comments. If a statement multiplies a number by 360, it's less easily understood than multiplying it by a constant named `degreesInACircle` that equals 360.

Q. Why did Jack Klugman have a 40-year feud with Norman Fell?

A. Klugman, the star of the TV shows *Quincy M.E.* and *The Odd Couple*, had a well-publicized long-running spat with Fell, the star of *Three's Company* and the landlord on *The Graduate*. No one seems to know the cause, but it did not end until Fell's death in 1998.

The movie reference site IMDb quotes Fell as saying, "I could have killed as Oscar. I would have been great as Quincy. I wouldn't have been so hammy. Klugman overacted every scene. You want the show to be good, pick me. You want a chain-smoking ------- who ruins any credibility for your project, I'll give you Klugman's number."

IMDb quotes Klugman as saying after Fell's funeral, "Best funeral I've ever been to. I've never laughed so hard in years. I had the time of my life."

The two actors, born in Philadelphia two years apart, bear some resemblance to each other and could have competed for the same roles over the decades they were acting in films and television. In reality, however, they were not enemies. As the blogger Tom Nawrocki found out in 2008, their feud was a 30-year joke they played on the media.

Workshop

Now that you've learned about variables and constants, you can answer a few questions and do a couple of exercises to firm up your knowledge about them.

Quiz

1. Why would you use unsigned over signed integers?

   A. They hold more numbers.

   B. They hold more positive numbers.

   C. There's no reason to prefer one over the other.

2. Are the variables `ROSE`, `rose`, and `Rose` the same?

   A. Yes

   B. No

   C. None of your business

3. What is the difference between a `#define` constant and `const`?

   A. Only one is handled by the preprocessor.

   B. Only one has a type.

   C. Both a and b

Answers

1. **B.** Unsigned integers hold more positive values and cannot be used to hold negative values. They hold the same number of values.

2. **B.** Because C++ is case sensitive, a `ROSE` is not a `rose` is not a `Rose`. Each reference is treated as a different variable by the compiler.

3. **C.** The preprocessor directive `#define` substitutes the specified value into your code every place it appears in code. It does not have a data type and is invisible to the compiler. A constant, created with the keyword `const`, has a data type and is handled by the compiler.

Activities

1. Create a program that uses constants for a touchdown (6 points), field goal (3 points), point after touchdown (1 point), and safety (2 point) and then adds them in the same order they were scored by the teams in the last Super Bowl. Display the final score. (For extra credit, make the Carolina Panthers win.)

2. Expand the Rectangle program so that it determines the area of a three-dimensional rectangle that has width, length, and height. To determine the area, use the multiplication operator * to multiply all three values.

To see solutions to these activities, visit this book's website at http://cplusplus.cadenhead.org.

HOUR 4
Using Expressions, Statements, and Operators

What You'll Learn in This Hour:

- ▶ How to write statements
- ▶ How to create expressions
- ▶ How to run code if a condition is met
- ▶ What the different operators accomplish

Statements

All C++ programs are made up of *statements*, which are commands that end with a semicolon. Each statement takes up one line by convention, but this is not a requirement—multiple statements can be put on a line as long as each ends with a semicolon. A statement controls the program's sequence of execution, evaluates an expression, or even can do nothing at all (the `null` statement). A common statement is an assignment:

```
x = a + b;
```

This statement assigns the variable `x` to equal the sum of `a + b`. The assignment operator `=` assigns the value on the right side of the operator to a variable on the left side. If `a` equals 4 and `b` equals 13, `x` will equal 17 after the statement is executed.

Whitespace

In the source code of a C++ program, any spaces, tabs, and newline characters are called *whitespace*. The compiler generally ignores whitespace, which serves the purpose of making the code more readable to programmers.

The previous assignment statement could be written in the following two ways and still work the same way:

```
x=a+b;
x       =      a       +       b       ;
```

The compiler ignores whitespace (or the lack of it). Whitespace cannot be used inside a variable name, so the variable `playerScore` could not be referred to as `player Score`.

The tabs or spaces that serve the purpose of indentation in programs are whitespace. Proper indentation makes it easier to see when a program block or function block begins and ends.

Compound Statements

Several statements can be grouped together as a *compound statement*, which begins with an opening brace { and ends with a closing brace }. A compound statement can appear anywhere a single statement could.

Although every statement in a compound statement must end with a semicolon, the compound statement itself does not end with a semicolon. Here's an example:

```
{
    temp = a;
    a = b;
    b = temp;
}
```

This compound statement swaps the values in the variables `a` and `b` using a variable named `temp` as a temporary holding place for one value.

Expressions

An *expression* is any part of a statement that returns a value, as in this simple example:

```
x = y + 13;
```

This statement makes the variable `x` equal to the variable `y` plus 13. So, if `y` equals 20, `x` equals 33. The entire statement returns the final value of `x`, so it's also an expression. To understand this better, consider a more complex statement:

```
z = x = y + 13;
```

This statement consists of three expressions:

- The result of the expression `y + 13` is stored in the variable `x`.
- The expression `x = y + 13` returns the value of `x`, which is stored in the variable `z`.
- The expression `z = x = y + 13` returns the value of `z`, which is not stored.

The assignment operator = causes the operand on the left side of the operator to have its value changed to the value on the right side of the operator.

Operand is a mathematical term referring to the part of an expression operated upon by an operator.

The Expression program in Listing 4.1 displays the values of three variables before and after they are used in a complex multiple-expression statement.

LISTING 4.1 The Full Text of `Expression.cpp`

```
 1: #include <iostream>
 2: int main()
 3: {
 4:     int x = 12, y = 42, z = 88;
 5:     std::cout << "Before -- x: " << x << " y: " << y;
 6:     std::cout << " z: " << z << "\n\n";
 7:     z = x = y + 13;
 8:     std::cout << "After -- x: " << x << " y: " << y;
 9:     std::cout << " z: " << z << "\n";
10:     return 0;
11: }
```

This program produces the following output:

```
Before -- x: 12 y: 42 z: 88

After -- x: 55 y: 42 z: 55
```

Three variables are declared and given initial values in line 4, then those values are displayed. An expression in line 7 assign values to `x` and `z`, in that order. The new values are displayed and the program ends.

Operators

An *operator* is a symbol that causes the compiler to take an action such as assigning a value or performing multiplication, division, or another mathematical operation.

Assignment Operator

An expression consists of an assignment operator, an operand to its left called an *l-value*, and an operand to its right called an *r-value*. In the expression `grade = 95`, the l-value is `grade`, and the r-value is 95.

Constants are r-values but cannot be l-values. The expression `95 = grade` is not permitted in C++ because the constant 95 cannot be assigned a new value.

The primary reason to learn the terms l-value and r-value is because they may appear in compiler error messages.

Mathematical Operators

There are five mathematical operators: addition (+), subtraction (–), multiplication (*), division (/), and modulus (%). C++, like C, does not have an exponentiation operator to raise a value to a specified power. There is a function to perform the task.

Addition, subtraction, and multiplication act as you'd expect, but division is more complex.

Integer division differs from ordinary division. When you divide 21 by 4, the result is a real number that has a fraction or decimal value. By contrast, integer division produces only integers, so the remainder is dropped. The value returned by 21 / 4 is 5.

The modulus operator `%` returns the remainder value of integer division, so 21 % 4 equals 1. The integer division 21 / 4 is 5, leaving a remainder of 1.

NOTE

When describing an expression using the modulus operator, it is called *modulo*, so 21 % 4 is "21 modulo 4." Modulo is the operation performed by the modulus operator and the result is called the modulus.

Finding the modulus can be useful in programming. If you want to display a statement every tenth time that a task is performed, the expression `taskCount % 10` can watch for this. The modulus ranges in value from 0 to 10. Every time it equals 0, the count of tasks is a multiple of 10.

Floating-point division is comparable to ordinary division. The expression 21 / 4.0 equals 5.25.

C++ decides which division to perform based on the type of the operands. If at least one operand is a floating-point variable or literal, the division is floating point. Otherwise, it is integer division.

Combining Operators

It is not uncommon to want to add a value to a variable and then to assign the result back into the variable. The following expression adds 10 to the value of a variable named `score`:

```
score = score + 10;
```

This expression takes the existing value of `score`, adds 10 to it, and stores the result in `score`.

This can be written more simply using the += self-assigned addition operator:

```
score += 10;
```

The self-assigned addition operator += adds the r-value to the l-value, and then assigns the result to the l-value. There are self-assigned subtraction (-=), division (/=), multiplication (*=), and modulus (%=) operators, as well.

These self-assignment operators do the same thing as longer expressions, so either form can be used at your discretion.

Increment and Decrement Operators

The most common value to add or subtract from a variable is 1. Increasing a variable by 1 is called *incrementing*, and decreasing it by 1 is called *decrementing*. C++ includes a ++ increment operator and -- decrement operator to accomplish these tasks:

```
score++;
zombies--;
```

These statements increase `score` by 1 and decrease `zombies` by 1, respectively. They are equivalent to these more verbose statements:

```
score = score + 1;
zombies = zombies - 1;
```

The ++ operator is said aloud as "plus-plus" and -- as "minus-minus."

NOTE

Now that you've been introduced to the increment operator, the name C++ should make more sense. The C++ programming language was intended by creator Bjarne Stroustrup as an incremental improvement over the C language. He named it like an expression, putting the increment operator in its name and causing countless people over the years to wonder why it's called "C-plus-plus" rather than "C-plus."

Prefix and Postfix Operators

The increment operator ++ and decrement operator -- can be used either before or after a variable's name to achieve different results. An operator placed before a variable's name is called a *prefix operator*, as in this statement:

```
++count;
```

An operator placed after the variable name is called the *postfix operator*:

```
count++;
```

In simple statements like the preceding examples, the operators accomplish the same thing. The `count` variable is increased by 1 in both statements.

The reason for the existence of prefix and postfix operators becomes apparent in complex expressions where a variable is being incremented or decremented and assigned to another variable. The prefix operator occurs before the variable's value is used in the expression. The postfix is evaluated after.

This will make more sense with a concrete example:

```
int x = 5;
int sum = ++x;
```

After these statements are executed, the x variable and `sum` variable both equal 6. The prefix operator in `++x` causes `x` to be incremented from 5 to 6 before it is assigned to `sum`.

Compare it to this example:

```
int x = 5;
int sum = x++;
```

This causes `sum` to equal 5 and `x` to equal 6. The postfix operator causes `x` to be assigned to `sum` before it is incremented from 5 to 6.

Listing 4.2 contains the Years program, which counts forward several years using prefix and postfix increment operators.

LISTING 4.2 The Full Text of `Years.cpp`

```
#include <iostream>

int main()
{
    int year = 2016;
    std::cout << "The year " << ++year << " passes.\n";
    std::cout << "The year " << ++year << " passes.\n";
    std::cout << "The year " << ++year << " passes.\n";

    std::cout << "\nIt is now " << year << ".";
    std::cout << " Have the Chicago Cubs won the World Series yet?\n";

    std::cout << "\nThe year " << year++ << " passes.\n";
    std::cout << "The year " << year++ << " passes.\n";
    std::cout << "The year " << year++ << " passes.\n";

    std::cout << "\nSurely the Cubs have won the Series by now.\n";
    return 0;
}
```

This program displays the following output:

```
The year 2017 passes.
The year 2018 passes.
The year 2019 passes.

It is now 2019. Have the Chicago Cubs won the World Series yet?

The year 2019 passes.
The year 2020 passes.
The year 2021 passes.

Surely the Cubs have won the Series by now.
```

The Years program counts forward the years, anticipating the first World Series victory by the Chicago Cubs, a Major League Baseball team that hasn't won a championship since 1908. The program begins by setting the `year` variable to 2016 in Line 5.

Line 6 produces the first output of the program: "The year 2017 passes." Take note that the year is 2017, not 2016 as it was originally set. This happens because the prefix operator in that line changes the value of year before it is displayed.

Several years pass, and in lines 10–11, the `year` equals 2019.

Line 13 produces this output: "The year 2019 passes." The `year` remains 2019 because the postfix operator changes the value of year after it is displayed.

NOTE

There are three ways of adding 1 to a variable in C++: `a = a + 1`, `a += 1`, and `a++`. This leads to some confusion about which one is best to use. There's no best way. As long as you know what your code is doing, all three ways are perfectly acceptable.

Operator Precedence

The values produced by complex expressions depend on the *order of precedence*, which is the order in which expressions are evaluated. Here's a complex expression with three operators:

```
int x = 5 + 3 * 8;
```

Without knowing the order of multiplication and addition, it's impossible to know what `x` equals after this statement executes.

This expression sets `x` to 64 if addition takes place before multiplication, because 8 times 8 equals 64. If multiplication takes place before addition, `x` equals 29 because 5 plus 24 equals 29.

Every operator has a precedence value in C++. Multiplication has higher precedence than addition, so the expression sets x to 29. The precedence of operators is shown in Table 4.1.

You are introduced to most of these operators in later hours. Operators are evaluated from the top of the table down. Operators with the same precedence are evaluated from left to right or right to left, as indicated in the table.

Looking at the table, you can see that the multiplication operator * and division operator / have higher precedence than the addition operator + and subtraction operator –. For this reason, multiplication and division are handled before addition and subtraction.

TABLE 4.1 Operator Precedence

<table>
<tr><th>Level</th><th>Operators</th><th>Evaluation Order</th></tr>
<tr><td>1 (highest)</td><td>( ) . [ ] → ::</td><td>Left to right</td></tr>
<tr><td>2</td><td>* & ! ~ ++ -- + -</td><td>Right to left</td></tr>
<tr><td></td><td>sizeof new delete</td><td>Left to right</td></tr>
<tr><td>3</td><td>.* → *</td><td>Left to right</td></tr>
<tr><td>4</td><td>* /</td><td>Left to right</td></tr>
<tr><td>5</td><td>+ –</td><td>Left to right</td></tr>
<tr><td>6</td><td><< >></td><td>Left to right</td></tr>
<tr><td>7</td><td>< <= >>=</td><td>Left to right</td></tr>
<tr><td>8</td><td>== !=</td><td>Left to right</td></tr>
<tr><td>9</td><td>&</td><td>Left to right</td></tr>
<tr><td>10</td><td>^</td><td>Left to right</td></tr>
<tr><td>11</td><td>|</td><td>Left to right</td></tr>
<tr><td>12</td><td>&&</td><td>Left to right</td></tr>
<tr><td>13</td><td>||</td><td>Left to right</td></tr>
<tr><td>14</td><td>?:</td><td>Right to left</td></tr>
<tr><td>15</td><td>= *= /= += -= %=</td><td>Right to left</td></tr>
<tr><td></td><td><<= >>= &= ^= |=</td><td>Right to left</td></tr>
<tr><td>16 (lowest)</td><td>,</td><td>Left to right</td></tr>
</table>

When two mathematical operators have the same precedence, they are performed in left-to-right order. Here's an expression with two multiplication operators and three addition operators:

```
int x = 5 + 3 + 8 * 9 + 6 * 4;
```

Because multiplication has higher precedence than addition and the same operators have left-to-right order, 8 times 9 is evaluated first and becomes 72:

```
int x = 5 + 3 + 72 + 6 * 4;
```

Next, 6 times 4 is evaluated:

```
int x = 5 + 3 + 72 + 24;
```

Now the addition operators are handled in left-to-right order. The final result is that `x` equals 104.

Some operators, such as assignment, are evaluated in right-to-left order:

```
int z = x = y + 13;
```

The first expression evaluated is `y + 13`, which is assigned to `x`. Next, `x` is assigned to `z`.

When precedence order doesn't meet your needs, you can use parentheses to impose a different order. Items within parentheses are evaluated at a higher precedence than any mathematical operators:

```
int totalSeconds = (minutesWork + minutesTravel) * 60;
```

This expression adds `minutesWork` and `minutesTravel`, multiplies the result by 60, and assigns it to `totalSeconds`.

Parentheses can be nested within each other. The innermost parenthesis are evaluated first:

```
totalSeconds = ((secondsWork * 60) + minutesTravel) * 60;
```

NOTE

When in doubt, use parentheses to make an expression's meaning clear. They do not affect a program's performance, so there's no harm in using them even in cases where they wouldn't be needed.

Relational Operators

Relational operators are used for comparisons to determine when two numbers are equal or one is greater or less than the other. Every relational expression returns either true or false. The relational operators are presented in Table 4.2.

TABLE 4.2 The Relational Operators

Name	Operator	Sample	Evaluates
Equals	`==`	`100 == 50;`	`false`
		`50 == 50;`	`true`
Not equal	`!=`	`100 != 50;`	`true`
		`50 != 50;`	`false`
Greater than	`>`	`100 > 50;`	`true`
		`50 > 50;`	`false`
Greater than or equals	`>=`	`100 >= 50;`	`true`
		`50 >= 50;`	`true`
Less than	`<`	`100 < 50;`	`false`
		`50 < 50;`	`false`
Less than or equals	`<=`	`100 <= 50;`	`false`
		`50 <= 50;`	`true`

If you have integer variables called `myAge` and `yourAge`, the expression `myAge == yourAge` determines whether they are equal. The following statement uses this expression:

```
std::cout << (myAge == yourAge) << "\n";
```

This statement displays 1 if they are equal and 0 if unequal.

CAUTION

Many novice C++ programmers confuse the assignment operator = with the equality operator ==, which can introduce bugs into a program that are difficult to spot. The compiler might give you a warning when you use the assignment operator in situations where the equality operator makes more sense, but it sometimes won't be detected until the program does not perform as intended.

`If-Else` Conditional Statements

The programs you have created thus far execute each line in order from top to bottom. The `if` keyword makes it possible to run code only if a condition is met, such as whether two variables are equal, one variable is larger than a specific value, or a `bool` variable has the value true.

The following `if` statement displays a message only when an integer called `zombies` meets a specific condition:

```
if (zombies == 0)
    std::cout << "No more zombies!\n";
```

This code displays the words "No more zombies!" if the `zombies` variable equals 0. The expression within parentheses is the condition. If the expression is true, the statement following the `if` is executed. If it is false, the statement is skipped.

For example, if the `zombies` variable equals 25 when this code runs, nothing is displayed.

The expression must be true for the conditional code to be executed. Because `bool` variables can be true or false, one can be used as the condition:

```
bool run = true;
if (run)
    std::cout << "Running\n";
```

This code displays the text "Running" only when the `bool` variable `run` equals true.

The `Else` Clause

A program can execute one statement if an `if` condition is true and another if it is false. The `else` keyword identifies the statement to execute when the condition is false:

```
if (zombies == 0)
    std::cout << "No more zombies!\n";
else
    std::cout << "Beware the zombie apocalypse!\n";
```

The Grader program in Listing 4.3 demonstrates the use of conditional statements.

LISTING 4.3 The Full Text of `Grader.cpp`

```
#include <iostream>

int main()
{
    int grade;
    std::cout << "Enter a grade (1-100): ";
    std::cin >> grade;

    if (grade >= 70)
        std::cout << "\nYou passed. Hooray!\n";
    else
        std::cout << "\nYou failed. Sigh.\n";

    return 0;
}
```

All the programs you've written so far have used `std::cout`, an object from the Standard C++ Library that displays information to a user. The directive in line 1 makes this object available in a program.

The Grader program uses another object from the input-output library: `std::cin`, which collects information from a user. Line 6 displays a query to the user: "Enter a grade (1–100)." Line 7 uses `std::cin` to receive keyboard input from the user, storing it in the integer variable `grade`.

Grader displays different output depending on what the user enters as a grade. This variability employs the `if-else` conditional in lines 9–12.

Here's an example of its output:

```
Enter a grade (1-100):
85

You passed. Hooray!
```

You got a B grade. Good work, but I know you can do better if you apply yourself and stop spending so much time on Snapchat when you should be studying.

Compound `If` Statements

Compound statements can be used anywhere in code that a single statement could be placed. The `if` and `if-else` conditionals often are followed by compound statements:

```
if (zombies == 0)
{
    std::cout << "No more zombies!\n";
    score += 5000;
}
```

This code does two things when `zombies` equals 0: It displays "No more zombies!" and adds 5,000 to the variable `score`. If `zombies` does not equal 0, neither of these things occurs.

Any statement can be used with an `if` conditional, even another `if` or `else` statement.

The NewGrader program in Listing 4.4 expands Grader by displaying a different message for A, B, C, and F grades.

LISTING 4.4 The Full Text of `NewGrader.cpp`

```
#include <iostream>

int main()
{
    int grade;
```

```
6:    std::cout << "Enter a grade (1-100): ";
7:    std::cin >> grade;
8:
9:    if (grade >= 70)
10:   {
11:       if (grade >= 90)
12:       {
13:           std::cout << "\nYou got an A. Great job!\n";
14:           return 0;
15:       }
16:       if (grade >= 80)
17:       {
18:           std::cout << "\nYou got a B. Good work!\n";
19:           return 0;
20:       }
21:       std::cout << "\nYou got a C. Perfectly adequate!\n";
22:   }
23:   else
24:       std::cout << "\nYou got an F. I failed as a parent!\n";
25:
26:   return 0;
27: }
```

The NewGrader program has a main `if-else` conditional that handles when the user-input `grade` is 70 or higher and when it isn't.

Grades of 70 or higher are handled in lines 10–22. Two `if` statements cover grades 90 or higher and 80 or higher and display messages for A and B students. After the message is displayed, the `return 0` statement immediately ends the `main()` function so the program ends.

If the program is still running when line 21 is reached, a message for C students is displayed.

The `else` conditional is paired with the `if` in line 9. It covers grades lower than 70 and displays a despondent message.

Here's sample output for the program:

```
Enter a grade (1-100): 93

You got an A. Great job!
```

With diligence and focus, you've improved your grades. Mother and I are very proud.

The NewGrader program uses braces only around compound statements. The `else` conditional is followed with a single statement, so it does not need braces.

Some programmers always use braces with conditionals and other blocks of code, even when unnecessary:

```
if (zombies == 0)
{
    std::cout << "No more zombies!\n";
}
else
{
    std::cout << "Beware the zombie apocalypse!\n";
}
```

This is permitted by the compiler and makes the `if` and `else` blocks of code more visually distinct. It also avoids bugs that occur when a single statement is turned into a compound statement by adding a new line but the programmer forgets to enclose it within braces.

NOTE

Remember that whitespace and indentation are meaningful to you as a programmer but entirely meaningless to the compiler. It doesn't care how `if` statements line up.

Logical Operators

The `if-else` conditionals used so far have a single expression as the condition. It's possible to test more than one condition using the logical operators `&&` (also called AND) and `||` (OR). The logical operator `!` (NOT) tests whether an expression is false.

These operators are listed in Table 4.3.

TABLE 4.3 The Logical Operators

Operator	Symbol	Example
AND	`&&`	`grade >= 70 && grade < 80`
OR	`||`	`grade > 100 || grade < 1`
NOT	`!`	`!grade >= 70`

AND Operator

The logical AND operator evaluates two expressions. If both expressions are true, the logical AND expression is true, as well. Consider this statement:

```
if ((x == 5) && (y == 5))
    // do something here
```

If x and y both equal 5, the expression is true. If either x or y does not equal 5, the expression is false. Both sides must be true for the entire expression to be true and for the conditional statement to execute.

OR Operator

The logical OR operator evaluates two expressions and if either one is true, the expression is true:

```
if ((x == 5) || (y == 5))
    // do something here
```

If either x or y equals 5 or both equal 5, the expression is true. In fact, if x equals 5, the compiler never checks y at all.

NOT Operator

A logical NOT statement reverses a normal expression, returning true if the expression is false and false if the expression is true. Here's a statement that uses one:

```
if (!(grade < 70))
```

This expression is true if grade is 70 or greater and false otherwise. The Grader and NewGrader programs used the expression grade >= 70 to check for passing grades. This NOT expression accomplishes the same thing by looking for grades that are not less than 70.

Relational Precedence

Relational operators and logical operators, like other operators, return a value of true or false and have a precedence order that determines which relations are evaluated first. This fact is important when determining the value of the statement such as the following:

```
if (x > 5 && y > 5 || z > 5)
```

The logical AND and OR operators have the same precedence, so they are evaluated in left-to-right order. For this expression to be true, both x and y must be greater than 5 or z must be greater than 5.

Parentheses can be used to impose a different order:

```
if (x > 5 && (y > 5 || z > 5))
```

For this expression to be true, x must be greater than 5 and either y or z must be greater than 5.

NOTE

It is a good idea to use extra parentheses in a complex logical expression just to clarify what the statement is doing. The left-to-right precedence of logical operators is easy for the compiler to understand, but not always clear to programmers. The goal always should be to write programs that work and that are easy to understand.

Tricky Expression Values

Expressions produce the values true or false. In C++, the value 0 also is considered false and any other value is true. Some C++ programmers take advantage of this feature in `if` statements:

```
if (zombies)
     std::cout << "There are " << x << " zombies left\n";
```

When `zombies` equals 0, the `if` expression is false and the zombie count is not displayed. When `zombies` equals any other number, the expression is true and the count is shown. This code is the same as the following:

```
if (zombies != 0)
     std::cout << "There are " << x << " zombies left\n";
```

Both statements are permitted in C++, but the latter is clearer. It is good programming practice to reserve the former method for true tests of logic, rather than for testing for non-zero values.

These two statements also are equivalent:

```
if (!x)
if (x == 0)
```

Both statements are true when `x` equals 0. The second statement is somewhat easier to comprehend.

Summary

During this hour, you learned about statements, expressions, and operators, the basic building blocks of a C++ program.

Statements are individual lines of code that perform specific tasks. A program consists of hundreds, thousands, or even millions of statements. Each statement ends with a semicolon.

Expressions are statements or portions of statements that produce a value. The value can be assigned to a variable using the assignment operator =.

Operators are symbols that cause the compiler to take action. Operators can assign values, perform mathematical operations such as addition or division, compare two values, and handle logical comparisons.

The conditional statements `if` and `else` can cause statements to be executed only if a specific condition is true. These conditions often are defined as expressions.

Q&A

Q. Because precedence determines which operators are acted on first, why use parentheses when you don't need them?

A. Precedence isn't always as clear to a programmer looking at code as it is to the C++ compiler. Using parentheses to make a program more understandable to the people working on it will pay off in the long run.

Q. What effect do tabs, spaces, and newline characters have on a program?

A. These characters, which are called whitespace, are ignored by the compiler and have no effect on the program. Their purpose is to make programs easier for humans to understand. Poor indentation can make it difficult to determine which statement belongs to an `if` conditional, where a compound statement begins and ends, and so on.

Q. Are negative numbers true or false?

A. Every number except for 0, whether positive and negative, is treated as true.

Q. Who gets to decide what a newly discovered animal is named?

A. The naming system for new species is guided by the International Code on Zoological Nomenclature, a set of rules that determine how the name is structured.

The person who discovers the animal usually gets to select its name, which is submitted for approval to the commission at the National History Museum in London, England.

If you have discovered a new species, visit the commission's web site at www.iczn.org.

Most discoverers base the name on themselves, but some have started selling the rights to raise money towards conservation efforts. In 2005, the online casino GoldenPalace.Com paid $650,000 to name a new primate *Callicebus aureipalati*. Aureipalatii means "golden palace" in Latin.

The German non-profit group Biopat sells naming rights to new species for a €2,600 Euro donation (currently around $2,870 U.S.). Visit the group's website at http://biopat.de/en for details.

Workshop

Now that you've learned about expressions and statements, it is time for you to answer a few questions and do a couple of exercises to firm up your knowledge about these topics.

Quiz

1. What is the difference between `x++` and `++x`?

   A. They increment the value of x at different times.

   B. The second form is not permitted in C++.

   C. One is a cat running left, the other a cat running right.

2. What is the difference between an l-value and an r-value?

   A. Only r-values can be used in expressions.

   B. Some r-values cannot be l-values, but all l-values can be r-values.

   C. Both a and b.

3. What does the modulo operator `%` do?

   A. It performs integer division.

   B. It produces the remainder of an integer division.

   C. It produces the square root of a number.

Answers

1. **A.** The first uses the postfix operator and the second uses the prefix operator. Postfix evaluates `x` before incrementing it, whereas prefix increments `x` before it is evaluated. The choice of postfix or prefix affects the value of `x` when it is used in an expression.
2. **B.** An l-value appears on the left side of an `=` assignment operator, whereas an r-value appears on the right. All l-values also can appear on the right side of the operator, but some r-values (such as literals) cannot act as l-values.
3. **B.** It calculates the remainder after performing integer division on the supplied operands.

Activities

1. Create a version of the NewGrader program that does not include the `return` statements, except for the final one. Run it with numerous test values until you spot the bug, and then figure out why it's happening.

2. Write a program that asks for a user's grade from 1 to 100, asks what the passing grade is on the same scale, and reports whether the user passed.

To see solutions to these activities, visit this book's website at http://cplusplus.cadenhead.org.

HOUR 5
Calling Functions

What You'll Learn in This Hour:

- ▶ What a function does
- ▶ How to declare and define functions
- ▶ How to call functions with arguments
- ▶ How to return a value from a function

What Is a Function?

A *function* is a section of a program that can act on data and return a value. Every C++ program has at least one function, the `main()` function called automatically when the program runs. This function can contain statements that call other functions, some of which might call others, and so on.

Each function has a name that's used to call the function. The execution of the program branches to the first statement in that function and continues until it reaches a `return` statement or the last statement of the function. At that point, execution resumes at the place where the function was called.

A well-designed function performs a specific task. Complicated tasks should be broken down into multiple functions, each of which can be called in turn. This makes your code easier to understand and maintain.

Declaring and Defining Functions

Before you can write the code for a function, you must declare it.

A function declaration tells the compiler the function's name, the type of data the function produces, and the types of any parameters received by the function. A function's declaration, which also is called its *prototype*, contains no code.

The declaration tells the compiler how the function works. The function prototype is a single statement, which ends with a semicolon.

The parameter list identifies each parameter and its type, separated by commas.

Here's a declaration for a function that determines a rectangle's area using `length` and `width` parameters:

```
int findArea(int length, int width);
```

The three parts of the declaration are the following:

- The return type, `int`
- The name, `findArea`
- The type and name of two parameters, an `int` named `length` and an `int` named `width`

The function prototype must match the three elements of the function or the program won't compile. The only thing that does not need to match are the names of the parameters. A function declaration doesn't need to name parameters at all. The previous declaration could be rewritten as follows:

```
int findArea(int, int);
```

Although this is permitted, it makes the function prototype less clear than if parameter names had been used.

The function's name is a short identifier that describes the task it performs. Because the name cannot contain spaces, a common convention is to capitalize each word in the name except for the first. That's why the *A* is capitalized in the name `findArea`.

All functions are structured the same as a program's `main()` function. The statements in the function are enclosed within an opening { brace and a closing } brace. If the function returns a value, there should be at least one `return` statement that returns a literal or variable of the proper return type. In a new feature of C++14, the `auto` keyword lets the compiler choose the data type returned by a function.

Any C++ data type can be returned by a function. If a function doesn't produce a value, the declaration should use `void` as the type. A function that returns `void` does not need a `return` statement, although one can still be used, as in this statement:

```
return;
```

Unlike the function declaration, the statement naming the function must not end with a semicolon.

Here's a definition of `findArea()` that determines the area of a rectangle by multiplying its length by its width:

```
int findArea(int length, int width)
{
    return length * width;
}
```

The only statement in the function returns the value of the two parameters multiplied by each other.

The Area program in Listing 5.1 uses this function.

LISTING 5.1 The Full Text of `Area.cpp`

```
#include <iostream>

int findArea(int length, int width); // function prototype

int main()
{
    int length;
    int width;
    int area;

    std::cout << "\nHow wide is your yard? ";
    std::cin >> width;
    std::cout << "\nHow long is your yard? ";
    std::cin >> length;

    area = findArea(length, width);

    std::cout << "\nYour yard is ";
    std::cout << area;
    std::cout << " square feet\n\n";
    return 0;
}

// function definition
int findArea(int l, int w)
{
     return l * w;
}
```

When the program is compiled and run, it produces the following output:

```
How wide is your yard? 32

How long is your yard? 25

Your yard is 800 square feet
```

The function prototype for the `findArea()` function is on line 3. The code for the function is contained on lines 25–28. Compare the prototype's name, return type and parameter types: They are the same, but the names of the parameters are `length` and `width` in the prototype and `l` and `w` in the function. This distinction does not matter because the parameter types match.

NOTE

If the definition of the function in `Area.cpp` was to be moved above its invocation, no prototype would be needed. Although this is a workable solution in small programs like the ones created in this book, on larger programming projects it will be more cumbersome to ensure that all functions are defined before they are used. Declaring all functions with prototypes frees you from having to think about this issue.

Using Variables with Functions

A function works with variables in several different ways. Variables can be specified as arguments when calling a function. Variables can be created in a function and cease to exist when the function completes. Variables also can be shared by the function and the rest of a program.

Local Variables

A variable created in a function is called a *local variable* because it exists only locally within the function itself. When the function returns, all of its local variables are no longer available for use in the program.

Local variables are created like any other variable. The parameters received by the function are also considered local variables. The Temperature program in Listing 5.2 uses local variables to convert a temperature value expressed in Fahrenheit scale to one using Celsius.

LISTING 5.2 The Full Text of `Temperature.cpp`

```
#include <iostream>

float convert(float);

int main()
{
    float fahrenheit;
    float celsius;

    std::cout << "Please enter the temperature in Fahrenheit: ";
    std::cin >> fahrenheit;
    celsius = convert(fahrenheit);
    std::cout << "\nHere's the temperature in Celsius: ";
```

```
14:     std::cout << celsius << "\n";
15:     return 0;
16: }
17:
18: // function to convert Fahrenheit to Celsius
19: float convert(float fahrenheit)
20: {
21:     float celsius;
22:     celsius = ((fahrenheit - 32) * 5) / 9;
23:     return celsius;
24: }
```

Here's output produced by running the program three times with the user input Fahrenheit values 77, 32, and 85:

```
Please enter the temperature in Fahrenheit: 77
Here's the temperature in Celsius: 25

Please enter the temperature in Fahrenheit: 32
Here's the temperature in Celsius: 0

Please enter the temperature in Fahrenheit: 85
Here's the temperature in Celsius: 29.4444
```

This program has a `convert()` function defined in lines 19–24 that takes one argument: a `float` value called `fahrenheit`.

A local variable named `celsius` is declared in line 21 and assigned a value in line 22. The value is determined using the three-step formula for converting Fahrenheit to Celsius:

1. Subtract 32 from the number.
2. Multiply the result by 5.
3. Divide that result by 9.

The converted value is returned by the function in line 23. When the function ends, the local variables `fahrenheit` and `celsius` cease to exist and no longer can be used.

In the `main()` method, a variable named `fahrenheit` is created to hold the value input by a user. A variable named `celsius` holds the converted version of that temperature. These variables have the same names as the local variables in the `convert()` function, but they are different variables.

The reason they are not the same is because they are created in a different scope. The scope of a variable is the portion of the program in which a variable exists. Scope determines how long a variable is available to your program and where it can be accessed. Variables declared within a block have the scope of that block. When the block ends with an ending } brace, the variable becomes unavailable.

You can declare variables within any block, such as an `if` conditional statement or a function.

Global Variables

Variables can be defined outside of all functions in a C++ program, including the `main()` function. These are called *global variables* because they are available everywhere in the program.

Variables defined outside of any function have global scope and thus are available from any function in the program, including `main()`.

The Global program in Listing 5.3 is a revised version of Temperature that makes use of global variables.

LISTING 5.3 The Full Text of `Global.cpp`

```
 1: #include <iostream>
 2:
 3: void convert();
 4:
 5: float fahrenheit;
 6: float celsius;
 7:
 8: int main()
 9: {
10:
11:     std::cout << "Please enter the temperature in Fahrenheit: ";
12:     std::cin >> fahrenheit;;
13:     convert();
14:     std::cout << "\nHere's the temperature in Celsius: ";
15:     std::cout << celsius << "\n";
16:     return 0;
17: }
18:
19: // function to convert Fahrenheit to Celsius
20: void convert()
21: {
22:     celsius = ((fahrenheit - 32) * 5) / 9;
23: }
```

When compiled and run, this program performs exactly like the Temperature program, despite the fact that the code has several significant differences.

The float variables `fahrenheit` and `celsius` are declared in lines 5–6, outside the `main()` function and `convert()` function. This makes them global variables that can be used anywhere without regard to scope.

Because the variables are global, the `convert()` function takes no parameters and uses the global `fahrenheit` to convert a Celsius value. The function also returns no value, using `void` as its return type, because it stores the converted temperature in the global `celsius`.

Although global variables might seem useful in this example, taking this approach is asking for trouble in more complex programs that you create. Global variables lend themselves to errors that are difficult to find. A value of a global variable can be changed on any statement in the program, so if there's an error you must check line by line until the error is found.

One of the advantages of variable scope is that it limits the section of a program that must be checked when a variable either contains a value you weren't expecting or has been used improperly.

The `Global` program is the only one in this book that makes use of global variables. Now that you know about them, forget everything you just learned.

Function Parameters

A function receives information in the form of function parameters. There can be more than one parameter as long as they are separated by commas, or a function can be called with no parameters at all. The parameters sent to a function don't have to be of the same data type. A function can be called with an integer, two longs, and a character as parameters, for instance.

Any valid C++ expression can be a function parameter, including constants, mathematical and logical expressions, and other functions that return a value.

The parameters passed to a function are local variables within that function, even if they have the same name as variables within the scope of the statement calling the function.

Consider the following sample code, which appears to swap the values of two variables:

```
int x = 4, y = 13;
swap(x, y);

void swap(int x, int y) {
    int temp = x;
    x = y;
    y = temp;
}
```

Contrary to what you might expect, the `swap()` function does not swap the variable values so that `x` equals 13 and `y` equals 4. Instead, the variables keep their original values. The reason is that the parameters received by the `swap()` function are local variables within that function. Changing their values does not affect the variables with the same name that were created right before `swap()` was called.

Changes made to function parameters do not affect the values in the calling function. This is called passing by value because values are passed to the function and a local copy is made of each parameter. These local copies are treated just like any other local variables.

The `swap()` function swaps the local variables received by the function as parameters, leaving the variables used to call `swap()` unchanged.

Because variables are passed by value to functions, the `swap()` function does not work.

Beginning in Hour 10, "Creating Pointers," you'll learn several alternatives to passing by value that enable functions to change variables passed to them.

Returning Values from Functions

Functions return a value or `void`.

To return a value from a function, the keyword `return` is followed by the value to return. The value can be a literal, a variable, or an expression, because all expressions produce a value. Here are some examples:

```
return 5;
return (x > 5);
return (convert(fahrenheit));
```

These are all permitted `return` statements, assuming that `convert()` returns a value. The value returned in the second statement is false if x is less than or equal to 5, true otherwise.

When a `return` statement is executed, program execution returns immediately to the statement that called the function. Any statements following `return` are not executed.

It is permissible to have more than one `return` statement in a function. This is demonstrated by the LeapYear program in Listing 5.4.

LISTING 5.4 The Full Text of `LeapYear.cpp`

```
#include <iostream>

bool isLeapYear(int year);

int main()
{
    int input;
    std::cout << "Enter a year: ";
    std::cin >> input;
    if (isLeapYear(input))
        std::cout << input << " is a leap year\n";
    else
```

```
13:         std::cout << input << " is not a leap year\n";
14:     return 0;
15: }
16:
17: bool isLeapYear(int year)
18: {
19:     if (year % 4 == 0)
20:     {
21:         if (year % 100 == 0)
22:         {
23:             if (year % 400 == 0)
24:                 return true;
25:             else
26:                 return false;
27:         }
28:         else
29:             return true;
30:     }
31:     else
32:         return false;
33: }
```

The LeapYear program determines whether a year is a leap year. Here's the output from four successive runs with different user input:

```
Enter a year: 2016
2016 is a leap year
Enter a year: 2017
2017 is not a leap year

Enter a year: 2100
2100 is not a leap year

Enter a year: 2000
2000 is a leap year
```

Leap years, which have 366 days rather than 365, follow three rules:

- If the year is divisible by 4, it is a leap year,
- Unless the year is also divisible by 100, in which case it is not a leap year,
- Unless the year is divisible by 400, and it's a leap year after all.

The `isLeapYear()` function in lines 17–33 uses several `if` and `else` statements to carry out these rules. The function returns the `bool` value `true` if a year is a leap year and `false` otherwise. The function takes an integer argument, the year to check.

There are four different `return` statements in the function, each of which ends the execution of the function in a different circumstance. Unlike other functions, the last line is not a `return` statement executed automatically. It is part of a conditional.

Default Function Parameters

When a function is declared in a prototype to receive one or more parameters, the function only can be called with parameters of the proper data types. Consider a function that takes one integer:

```
bool isLeapYear(int year);
```

The `isLeapYear()` function must take an integer as the parameter, a requirement the compiler will check. Calling a function with a missing or invalid value causes a compiler error.

There's one exception to this rule: If the function prototype declares a default value for a parameter, the function can be called without that parameter. The default value is used whenever the parameter is omitted. Here's a revised prototype of `isLeapYear()` that includes a default year:

```
bool isLeapYear(int year = 2016);
```

If the `isLeapYear()` function is called without specifying a year, the default of 2016 is used.

A function's definition does not change when default parameters are declared in the prototype.

When a function has more than one parameter, default values are assigned based on the order of the parameters. Any parameter can be assigned a default value, with one important restriction: If a parameter does not have a default value, no previous parameter may have a default value.

Here's a prototype with four parameters:

```
long set4DPoint(int x, int y, int z, int t);
```

The following change is not permitted:

```
long set4DPoint(int x, int y, int z = 1, int t);
```

The reason it doesn't work is because the `t` parameter lacks a default value. Here's a permitted prototype:

```
long set4DPoint(int x, int y, int z = 1, int t = 2000);
```

The function created from this prototype could be called with this statement:

```
set4DPoint(130, 85);
```

The argument values would be 130 for `x`, 85 for `y`, 1 for `z`, and 2000 for `t`.

The AreaCube program in Listing 5.5 calculates the area of a three-dimensional cube, using default function parameter values for two of the dimensions.

LISTING 5.5 **The Full Text of** `AreaCube.cpp`

```
1: #include <iostream>
2:
3: int findArea(int length, int width = 20, int height = 12);
4:
5: int main()
6: {
7:     int length = 100;
8:     int width = 50;
9:     int height = 2;
10:    int area;
11:
12:    area = findArea(length, width, height);
13:    std::cout << "First area: " << area << "\n\n";
14:
15:    area = findArea(length, width);
16:    std::cout << "Second area: " << area << "\n\n";
17:
18:    area = findArea(length);
19:    std::cout << "Third area: " << area << "\n\n";
20:    return 0;
21: }
22:
23: int findArea(int length, int width, int height)
24: {
25:     return (length * width * height);
26: }
```

The program produces the following output:

```
First area: 10000

Second area: 60000

Third area: 24000
```

On line 3, the `findArea()` prototype specifies that the function takes three integer parameters, the last two with default values.

The function computes the area of a cube. If no `height` is provided, a `height` of 12 is used. If no `width` is provided, a `width` of 20 and `height` of 12 are used. It is not possible to provide a `height` without providing a `width`.

On lines 7–9, the dimensions `length`, `height`, and `width` are initialized. They are passed to the `findArea()` function on line 12. The values are computed, and the result is displayed.

On line 15 `findArea()` is called again with no value for `height`. The default value is used and the area of the computed cube is displayed.

On line 18, `findArea()` is called with neither `width` nor `height`. Execution branches off for a third time to the function. The default values for both are used and the cube's area is displayed.

Overloading Functions

In C++, more than one function can have the same name as long as there are differences in their arguments, a practice called *function overloading*. The functions must have different data types for parameters, a different number of parameters, or both. Here are three prototypes for overloaded functions:

```
int store(int, int);
int store(long, long);
int store(long);
```

The `store()` function is overloaded with three different parameter lists. The first and second differ in the data types and the third differs in the number of parameters.

The parameters the function is called with determine which function will be called.

The return types for overloaded functions do not factor into whether they are different. Several overloaded functions can have the same return type, as in the preceding example, or different types. You can't overload by making the return different, however. The parameter types or number of parameters must differ.

Function overloading also is called *function polymorphism*.

Overloading makes it possible to create a function that performs a similar task on different types of data without creating unique names for each function. If your program needs to average two numbers expressed in different formats, it could have functions named `averageInts()`, `averageDoubles()`, and `averageFloats()`.

To simplify, an overloaded function called `average()` could be used with these prototypes:

```
int average(int, int);
long average(long, long);
float average(float, float);
```

You just pass in the right data when calling `average()` and the proper function is called.

Inline Functions

When you define a function, the C++ compiler creates just one set of instructions in memory. Execution of the program jumps to those instructions when the function is called and jumps back after the function returns to the next line in the calling function. If the program calls the function 10 times, it jumps to the same set of instructions each time. There only is one copy of the instructions that make up the function, not 10 copies.

Some performance overhead is required to jump in and out of functions. When a function consists of a small number of statements, you can gain some efficiency if the program avoids making the jumps. The program runs faster if the function call can be avoided.

If a C++ function is declared with the keyword `inline`, the compiler does not create a real function. Instead, it copies the code from the inline function directly into the place where the function was called. It is just as if you had written the statements of the function right there.

If an inline function is called 10 times, the inline code is copied all 10 times. The tiny improvement in speed could be swamped by the increase in size of the executable program.

NOTE

The `inline` keyword is a hint to the compiler that you would like the function to be inlined. The compiler is free to ignore the hint and make a real function call. Current compilers do a terrific job on their own of making C++ code execute quickly, so there's often little to be gained from declaring a function inline.

The inline keyword is used in the function prototype:

```
inline int double(int);
```

The function itself does not change:

```
int double(int target)
{
    return 2 * target;
}
```

Auto-Typed Return Values

One of the features added to C++ with version C++14 is the automatic deduction of a function's return type with the `auto` keyword. You already could create variables with `auto` whose data type was figured out by the compiler based on the value assigned to it. This takes that convenience a step further.

To make a function's return type determined by deduction, use `auto` where the return type is specified, as in this simple function:

```
auto subtract(int x, int y)
{
    return x - y;
}
```

Because both x and y are integers, the sum of subtracting one from the other also is an `int`.

There are a few things to keep in mind when using this capability.

If a function has more than one return statement, they all must return the same data type.

The function must be defined above the code that makes use of it.

LISTING 5.6 The Full Text of `AutoCube.cpp`

```
#include <iostream>

auto findArea(int length, int width = 20, int height = 12);

auto findArea(int length, int width, int height)
{
    return (length * width * height);
}

int main()
{
    int length = 100;
    int width = 50;
    int height = 2;
    int area;

    area = findArea(length, width, height);
    std::cout << "First area: " << area << "\n\n";

    area = findArea(length, width);
    std::cout << "Second area: " << area << "\n\n";

    area = findArea(length);
    std::cout << "Third area: " << area << "\n\n";
    return 0;
}

```

Because the program makes use of a new feature introduced in C++14, you may need to compile it with the flag `--std=c++14`, as in this command:

```
g++ -o AutoCube.exe --std=c++14 AutoCube.cpp
```

In Listing 5.6, the `auto` keyword appears in the function prototype in line 5 and the function declaration two lines later. The function was moved above the `main()` function in the source code. If it hadn't been, the compiler would have halted with the following error message:

```
AreaCube.cpp:12:12: error: use of 'auto findArea(int, int, int)'
before deduction of auto
```

The program produces the same output as AreaCube.

Summary

Functions are the workhorses of a C++ program. Every task a program performs is represented by a function. When that task can be broken down into smaller tasks, each of those can be a function, as well.

All functions should be declared using function prototypes, which are statements that identify the function's name, the order and data type of parameters, and the data type that it returns. A function's return type can be figured out by the compiler by putting `auto` in its place, a new capability of C++.

The functions in this hour's programs are named like commands: `findArea()`, `convert()`, and `average()`. Functions are commands. You're telling the computer to do something, such as find an area, convert a value, or average two numbers.

Each function that you write in a program is a discrete task. The more specific the task, the shorter the function will be.

Function overloading makes it possible to use the same function name on several related functions. The data type and number of parameters to the function are used to differentiate between them. The C++ compiler figures out which function to execute based on these differences.

Q&A

Q. Why not make all variables global?

A. Although this used to be common in programming, as programs became more complex it became extremely difficult to find bugs in programs with globally accessible variables. The reason is because data could be misused in any `part` of the program. To minimize the chance of error and make debugging easier, data should be kept in as local a scope as possible.

Q. Why aren't changes to the value of function parameters reflected in the calling function?

A. Parameters passed to a function are passed by value. That means that the `parameter` received by the function is actually a copy of the original value, even if it shares the same variable name. You learn how to pass a changeable parameter to a function when you begin working with pointers and references in Hour 10.

Q. What happens if I have the following two functions?

```
int findArea(int width, int length = 1);
int findArea(int size);
```

Will these overload? There are a different number of parameters, but the first one has a default value.

A. The declarations will compile, but calling the `findArea()` with one parameter `will` cause a compile-time error about "ambiguity between `findArea(int, int)` and `findArea(int)`."

Q. Why doesn't anyone ever use a No. 1 pencil?

A. `Pencils` are produced according to a grading system that rates them based on how soft the lead is, which dictates the darkness of the mark it produces. The softer the lead, the darker the mark.

The `grades` of pencils sold in the United States are No. 1, 2, 2.5, 3, and 4.

The No. 1 produces the darkest mark, but the soft lead breaks more easily `and` requires sharpening more often. The No. 4 has the hardest lead and produces the faintest mark.

No. 2, by striking a balance between lead softness and mark darkness, is so popular that most people aren't aware any of the others exist.

`The` others can be found at art supply stores, though they may use another grading system entirely that uses "B" for the softest leads and "H" for the hardest. The range goes "9B", "8B", "7B" on down to a middle value of "B", then goes from "H" to "2H", "3H", "4H" up to a maximum of "9H".

Also, pencil leads aren't made of lead. They're graphite.

`Who` knew pencils were so complicated? If you need to take notes while you figure all of this out, use a No. 2 pencil.

Workshop

Now that you've had the chance to see functions, you can answer a few questions and do a couple of exercises to firm up your knowledge of function prototypes and function parameters.

Quiz

1. What happens when a variable is a parameter received by a called function?

   A. A copy of the variable is passed to the function.

   B. The actual variable is passed to the function.

   C. A compiler error occurs.

2. When three overloaded functions have the same name, how does C++ know which one to call?

   A. The function's return types are different.

   B. The functions parameters are different.

   C. The order of the function from top to bottom.

3. How many values can a `return` statement return?

   A. One

   B. One or more

   C. None or one

Answers

1. **A.** A copy is made of the variable, which is called passing by value. Any changes to the variable within the function do not affect the original variable.

2. **B.** Overloaded functions must have parameters of different types or a different number of parameters. The compiler uses this difference to determine which function to call. The return type of the functions does not matter.

3. **C.** A function can return no more than one value, although the function can have several `return` statements to return that value. When a function does not return any value, the `void` data type indicates this fact.

Activities

1. Write a program that converts a temperate from Celsius to Fahrenheit. The formula to do this is to multiply the Celsius temperate by 9, divide the result by 5, and then add 32.

2. Write a program that can calculate the average of two integers, two long integers or two floating-point values using an overloaded function named `average()`.

To see solutions to these activities, visit this book's website at http://cplusplus.cadenhead.org.

HOUR 6
Controlling the Flow of a Program

What You'll Learn in This Hour:

- What loops are and how they are used
- How to build various loops
- Using `switch-case` for complex conditional tests

Looping

One of the things that a computer excels at is doing the same thing over and over again. Software doesn't get tired.

Many tasks in a program are accomplished by doing the same thing either a fixed number of times or until a specific condition is met. A block of code that's executed more than once in a row in a program is called a *loop*. Each pass through the loop is called an *iteration*.

These terms will come in handy as you learn during this hour about `while` loops, `do-while` loops, and `for` loops.

`while` Loops

A `while` loop causes a program to repeat a group of statements as long as a starting condition remains true. The `while` keyword is followed by an expression in parentheses. If the expression is true, the statements inside the loop block are executed. They are executed repeatedly until the expression is false.

Here's a `while` loop that displays the numbers 0 through 99:

```
int x = 0;
while (x < 100)
{
    std::cout << x << "\n";
    x++;
}
```

The `while` keyword is followed by an expression within parentheses. This statement does not end in a semicolon. The statements inside the loop are a block statement surrounded by { and } braces.

The loop has the conditional expression `x < 100`. Each time that x is less than 100, the body of the loop is executed, and the value of x is displayed.

When x is equal to 100, the loop ends.

Without the `x++` increment statement, the value of x would remain 0, and the loop would never end. This is called an *infinite loop*.

The Thirteens program in Listing 6.1 uses a `while` loop to display all multiples of 13 lower than 500.

LISTING 6.1 The Full Text of `Thirteens.cpp`

```
 1: #include <iostream>
 2:
 3: int main()
 4: {
 5:     int counter = 0;
 6:
 7:     while (counter < 500)
 8:     {
 9:         counter++;
10:         if (counter % 13 == 0)
11:         {
12:             std::cout << counter << " ";
13:         }
14:     }
15:
16:     std::cout << "\n";
17:     return 0;
18: }
```

This program produces the following output:

```
13 26 39 52 65 78 91 104 117 130 143 156 169 182 195
208 221 234 247 260 273 286 299 312 325 338 351 364
377 390 403 416 429 442 455 468 481 494
```

The Thirteens program demonstrates the fundamentals of the `while` loop. A condition is tested and the body of the `while` loop is executed while it is true. The condition tested on line 7 is whether the `counter` variable is less than 500. For as long as the condition is true, the body of the loop is executed.

On line 9, the counter is incremented. On line 10, an `if` statement checks whether the current value of `counter` is evenly divisible by 13. If it is, the value is displayed.

The conditional on line 7 is false when `counter` is no longer less than 500, causing the `while` loop to end. Program execution skips lines 9–13 and continues with line 16.

Breaking Out of Loops

The `break` statement causes a loop to end immediately, instead of waiting for its condition to be false. This statement appears inside a loop and is demonstrated in the Fourteens program in Listing 6.2, which displays the first 20 multiples of 14.

LISTING 6.2 The Full Text of `Fourteens.cpp`

```
 1: #include <iostream>
 2:
 3: int main()
 4: {
 5:     int counter = 0;
 6:     int multiples = 0;
 7:
 8:     while (true)
 9:     {
10:         counter++;
11:         if (counter % 14 == 0)
12:         {
13:             std::cout << counter << " ";
14:             multiples++;
15:         }
16:         if (multiples > 19)
17:             break;
18:     }
19:
20:     std::cout << "\n";
21:     return 0;
22: }
```

This program produces this output:

```
14 28 42 56 70 84 98 112 126 140 154 168 182 196 210 224
238 252 266 280
```

This program is similar to the Thirteens program. A counter variable is incremented from 0 upward, and every time the variable is evenly divisible by 14 (line 11), its value is displayed.

The `while` conditional in line 8 of the program has an unusual conditional expression:

```
while (true)
```

Because a `while` loop executes as long as its condition is true, this loop is designed to loop forever.

The `break` statement in line 17 is what causes the loop to end. A `multiples` variable tracks the number of times a multiple of 14 has been displayed. When this variable exceeds 19, `break` ends the loop.

CAUTION

Infinite loops such as `while(true)` can cause a program to run forever if the exit condition is never reached. Press Ctrl+C to end execution of a program that isn't ending on its own. Use `while(true)` with care and test the code thoroughly.

Continuing to the Next Loop

A `continue` statement is another way to alter the performance of a loop. When a continue is encountered within a loop, the execution skips all remaining statements and begins a new iteration of the loop.

The Fifteens program in Listing 6.3 displays the first 20 multiples of 15 using a continue statement inside the `while` loop.

LISTING 6.3 The Full Text of `Fifteens.cpp`

```
#include <iostream>

int main()
{
    int counter = 0;
    int multiples = 0;

    while (multiples < 19)
    {
        counter++;
        if (counter % 15 != 0)
            continue;
        std::cout << counter << " ";
        multiples++;
    }

    std::cout << "\n";
    return 0;
}
```

Here's the program's output:

```
15 30 45 60 75 90 105 120 135 150 165 180 195
210 225 240 255 270 285
```

The Fifteens program uses a `while` loop to iterate through a `counter` variable, like the preceding two projects of the hour. The `while` statement in line 8 causes the loop to keep going until 20 multiples of 15 have been displayed.

The counter variable is incremented in line 10.

An `if` statement in line 11 tests whether the `counter` variable is not evenly divisible by 15. If this condition is true, the `continue` statement in line 12 is executed, and the rest of the loop is skipped. Execution of the program resumes with line 8.

If the counter variable is evenly divisible by 15, `continue` is ignored and lines 13–14 of the loop are executed. The value of `counter` is displayed and the `multiples` variable is incremented.

As loops demonstrate, C++ often offers several different ways to accomplish the same task. As long as the program that you write does what's needed, you can choose the technique that you prefer.

do-while Loops

The `while` loop tests a conditional expression before executing the statements in the loop. If the condition is never true, the statements never execute.

A loop can test the condition at the end of the loop with the `do-while` statement.

Consider the following loop:

```
int x = 60;
do
{
   std::cout << x << "\n";
   x++;
} while (x < 50);
```

This loop's conditional only is true when `x < 50`. Because `x` begins with an initial value of 60, this condition is never met.

In spite of this, the body of the loop executes once and the `x` value of 60 is displayed. This occurs because the `do-while` loop does not consider the condition for the first time until after the loop's statements are executed.

A `do-while` loop always executes the body at least once.

The Badger program in Listing 6.4 uses one of these loops to display a word a user-selected number of times.

LISTING 6.4 The Full Text of `Badger.cpp`

```
1: #include <iostream>
2:
3: int main()
4: {
5:     int badger;
6:     std::cout << "How many badgers? ";
7:     std::cin >> badger;
8:
9:     do
10:    {
11:        std::cout << "Badger ";
12:        badger--;
13:    } while (badger > 0);
14:
15:    std::cout << "\n";
16:    return 0;
17: }
```

When you run the program, it asks the question "How many badgers?" and displays the word *Badger* that many times.

```
How many badgers? 5
Badger Badger Badger Badger Badger
```

Run this program a second time and enter **0**. You will see this output:

```
How many badgers? 0
Badger
```

The user is prompted for a starting value on line 7, which is stored in the integer variable `badger`. In the `do-while` loop, the body of the loop is entered before the condition is tested, and therefore guaranteed to be executed at least once. On line 11, the word "Badger" is displayed, on line 12 the counter is decremented, and on line 13 the condition is tested. If the condition is true, execution jumps to the top of the loop on line 11; otherwise, it falls through to line 14.

The `continue` and `break` statements work in a `do-while` loop exactly as they do in a `while` loop. The only difference between a `while` loop and a `do-while` loop is when the condition is tested.

`for` Loops

When using loops in a program, you often find yourself setting up a counter variable, testing to see whether the counter meets a condition and changing the variable's value each time through the loop, as in this sample `while` loop:

```
int x = 0;
while (x < 13)
{
    std::cout << "X";
    x++;
}
std::cout << "\n";
```

This code displays an "X" 13 times on one line of output.

A for loop is a sophisticated loop that combines all three of these steps together into a single statement. The statement consists of the keyword for followed by a pair of parentheses. Within the parentheses are three statements separated by semicolons:

- The initialization of the counter
- The conditional test
- The change to the counter

The following code rewrites the preceding while loop to produce the same output:

```
for (int x = 0; x < 13; x++)
{
    std::cout << "X";
}
std::cout << "\n";
```

The first section of a for loop is the initialization. Any C++ statement can be put here, but typically it is used to create and initialize a counter variable.

The second section is the test, which can be any legal C++ expression. This serves the same purpose as the condition in a while or do-while loop.

The third section is the action that changes the counter. This typically is a statement that increments or decrements the counter's value, but any legal C++ statement can be used here.

The MultTable program in Listing 6.5 creates a multiplication table for a user-selected number. The first 10 multiples of that number are displayed using a for loop.

LISTING 6.5 The Full Text of MultTable.cpp

```
#include <iostream>

int main()
{
    int number;
    std::cout << "Enter a number: ";
```

```
 7:       std::cin >> number;
 8:
 9:       std::cout << "\nFirst 10 Multiples of " << number << "\n";
10:
11:       for (int counter = 1; counter < 11; counter++)
12:       {
13:            std::cout << number * counter << " ";
14:       }
15:       std::cout << "\n";
16:
17:       return 0;
18: }
```

Here's sample output for the user input 11:

```
Enter a number: 11

The First 10 Multiples of 11:
11 22 33 44 55 66 77 88 99 110
```

The `for` statement on line 11 combines on one line the initialization of the integer variable `counter`, the test that `counter` is less than 11, and the action to increment to `counter` all into one line. The body of the `for` loop is line 13.

CAUTION

A common mistake is using a comma (,) instead of a semicolon (;) to separate the sections of a `for` statement, which results in a compiler error. Another common mistake is to place a semicolon (;) after the closing parenthesis of the `for` statement. This makes the loop do nothing but loop. Because there are times it makes sense to do this, the compiler does not report an error.

Advanced `for` Loops

A `for` loop can be powerful and flexible. It is not uncommon to initialize more than one variable, test a compound logical expression, and execute more than one statement.

When the initialization and action sections contain more than one statement, they are separated by commas. Here's an example:

```
for (int x = 0, y = 0; x < 10; x++, y++)
{
    std::cout << x * y << "\n";
}
```

This loop has an initialization section that sets up two integer variables: `x` and `y`. Take note of the comma between the two declarations.

The loop's test section tests whether `x < 10`.

The loop's action section increments both integer variables, using a comma between the statements.

The body of the loop displays the product of multiplying the variables together.

Each section of a `for` loop also can be empty. The semicolons are still there to separate sections, but some of them contain no code. Here's an example:

```
int x = 0;
int y = 0;
for ( ; x < 10; x++, y++)
{
    std::cout << x * y << "\n";
}
```

Nested Loops

Loops can be nested with one loop sitting in the body of another. The inner loop will be executed in its entirety for every execution of the outer loop.

The BoxMaker program in Listing 6.6 uses one `for` loop nested inside another to display a box made of a user-selected character with a user-specified height and width.

LISTING 6.6 **The Full Text of** `BoxMaker.cpp`

```
#include <iostream>

int main()
{
    int rows, columns;
    char character;

    std::cout << "How many rows? ";
    std::cin >> rows;
    std::cout << "How many columns? ";
    std::cin >> columns;
    std::cout << "What character to display? ";
    std::cin >> character;

    std::cout << "\n";
    for (int i = 0; i < rows; i++)
    {
        for (int j = 0; j < columns; j++)
        {
            std::cout << character;
        }
```

```
22:         std::cout << "\n";
23:     }
24:     return 0;
25: }
```

When you run the program, you are asked to select the row and column width of the rectangle. Next, you're asked what character to use when drawing the box.

Here's output for a 10-by-15 rectangle made up of asterisks:

```
How many rows? 10
How many columns? 15
What character? *

***************
***************
***************
***************
***************
***************
***************
***************
***************
***************
```

The first `for` loop, on line 16, initializes a counter named i to 0 and then the body of the loop is run.

On line 18, the first line of the outer `for` loop, an inner `for` loop is established. This loop initializes a counter named `j` to 0, and the body of the inner `for` loop is executed. On line 20, the chosen character is printed, and control returns to the header of the inner `for` loop.

The inner `for` loop is only one statement, which displays the character. The condition is tested (`j < columns`); if it evaluates to true, `j` is incremented and the next character is displayed. This continues until `j` equals the number of columns.

When the inner `for` loop fails its test, in the preceding example after 15 asterisks are printed, execution falls through to line 22, and a new line is printed. The outer `for` loop now returns to its header, where its condition (`i < rows`) is tested. If this evaluates to true, `i` is incremented and the body of the loop is executed.

In the second iteration of the outer `for` loop, the inner `for` loop is started over. Thus, `j` is reinitialized to 0, and the entire inner loop is run again.

When you use a nested loop, the inner loop is executed for each iteration of the outer loop. Therefore, the character is printed `columns` times for each `row`.

switch Statements

When you use a series of if or if-else conditionals on the same variable, your C++ code can become excessively confusing and cumbersome. An alternative is to use switch, a conditional that tests one expression for multiple values to decide which of several blocks of code to execute.

A switch statement consists of the keyword switch followed by an expression to test one or more case sections with possible values of that expression, and possibly a default section when no case matches.

The following switch statement displays a singular or plural ending to the word "zombie," depending on how many zombies you have killed:

```
std::cout << "You have killed " << zombies << " zombie";
switch (zombies)
{
    case 0:
        std::cout << "s\n";
        break;
    case 1:
        std::cout << "\n";
        break;
    default:
        std::cout << "s\n";
}
```

The switch expression is the variable zombies. The two case sections catch different values of zombies. If the value is 0, the character 's' makes the display text "You have killed 0 zombies" with the trailing s. If the value is 1, the text is "You have killed 1 zombie" with no trailing s.

The default section handles all other values for zombies, displaying "You have killed" followed by the number and the word zombies.

The evaluation in the case sections of a switch statement only can be for equality. There's no way to test relational operators or Boolean operations. If one of the case values matches the expression, execution jumps to those statements and continues to the end of the switch block unless a break statement is encountered. If nothing matches, execution branches to the optional default statement. If there is no default and no matching value, execution falls through the switch statement, and the statement ends.

TIP

It's good programming practice to have a default case in switch statements even when you don't have a reason to employ one. The default can be used to display an error when a value defies your expectations and doesn't match any of the case sections.

In the preceding example, each case section ends with a break statement that exits the switch statement. If there is no break statement at the end of a case section, execution falls through to the next case, and its section is executed also. Although it comes in handy in limited situations to execute multiple cases, in most situations you will want a break ending each section.

The BadTeacher program in Listing 6.7 uses a switch statement to deliver a custom comment to a student in response to the grade received on a test.

LISTING 6.7 The Full Text of BadTeacher.cpp

```
#include <iostream>

int main()
{
    char grade;
    std::cout << "Enter your letter grade (ABCDF): ";
    std::cin >> grade;
    switch (grade)
    {
    case 'A':
        std::cout << "Finally!\n";
        break;
    case 'B':
        std::cout << "You can do better!\n";
        break;
    case 'C':
        std::cout << "I'm disappointed in you!\n";
        break;
    case 'D':
        std::cout << "You're not smart!\n";
        break;
    case 'F':
        std::cout << "Get out of my sight!\n";
        break;
    default:
        std::cout << "That's not even a grade!\n";
        break;
    }
    return 0;
}
```

This program asks a user to report a letter grade of A, B, C, D, or F, and then responds to this input with an abusive response. Here are three examples of output:

```
Enter your letter grade (ABCDF): C
I'm disappointed in you!

Enter your letter grade (ABCDF): F
Get out of my sight!

Enter your letter grade (ABCDF): Z
That's not even a grade!
```

The user is prompted for a letter. That letter is tested in the `switch` statement in line 8. The `case` statement on line 10 tests for the character 'A'. If it's a match, line 11 is executed, and the comment "Finally!" is displayed, and the `break` on the following line ends the statement.

The other four letter grades are tested in their own `case` sections. If none of these matches, the `default` section on lines 26–27 is executed.

Summary

The loops and conditionals you learned about during this hour add considerable brainpower to C++ programs.

The `while` loop runs a block of code until a condition is no longer true. If the condition is never true, the code is never executed.

By contrast, the `do-while` loop runs a block of code at least once, even if the tested condition is never true.

A `for` loop is designed using initialization, test, and action sections. These sections make it possible to create a counter variable, test its value, and change its value all within the `for` statement that creates the loop.

Sophisticated loops can be developed with the `continue` statement, which skips to the beginning of the next iteration through a loop, and the `break` statement, which ends a loop entirely.

The `switch-case` conditional simplifies the process of checking the same variable for a set of different equality values. Although the same task could be achieved by a series of `if` or `if-else` conditionals, `switch` is simpler to develop and debug.

Q&A

Q. **How do you choose between `if-else` and `switch`?**

A. If there's more than one or two `else` clauses and all are testing the same value, consider using a `switch` statement. If you need to compare relationships (a > b for instance), you cannot use the `switch` statement. Otherwise, you can choose any conditional. There's no wrong answer as long as your program works.

Q. **How do you choose between `while` and `do-while`?**

A. If the body of the `loop` always should execute at least once, consider a `do-while` loop; otherwise, use the `while` loop.

Q. **How do you choose between `while` and `for`?**

A. If you are executing a statement (or block of statements) a fixed number of times based on the value of a variable that is being incremented, consider the `for` loop. If your variable is already initialized or is not incremented on each loop, a `while` loop might be the better choice.

Q. **Why is an airplane's black box orange?**

A. The boxes are painted fluorescent orange to make them easier to spot in the wreckage of a plane crash. It is a historical misnomer to describe them as black, since even the earliest prototypes were brightly colored. One of the first was nicknamed the "red egg."

The boxes are normally placed at the spot most likely to survive a crash: the rear of the plane near the juncture of the fuselage and the upper tail fin. They are designed to endure a temperature of 1,100 degrees Celsius for 30 minutes and an impact force 3,500 times as strong as gravity. There's actually two boxes—a flight data recorder and cockpit voice recorder.

The inventor of the device, Australian aeronautical engineer David Warren, was nine years old when his father died in a plane crash in the 1930s.

Efforts are underway to make black boxes obsolete by transmitting flight data and pilot voice recordings to satellites throughout a flight.

As to why they're called black boxes, that appears to be borrowed from an early type of flight data recorder. Francois Hussenot and Paul Beaudouin devised a recorder in France that used photographic film and a thin ray of light in a pitch-black box.

Workshop

You learned about some complex program flow this hour, and you should answer a few questions and do a couple of exercises to firm up your knowledge of the topic.

Quiz

1. What data type should be used in a `for` loop?

   A. Integer

   B. Integer or float

   C. Any type is acceptable

2. Which loop cannot use the `break` or `continue` statements?

   A. `for`

   B. `for` or `while`

   C. None

3. What does the `break` command do within a `switch` statement?

   A. Skip to the next `case`

   B. End the `switch` statement

   C. Skip to the `default` section

Answers

1. **C.** Most programmers limit their use of the `for` statement to integers. But that is not a limitation of the language; you can work with floats or strings or other data types.

2. **C.** The `break` and `continue` statements can be used in any type of loop, although they are less common in `for` loops. The reason is that those loops often loop a fixed number of times.

3. **B.** Within a `switch` statement, the `break` command causes execution to resume outside of the body of the `switch` statement. Without it, commands are executed from the first case condition that is true until the end of the switch body.

Activities

1. Write a program that displays the first 100 multiples of 16.

2. Modify the BadTeacher program so that it handles the grades E and G through H, displaying abusive responses tailored to such ignorant prattle.

To see solutions to these activities, visit this book's website at http://cplusplus.cadenhead.org.

HOUR 7
Storing Information in Arrays and Strings

What You'll Learn in This Hour:

- How to store related data in arrays
- How to declare arrays
- How to create strings from character arrays
- How to copy strings

What Is an Array?

An *array* is a collection of related data of the same data type. An array can be envisioned as a series of data storage locations. Each storage location is called an *element* of the array.

An array is declared by writing the data type and array name followed by the number of elements the array holds inside square brackets. Here's an example:

```
long peaks[25];
```

The peaks array holds 25 long integers. This declaration causes the compiler to set aside enough memory to hold all 25 elements. Because each long integer requires 4 bytes, this declaration sets aside 100 contiguous bytes of memory.

Array elements are numbered from 0 up to the largest element, so the peaks array holds elements from 0 through 24. Each element is accessed by using its number in square braces. This statement assigns a value to the first peaks element:

```
peaks[0] = 29029;
```

This statement assigns a value to the last:

```
peaks[24] = 7804;
```

The number of an array element also is called its *subscript*.

The zero-based numbering of array elements can be confusing—an array with three elements has elements numbered 0, 1, and 2 (not 1, 2, and 3).

The WeightGoals program in Listing 7.1 uses an array to calculate weight-loss milestones for a dieting person. The array holds floating-point values that represent progress of 10%, 25%, 50%, and 75% toward the dieter's goal weight.

LISTING 7.1 The Full Text of `WeightGoals.cpp`

```
#include <iostream>

int main()
{
    float goal[4];
    goal[0] = 0.9;
    goal[1] = 0.75;
    goal[2] = 0.5;
    goal[3] = 0.25;
    float weight, target;

    std::cout << "Enter current weight: ";
    std::cin >> weight;
    std::cout << "\nEnter goal weight: ";
    std::cin >> target;
    std::cout << std::endl;

    for (int i = 0; i < 4; i++)
    {
        float loss = (weight - target) * goal[i];
        std::cout << "Goal " << i << ": ";
        std::cout << target + loss << std::endl;
    }

    return 0;
}
```

This program asks a user's current weight and goal weight, and then displays four intermediate weight milestones:

```
Enter current weight: 265

Enter goal weight: 220

Goal 0: 260.5
Goal 1: 253.75
Goal 2: 242.5
Goal 3: 231.25
```

The program stores the user's current weight in the variable `weight` and the user's target in the variable `target`. Both hold floating-point variables.

The goal array holds four values that will be used to calculate the weight milestones. The four-element array is created (line 5) and values of 0.9, 0.75, 0.5, and 0.25 are assigned to those elements (lines 6–9).

A `for` loop iterates through the elements of the array. The amount to reach a milestone is stored in the `loss` variable (line 20). This variable is the total amount of weight to lose multiplied by the percentage.

The `loss` total is added to `target` and displayed as a milestone (line 21).

NOTE

The fact that arrays count up from 0 rather than 1 is a common cause of bugs in programs written by C++ novices. When you use an array, remember that an array with 10 elements counts from `array[0]` to `array[9]`.

Writing Past the End of Arrays

When you assign a value to an array element, the compiler computes where to store the value in memory based on the size of each element and its subscript. If you store a new value in `goal[3]`, the compiler multiplies the offset of 3 by the size of each element, which for `long` integers is four bytes. The compiler then moves that many bytes, 12, from the beginning of the array and stores the new value at that location.

The `goal` array in the WeightGoals program only has four elements. If you try to store something in `goal[4]`, the compiler ignores the fact that there is no such element. Instead, it stores it in memory 20 bytes past the beginning of the first element, replacing whatever data is at that location. This can be almost any data, so writing the new out-of-bounds value might have unpredictable results, such as the program crashing or running with strange results.

These errors can be difficult to spot as a program runs, so it's important to pay attention to the size of arrays when they are accessed.

It is so common to write data one element past the end of an array that the bug has its own name: a *fence post error*. The name refers to the problem of counting how many posts you need for a 10-foot fence if you need one post for every foot. Some people answer 10, but you need 11, as shown in Figure 7.1.

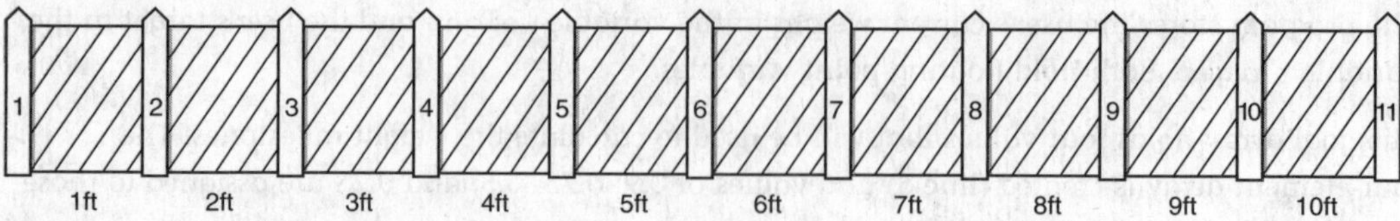

FIGURE 7.1
Counting fence posts.

This sort of "off by one" mistake can be the bane of any programmer's life. Over time, however, you'll get used to the idea that a 25-element array counts only to element 24 and that everything counts from zero.

Initializing Arrays

You can initialize a simple array of built-in types, such as integers or characters, when you first declare the array. After the array name, put an equal sign and a list of comma-separated values enclosed in braces:

```
int post[10] = { 0, 10, 20, 30, 40, 50, 60, 70, 80, 90 };
```

This declares `post` to be an array of 10 integers. It assigns `post[0]` the value 0, `post[1]` the value 10, and so forth up to `post[9]` equaling 90.

If you omit the size of the array, an array just big enough to hold the initialization is created. Consider this statement:

```
int post[] = { 10, 20, 30, 40, 50 };
```

An integer array with five elements is created with `post[0]` equal to 10, `post[1]` equal to 20, and so on.

The built-in C++ function `sizeof()` can be used to count the number of elements in an array:

```
const int size = sizeof(post) / sizeof(post[0]);
```

This example obtains the size of the `post` array by dividing the size of the entire array by the size of an individual element in the array. The result is the number of members in the array.

You cannot initialize more elements than you've declared for the array. This statement generates a compiler error:

```
int post[5] = { 10, 20, 30, 40, 50, 60 };
```

The error occurs because a five-element array has been initialized with six values. It is permitted to initialize an array with fewer values than it holds, as in this statement:

```
int long[5] = { 10, 20 };
```

Multidimensional Arrays

An array can be thought of as a single row of data. A second dimension could be conceptualized as a grid of data consisting of rows and columns. This is a two-dimensional array of data, with one dimension representing each row and the second dimension representing each column. A three-dimensional array could be a cube, with one dimension representing width, a second dimension representing height, and a third dimension representing depth. You even can have arrays of more than three dimensions, although they are harder to imagine as objects in space.

When you declare arrays, each dimension is represented as a subscript in the array. A two-dimensional array has two subscripts:

```
int grid[5, 13];
```

A three-dimensional array has three subscripts:

```
int cube[5, 13, 8];
```

Arrays can have any number of dimensions, although it is likely that most of the arrays you create will have one or two dimensions.

A good example of a two-dimensional array is a chessboard. One dimension represents the eight rows; the other dimension represents the eight columns. Figure 7.2 illustrates this idea.

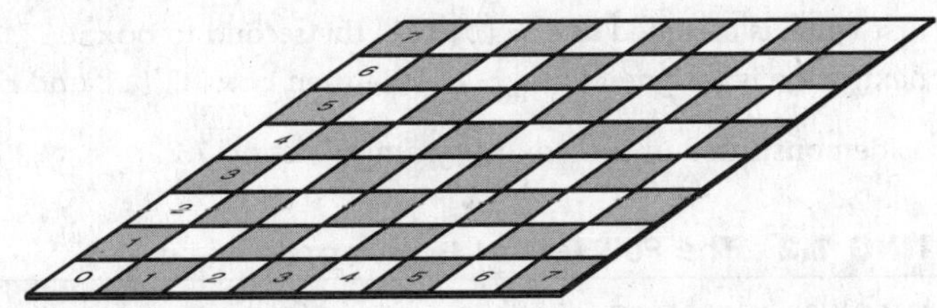

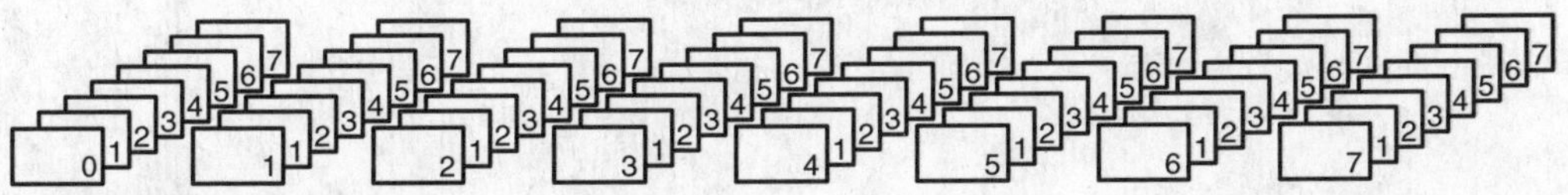

FIGURE 7.2
A chessboard is a two-dimensional array of squares.

Suppose that you have an array of char values named board that represents the board. Each element could equal 'w' if a white piece occupies the square, 'b' if a black piece does and '' (no character) otherwise. The following statement creates the array:

```
int board[8][8];
```

You also could represent the same data with a one-dimensional, 64-square array:

```
int board[64];
```

This doesn't correspond as closely to the real-world object as the two-dimensional array, however. When the game begins, the king is located in the fourth position in the first row. Counting from zero, that position corresponds to `board[0][3]`, assuming that the first subscript corresponds to `row` and the second to `column`. The layout of positions for the entire board is illustrated in Figure 7.2.

CAUTION

Multidimensional arrays can rapidly grow to exceed available memory, so keep that in mind when creating large arrays with multiple dimensions.

Initializing Multidimensional Arrays

You can initialize multidimensional arrays with values just like single-dimension arrays. Values are assigned to array elements in order, with the last array subscript changing and each of the former ones holding steady. Here's an example:

```
int box[5][3] = { 8, 6, 7, 5, 3, 0, 9, 2, 1, 7, 8,
    9, 0, 5, 2 };
```

The first value is assigned to `box[0][0]`, the second to `box[0][1]`, and the third to `box[0][2]`. The next value is assigned to `box[1][0]`, then `box[1][1]` and `box[1][2]`.

This is demonstrated in the Box program in Listing 7.2.

LISTING 7.2 **The Full Text of** `Box.cpp`

```
#include <iostream>

int main()
{
    int box[5][3] = { 8, 6, 7, 5, 3, 0, 9, 2, 1, 7, 8,
        9, 0, 5, 2 };

    for (int i = 0; i < 5; i++)
    {
        for (int j = 0; j < 3; j++)
        {
            std::cout << "box[" << i << "]";
            std::cout << "[" << j << "] = ";
            std::cout << box[i][j] << "\n";
        }
    }
}
```

The program's output displays the contents of each array element, which can be compared to the assignment statement in lines 5–6:

```
box[0][0] = 8
box[0][1] = 6
box[0][2] = 7
box[1][0] = 5
box[1][1] = 3
box[1][2] = 0
box[2][0] = 9
box[2][1] = 2
box[2][2] = 1
box[3][0] = 7
box[3][1] = 8
box[3][2] = 9
box[4][0] = 0
box[4][1] = 5
box[4][2] = 2
```

The `box` variable holds a two-dimensional array that has five integers in the first dimension and two integers in the second. This creates a 5-by-3 grid of elements.

Two `for` loops are used to cycle through the array, displaying each array element and its value.

For the sake of clarity, you could group the initializations with braces, organizing each row on its own line:

```
int box[5][3] = {
    {8, 6, 7},
    {5, 3, 0},
    {9, 2, 1},
    {7, 8, 9},
    {0, 5, 2} };
```

The compiler ignores the inner braces. This makes it easier to see how the numbers are distributed.

Each value must be separated by a comma without regard to the braces. The entire initialization set must be within braces, and it must end with a semicolon.

A Word About Memory

When you declare an array, you tell the compiler exactly how many elements you expect to store in it. The compiler sets aside the proper amount of memory for an array given the size of the data type and the number of elements it contains. Arrays are suitable for data that consists of a known number of elements, such as squares on a chessboard (64) or years in a century (100).

When you have no idea how many elements are needed, you must use more advanced data structures.

Future hours of this book cover arrays of pointers, arrays built on the heap, and other structures. In Hour 19, "Storing Information in Linked Lists," you learn about an advanced data structure known as a linked list.

Character Arrays

Familiarity with arrays makes it possible to work with longer text than the single characters represented by the `char` data type. A string is a series of characters. The only strings you've worked with up to this point have been string literals used in `std::cout` statements:

```
std::cout << "Solidum petit in profundis!\n";
```

In C++, a string is an array of characters ending with a `null` character, a special character coded as `'\0'`. You can declare and initialize a string like any other array:

```
char yum[] = { 'Z', 'o', 'm', 'b', 'i', 'e',
    ' ','E','a','t',' ', 'B', 'r', 'a', 'i', 'n',
    's', '\0' };
```

The last character, `'\0'`, is the `null` character that terminates the string.

Because this character-by-character approach is difficult to type and admits too many opportunities for error, C++ enables a shorthand form of string initialization using a literal:

```
char yum[] = "Zombie Eat Brains";
```

This form of initialization doesn't require the `null` character; the compiler adds it automatically.

The string "Zombie Eat Brains" is 18 bytes, including `null`.

You also can create uninitialized character arrays, which are called buffers. As with all arrays, it is important to ensure that you don't put more into the buffer than there is room for.

Buffers can be used to store input typed by a user. Several programs created in past hours used the `std::cin` object to collect user input and store it in a variable:

```
std::cin >> yum;
```

Although this approach works, two major problems arise. First, if the user enters more characters than the size of the buffer, `cin` writes past the end of the buffer, making the program run improperly and causing security concerns. Second, if the user enters a space, `cin` treats it as the end of the string and stops writing to the buffer.

To solve these problems, you must call a function of the `cin` object called `getline()` with two arguments:

- The buffer to fill
- The maximum number of characters to get

NOTE

You may be wondering how a function can be called by adding a period "." to something called an object, because objects have yet to be fully introduced in this book. A function that refers to an object followed by a period and a name, like `std::cin.getline()`, is called a member function. This concept will be covered in Hour 8, "Creating Basic Classes."

The following statement stores user input of up to 18 characters (including `null`) and stores it in the `yum` character array:

```
std::cin.getline(yum, 18);
```

The method also can be called with a third argument, the delimiter that terminates input:

```
std::cin.getline(yum, 18,' ');
```

This statement terminates input at the first space. When the third argument is omitted, the newline character (`'\n'`) is the delimiter.

The BridgeKeeper program in Listing 7.3 asks three famous questions from a classic movie, storing them in buffers.

LISTING 7.3 The Full Text of `BridgeKeeper.cpp`

```
#include <iostream>

int main()
{
    char name[50];
    char quest[80];
    char velocity[80];

    std::cout << "\nWhat is your name? ";
    std::cin.getline(name, 49);

    std::cout << "\nWhat is your quest? ";
    std::cin.getline(quest, 79);

    std::cout << "\nWhat is the velocity of an unladen swallow? ";
    std::cin.getline(velocity, 79);
```

```
17:
18:     std::cout << "\nName: " << name << std::endl;
19:     std::cout << "Quest: " << quest << std::endl;
20:     std::cout << "Velocity: " << velocity << std::endl;
21:     return 0;
22: }
```

This program produces output like the following:

```
What is your name? Rogers Cadenhead

What is your quest? Time-based C++ tutelage

What is the airspeed velocity of an unladen
swallow? I don't know-- aagh!

Name: Rogers Cadenhead
Quest: Time-based C++ tutelage
Velocity: I don't know-- aagh!
```

Line 10 calls the function `getLine()` of `cin`. The buffer declared in line 5 is passed in as the first argument. The second argument is the maximum number of characters to allow as input. Because the `name` buffer can hold 50 characters, the argument must be 49 to allow for the terminating `null`. There is no need to provide a terminating character as a third argument because the default value of `newline` is sufficient.

The film in question, if you haven't recognized it already (or even if you did), is *Monty Python and the Holy Grail*. The Bridge of Death is guarded by a bridgekeeper who demands that three questions be answered correctly. Get one wrong and you are thrown off to your doom.

The correct answers, in case you ever run into this problem on your travels:

- It is Arthur, King of the Britons
- To seek the Holy Grail
- What do you mean? An African or European swallow?

Copying Strings

C++ inherits from C a library of functions for dealing with strings. This library can be incorporated in a program by including the header file `string.h`:

```
#include <string.h>
```

Among the many functions provided are two for copying one string into another: `strcpy_s()` and `strncpy_s()`.

The `strcpy_s()` function copies the entire contents of one string into a designated buffer, as demonstrated by the StringCopier program in Listing 7.4.

LISTING 7.4 The Full Text of `StringCopier.cpp`

```
 1: #include <iostream>
 2: #include <string.h>
 3:
 4: int main()
 5: {
 6:     char string1[] = "Free the bound periodicals!";
 7:     char string2[80];
 8:
 9:     strcpy_s(string2, string1);
10:
11:     std::cout << "String1: " << string1 << std::endl;
12:     std::cout << "String2: " << string2 << std::endl;
13:     return 0;
14: }
```

Run this program to eyeball the following output:

```
String1: Free the bound periodicals!
String2: Free the bound periodicals!
```

A character array is created on Line 6 and initialized with the value of a string literal. The `strcpy()` function on Line 9 takes two character arrays: a destination that will receive the copy and a source that will copy it. If the source array is larger than the destination, `strcpy()` writes data past the end of the buffer.

To protect against this, the standard library also includes the function `strncpy()`. This version takes a third argument that specifies the maximum number of characters to copy:

```
strncopy(string1, string2, 80);
```

Reading Arrays with Foreach Loops

One disadvantage of C++ relative to languages such as Java has been the amount of code required to do one of the most common tasks in programming. When you loop through the elements of an array (or other data structures), the code is a bit cumbersome.

A recent addition to C++ is a new `for` loop that can loop through every element in an array. It's commonly called a foreach loop because it iterates through a loop once for each element.

This foreach loop uses the keyword `for`, just like other `for` loops. Unlike other `for` loops, the foreach has two sections separated by a colon (:) instead of three separated by semicolons.

The first section is a variable that will hold an element of the array. The second is the name of the array.

The Production program in Listing 7.5 uses a foreach loop to display the contents of an integer array, five totals that represent one year's production of a commodity.

LISTING 7.5 The Full Text of `Production.cpp`

```
 1: #include <iostream>
 2:
 3: int main()
 4: {
 5:    int production[] = { 10500, 16000, 5800, 4500, 13900 };
 6:
 7:    for (int year : production)
 8:    {
 9:       std::cout << "Output: " << year << std::endl;
10:    }
11: }
```

Because this program uses a recent addition to C++, you may need to use the `std=c++14` flag when you compile it.

Run it to see this output:

```
Output: 10500
Output: 16000
Output: 5800
Output: 4500
Output: 13900
```

The program defines a `production` array of integers in line 5 with five elements. They are assigned values in the same statement.

In line 7, a loop is declared that will iterate once for each element in `production`. The element's value is stored in an `int` variable named `year`.

This value is displayed in line 9.

As you learn about data structures more advanced than arrays, you will find more uses for the foreach loop.

Summary

One thing that makes software so useful is the ability to process large amounts of similar data. Arrays are collections of data that share the same data type. This hour demonstrated them with only the simple data types, but you learn in upcoming hours that arrays can be put to use on more complex forms of data.

Although strings are just character arrays in C++, they're commonly referred to as strings because they serve so many useful purposes. Strings can collect user input, present text, and store textual data from files, web documents, and other sources.

There are many other ways to represent data in C++ more sophisticated than simple data types and arrays.

Q&A

Q. What happens if I write to element 25 in a 24-member array?

A. The end of the world as we know it. Not really, but it's pretty bad. When you store a value past the end of an array, you write to other memory with potentially disastrous effects on your program. Memory used by the program could be overwritten and the software could run improperly.

This mistake is called a buffer overflow. According to security experts, the most common software exploit used by malicious programmers is to write data past a buffer and use this error to execute new code. The new code often can do anything, such as altering or deleting files, granting system privileges to untrusted users, and replicating viruses.

Q. What is in an uninitialized array element?

A. An array element that has not been assigned a value. The value is whatever happens to be in memory at a given time. The results of using this element without assigning a value are unpredictable.

Q. Why did the number 13 become associated with bad luck?

A. Thirteen has been getting bad press since the Middle Ages, partially from the observation that the presence of Judas made the Last Supper a table for 13.

Additionally, the Norse god Loki arrived at a party attended by 12 of his colleagues and ruined the proceedings, according to one myth.

Furthermore, when ancient calendars in Sumer and Babylon ventured too far off the mark, a thirteenth month was added to bring things into line with the seasons. This kludge affected planting schedules and crop yield, so month 13 was not welcome.

Thirteen is also one past a dozen and 12 is considered to be a suitable number for a wide variety of things. This makes 13 one too many and represents transgression and discord.

The number 13 is so terrifying there's a word to describe the fear of it: *triskaidekaphobia*.

As a person whose birthday falls on April 13, I think the number gets a bad rap.

Workshop

You just spent the past hour learning about arrays. Now is the time to answer a few questions and perform a couple of exercises to firm up your knowledge of them.

Quiz

1. What is the minimum array subscript for a particular array?

   A. 0

   B. 1

   C. There's a two-drink minimum.

2. What happens if you try to store data beyond the maximum allowed array subscript?

   A. The compiler reports an error.

   B. The data is ignored.

   C. The data is written in memory past the array.

3. What is another name for a character array that does not have an initial value?

   A. A string

   B. A buffer

   C. A `null` character

Answers

1. **A.** All arrays start with zero. The last element is the size of the array minus 1, so the array `brains[50]` would hold 49.

2. **C.** The data is written to the address right after the end of the array. It is difficult to tell what will happen. If you are lucky, the data is stored in an area of memory the computer doesn't want you to access, and an error results. If you are unlucky, another variable is changed in some strange way that is difficult to debug.

3. **B.** A buffer can be used to store user input or any other character data.

Activities

1. Write a program that asks a user's first and last name and displays it as part of a sentence greeting the user.

2. Modify the WeightGoals program to use a foreach loop and add a new milestone for 10%.

To see solutions to these activities, visit this book's website at http://cplusplus.cadenhead.org.

HOUR 8
Creating Basic Classes

What You'll Learn in This Hour:

- What types are
- What classes and objects are
- How to define a new class and create objects of that class

What Is a Type?

One of the things that distinguishes humans is our ability to categorize. We don't see hundreds of vague shapes in nature; we see animals, rocks, insects, and trees. We don't just see animals; we see bears, foxes, chupacabras, sasquatches, and so forth. We divide things into various classes that tell us what type of thing they are.

A sasquatch is a type of mammal. A mammal is a type of animal. An animal is a type of living thing.

In C++, a *type* is an object with data and a set of abilities. You've worked with built-in types such as `int`, `long`, and `float` numbers. You also can create your own types, as you discover this hour.

Computer programs are written to solve real-world problems, such as keeping track of employee paychecks or scheduling the games in a childrens soccer league. One of the best ways to write a program to accomplish large, complex tasks is to create representations of the objects that work together to perform the task.

So, if you're creating a league schedule, you could have objects to represent each team in the league, each day that games can be played and each game on the schedule. The closer these objects correspond to reality, the easier it is to write the program.

Creating New Types

As you work with built-in types in C++, each variable's type tells you quite a bit about it. For example, if you write a program with `height` and `width` declared as unsigned short integers, you know that each variable one can hold a number between 0 and 65,535.

The type also tells you capabilities of the variable. Short integers can be added together, so by declaring `height` and `width` as that type, you know they can be added together.

The type of a variable tells you several things:

- Its size in memory
- The information it can hold
- The actions that can be performed on it

In C++ you define your own types to model a problem you are trying to solve. The mechanism for declaring a new type is to create a class. A *class* is a definition of a new type.

Classes and Members

A C++ class is a template used to create objects. After you define a class, objects created from that class can be put to use like any other data type.

A class is a collection of related variables and functions bundled together. The variables can be of any other type, including other classes.

Variables make up the data in the class, and functions perform tasks using that data. Bundling these together is called *encapsulation*.

This will make more sense in relation to a real object, such as the red tricycle my parents left behind during a move from Wichita Falls, Texas, to Dallas when I was four years old. (The U-Haul ran out of room. This is a touchy subject for me.)

One way to think about a tricycle is that it's a collection of objects connected together—wheels, a seat, handlebars, and pedals. Another way is in terms of what it can do: move, accelerate, stop, and impress other four-year-olds.

Combining these together—the physical aspects and performance—is encapsulating the object.

Encapsulation of a class makes it possible for other programs to use the class without knowing how it works. Users of your class only need to know what it does, not how it does it.

The variables of the class are called its *member variables*. A `Tricycle` class might have member variables representing the wheel size, top speed, and the height of its fluorescent orange safety flag.

Member variables, also known as *data members* or *instance variables*, are part of your class, just like the wheel and brake are part of a trike.

The functions in the class use and modify the member variables. They are called the member *functions* (or *methods*) of the class. Member functions of the `Tricycle` class might include `pedal()` and `brake()`.

Member functions are as much a part of your class as member variables. They determine what the objects of your class can do.

Declaring a Class

To declare a class, use the `class` keyword followed by information about the member variables and member functions of the class. An opening brace and closing brace enclose the class definition. Here's an example for a `Tricycle` class:

```
class Tricycle
{
public:
    unsigned int speed;
    unsigned int wheelSize;
    pedal();
    brake();
};
```

This code creates a class called `Tricycle` with two member variables, `speed` and `wheelSize`, and two member functions, `pedal()` and `brake()`. All four can be used by other classes because the `public` keyword precedes them in the class definition. You learn more about this keyword later in the hour.

Declaring this class does not allocate memory for a `Tricycle`. It just tells the compiler what the `Tricycle` class is, what data it contains (`speed` and `wheelSize`) and what it can do (`pedal()` and `brake()`).

It also tells the compiler how much room the compiler must set aside for each of the Tricycle objects that you create. In this example, if an integer is four bytes, `Tricycle` is only eight bytes total: `speed` is four bytes and `wheelSize` is another four. The two functions take up no room because no storage space is set aside for member functions.

Defining an Object

An object is created from a class by specifying its class and a variable name, just as you've done with built-in types in the preceding seven hours. For example:

```
Tricycle wichita;
```

This statement creates a `Tricycle` object named `wichita`. The `Tricycle` class is used as a template for the object. The object will have all member variables and member functions defined for the class.

C++ differentiates between the class `Tricycle`, which is the concept of a tricycle, and each individual `Tricycle` object.

An *object* is just an individual instance of a class. When you create an object, you are said to "instantiate" it from the class.

NOTE

Because C++ is case sensitive, all class names should follow the same convention to minimize errors. Instead of having to remember whether a class is called `Tricycle`, `tricycle`, or `TRICYCLE`, if you always capitalize the first letter of a class name you'll know it is `Tricycle`. Some programmers prefix every class name with a particular lowercase letter (for example, `cTricycle` or `cSkateboard`). The convention used in this book is initial capitalization, as in `Tricycle` and `Sasquatch`.

Member variables and functions also should follow the same naming rules. This book begins both with lowercase letters, as in `speed` and `pedal()`, and a capital letter beginning each subsequent word (if any), as in `bringMyTrike()`.

Accessing Class Members

After you create an object, you use the dot operator (`.`) to access the member functions and variables of that object. As you might recall, the `Tricycle` class has a member variable called `speed`. To set this variable, use the dot operator:

```
Tricycle wichita;
wichita.speed = 6;
```

After the member function `pedal()` function has been defined, the dot operator is used to call it:

```
wichita.pedal();
```

Private Versus Public Access

The `Tricycle` class has two public member variables and two public member functions. The `public` keyword makes these parts of the class available to the public—in other words, other classes and programs that use `Tricycle` objects.

All member variables and functions are private by default. Private members can be accessed only within functions of the class itself. Public members can be accessed everywhere else. Here's a modified definition of `Tricycle`:

```
class Tricycle
{
    unsigned int speed;
    unsigned int wheelSize;
    pedal();
    brake();
};
```

When the `public` keyword appears in a class definition, all member variables and functions after the keyword are public:

```
class Tricycle
{
    int model = 110;
public:
    unsigned int speed;
    unsigned int wheelSize;
    pedal();
    brake();
};
```

The preceding code declares everything in the `Tricycle` class public except for the `model` member variable.

There's also a `private` keyword to make all subsequent member variables and functions private.

Each use of `public` or `private` changes access control from that point on to the end of the class or until the next access control keyword.

Keeping member data private limits access and controls how their values can be changed.

Although member variables can be public, it's a good idea to keep them all private and make them available only via functions.

A function used to set or get the value of a private member variable is called an *accessor*. Other classes must call the accessor instead of working directly with the variable.

Accessors enable you to separate the details of how the data is stored from how it is used. If you later change how the data is stored, you don't need to rewrite functions that use the data.

You create accessors in the next section.

Implementing Member Functions

Every class member function that you declare also must be defined.

A member function definition begins with the name of the class followed by the scope resolution operator (::) and the name of the function. Here's an example:

```
void Tricycle::pedal()
{
    std::cout << "Pedaling trike\n";
}
```

Class functions have the same capabilities as functions; they can have parameters and return a value.

The Tricycle program in Listing 8.1 defines a `Tricycle` class and takes it for a test drive.

LISTING 8.1 The Full Text of `Tricycle.cpp`

```
#include <iostream>

class Tricycle
{
public:
    int getSpeed();
    void setSpeed(int speed);
    void pedal();
    void brake();
private:
    int speed;
};

// get the trike's speed
int Tricycle::getSpeed()
{
    return speed;
}

// set the trike's speed
void Tricycle::setSpeed(int newSpeed)
{
    if (newSpeed >= 0)
    {
        speed = newSpeed;
    }
}

// pedal the trike
```

```
30: void Tricycle::pedal()
31: {
32:     setSpeed(speed + 1);
33:     std::cout << "\nPedaling; tricycle speed " << speed << " mph\n";
34: }
35:
36: // apply the brake on the trike
37: void Tricycle::brake()
38: {
39:     setSpeed(speed - 1);
40:     std::cout << "\nBraking; tricycle speed " << speed << " mph\n";
41: }
42:
43: // create a trike and ride it
44: int main()
45: {
46:     Tricycle wichita;
47:     wichita.setSpeed(0);
48:     wichita.pedal();
49:     wichita.pedal();
50:     wichita.brake();
51:     wichita.brake();
52:     wichita.brake();
53:     return 0;
54: }
```

The Tricycle program creates a `Tricycle` object, sets its initial speed to 0 and calls the `pedal()` and `brake()` member functions several times. These functions increase and decrease the speed, respectively. Here's the output:

```
Pedaling; tricycle speed 1 mph

Pedaling; tricycle speed 2 mph

Braking; tricycle speed 1 mph

Braking; tricycle speed 0 mph

Braking; tricycle speed 0 mph
```

Lines 3–12 contain the definition of the `Tricycle` class. Line 5 contains the keyword `public`, which tells the compiler that what follows is a set of public members. Line 6 has the declaration of the public accessor `getSpeed()`, which provides access to the private member variable `speed` declared on line 11. Line 7 has the public accessor `setSpeed()`, which takes an integer as an parameter and sets `speed` to the value of that parameter.

Line 10 begins the private section, which includes only the declaration of the private member variable `speed`.

Lines 15–18 contain the definition of the member function `getSpeed()`. This function takes no parameters; it returns an integer. Note that class member functions include the class name followed by two colons and the function's name. This syntax tells the compiler that the `getSpeed()` function you are defining here is the one that you declared in the `Tricycle` class. With the exception of this header line, the `getSpeed()` function is created like any function.

The `getSpeed()` function is only one statement, which returns the value in the member variable `speed`. The program's `main()` function cannot access `speed` because it is private in the `Tricycle` class. The `main()` function has access to the public function `getSpeed()`. Because `getSpeed()` is a function of the class, it has full access to its `speed` variable. This access enables the function to return the value of `speed` to `main()`.

Lines 21–27 contain the definition of the `setSpeed()` function. It takes an integer parameter and sets the value of `speed` to the value of that parameter, but only if the parameter is greater than or equal to 0. By using an accessor and making `speed` private, the class controls how the variable is set. This restriction against negative speeds is an example of that.

Line 30 begins the `pedal()` function. This function increases the speed of the trike by 1 by calling `setSpeed()` and displays the current speed after acceleration.

Line 37 begins the `brake()` function, which decreases the speed by 1 with a call to `setSpeed()` and displays the current speed. The attempt to decrease the speed fails if `speed` equals 0, because 0 miles per hour is the slowest the trike can travel.

Line 44 begins the body of the program with the `main()` function. A `Tricycle` object named `wichita` is created and given an initial speed of 0. The `Tricycle` object's `pedal()` and `brake()` function are called to change the rate of speed.

The last call to `brake()` in line 52 shows that the speed won't go below 0. The trike already had stopped as of line 51, as the output illustrates.

Creating and Deleting Objects

There are two ways to define built-in types such as integers. One way is to define the variable and then assign a value to it later in the program:

```
int weight;
weight = 7;
```

Alternatively, you can define the integer and immediately initialize it:

```
int weight = 7;
```

Initialization combines the definition of the variable with its initial assignment. Nothing stops you from changing that value later, but initialization ensures that the variable always has a value.

Classes have a special member function called a *constructor* that is called when an object of the class is instantiated. The job of the constructor is to create a valid object of the class, which often includes initializing its member data. The constructor is a function with the same name as the class but no return value. Constructors may or may not have parameters, just like any other function of the class.

Here's a constructor for the `Tricycle` class:

```
Tricycle::Tricycle(int initialSpeed)
{
    setSpeed(initialSpeed);
}
```

This constructor sets the initial value of the `speed` member variable using a parameter.

When you declare a constructor, you also should declare a destructor. Just as constructors create and initialize objects of your class, destructors clean up after objects and free any memory that was allocated for them. A destructor always has the name of the class preceded by a tilde (~). Destructors take no parameters and have no return value.

Here's a `Tricycle` destructor:

```
Tricycle::~Tricycle()
{
    // do nothing
}
```

As currently written, the class requires no special actions to free up memory, so the destructor only includes a comment.

Default Constructors

There are several ways to call constructors when setting up an object.

One is to specify one or more parameters in parentheses:

```
Tricycle wichita(5);
```

The parameter (or parameters) is sent to the constructor. In this example, it sets the initial speed of the trike.

You also can set an object up without specifying parameters:

```
Tricycle wichita;
```

This calls the default constructor of the class, which is a constructor with no parameters.

Constructors Provided by the Compiler

If you declare no constructors, as you did in the Tricycle program in Listing 8.1, the compiler creates a default constructor.

The default constructor the compiler provides takes no action; it is as if you declared a constructor with no parameters whose body was empty.

There are two important points to note:

- The default constructor is any constructor that takes no parameters. You can define it yourself or be provided one as a default from the compiler.
- If you define any constructor (with or without parameters), the compiler does not provide a default constructor for you. In that case, if you want a default constructor, you must define it yourself.

If you fail to define a destructor, the compiler also provides one of those, which also has an empty body and does nothing.

If you define a constructor, it's a good practice to define a destructor even if your destructor does nothing. This helps you remember to make use of the destructor when you need to take explicit steps to free memory.

The NewTricycle program in Listing 8.2 rewrites the `Tricycle` class to use a constructor to initialize the object, setting its speed to an initial value. It also demonstrates where the destructor is called.

LISTING 8.2 The Full Text of `NewTricycle.cpp`

```
#include <iostream>

class Tricycle
{
public:
    Tricycle(int initialAge);
    ~Tricycle();
    int getSpeed();
    void setSpeed(int speed);
    void pedal();
    void brake();
private:
    int speed;
};

// constructor for the object
Tricycle::Tricycle(int initialSpeed)
{
    setSpeed(initialSpeed);
```

```
}

// destructor for the object
Tricycle::~Tricycle()
{
    // do nothing
}

// get the trike's speed
int Tricycle::getSpeed()
{
    return speed;
}

// set the trike's speed
void Tricycle::setSpeed(int newSpeed)
{
    if (newSpeed >= 0)
    {
        speed = newSpeed;
    }
}

// pedal the trike
void Tricycle::pedal()
{
    setSpeed(speed + 1);
    std::cout << "\nPedaling; tricycle speed " << getSpeed() << " mph\n";
}

// apply the brake on the trike
void Tricycle::brake()
{
    setSpeed(speed - 1);
    std::cout << "\nBraking; tricycle speed " << getSpeed() << " mph\n";
}

// create a trike and ride it
int main()
{
    Tricycle wichita(5);
    wichita.pedal();
    wichita.pedal();
    wichita.brake();
    wichita.brake();
    wichita.brake();
    return 0;
}
```

This program produces the following output, which reflects an initial trike speed of 5 mph:

```
Pedaling; tricycle speed 6 mph

Pedaling; tricycle speed 7 mph

Braking; tricycle speed 6 mph

Braking; tricycle speed 5 mph

Braking; tricycle speed 4 mph
```

The `Tricycle` class definition in Listing 8.2 has two new additions: a declaration for a constructor that takes an integer parameter and a declaration for a constructor.

Lines 17–20 show the implementation of the constructor, which is similar to the implementation of the `SetAge()` accessor function. There is no return value.

Lines 23–26 show the implementation of the destructor `~Tricycle()`.

A `Tricycle` object is created in Line 60 and given an initial value of 5 with a parameter to the constructor.

Summary

Over the history of computer programming there have been several popular methodologies for creating programs. The one introduced in this hour is called *object-oriented programming* (OOP) because of how it conceives of programs.

In OOP, a program consists of one or more objects, each of which has its own data in the form of member data and functions in the form of functions. The objects are separate from each other and specialize in a specific and narrow purpose.

By designing objects to be independent of each other, you create code that's more easily reused elsewhere. If you created a `Printer` class in a program to print documents, that class can be used by other programs you write if they need printing capabilities.

You learn more about OOP in the next hour as you delve deeper into classes.

Q&A

Q. How big is a class object?

A. A class object's size in memory is determined by the sum of the sizes of its member variables. Class functions don't take up room as part of the memory set aside for the object.

Some compilers align variables in memory in such a way that two-byte variables actually consume somewhat more than two bytes.

Q. Why shouldn't I make all the member data public?

A. Making member data private enables the client of the class to use the data without worrying about how it is stored or computed. For example, if the `Tricycle` class has a member function `getSpeed()`, clients of the `Tricycle` class can ask for the trike's speed without knowing if the trike stores its speed in a member variable or computes it on-the-fly. Public data is like global data—any code that uses the object can access the data. So if it becomes changed, there's often a difficult time figuring out where it happened.

Q. Why do lawn gnomes protect our yards instead of lawn elves, lawn dwarves, lawn halflings, lawn half-elves, or lawn half-orcs?

A. Lawn gnomes date back to 19th century Germany, where in the village of Thuringia the ceramic artisan Phillip Griebel created the first yard protectors in honor of local myths about how gnomes protected gardens at night.

The gnomes proved popular enough to spread all over Germany, then over to England, and finally the world. They're typically bearded males with a red hat who smoke pipes.

A popular prank in recent years is "gnoming," which is stealing someone's lawn gnome and having him photographed at remote locations, perhaps even on a foreign vacation. In France in the late 1990s, a group calling itself the Garden Gnome Liberation Front stole more than 150 in a bid to give them their freedom.

Workshop

Now that you've gotten to see classes and objects, you can answer a few questions and complete a couple of exercises to firm up your knowledge and understanding.

Quiz

1. Which of the following does not take up computer memory?

A. Class

B. Object

C. Both

2. What keyword prevents some member data and functions from being used outside of the class?

   A. `public`

   B. `private`

   C. Neither

3. Why did the author's parents leave his tricycle behind when he was four?

   A. Cruel indifference

   B. A moving truck ran out of room

   C. Because adversity builds character

Answers

1. **A.** A class occupies no memory because it is just a definition of how an object would be created. An object is the implementation of that class.
2. **B.** Private data and functions can be accessed only within the class itself. Public data and functions can be accessed outside of the class. You generally want to keep all your class data items private and the functions public (so they can be called).
3. **B.** The U-Haul van they were renting ran out of room. I've been told I received a new tricycle shortly after we arrived in Dallas, but I don't remember it. Watch the movie *Citizen Kane* to understand more about toy-based childhood lamentation.

Activities

1. Modify the `Tricycle` application to add a second trike. Give it an initial value and try the `pedal()` and `brake()` member functions on it.
2. Modify the `NewTricycle` application to add a member variable called `wheelSize` that must be at least 4 in value when set with an accessor.

To see solutions to these activities, visit this book's website at http://cplusplus.cadenhead.org.

HOUR 9

Moving into Advanced Classes

What You'll Learn in This Hour:

- ▶ What constant member functions are
- ▶ How to separate the class interface from its implementation
- ▶ How to manage your classes
- ▶ How to find and avoid bugs

`const` Member Functions

If you declare a member function to be constant with the `const` keyword, it indicates that the function won't change the value of any members of the class. To declare a function as constant, put the keyword `const` after the parentheses, as in this example:

```
void displayPage() const;
```

Accessors used to retrieve a variable's value, which also are called getter functions, often are constant functions. The `Tricycle` class from the preceding hour had two accessors:

```
void setSpeed(int newSpeed);
int getSpeed();
```

The `setSpeed()` function cannot be `const` because it changes the member variable `speed`. The `getSpeed()` function, on the other hand, can be `const` because it doesn't change the class at all. It simply returns the current value of the member variable `speed`. Therefore, the declaration of the function can become this:

```
int getSpeed() const;
```

If you declare a function to be `const` and the implementation of that function changes the object by changing the value of any of its members, the compiler will flag it as an error.

It is good programming practice to declare as many functions to be `const` as possible. When you do, this enables the compiler to catch unintended changes to member variables, instead of letting these errors show up when your program is running.

Interface Versus Implementation

The parts of a program that create and use objects are the clients of the class. The class declaration serves as a contract with these clients. The contract tells clients what data the class has available and what the class can do.

For example, in the `Tricycle` class declaration, you promise in the contract that every `Tricycle` object will be able to retrieve its speed, that you can initialize the speed at construction and set or retrieve it later, and that every `Tricycle` will know how to `pedal()` and `brake()`.

If you make `getSpeed()` a `const` function, the contract also promises that it won't change the `Tricycle` on which it is called in that function.

Organizing Class Declarations and Function Definitions

Class definitions often are kept separate from their implementations in the source code of C++ programs. Each function that you declare for your class must have a definition. Like functions, the definition of a class function has a header and a body.

The definition must be in a file that the compiler can find. Most C++ compilers expect that file to end with `.cpp`.

Although you can put the declaration in the source code file, a convention that most programmers adopt is putting the declaration in a header file with the same name ending with the file extension `.hpp` (or less commonly `.h` or `.hp`).

So if you put the declaration of the `Tricycle` class in a file named `Tricycle.hpp`, the definition of the class functions would be in `Tricycle.cpp`. The header file can be incorporated into the `.cpp` file with a preprocessor directive:

```
#include "Tricycle.hpp"
```

The reason to separate them is because clients of a class don't care about the implementation specifics. Everything they need to know is in the header file.

Inline Implementation

Just as you can tell the compiler to make a regular function inline, you can make member functions inline. The keyword `inline` appears before the return value, as in this example:

```
inline int Tricycle::getSpeed()
{
    return speed;
}
```

You also can put the definition of a function in the declaration of the class, which automatically makes that function inline. Here's an example:

```
class Tricycle
{
public:
    int getSpeed() const { return speed; }
    void setSpeed(int newSpeed);
};
```

The `getSpeed()` definition has changed. Instead of a semicolon after the keyword `const`, there's a short block of code within braces. The body of the inline function begins immediately after the declaration of the member function; there's no semicolon after the parentheses. Whitespace doesn't matter, so the declaration could be formatted like this:

```
class Tricycle
{
public:
   int getSpeed() const
   {
      return speed;
   }
   void setSpeed(int newSpeed);
};
```

Listings 9.1 and 9.2 re-create the `Tricycle` class, moving the declaration to `Tricycle.hpp` and the implementation of the functions to `Tricycle.cpp`. Listing 9.1 also changes the `getSpeed()` accessor and the `pedal()` and `brake()` functions to inline.

LISTING 9.1 The Full Text of `Tricycle.hpp`

```
#include <iostream>

class Tricycle
{
public:
    Tricycle(int initialSpeed);
    ~Tricycle();
    int getSpeed() const { return speed; }
    void setSpeed(int speed);
    void pedal()
    {
        setSpeed(speed + 1);
        std::cout << "Pedaling " << getSpeed() << " mph\n\n";
    }
    void brake()
    {
        setSpeed(speed - 1);
```

```
        std::cout << "Pedaling " << getSpeed() << " mph\n";
    }
private:
    int speed;
};
```

LISTING 9.2 The Full Text of `Tricycle.cpp`

```
#include "Tricycle.hpp"

// constructor for the object
Tricycle::Tricycle(int initialSpeed)
{
    setSpeed(initialSpeed);
}

// destructor for the object
Tricycle::~Tricycle()
{
    // do nothing
}

// set the trike's speed
void Tricycle::setSpeed(int newSpeed)
{
    if (newSpeed >= 0)
        speed = newSpeed;
}

// create a trike and ride it
int main()
{
    Tricycle wichita(5);
    wichita.pedal();
    wichita.pedal();
    wichita.brake();
    wichita.brake();
    wichita.brake();
    return 0;
}
```

```
Pedaling 6 mph

Pedaling 7 mph

Pedaling 6 mph
Pedaling 5 mph
Pedaling 4 mph
```

The `getSpeed()` function is declared on line 8 of Listing 9.1 and its inline implementation is provided. Lines 9–19 provide more inline functions.

Line 1 of Listing 9.2 is a preprocessor directive to include the header file `Tricycle.hpp` in the source code.

Classes with Other Classes as Member Data

It is not uncommon to build a complex class by declaring simpler classes and including them in the declaration of the more complicated class.

For example, you might declare the classes `Wheel`, `Motor`, `Transmission`, and so forth, then combine them together in a `Car` class. This arrangement declares a "has-a" relationship: A car has a motor, it has a set of wheels, and it has a transmission.

Consider a second example. A rectangle is composed of four lines. Each line is defined by two points. A point is defined by x and y coordinates. Listing 9.3 shows a complete declaration of a `Rectangle` class as it might appear in `Rectangle.hpp`.

Because a rectangle is defined as four lines connecting four points, and each point refers to a coordinate on a graph, a `Point` class is first declared to hold the x and y coordinates of each point. Listing 9.4 shows a complete declaration of both classes.

LISTING 9.3 The Full Text of `Rectangle.hpp`

```
#include <iostream>

class Point
{
    // no constructor, use default
public:
    void setX(int newX) { x = newX; }
    void setY(int newY) { y = newY; }
    int getX() const { return x; }
    int getY() const { return y; }
private:
    int x;
    int y;
};

class  Rectangle
{
public:
    Rectangle(int newTop, int newLeft, int newBottom, int newRight);
    ~Rectangle() {}

    int getTop() const { return top; }
```

```
    int getLeft() const { return left;}
    int getBottom() const { return bottom; }
    int getRight() const { return right; }

    Point getUpperLeft() const { return upperLeft; }
    Point getLowerLeft() const { return lowerLeft; }
    Point getUpperRight() const { return upperRight; }
    Point getLowerRight() const { return lowerRight; }

    void setUpperLeft(Point location);
    void setLowerLeft(Point location);
    void setUpperRight(Point location);
    void setLowerRight(Point location);

    void setTop(int newTop);
    void setLeft (int newLeft);
    void setBottom (int newBottom);
    void setRight (int newRight);

    int getArea() const;

private:
    Point upperLeft;
    Point upperRight;
    Point lowerLeft;
    Point lowerRight;
    int top;
    int left;
    int bottom;
    int right;
};
```

LISTING 9.4 The Full Text of `Rectangle.cpp`

```
#include "Rectangle.hpp"

Rectangle::Rectangle(int newTop, int newLeft, int newBottom, int newRight)
{
    top = newTop;
    left = newLeft;
    bottom = newBottom;
    right = newRight;

    upperLeft.setX(left);
    upperLeft.setY(top);

    upperRight.setX(right);
    upperRight.setY(top);
```

```

    lowerLeft.setX(left);
    lowerLeft.setY(bottom);

    lowerRight.setX(right);
    lowerRight.setY(bottom);
}

void Rectangle::setUpperLeft(Point location)
{
    upperLeft = location;
    upperRight.setY(location.getY());
    lowerLeft.setX(location.getX());
    top = location.getY();
    left = location.getX();
}

void Rectangle::setLowerLeft(Point location)
{
    lowerLeft = location;
    lowerRight.setY(location.getY());
    upperLeft.setX(location.getX());
    bottom = location.getY();
    left = location.getX();
}

void Rectangle::setLowerRight(Point location)
{
    lowerRight = location;
    lowerLeft.setY(location.getY());
    upperRight.setX(location.getX());
    bottom = location.getY();
    right = location.getX();
}

void Rectangle::setUpperRight(Point location)
{
    upperRight = location;
    upperLeft.setY(location.getY());
    lowerRight.setX(location.getX());
    top = location.getY();
    right = location.getX();
}

void Rectangle::setTop(int newTop)
{
    top = newTop;
    upperLeft.setY(top);
```

```
    upperRight.setY(top);
}

void Rectangle::setLeft(int newLeft)
{
    left = newLeft;
    upperLeft.setX(left);
    lowerLeft.setX(left);
}

void Rectangle::setBottom(int newBottom)
{
    bottom = newBottom;
    lowerLeft.setY(bottom);
    lowerRight.setY(bottom);
}

void Rectangle::setRight(int newRight)
{
    right = newRight;
    upperRight.setX(right);
    lowerRight.setX(right);
}

int Rectangle::getArea() const
{
    int width = right - left;
    int height = top - bottom;
    return (width * height);
}

// compute area of the rectangle by finding corners,
// establish width and height and then multiply
int main()
{
    // initialize a local Rectangle variable
    Rectangle myRectangle(100, 20, 50, 80);

    int area = myRectangle.getArea();

    std::cout << "Area: " << area << std::endl;
    std::cout << "Upper Left X Coordinate: ";
    std::cout << myRectangle.getUpperLeft().getX() << std::endl;
    return 0;
}
```

When the Rectangle program in Listing 9.4 is run, here's the output:

```
Area: 3000
Upper Left X Coordinate: 20
```

Lines 3–14 in Listing 9.3 declare the class `Point`, which is used to hold a specific x, y coordinate on a graph.

The member variables `x` and `y` are declared in lines 12–13 to hold the values of the coordinates. Under the Cartesian coordinate system this class uses, as the *x* coordinate increases, the point moves to the right on the graph. As the *y* coordinate increases, the point moves upward. Other graphs use different systems.

The `Point` class uses inline accessors to get and set the `x` and `y` points declared in lines 7–10. Because the `Point` class uses the default constructor and destructor, their coordinates must be set explicitly.

Line 16 begins the declaration of a `Rectangle` class. A `Rectangle` consists of four points that represent the corners of the `Rectangle`.

The constructor for the `Rectangle` (line 19) takes four integers, called `newTop`, `newLeft`, `newBottom`, and `newRight`. The four parameters to the constructor are copied into four member variables, and then the four `Points` are established.

In addition to the accessor functions, `Rectangle` has a function named `getArea()` declared in line 42. Instead of storing the area as a variable, the `getArea()` function computes the area in lines 87–92 of Listing 9.4. To do this, it computes the width and the height of the rectangle and then multiplies those two values.

Getting the x coordinate of the upper-left corner of the rectangle requires that you access the `upperLeft` point and ask that point for its `x` value. Because `getUpperLeft()` is a function of `Rectangle`, it can directly access the private data of `Rectangle`, including the `upperLeft` member variable. Because `upperLeft` is a `Point` and a point's `x` value is private, `getUpperLeft()` cannot directly access this data. Instead, it must use the public accessor `getX()` to obtain the value.

Line 96 of Listing 9.4 is the beginning of the body of the actual program. Until line 99, no memory has been allocated and nothing has been executed. The only thing accomplished in the preceding lines is to tell the compiler how to make `Point` and `Rectangle` objects, in case they are ever needed.

A `Rectangle` is defined in line 99 by passing in values for `top`, `left`, `bottom`, and `right`.

In line 101, a local integer variable, `area`, is declared. This variable holds the area of the `Rectangle` that was created, initializing it with the value returned by `Rectangle's getArea()` function.

A client of `Rectangle` could create a `Rectangle` object and get its area without ever looking at the implementation of `getArea()`.

By looking at the header file in Listing 9.3, which contains the declaration of the `Rectangle` class, a programmer knows that `getArea()` returns an `int`. How `getArea()` accomplishes this is not a concern to users of class `Rectangle`. In fact, the author of `Rectangle` could change the function without affecting programs that use the `Rectangle` class.

Summary

A C++ programmer doesn't have to use classes or objects at all. Programs could consist simply of variables and functions, removing the need to master the complex concepts of object-oriented programming.

Few programmers go this route. Why? Because you can be much more effective if you design a program as a series of classes that interact with each other.

Developing classes makes code more reusable. If an object that's useful in one program would be useful in another, the class can be reused. A word processor's `Spellchecker` class could be added to a web browser or any other tool where users write text. The spell-checking object's capabilities would work the same in any program.

Classes also make code more reliable. The tasks a program requires are packaged with the data necessary to get that work done. By thinking of a program as a set of objects that each have specific tasks to perform, the work is spread out and organized. When problems crop up, it's easier to determine the class where the error occurs.

Q&A

Q. If using a `const` function to change a class may cause a compiler error, why shouldn't I just leave out the word `const` and be sure to avoid errors?

A. If your function logically shouldn't change the class, using the keyword `const` is a good way to enlist the compiler in helping you find silly mistakes. For example, consider what happens if the `getSpeed()` function has this line

```
if (speed = 100) std::cout << "Maximum speech reached\n";
```

This code contains an error that the compiler will catch if the `getSpeed()` function is declared `const`. The statement, which is supposed to check whether `speed` equals `100`, accidentally assigns the value `100` to the member variable. (The assignment operator = is used by mistake instead of the equality operator ==.) Because this assignment changes the class in a constant function, the compiler will find the error.

This kind of mistake can be tough to find simply by scanning the code—the eye often sees only what it expects to see. More importantly, the program might appear to run correctly, but `speed` has now been set to a bogus number.

Q. How did grasshopper ice cream get its name, considering the fact that insects would be disgusting dessert ingredients?

A. Blame a drink from New Orleans.

The term grasshopper has been used to describe several different green foods and liquids, including desserts, pies, and cocktails. If you go to a bar and order a grasshopper, you get a deep-green drink flavored by crème de menthe, crème de cacao, and fresh cream. A grasshopper pie is made with Oreo cookies, melted marshmallows, crème de menthe, crème de cacao, and whipped cream.

Grasshopper milkshakes and ice cream are made with crème de menthe-flavored mint ice cream.

The origin for all these grasshoppers is Tujague's, the second-oldest restaurant in New Orleans and the place the cocktail was first mixed. When Philibert Guichet invented the drink in 1919, he chose the name because of its "grasshopper green" color.

Workshop

You learned even more about classes in this hour, and it is time for you to answer a few questions and do a couple of exercises to firm up your knowledge.

Quiz

1. Which of the following is not a common filename extension for C++ header files?

   A. `.hpp`

   B. `.cpp`

   C. `.h`

2. What happens in `Rectangle.cpp` and `Rectangle.hpp` if the `Point` class is not defined?

   A. A compiler error occurs.

   B. The program runs incorrectly.

   C. The results vary.

3. Where can you make a class function inline?

   A. In the class declaration

   B. In the class implementation

   C. Both

Answers

1. **B.** C++ header files usually end in `.hpp` (and less commonly `.h`). C++ programs end in `.cpp`.
2. **A.** Assuming that `Point` is not defined somewhere else, the compiler reports an error about an undefined reference. It is common to have classes rely on other classes and build on them.
3. **C.** A class function that's included in a class declaration automatically is an inline function. Otherwise, a class function must include the `inline` keyword to request that the method be executed inline for faster performance.

Activities

1. Split the `Point` class out of `Rectangle.hpp` into its own header file and include it in `Rectangle.hpp`. How does this change the compilation of `Rectangle.cpp`? Do the results change?
2. Create a `Line` class that consists of two connected points, using the `Point` class.

To see solutions to these activities, visit this book's website at http://cplusplus.cadenhead.org.

HOUR 10

Creating Pointers

What You'll Learn in This Hour:

- What pointers are
- How to declare and use pointers
- What the heap is and how to manipulate memory

Understanding Pointers and Their Usage

One of the most powerful tools available to a C++ programmer is the pointer. Pointers provide the capability to manipulate computer memory directly. That power comes at a price: Pointers are one of the most difficult aspects of C++ for beginners to learn.

A variable is an object that can hold a value. An integer variable holds a number. A character variable holds a letter. A pointer is a variable that holds a memory address.

Okay, so what is a memory address? To fully understand this, you must know a little about computer memory.

Computer memory is where variable values are stored. By convention, computer memory is divided into sequentially numbered memory locations. Each of these locations is a memory address.

Every variable of every type is located at a unique address in memory. Figure 10.1 shows a schematic representation of the storage of an `unsigned long` integer variable, `theAge`.

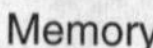

theAge

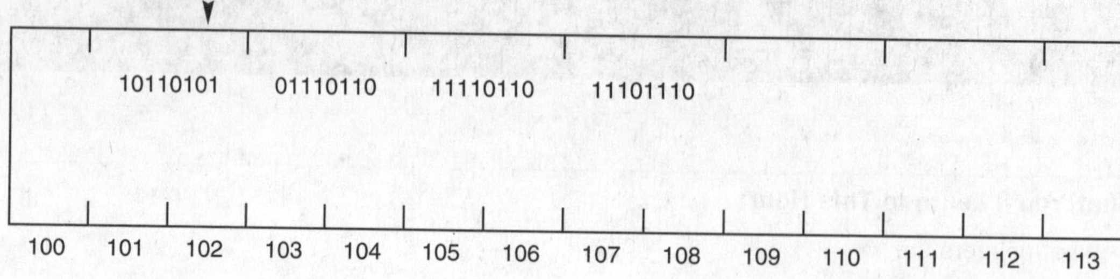

each location = 1 byte

unsigned long int theAge = 4 bytes = 32 bits
variable name theAge points to 1st byte
the address of theAge is 102

FIGURE 10.1
A schematic representation of `theAge`.

Different computers number the memory using different complex schemes. Usually, programmers don't need to know the particular address of any given variable because the compiler handles the details. If you want this information, you can use the address-of operator `&`, which is demonstrated in the Addresser program in Listing 10.1.

LISTING 10.1 The Full Text of `Addresser.cpp`

```
#include <iostream>

int main()
{
    unsigned short shortVar = 5;
    unsigned long  longVar = 65535;
    long sVar = -65535;

    std::cout << "shortVar:\t" << shortVar;
    std::cout << "\tAddress of shortVar:\t" << &shortVar << "\n";
    std::cout << "longVar:\t"  << longVar;
    std::cout << "\tAddress of longVar:\t"  << &longVar  << "\n";
    std::cout << "sVar:\t\t"   << sVar;
    std::cout << "\tAddress of sVar:\t"     << &sVar     << "\n";

    return 0;
}
```

Addresser produces output like the following:

```
shortVar:       5           Address of shortVar:      0x60fe9e
longVar:        65535       Address of longVar:       0x60fe98
sVar:           -65535      Address of sVar:          0x60fe94
```

The actual address of each pointer will differ because each computer stores variables at different addresses, depending on what else is in memory and how much memory is available.

NOTE

The special character `\t` in lines 9–14 of Listing 10.1 causes a tab character to be inserted in the output. This is a simple way of creating columns. There are other useful characters like this in addition to the newline character `\n`.

The `\\` character is used to display a backslash.

The `\"` character is used to display a double quote.

The `\'` character is used to display a single quote.

Three variables are declared and initialized: a `short` in line 5, an `unsigned long` in line 6, and a `long` in line 7. Their values and addresses are displayed in lines 9–14 by using the address-of operator `&`.

The value of `shortVar` is `5` (as expected), and its address is 0x60fe9e. This complicated address is computer-specific and can change slightly each time the program is run. Your results will differ. What doesn't change, however, is that the difference in the first two addresses is four bytes if your computer uses four-byte `short` integers. The difference between the second and third is four bytes if your computer uses four-byte `long` integers. Figure 10.2 illustrates how the variables in this program would be stored in memory. (Note that on some computers the difference will be four bytes on both, depending on how your compiler is configured.)

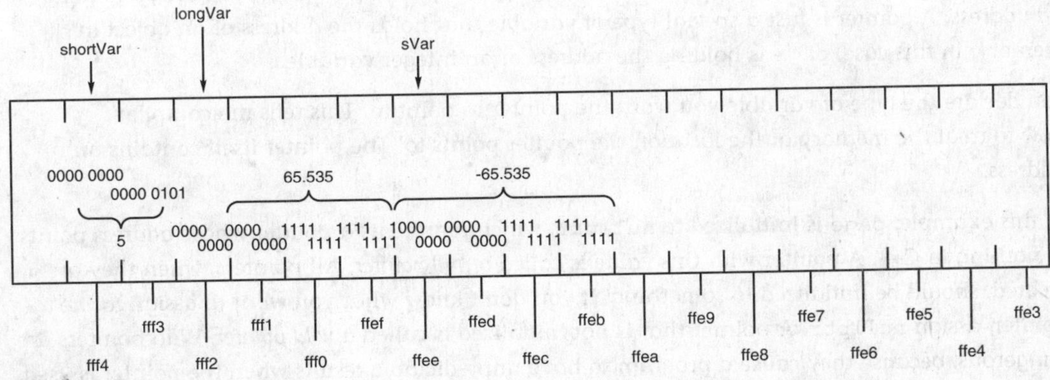

FIGURE 10.2
Illustration of variable storage.

There is no reason why you would need to know the actual numeric value of the address of each variable. What you care about is that each one has an address and that the right amount of memory is set aside.

How does the compiler know how much memory each variable needs? You tell the compiler how much memory to allow for your variables by declaring the variable's type.

Therefore, if you declare your variable to be of type `unsigned long`, the compiler knows to set aside four bytes of memory because every `unsigned long` takes four bytes. The compiler takes care of assigning the actual address.

When a pointer is allocated, the compiler assigns enough memory to hold an address in your hardware and operating system environment. The size of a pointer might or might not be the same size as an integer, so be sure you make no assumptions.

Storing the Address in a Pointer

Every variable has an address. Even without knowing the specific address of a given variable, you can store that address in a pointer.

For example, suppose that the variable `howOld` is an integer. To declare a pointer called `pAge` to hold its address, you write the following statement:

```
int *pAge = nullptr;
```

This declares `pAge` to be a pointer to `int`. That is, `pAge` is declared to hold the address of an `int`.

Pointers can have any name that is legal for other variables. This book follows the convention of naming all pointers with an initial `p` and a second letter capitalized, as in `pAge` or `pHeap`.

Note that `pAge` is a variable like any other variable. When you declare an integer variable, it is set up to hold an integer. When you declare a pointer variable like `pAge`, it is set up to hold an address. A pointer is just a special type of variable that holds the address of an object in memory; in this case, `pAge` is holding the address of an integer variable.

You declare the type of variable you want the pointer to point to. This tells the compiler how to treat the memory at the location the pointer points to. The pointer itself contains an address.

In this example, `pAge` is initialized to `nullptr`, which represents a pointer whose address points to nothing in C++. A pointer with this value is called a *null pointer*. All pointers, when they are created, should be initialized to something. If you don't know what you want to assign to the pointer, assign `nullptr`. A pointer that is not initialized is called a *wild pointer*. Wild pointers are dangerous, because they cause a program to have unpredictable results when the pointer is used.

You also might see pointers initialized to 0, like this:

```
int *pAge = 0;
```

The result should be the same as if you initialized it to `nullptr`, but technically 0 is an integer constant, and `nullptr` is an address constant equivalent to `NULL`.

TIP

In earlier versions of C++, pointers without an address were set to `NULL` instead of `nullptr`. The result was largely the same, but there were some minor issues for developers of C++ libraries that were resolved by being more precise. If you are using a C++ compiler that does not support C++14 or C++11, use `NULL` instead of 0 or `nullptr`.

If you initialize the pointer to `nullptr`, you must specifically assign the address of `howOld` to `pAge`. Here's code to do that:

```
int howOld = 50;          // make a variable
int *pAge = nullptr;           // make a pointer
pAge = &howOld;           // put howOld's address in pAge
```

The first line creates a variable `howOld`, whose type is `unsigned short int`, and initializes it with the value 50. The second line declares `pAge` to be a pointer to type `unsigned short int` and initializes the address to `nullptr`. You know that `pAge` is a pointer because of the asterisk (*) after the variable type and before the variable name.

The third line assigns the address of `howOld` to the pointer `pAge`. You can tell that the address of `howOld` is being assigned to the pointer because of the address-of operator `&`. If the address-of operator was not used, the value of `howOld` would be assigned instead of its address. That value might be a valid address somewhere in memory, but that would be entirely a coincidence.

NOTE

Assigning a non-pointer to a pointer variable is a common error. Fortunately, the compiler will detect this and fail with an "invalid conversion" error.

At this point, `pAge` has as its value the address of `howOld` and `howOld` has the value 50. You could have accomplished this with fewer steps:

```
unsigned short int howOld = 50;        // make a variable
unsigned short int *pAge = &howOld;    // make pointer to howOld
```

`pAge` is a pointer that now contains the address of the `howOld` variable. Using `pAge`, you can determine the value of `howOld`, which in this case is 50. Accessing `howOld` by using the pointer pAge is called *indirection* because you are indirectly accessing howOld by means of pAge. Later this hour you see how to use indirection to access a variable's value.

Indirection accesses the value at the address held by a pointer. The pointer provides an indirect way to get the value held at that address.

The Indirection Operator, or Using Pointers Indirectly

The indirection operator * also is called the dereference operator. When a pointer is dereferenced, the value at the address stored by the pointer is retrieved. Consider the following statements to assign one variable's value to another:

```
unsigned short int howOld = 50;
unsigned short int yourAge;
yourAge = howOld;
```

A pointer provides indirect access to the value of the variable whose address it stores. To assign the value in howOld to the new variable yourAge by way of the pointer pAge, you write the following:

```
unsigned short int howOld = 50;            // create the variable howOld
unsigned short int *pAge = &howOld;        // pAge points to the address of howOld
unsigned short int yourAge;                // create another variable
yourAge = *pAge;                           // assign value at pAge (50) to yourAge
```

The indirection operator * in front of the variable pAge means "the value stored at." This assignment says, "Take the value stored at the address in pAge and assign it to yourAge." Another way of thinking about it is "don't affect the pointer, affect the item stored at the address in the pointer."

NOTE

The indirection operator * is used in two distinct ways with pointers: declaration and dereference. When a pointer is declared, the star indicates that it is a pointer, not a normal variable. For example:

```
unsigned short *pAge = nullptr; // make a pointer to an unsigned short
```

When the pointer is dereferenced, the indirection operator indicates that the value at the memory location stored in the pointer is to be accessed, rather than the address itself:

```
*pAge = 5; // assign 5 to the value at pAge
```

Also note that this same character (*) is used as the multiplication operator. The compiler knows which operator to call based on context.

We deal with indirection in our daily lives all the time. If you want to call a friend, you pick their name in your phone's list of contacts (or tell your phone to call that person). The name is a reference to the actual phone number, which the phone dials. When you do that, you rely on indirection.

Pointers, Addresses, and Variables

It is important to distinguish between a pointer, the address that the pointer holds, and the value at the address held by the pointer. This is the source of much of the confusion about pointers.

Consider the following code fragment:

```
int theVariable = 5;
int *pPointer = &theVariable;
```

`theVariable` is declared to be an integer variable initialized with the value 5. `pPointer` is declared to be a pointer to an integer; it is initialized with the address of `theVariable`. The address that `pPointer` holds is the address of `theVariable`. The value at the address that `pPointer` holds is 5. Figure 10.3 shows a schematic representation of `theVariable` and `pPointer`.

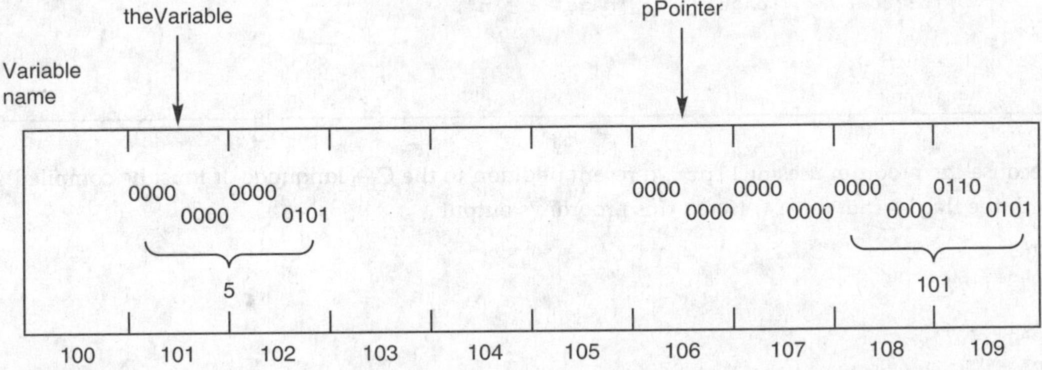

FIGURE 10.3
A schematic representation of memory.

Manipulating Data by Using Pointers

After a pointer is assigned the address of a variable, you can use that pointer to access the data in that variable. The Pointer program in Listing 10.2 demonstrates how the address of a local variable is assigned to a pointer and how the pointer manipulates the values in that variable.

LISTING 10.2 The Full Text of `Pointer.cpp`

```
 1: #include <iostream>
 2:
 3: int main()
 4: {
 5:     int myAge;               // a variable
 6:     int *pAge = nullptr;     // a pointer
 7:
 8:     myAge = 5;
 9:     pAge = &myAge;        // assign address of myAge to pAge
10:     std::cout << "myAge: " << myAge << "\n";
11:     std::cout << "*pAge: " << *pAge << "\n\n";
12:
13:     std::cout << "*pAge = 7\n";
14:     *pAge = 7;            // sets myAge to 7
15:     std::cout << "*pAge: " << *pAge << "\n";
16:     std::cout << "myAge: " << myAge << "\n\n";
17:
18:     std::cout << "myAge = 9\n";
19:     myAge = 9;
20:     std::cout << "myAge: " << myAge << "\n";
21:     std::cout << "*pAge: " << *pAge << "\n";
22:
23:     return 0;
24: }
```

Because the program uses `nullptr`, a recent addition to the C++ language, it must be compiled with the flag `--std=c++14`. Here's this program's output.

```
myAge: 5
*pAge: 5

*pAge = 7
*pAge: 7
myAge: 7

myAge = 9
myAge: 9
*pAge: 9
```

This program declares two variables: an `int` `myAge` and a pointer `pAge`, which is a pointer to an `int` and holds the address of `myAge`. `myAge` is assigned the value 5 in line 8; this is verified by the output.

In line 9, `pAge` is assigned the address of `myAge`. In line 11, `pAge` is dereferenced and displayed, showing that the value at the address that `pAge` stores is the 5 stored in `myAge`. In line 14, the value 7 is assigned to the variable at the address stored in `pAge`. This sets `myAge` to 7, and the output confirms this.

In line 19, the value 9 is assigned to the variable `myAge`. This value is obtained directly in line 20 and indirectly—by dereferencing `pAge`—in line 21.

Examining Addresses Stored in Pointers

Pointers enable you to manipulate addresses without ever knowing their real value. After this hour, you'll take it on faith that when you assign the address of a variable to a pointer, the pointer really has the address of that variable as its value. But just this once, why not check to make sure? The PointerCheck program in Listing 10.3 puts a pointer to the test.

LISTING 10.3 The Full Text of `PointerCheck.cpp`

```
#include <iostream>

int main()
{
    unsigned short int myAge = 5, yourAge = 10;
    unsigned short int *pAge = &myAge;  // a pointer

    std::cout << "myAge:\t" << myAge;
    std::cout << "\t\tyourAge:\t" << yourAge << "\n";
    std::cout << "&myAge:\t" << &myAge;
    std::cout << "\t&yourAge:\t" << &yourAge <<"\n";

    std::cout << "pAge:\t" << pAge << "\n";
    std::cout << "*pAge:\t" << *pAge << "\n\n";

    pAge = &yourAge;        // reassign the pointer

    std::cout << "myAge:\t" << myAge;
    std::cout << "\t\tyourAge:\t" << yourAge << "\n";
    std::cout << "&myAge:\t" << &myAge;
    std::cout << "\t&yourAge:\t" << &yourAge <<"\n";

    std::cout << "pAge:\t" << pAge << "\n";
    std::cout << "*pAge:\t" << *pAge << "\n\n";

    std::cout << "&pAge:\t" << &pAge << "\n";
    return 0;
}
```

This program produces the following output:

```
myAge:   5              yourAge:   10
&myAge:  0x60fe9e       &yourAge:  0x60fe9c
pAge:    0x60fe9e
*pAge:   5

myAge:   5              yourAge:   10
&myAge:  0x60fe9e       &yourAge:  0x60fe9c
pAge:    0x60fe9c
*pAge:   10

&pAge:   0x60fe98
```

Your output will differ because each computer stores variables at different addresses, depending on what else is in memory and how much memory is available.

In line 5, `myAge` and `yourAge` are declared to be variables of type `unsigned short` integer. In line 6, `pAge` is declared to be a pointer to an `unsigned short` integer, and it is initialized with the address of the variable `myAge`.

Lines 8–11 print the values and the addresses of `myAge` and `yourAge`. Line 13 displays the contents of `pAge`, which is the address of `myAge`. Line 14 displays the result of dereferencing `pAge`, which displays the value at `pAge`—the value in `myAge`, or 5.

This is the essence of pointers. Line 13 shows that `pAge` stores the address of `myAge`, and line 14 shows how to get the value stored in `myAge` by dereferencing the pointer `pAge`. Make sure that you understand this fully before you go on. Study the code and look at the output.

In line 16, `pAge` is reassigned to point to the address of `yourAge`. The values and addresses are displayed again. The output shows that `pAge` now has the address of the variable `yourAge`, and that dereferencing obtains the value in `yourAge`.

Line 26 displays the address of `pAge` itself. Like any variable, it too has an address, and that address can be stored in a pointer. (Assigning the address of a pointer to another pointer will be discussed shortly.)

Why Use Pointers?

So far, you've seen step-by-step details of assigning a variable's address to a pointer. In practice, though, you would never do this. After all, why bother with a pointer when you already have a variable with access to that value? The only reason for this kind of pointer manipulation of a variable is to demonstrate how pointers work.

Now that you are comfortable with the syntax of pointers, you can put them to better use. Pointers are employed most often for three tasks:

- Managing data on the heap
- Accessing class member data and functions
- Passing variables by reference to functions

The rest of this hour focuses on managing data on the heap and accessing class member data and functions. In Hour 12, "Creating References," you learn about passing variables by reference.

The Stack and the Heap

Programmers generally deal with five areas of memory:

- Global name space
- The heap
- Registers
- Code space
- The stack

Local variables are on the stack, along with function parameters. Code is in code space, of course, and global variables are in global name space. The registers are used for internal housekeeping functions, such as keeping track of the top of the stack and the instruction pointer. Just about all remaining memory is given over to the heap, which is sometimes referred to as the free store.

The limitation of local variables is that they don't persist. When the function returns, the local variables are thrown away. Global variables solve that problem at the cost of being accessible without restriction throughout the program, which leads to the creation of bug-prone code that is more difficult to understand and maintain. Putting data in the heap solves both of these problems.

You can think of the heap as a massive section of memory in which thousands of sequentially numbered cubbyholes lie waiting for your data. You can't label these cubbyholes, though, as you can with the stack. You must ask for the address of the cubbyhole that you reserve and then stash that address away in a pointer.

One way to think about this is with an analogy: While camping, to avoid getting lost you set the location of your tent in a GPS device and give it the descriptive name "Camp." The device saves the latitude and longitude of that location, but you don't memorize them yourself.

When you use the device later, you don't know the exact latitude and longitude, only that the name Camp will lead you to that place.

The name Camp is your data on the heap. You don't know where it is, but you know how to get to it. You access it by using its address. You don't have to know that number; you just have to put it into a pointer. The pointer gives you access to your data without bothering you with the details.

The stack is cleaned automatically when a function returns. All the local variables go out of scope, and they are removed from the stack. The heap is not cleaned until your program ends, and it is your responsibility to free any memory that you've reserved when you are done with it. Leaving items hanging around in the heap when you no longer need them is known as a memory leak, a topic covered later in this hour.

The advantage to the heap is that the memory you reserve remains available until you explicitly free it. If you reserve memory on the heap while in a function, the memory is still available when the function returns.

The advantage of accessing memory in this way, rather than using global variables, is that only functions with access to the pointer have access to the data. This provides a tightly controlled interface to that data, and it eliminates the problem of one function changing that data in unexpected and unanticipated ways.

For this to work, you must be able to create a pointer to an area on the heap. The following sections describe how to do this.

Using the `new` Keyword

You allocate memory on the heap in C++ by using the `new` keyword followed by the type of the object that you want to allocate so that the compiler knows how much memory is required. Therefore, `new unsigned short int` allocates two bytes in the heap, and `new long` allocates four.

The return value from `new` is a memory address. It must be assigned to a pointer. To create an `unsigned short` on the heap, you might write the following:

```
unsigned short int *pPointer;
pPointer = new unsigned short int;
```

You can, of course, initialize the pointer at its creation:

```
unsigned short int *pPointer = new unsigned short int;
```

In either case, `pPointer` now points to an `unsigned short int` on the heap. You can use this like any other pointer to a variable and assign a value into that area of memory:

```
*pPointer = 72;
```

This means "put 72 at the value in `pPointer`" or "assign the value 72 to the area on the heap to which `pPointer` points."

If new cannot create memory on the heap—because memory is a limited resource—it throws an exception. Exceptions are error-handling objects covered in detail in Hour 24, "Dealing with Exceptions and Error Handling."

NOTE

Some older compilers return a pointer that equals NULL. If you have an older compiler, check your pointer for NULL each time you request new memory. All modern compilers can be counted on to throw an exception.

Using the delete Keyword

When you have finished with your area of memory, you must call delete on the pointer, which returns the memory to the heap. Remember that the pointer itself—as opposed to the memory it points to—is a local variable. When the function in which it is declared returns, that pointer goes out of scope and is lost. The memory allocated with the new operator is not freed automatically, however. That memory becomes unavailable. This situation is called a memory leak because that memory can't be recovered until the program ends. It is as though the memory has leaked out of your computer.

To restore the memory to the heap, you use the keyword delete. For example:

```
delete pPointer;
```

When you delete the pointer, what you are really doing is freeing up the memory whose address is stored in the pointer. You are saying, "Return to the heap the memory that this pointer points to." The pointer is still a pointer, and it can be reassigned.

When you call delete on a pointer, the memory it points to is freed. Calling delete on that pointer again will crash your program! When you delete a pointer, set it to nullptr. Calling delete on a null pointer is guaranteed to be safe. For example:

```
Animal *pDog = new Animal;
delete pDog; // frees the memory
pDog = nullptr; // sets pointer to null
// ...
delete pDog; // harmless
```

Don't worry if the preceding code looks confusing. We'll look at allocating objects on the heap in the next hour. This also works with data types like int, as shown here:

```
int *pNumber = new int;
delete pNumber; // frees the memory
pNumber = nullptr; // sets pointer to null
// ...
delete pNumber; // harmless
```

The Heap program in Listing 10.4 demonstrates allocating a variable on the heap, using that variable, and deleting it.

LISTING 10.4 The Full Text of `Heap.cpp`

```
1: #include <iostream>
2:
3: int main()
4: {
5:     int localVariable = 5;
6:     int *pLocal= &localVariable;
7:     int *pHeap = new int;
8:     if (pHeap == nullptr)
9:     {
10:        std::cout << "Error! No memory for pHeap!!";
11:        return 1;
12:    }
13:    *pHeap = 7;
14:    std::cout << "localVariable: " << localVariable << "\n";
15:    std::cout << "*pLocal: " << *pLocal << "\n";
16:    std::cout << "*pHeap: " << *pHeap << "\n";
17:    delete pHeap;
18:    pHeap = new int;
19:    if (pHeap == nullptr)
20:    {
21:        std::cout << "Error! No memory for pHeap!!";
22:        return 1;
23:    }
24:    *pHeap = 9;
25:    std::cout << "*pHeap: " << *pHeap << "\n";
26:    delete pHeap;
27:    return 0;
28: }
```

The program has the following output:

```
localVariable: 5
*pLocal: 5
*pHeap: 7
*pHeap: 9
```

Line 5 declares and initializes a local variable. Line 6 declares and initializes a pointer with the address of the local variable. Line 7 declares another pointer but initializes it with the result obtained from calling `new int`. This allocates space on the heap for an `int`. Line 13 assigns the value 7 to the newly allocated memory. Line 14 displays the value of the local variable, and line 15 prints the value pointed to by `pLocal`. As expected, these are the same. Line 16 prints the value pointed to by `pHeap`. It shows that the value assigned in line 13 is, in fact, accessible.

In line 17, the memory allocated in line 7 is returned to the heap by a call to `delete`. This frees the memory and disassociates the pointer from that memory location. `pHeap` is now free to point to other memory. It is reassigned in lines 18 and 24, and line 25 displays the result. Line 26 again restores that memory to the heap.

NOTE

Although line 26 is redundant (the end of the program would have returned that memory), it is a good idea to free this memory explicitly. If the program changes or is extended, it will be beneficial that this step was already taken care of.

Avoiding Memory Leaks

Another way you might inadvertently create a memory leak is by reassigning your pointer before deleting the memory to which it points. Consider this code:

```
1: unsigned short int *pPointer = new unsigned short int;
2: *pPointer = 72;
3: pPointer = new unsigned short int;
4: *pPointer = 84;
```

Line 1 in this fragment creates `pPointer` and assigns it the address of an area on the heap. Line 2 stores the value 72 in that area of memory. Line 3 reassigns `pPointer` to another area of memory. Line 4 places the value 84 in that area. The original area—in which the value 72 is now held—is unavailable because the pointer to that area of memory has been reassigned. There is no way to access that original area of memory, nor is there any way to free it before the program ends.

The code should have been written like this:

```
1: unsigned short int *pPointer = new unsigned short int;
2: *pPointer = 72;
3: delete pPointer;
4: pPointer = new unsigned short int;
5: *pPointer = 84;
```

Now the memory originally pointed to by `pPointer` is deleted—and thus freed—in line 3 of the preceding fragment.

NOTE

For every time in your program that you call `new`, there should be a call to `delete`. It is important to keep track of which pointer owns an area of memory and to ensure that the memory is returned to the heap when you are done with it.

Null Pointer Constant

As you learned earlier this hour, it's important when using pointers to make sure they always have a value. A pointer that is not initialized could be pointing to anything in memory. These wild pointers pose a security and stability risk to your programs.

In earlier versions of C++, a pointer was assigned a null value when created by using either 0 or `NULL` as the value, as in these statements:

```
int *pBuffer = 0;
int *pBuffer = NULL;
```

These accomplish the same thing because `NULL` is a preprocessor macro that is converted to either 0 (an integer) or 0L (a long).

Setting null pointers like this worked well in almost all circumstances, but it created an ambiguity when a class relies on function overloading. Consider an overloaded function that takes either a character pointer or an integer as an argument:

```
void displayBuffer(char *);
void displayBuffer(int);
```

If this function is called with a null pointer, the `displayBuffer(int)` member function will be called, despite the fact that this is probably not what the programmer intended.

The `nullptr` keyword you already have been using solves this pointer problem:

```
int *pBuffer = nullptr;
```

The constant 0 also remains valid as a null pointer value, for reasons of backward compatibility, but `nullptr` is preferred.

A `nullptr` value is not implicitly converted to integer types, except for `bool` values, where a `nullptr` converts to the value `false`.

The Swapper program (Listing 10.5) gives one variable the value of another using a pointer.

LISTING 10.5 The Full Text of `Swapper.cpp`

```
#include <iostream>

int main()
{
    int value1 = 12500;
    int value2 = 1700;
    int *pointer2 = nullptr;

    // give pointer the address of value2
    pointer2 = &value2;
```

```
11:     // dereference the pointer and assign to value1
12:     value1 = *pointer2;
13:     pointer2 = 0;
14:
15:     std::cout << "value1 = " << value1 << "\n";
16:
17:     return 0;
18: }
```

This program must be compiled with the `--std=c++14` flag because `nullptr` is a new addition to C++. After you successfully compile it, run Swapper to produce the following output:

```
value1 = 1700
```

The `pointer2` variable is initialized as a null pointer, then assigned the address of the value2 variable on line 10. This is dereferenced and stored in value1 (line 12), replacing its original value.

Summary

This hour was the first of two devoted to pointers, a subject that trips up more beginning C++ programmers than any other aspect of the language.

Variable values are stored in computer memory, which is organized into sequential memory locations. Each location is a memory address. Pointers are special variables to one of those addresses.

Pointers make it possible to manipulate computer memory directly in a program. When you know the memory address of data, you don't have to use a variable to access that data. You can work with a pointer to that address instead.

There are tasks where it makes more sense to use pointers than variables. Pointers are one of the most powerful parts of the C++ language.

If they're still a point of confusion, you should find they make more sense the further you progress through the book.

Q&A

Q. Why are pointers so important?

A. As you saw during this hour, pointers are important because they are used to hold the address of objects on the heap and pass arguments by reference. In addition, in Hour 14, "Calling Advanced Functions," you'll see how pointers are used in a technique called class polymorphism.

Q. Why should I bother to declare anything on the heap?

A. Objects on the heap persist after the return of a function. In addition, the capability to store objects on the heap enables you to decide at runtime how many objects you need, instead of having to declare this in advance. This is explored in greater depth in Hour 11, "Developing Advanced Pointers."

Q. If George Washington had accepted the offer to become the king of the United States, who would be the country's king today?

A. Assuming that the United States followed the same rules of succession as England, for many years the king of America was Paul Emery Washington, a building supply company manager in San Antonio, Texas.

George Washington had no blood descendants, so when he died in 1799 the throne would pass to one of his brothers' children. Some other Washingtons in the line also died childless or had no living male descendants, so the issue becomes complicated.

When the genealogical web site Ancestry.Com researched the American king succession in 2008, they found 8,000 of George Washington's relatives could factor into the decision. There were four likely succession paths, and Paul Washington was at the end of two of them.

"I doubt if I'd be a very good king," Paul told NBC's *Today Show*. "We've done so well as a country without a king, so I think George made the best decision."

Though he rejected his monarchial birthright, Paul started calling his oldest son Bill "Prince William." When Paul died in 2014 at age 87, Bill ascended to the hypothetical throne.

Workshop

Now that you've learned about pointers, you can answer a few questions and complete a couple of exercises to firm up your knowledge.

Quiz

1. What is the difference between 0 and `nullptr` when initializing a pointer?

A. `nullptr` creates a null pointer.

B. 0 creates a null pointer.

C. Both create null pointers.

2. What is it called when you don't free heap space after you're done with it?

A. A memory leak

B. A memory hole

C. I forgot the question

3. How do I free up memory allocated with `new`?

   A. `return`

   B. `delete`

   C. `*`

Answers

1. **C.** Both 0 and `nullptr` initialize a pointer to no address, making it a null pointer. Using `nullptr` is more clear because it's obviously a pointer, while the value 0 serves many other purposes in C++. When supported, the new constant `nullptr` should be used instead of either 0 or NULL.

2. **A.** Memory leak. The program continues to allocate new space as it needs it, but less and less memory is available.

3. **B.** Use the `delete` keyword. It is good practice to `delete` as soon as you are done with the contents of a variable on the heap.

Activities

1. Modify the PointerCheck program to multiply `yourAge` and `*pAge` and store the result in a new variable. Display that variable. Think about how the compiler can tell the difference between the `*` operator for multiplication and `*` for dereferencing `pAge`.

2. Further modify PointerCheck to use dereferenced pointer `*pAge` to change the contents of `myAge` or `yourAge`.

To see solutions to these activities, visit this book's website at http://cplusplus.cadenhead.org.

HOUR 11
Developing Advanced Pointers

What You'll Learn in This Hour:

- How to create objects on the heap
- How to use pointers effectively
- How to prevent memory problems when using pointers

Creating Objects on the Heap

One of the most powerful tools available to a C++ programmer is the capability to directly manipulate computer memory by using pointers.

Just as you can create a pointer to an integer, you can create a pointer to any object. If you have declared an object of type `Cat`, you can declare a pointer to that class and instantiate a `Cat` object on the heap, just as you can make one on the stack. The syntax is the same as for integers:

```
Cat *pCat = new Cat;
```

This calls the default constructor—the constructor that takes no parameters. A constructor is called whenever an object is created on the stack or on the heap.

Deleting Objects

When you call `delete` on a pointer to an object on the heap, the object's destructor is called before the memory is released. This gives your class a chance to clean up, just as it does for objects destroyed on the stack.

The HeapCreator program in Listing 11.1 shows how to create and delete objects on the heap.

LISTING 11.1 The Full Text of `HeapCreator.cpp`

```
#include <iostream>

class SimpleCat
{
public:
    SimpleCat();
    ~SimpleCat();
private:
    int itsAge;
};

SimpleCat::SimpleCat()
{
    std::cout << "Constructor called\n";
    itsAge = 1;
}

SimpleCat::~SimpleCat()
{
    std::cout << "Destructor called\n";
}

int main()
{
    std::cout << "SimpleCat Frisky ...\n";
    SimpleCat Frisky;

    std::cout << "SimpleCat *pRags = new SimpleCat ...\n";
    SimpleCat * pRags = new SimpleCat;

    std::cout << "delete pRags ...\n";
    delete pRags;

    std::cout << "Exiting, watch Frisky go ...\n";
    return 0;
}
```

The program displays the following output:

```
SimpleCat Frisky ...
Constructor called
SimpleCat *pRags = new SimpleCat ...
Constructor called
delete pRags ...
Destructor called
Exiting, watch Frisky go ...
Destructor called
```

Lines 3–10 declare the stripped-down class `SimpleCat`. On line 26, `Frisky` is created on the stack, which causes the constructor to be called. On line 29, the `SimpleCat` pointed to by `pRags` is created on the heap; the constructor is called again. On line 32, `delete` is called on `pRags`, and the destructor is called. When the function ends, `Frisky` goes out of scope, and the destructor is called.

Accessing Data Members Using Pointers

Data members and functions are accessed by using the dot operator (`.`) for `Cat` objects created locally. To access the `Cat` object on the heap, you must dereference the pointer and call the dot operator on the object pointed to by the pointer. Therefore, to access the `GetAge` member function, you write the following:

```
(*pRags).GetAge();
```

Parentheses are used to assure that `pRags` is dereferenced before `GetAge()` is accessed.

Because this is cumbersome, C++ provides a shorthand operator for indirect access: the points-to operator `->`, which is created by typing a dash followed by the greater than symbol. C++ treats this as a single symbol.

The HeapAccessor program in Listing 11.2 demonstrates accessing member variables and functions of objects created on the heap.

LISTING 11.2 The Full Text of `HeapAccessor.cpp`

```
#include <iostream>

class SimpleCat
{
public:
    SimpleCat() { itsAge = 2; }
    ~SimpleCat() {}
    int GetAge() const { return itsAge; }
    void SetAge(int age) { itsAge = age; }
private:
    int itsAge;
};

int main()
{
    SimpleCat *Frisky = new SimpleCat;
    std::cout << "Frisky is " << Frisky->GetAge()
              << " years old" << std::endl;

    Frisky->SetAge(5);
```

```
21:     std::cout << "Frisky is " << Frisky->GetAge()
22:               << " years old" << std::endl;
23:
24:     delete Frisky;
25:     return 0;
26: }
```

HeapAccessor produces this output:

```
Frisky is 2 years old
Frisky is 5 years old
```

On line 16, a `SimpleCat` object is instantiated on the heap. The default constructor in line 6 sets its age to 2, and the `GetAge()` member function is called on line 17. Because this is a pointer, the points-to operator `->` is used to access the member data and functions. On line 20, the `SetAge()` function is called, and `GetAge()` is accessed again on line 21.

Member Data on the Heap

One or more of the data members of a class can be a pointer to an object on the heap. The memory can be allocated in the class constructor or in one of its functions, and it can be deleted in its destructor, as the DataMember program in Listing 11.3 illustrates.

LISTING 11.3 The Full Text of `DataMember.cpp`

```
#include <iostream>

class SimpleCat
{
public:
    SimpleCat();
    ~SimpleCat();
    int GetAge() const { return *itsAge; }
    void SetAge(int age) { *itsAge = age; }

    int GetWeight() const { return *itsWeight; }
    void setWeight (int weight) { *itsWeight = weight; }

private:
    int *itsAge;
    int *itsWeight;
};

SimpleCat::SimpleCat()
{
    itsAge = new int(2);
```

```
22:     itsWeight = new int(5);
23: }
24:
25: SimpleCat::~SimpleCat()
26: {
27:     delete itsAge;
28:     delete itsWeight;
29: }
30:
31: int main()
32: {
33:     SimpleCat *Frisky = new SimpleCat;
34:     std::cout << "Frisky is " << Frisky->GetAge()
35:               << " years old" << std::endl;
36:
37:     Frisky->SetAge(5);
38:     std::cout << "Frisky is " << Frisky->GetAge()
39:               << " years old" << std::endl;
40:
41:     delete Frisky;
42:     return 0;
43: }
```

This program produces the following output:

```
Frisky is 2 years old
Frisky is 5 years old
```

The class `SimpleCat` has two member variables—both of which are pointers to integers. The constructor (lines 19–23) initializes the pointers to memory on the heap and to the default values.

The destructor (lines 25–29) cleans up the allocated memory. Because this is the destructor, there is no point in assigning these pointers to `nullptr` because they will no longer be accessible. This is one of the safe places to break the rule that deleted pointers should be assigned to `nullptr`, although following the rule doesn't hurt.

The calling function—in this case, `main()`—is unaware that `itsAge` and `itsWeight` are pointers to memory on the heap. `main()` continues to call `GetAge()` and `SetAge()` and the details of the memory management are hidden in the implementation of the class, as they should be.

When `Frisky` is deleted on line 41, its destructor is called. The destructor deletes each of its member pointers. If these in turn point to objects of other user-defined classes, their destructors are also called.

This is an excellent example of why to write your own destructor rather than use the compiler's default. By default, the `delete` statements on lines 27–28 would not happen. Without those deletes, the object goes away with the `delete` on line 41 (including the pointers to the heap)—but not the entries on the heap itself. Without the destructor, there would be a memory leak.

The `this` Pointer

Every class member function has a hidden parameter: the `this` pointer, which points to the individual object in which the function is running. So in each call to `GetAge()` or `SetAge()`, the `this` pointer for the object can be referenced.

The job of the `this` pointer is to point to the individual object whose function has been invoked. Usually, you don't need `this`; you just call functions and set member variables. Occasionally, however, you need to access the object itself (perhaps to return a pointer to the current object). It is at that point that the `this` pointer becomes so helpful.

Normally, you don't need to use the `this` pointer to access the member variables of an object from within functions of that object. You can, however, explicitly call the `this` pointer if you want to. The This program in Listing 11.4 illustrates how to make use of the `this` pointer.

LISTING 11.4 The Full Text of `This.cpp`

```
#include <iostream>

class Rectangle
{
public:
    Rectangle();
    ~Rectangle();
    void SetLength(int length) { this->itsLength = length; }
    int GetLength() const { return this->itsLength; }
    void SetWidth(int width) { itsWidth = width; }
    int GetWidth() const { return itsWidth; }

private:
    int itsLength;
    int itsWidth;
};

Rectangle::Rectangle()
{
    itsWidth = 5;
    itsLength = 10;
}

Rectangle::~Rectangle()
{}

```

```
27: int main()
28: {
29:     Rectangle theRect;
30:     std::cout << "theRect is " << theRect.GetLength()
31:               << " feet long." << std::endl;
32:     std::cout << "theRect is " << theRect.GetWidth()
33:               << " feet wide." << std::endl;
34:
35:     theRect.SetLength(20);
36:     theRect.SetWidth(10);
37:     std::cout << "theRect is " << theRect.GetLength()
38:               << " feet long." << std::endl;
39:     std::cout << "theRect is " << theRect.GetWidth()
40:               << " feet wide." << std::endl;
41:
42:     return 0;
43: }
```

When you run the program, the following output is displayed:

```
theRect is 10 feet long.
theRect is 5 feet wide.
theRect is 20 feet long.
theRect is 10 feet wide.
```

The `SetLength()` and `GetLength()` accessor functions in lines 8–9 explicitly use the `this` pointer to access the member variables of the `Rectangle` object. The `SetWidth` and `GetWidth` accessors in lines 10–11 do not. There is no difference in their behavior, although the function without the `this` pointer may be easier to read.

NOTE

If that's all there were to the `this` pointer, there would be little point in bothering you with it. But because `this` is a pointer, it stores the memory address of an object and can be a powerful tool. You'll see a practical use for the `this` pointer in Hour 15, "Using Operator Overloading."

You don't have to worry about creating or deleting the `this` pointer. The C++ compiler takes care of that.

Stray or Dangling Pointers

A source of bugs that are nasty and difficult to find is stray pointers. A stray pointer is created when you call `delete` on a pointer—thereby freeing the memory that it points to—and later try to use that pointer again without reassigning it.

It is as though someone on your camping trip moved your tent, so even if you press the Camp button on your GPS device, you won't be taken to the correct location.

Take care not to use a pointer after you have called `delete` on it. The pointer still points to the old area of memory, but the compiler is free to put other data there; using the pointer can cause your program to crash. Worse, your program might proceed merrily on its way and crash several minutes later. This is called a *time bomb*, and it is no fun. To be safe, after you delete a pointer, set it to `nullptr`. This disarms the pointer.

NOTE

Stray pointers are often called *wild pointers* or *dangling pointers*.

`const` Pointers

You can use the keyword `const` for pointers before the type, after the type, or in both places. For example, all the following are legal declarations:

```
const int *pOne;
int * const pTwo;
const int * const pThree;
```

These three statements do not all mean the same thing. `pOne` is a pointer to a constant integer. The value that is pointed to can't be changed using this pointer. That means you can't write the following:

```
*pOne = 5;
```

If you try to do so, the compiler fails with an error.

`pTwo` is a constant pointer to an integer. The integer can be changed, but `pTwo` can't point to anything else. A constant pointer can't be reassigned. That means you can't write this:

```
pTwo = &x;
```

`pThree` is a constant pointer to a constant integer. The value that is pointed to can't be changed and `pThree` can't be changed to point to anything else.

Draw an imaginary line just to the right of the asterisk. If the word `const` is to the left of the line, that means the object is constant. If the word `const` is to the right of the line, the pointer itself is constant:

```
const int *p1;   // the int pointed to is constant
int * const p2;  // p2 is constant, it can't point to anything else
```

const Pointers and const Member Functions

In Hour 8, "Creating Basic Classes," you learned that you can apply the const keyword to a member function. When a function is declared as const, the compiler flags as an error any attempt to change data in the object from within that function.

If you declare a pointer to a const object, the only functions that you can call with that pointer are const functions. The ConstPointer program in Listing 11.5 illustrates this.

LISTING 11.5 The Full Text of ConstPointer.cpp

```
#include <iostream>

class Rectangle
{
public:
    Rectangle();
    ~Rectangle();
    void SetLength(int length) { itsLength = length; }
    int GetLength() const { return itsLength; }

    void SetWidth(int width) { itsWidth = width; }
    int GetWidth() const { return itsWidth; }

private:
    int itsLength;
    int itsWidth;
};

Rectangle::Rectangle():
itsWidth(5),
itsLength(10)
{}

Rectangle::~Rectangle()
{}

int main()
{
    Rectangle* pRect =  new Rectangle;
    const Rectangle *pConstRect = new Rectangle;
    Rectangle * const pConstPtr = new Rectangle;

    std::cout << "pRect width: "
              << pRect->GetWidth() << " feet\n";
    std::cout << "pConstRect width: "
              << pConstRect->GetWidth() << " feet\n";
```

```
37:     std::cout << "pConstPtr width: "
38:               << pConstPtr->GetWidth() << " feet\n";
39:
40:     pRect->SetWidth(10);
41:     // pConstRect->SetWidth(10);
42:     pConstPtr->SetWidth(10);
43:
44:     std::cout << "pRect width: "
45:               << pRect->GetWidth() << " feet\n";
46:     std::cout << "pConstRect width: "
47:               << pConstRect->GetWidth() << " feet\n";
48:     std::cout << "pConstPtr width: "
49:               << pConstPtr->GetWidth() << " feet\n";
50:     return 0;
51: }
```

This program displays the following output:

```
pRect width: 5 feet
pConstRect width: 5 feet
pConstPtr width: 5 feet
pRect width: 10 feet
pConstRect width: 5 feet
pConstPtr width: 10 feet
```

Lines 3–17 declare `Rectangle`. Line 12 declares the `GetWidth()` member function `const`. Line 29 declares a pointer to a `Rectangle`. Line 30 declares `pConstRect`, which is a pointer to a constant `Rectangle`. Line 31 declares `pConstPtr`, which is a constant pointer to `Rectangle`.

Lines 33–38 print the values of the widths.

In line 40, `pRect` is used to set the width of the rectangle to `10`. In line 41, `pConstRect` would be used, but it was declared to point to a constant `Rectangle`. Therefore, it cannot legally call a non-`const` member function and is commented out. On line 31, `pConstPtr` is declared to be a constant pointer to a rectangle. In other words, the pointer is constant and cannot point to anything else, but the rectangle is not constant.

NOTE

When you declare an object to be `const`, you are, in effect, declaring that the `this` pointer is a pointer to a `const` object. A `const this` pointer can be used only with `const` member functions. Constant objects and constant pointers are discussed again in the next hour, when references to constant objects are discussed.

Summary

Pointers can be created to point to simple data types like integers and to objects as well.

Objects can be created and deleted on the heap. If you have declared an object, you can declare a pointer to that class and instantiate the object on the heap.

Data members of a class can be pointers to objects on the heap. Memory can be allocated in the class constructor or one of its functions and deleted in the destructor.

The ability to directly access computer memory by using pointers is one of the most powerful tools available to a C++ programmer.

Q&A

Q. Why should I declare an object as `const` if it limits what I can do with it?

A. As a programmer, you want to enlist the compiler in helping you find bugs. One serious bug that is difficult to find is a function that changes an object in ways that aren't obvious to the calling function. Declaring an object `const` prevents such changes.

Q. Why should I bother to declare anything on the heap?

A. Objects on the heap persist after the return of a function. They also are dynamic—you can allocate as many as you need for a particular application or set of input data. In addition, objects declared on the heap can be used to create complex data structures as explored in Hour 19, "Storing Information in Linked Lists."

Q. Why do people have creepy red eyes in photographs?

A. That happens when the camera's bright flash reflects off a person's retinas, revealing the red color of blood vessels that nourish the eyes and giving pupils a demonic appearance.

Some cameras offer a "red eye reduction" feature that reduces this effect by firing two flashes—one before the picture is taken. The first flash causes the photo subject's pupils to contract, minimizing the red-eye effect.

Pupils that appear white in a photo are a possible indicator of eye disease such as *retinoblastoma*, a highly treatable cancer if detected early. If a photo shows a white-eye effect, the subject should see an ophthalmologist to ensure his or her eyes are healthy.

Workshop

We spent the past hour advancing your knowledge of pointers, and it is now time for you to answer a few questions and complete a couple of exercises to firm up that knowledge.

Quiz

1. What keywords are used to allocate and release space from the heap in C++?
   A. `alloc` and `dealloc`
   B. `public` and `private`
   C. `new` and `delete`
2. When is an object deleted (the destructor called) if you do not issue the delete yourself?
   A. When the program ends
   B. When the object's scope ends
   C. Never
3. What is a pointer called that is used after a `delete` was performed on that pointer?
   A. A null pointer
   B. A stray pointer
   C. A pointer sister

Answers

1. **C.** `new` is used to allocate space on the heap and `delete` is used to release it.
2. **B.** When the scope for an object is exited, that object is automatically deleted. If an object is created in `main()` and not deleted by the programmer, when `main()` is exited, the destructor is called. The output from Listing 11.1 shows this happening.
3. **B.** A stray pointer. You don't really know what that memory location is being used for!

Activities

1. Add a cat named Spooky to the HeapCreator program.
2. Modify the HeapAccessor program so that it does not use the points-to operator.

To see solutions to these activities, visit this book's website at http://cplusplus.cadenhead.org.

HOUR 12
Creating References

What You'll Learn in This Hour:

- What references are
- How references differ from pointers
- How to create and use references
- What the limitations of references are
- How to pass values and objects into and out of functions by reference

What is a Reference?

In the past two hours, you learned how to use pointers to manipulate objects on the heap and refer to those objects indirectly. References, the topic of this hour, give you almost all the power of pointers with a much easier syntax.

A *reference* is an alias. When you create a reference, you initialize it with the name of another object, the target. From that moment on, the reference acts as an alternative name for the target, and anything you do to the reference is really done to the target.

You might read elsewhere that references are pointers, but that is not correct. Although references are often implemented using pointers, that is a matter of concern only to creators of compilers; as a programmer, you must keep these two ideas distinct.

Pointers are variables that hold the address of another object. References are aliases to an object.

Creating a Reference

You create a reference by writing the type of the target object, followed by the reference operator `&`, followed by the name of the reference. References can use any legal variable name, but in this book all reference names are prefixed with `r` and the second letter is capitalized. So, if you have an integer variable named `someInt`, you can make a reference to that variable with the following statement:

```
int &rSomeRef = someInt;
```

This is read as "`rSomeRef` is a reference to an integer that is initialized to refer to `someInt`." The Reference program in Listing 12.1 shows how references are created and used.

LISTING 12.1 The Full Text of `Reference.cpp`

```
 1: #include <iostream>
 2:
 3: int main()
 4: {
 5:     int intOne;
 6:     int &rSomeRef = intOne;
 7:
 8:     intOne = 5;
 9:     std::cout << "intOne: " << intOne << std::endl;
10:     std::cout << "rSomeRef: " << rSomeRef << std::endl;
11:
12:     rSomeRef = 7;
13:     std::cout << "intOne: " << intOne << std::endl;
14:     std::cout << "rSomeRef: " << rSomeRef << std::endl;
15:     return 0;
16: }
```

Reference produces the following output:

```
intOne: 5
rSomeRef: 5
intOne: 7
rSomeRef: 7
```

On line 5, a local `int` variable, `intOne`, is declared. On line 6, a reference to an `int`, `rSomeRef`, is declared and initialized to refer to `intOne`. If you declare a reference but don't initialize it, you get a compiler error. References must be initialized.

On line 8, `intOne` is assigned the value 5. On lines 9–10, the values in `intOne` and `rSomeRef` are displayed, and are the same because `rSomeRef` is simply the reference to `intOne`.

On line 12, 7 is assigned to `rSomeRef`. Because this is a reference, it is an alias for `intOne`, and therefore the 7 is really assigned to `intOne`, as is shown by the display on lines 13–14.

NOTE

The reference operator & is the same symbol as the one used for the address-of operator. In this case, it is used in the declaration.

Remember, with pointers, an asterisk (*) in the declaration means that the variable is a pointer. In a statement, it is the indirection operator when used with pointers or the multiplication operator when used in a mathematical expression.

Using the Address of Operator on References

If you ask a reference for its address, it returns the address of its target. That is the nature of references—they are aliases for the target.

The Reference2 program in Listing 12.2 demonstrates this concept.

LISTING 12.2 The Full Text of `Reference2.cpp`

```
#include <iostream>

int main()
{
    int  intOne;
    int &rSomeRef = intOne;

    intOne = 5;
    std::cout << "intOne: " << intOne << std::endl;
    std::cout << "rSomeRef: " << rSomeRef << std::endl;

    std::cout << "&intOne: "  << &intOne << std::endl;
    std::cout << "&rSomeRef: " << &rSomeRef << std::endl;

    return 0;
}
```

Here's the output for the Reference2 program:

```
intOne: 5
rSomeRef: 5
&intOne: 0x60fe98
&rSomeRef: 0x60fe98
```

Once again, `rSomeRef` is initialized as a reference to `intOne`. This time the addresses of the two variables are displayed and they are identical. C++ gives you no way to access the address of the reference itself because it is not meaningful, as it would be if you were using a pointer or other variable. References are initialized when created and always act as a synonym for their target, even when the address-of operator is applied.

For example, if you have a class called `President`, you might declare an instance of that class as follows:

```
President Millard_Fillmore;
```

You might then declare a reference to `President` and initialize it with this object:

```
President &Fillmore = Millard_Fillmore;
```

There is only one `President`; both identifiers refer to the same object of the same class. Any action you take on `Fillmore` will be taken on `Millard_Fillmore`, as well.

Be careful to distinguish between the `&` symbol on line 6 of Listing 12.2, which declares a reference to `int` named `rSomeRef`, and the `&` symbols on lines 12 and 13, which return the addresses of the integer variable `intOne` and the reference `rSomeRef`.

Normally, when you use a reference, you do not use the address-of operator. You just use the reference as you would use the target variable. This is shown on line 10.

Even experienced C++ programmers, who know the rule that references cannot be reassigned and are always aliases for their target, can be confused by what happens when you try to reassign a reference: What appears to be a reassignment turns out to be the assignment of a new value to the target.

This is demonstrated by the Assignment program in Listing 12.3.

LISTING 12.3 The Full Text of `Assignment.cpp`

```
#include <iostream>

int main()
{
    int intOne;
    int &rSomeRef = intOne;

    intOne = 5;
    std::cout << "intOne:\t" << intOne << std::endl;
    std::cout << "rSomeRef:\t" << rSomeRef << std::endl;
    std::cout << "&intOne:\t"  << &intOne << std::endl;
    std::cout << "&rSomeRef:\t" << &rSomeRef << std::endl;

    int intTwo = 8;
    rSomeRef = intTwo; // not what you think!
    std::cout << "\nintOne:\t" << intOne << std::endl;
    std::cout << "intTwo:\t" << intTwo << std::endl;
```

```
18:     std::cout << "rSomeRef:\t" << rSomeRef << std::endl;
19:     std::cout << "&intOne:\t"  << &intOne << std::endl;
20:     std::cout << "&intTwo:\t"  << &intTwo << std::endl;
21:     std::cout << "&rSomeRef:\t" << &rSomeRef << std::endl;
22:     return 0;
23: }
```

The program displays this output:

```
intOne: 5
rSomeRef:       5
&intOne:        0x60fe98
&rSomeRef:      0x60fe98

intOne: 8
intTwo: 8
rSomeRef:       8
&intOne:        0x60fe98
&intTwo:        0x60fe94
&rSomeRef:      0x60fe98
```

Once again, an integer variable and a reference to an integer are declared, on lines 5–6. The integer is assigned the value 5 on line 8, and the values and their addresses are printed on lines 9–11.

On line 14 a new variable, `intTwo`, is created and initialized with the value 8. On line 15, the program tries to reassign `rSomeRef` to now be an alias to the variable `intTwo`, but that is not what happens.

Instead, rSomeRef continues to act as an alias for `intOne`, so this assignment is exactly equivalent to the following:

```
intOne = intTwo;
```

Sure enough, when the values of `intOne` and `rSomeRef` are displayed (lines 16–18) they are the same as `intTwo`. In fact, when the addresses are printed on lines 19–21, you see that `rSomeRef` continues to refer to `intOne` and not `intTwo`.

What Can Be Referenced?

Any object can be referenced, including user-defined objects. Note that you create a reference to an object, not to a class or a data type such as `int`. You do not write this:

```
int &rIntRef = int; // wrong
```

You must initialize rIntRef to a particular integer, such as this:

```
int howBig = 200;
int &rIntRef = howBig;
```

In the same way, you don't initialize a reference to a Cat:

```
Cat &rCatRef = Cat; // wrong
```

You must initialize rCatRef to a particular Cat object:

```
Cat Frisky;
Cat &rCatRef = Frisky;
```

References to objects are used just like the object itself. Member data and functions are accessed using the normal class member access operator (.). As with the built-in types, the reference acts as an alias to the object.

Null Pointers and Null References

When pointers are not initialized, or when they are deleted, they ought to be assigned to nullptr. This is not true for references. In fact, a reference cannot be null, and a program with a reference to a null object is considered an invalid program. When a program is invalid, just about anything can happen. It can appear to work, run with an insignificant error, or erase important files on your hard drive. All are possible outcomes of an invalid program.

Most compilers support null references without much complaint, crashing only if you try to use the reference in some way. Taking advantage of this, however, is not a good idea. When you move your program to another computer or a different compiler, mysterious bugs might occur if you have null references.

Passing Function Arguments by Reference

In Hour 5, "Calling Functions," you learned that functions have two limitations: Arguments are passed by value and the return statement only can return one value.

Passing values to a function by reference can overcome both of these limitations. In C++, passing by reference is accomplished in two ways: using pointers and using references. The syntax is different, but the net effect is the same: Rather than a copy being created within the scope of the function, the actual original object is passed into the function.

Passing an object by reference enables the function to change the object being referred to.

The ValuePasser program in Listing 12.4 creates a swap function and passes in its parameters by value.

LISTING 12.4 The Full Text of `ValuePasser.cpp`

```
#include <iostream>

void swap(int x, int y);

int main()
{
    int x = 5, y = 10;

    std::cout << "Main. Before swap, x: " << x
              << " y: " << y << std::endl;
    swap(x,y);
    std::cout << "Main. After swap, x: " << x
              << " y: " << y << std::endl;
    return 0;
}

void swap (int x, int y)
{
    int temp;

    std::cout << "Swap. Before swap, x: " << x
              << " y: " << y << std::endl;

    temp = x;
    x = y;
    y = temp;

    std::cout << "Swap. After swap, x: " << x
              << " y: " << y << std::endl;

}
```

The following output is displayed:

```
Main. Before swap, x: 5 y: 10
Swap. Before swap, x: 5 y: 10
Swap. After swap, x: 10 y: 5
Main. After swap, x: 5 y: 10
```

This program initializes two variables in `main()` and then passes them to the `swap()` function, which appears to swap them. But when they are examined again in `main()`, they are unchanged!

The problem here is that x and y are being passed to swap() by value. Local copies were made in the function and those copies were swapped, but the originals remained unchanged. What you want to do is pass x and y by reference.

There are two ways to solve this problem in C++: You can make the parameters of swap() pointers to the original values or you can pass in references to the original values.

Making swap() Work with Pointers

When you pass in a pointer, you pass in the actual address of the object. Thus, the function can manipulate the value at that address.

To make swap() change the actual values using pointers, the function should be declared to accept two int pointers. Then, by dereferencing the pointers, the values of x and y will, in fact, be swapped. The PointerSwap program in Listing 12.5 demonstrates this idea.

LISTING 12.5 The Full Text of PointerSwap.cpp

```
#include <iostream>

void swap(int *x, int *y);

int main()
{
    int x = 5, y = 10;

    std::cout << "Main. Before swap, x: " << x
              << " y: " << y << std::endl;
    swap(&x, &y);
    std::cout << "Main. After swap, x: " << x
              << " y: " << y << std::endl;
    return 0;
}

void swap(int *px, int *py)
{
    int temp;

    std::cout << "Swap. Before swap, *px: " << *px
              << " *py: " << *py << std::endl;

    temp = *px;
    *px = *py;
    *py = temp;

    std::cout << "Swap. After swap, *px: " << *px
              << " *py: " << *py << std::endl;
}
```

The PointerSwap program demonstrates the results of the swap attempt in the output:

```
Main. Before swap, x: 5 y: 10
Swap. Before swap, *px: 5 *py: 10
Swap. After swap, *px: 10 *py: 5
Main. After swap, x: 10 y: 5
```

Success! On line 3, the prototype of `swap()` is changed to indicate that its two parameters will be pointers to `int` rather than `int` variables. The asterisk between the variable type and its name indicates that it's a pointer.

When `swap()` is called on line 11, the addresses of `x` and `y` are passed as the arguments.

On line 19, the local variable `temp` is declared in the `swap()` function. There's no need for temp to be a pointer; it will just hold the value of `*px` (the value of `x` in the calling function) for the life of the function. After the function returns, `temp` is no longer needed.

On line 24, `temp` is assigned the value at `px`. On line 25, the value at `px` is assigned to the value at `py`. On line 26, the value stashed in `temp` (that is, the original value at `px`) is put into `py`.

The values in the calling function, whose address was passed to `swap()`, are swapped.

Implementing `swap()` with References

The preceding program works, but the syntax of the `swap()` function is cumbersome in two ways. First, the repeated need to dereference the pointers in the swap`()` function makes it error-prone and hard to read. Second, the need to pass the address of the variables in the calling function makes the inner workings of `swap()` overly apparent to its users.

A useful goal in C++ is to prevent the caller of a function from worrying about how it works, instead of just focusing on what it does and the value it returns. Passing by pointers puts the burden on the calling function, which is not where it belongs. The calling function must know to pass in the address of the object it wants to swap.

The burden of understanding reference semantics should be on the function implementing the swap. To accomplish this, you use references. The ReferenceSwap program in Listing 12.6 rewrites the `swap()` function using references.

Now the calling function just passes in the object, and because the parameters are declared to be references, the semantics are passed by reference. The calling function doesn't need to do anything special.

LISTING 12.6 The Full Text of ReferenceSwap.cpp

```
 1: #include <iostream>
 2:
 3: void swap(int &x, int &y);
 4:
 5: int main()
 6: {
 7:     int x = 5, y = 10;
 8:
 9:     std::cout << "Main. Before swap, x: " << x
10:               << " y: " << y << std::endl;
11:     swap(x, y);
12:     std::cout << "Main. After swap, x: " << x
13:               << " y: " << y << std::endl;
14:     return 0;
15: }
16:
17: void swap(int &rx, int &ry)
18: {
19:     int temp;
20:
21:     std::cout << "Swap. Before swap, rx: " << rx
22:               << " ry: " << ry << std::endl;
23:
24:     temp = rx;
25:     rx = ry;
26:     ry = temp;
27:
28:     std::cout << "Swap. After swap, rx: " << rx
29:               << " ry: " << ry << std::endl;
30: }
```

In the program's output, the success of the swap is demonstrated:

```
Main. Before swap, x: 5 y: 10
Swap. Before swap, rx: 5 ry: 10
Swap. After swap, rx: 10 ry: 5
Main. After swap, x: 10 y: 5
```

Just as in the example with pointers, two variables are declared (line 7), and their values are displayed on lines 9–10. On line 11 the function `swap()` is called, but note that `x` and `y` are passed, not their addresses. The calling function simply passes the variables.

When `swap()` is called, program execution jumps to line 17, where the variables are identified as references by the reference operator `&` between the argument's type and name. The values of `x` and `y` are displayed on lines 21–22, but note that no special operators are required. These are aliases for the original values and can be used as such.

On lines 24–26 the values are swapped, then they're displayed on lines 28–29. Program execution jumps back to the calling function, and on lines 12–13 the values are displayed in `main()`. Because the parameters to `swap()` are declared to be references, the values from `main()` are passed by reference, and thus are changed in `main()`, as well.

References provide the convenience and ease of use of normal variables with the power and pass-by-reference capability of pointers.

Understanding Function Headers and Prototypes

The `swap()` function that takes references is easier to use and the code is easier to read. But how does the calling function know if the values are passed by reference or by value? As a user of `swap()`, the programmer must ensure that `swap()` will in fact change the parameters.

This is another use for the function prototype. By examining the parameters declared in the prototype, which is typically in a header file along with all the other prototypes, the programmer knows that the values passed into `swap()` are passed by reference and thus will be swapped properly.

If `swap()` had been a member function of a class, the class declaration, also available in a header file, would have supplied this information.

In C++, users of classes (any other class's function using the class) rely on the header file to tell all that is needed. This file acts as the interface to the class or function. The actual implementation is hidden from the client, which enables the programmer to focus on the problem at hand and to use the class or function without concern for how it is implemented.

Returning Multiple Values

As discussed, functions can return only one value. What if you need to get two values back from a function? One way to solve this problem is to pass two objects into the function by reference. The function then can fill the objects with the correct values. Because passing by reference enables a function to change the original objects, this effectively lets the function return two pieces of information. This approach bypasses the return value of the function, which then can be reserved for reporting errors.

Once again, this can be done with references or pointers. The ReturnPointer program in Listing 12.7 demonstrates a function that returns three values, two as pointer parameters and one as the return value of the function.

LISTING 12.7 The Full Text of `ReturnPointer.cpp`

```
#include <iostream>

short factor(int, int*, int*);

int main()
{
    int number, squared, cubed;
    short error;

    std::cout << "Enter a number (0 - 20): ";
    std::cin >> number;

    error = factor(number, &squared, &cubed);

    if (!error)
    {
        std::cout << "number: " << number << "\n";
        std::cout << "square: " << squared << "\n";
        std::cout << "cubed: "  << cubed   << "\n";
    }
    else
        std::cout << "Error encountered!!\n";
    return 0;
}

short factor(int n, int *pSquared, int *pCubed)
{
    short value = 0;
    if (n > 20)
    {
        value = 1;
    }
    else
    {
        *pSquared = n*n;
        *pCubed = n*n*n;
        value = 0;
    }
    return value;
}
```

The ReturnPointer program produces the following output:

```
Enter a number (0 - 20): 13
number: 13
square: 169
cubed: 2197
```

On line 7, `number`, `squared`, and `cubed` are defined as `int`. `number` is assigned a value based on user input. This number and the addresses of `squared` and `cubed` are passed to the function `factor()`.

`factor()` examines the first parameter, which is passed by value. If it is greater than 20 (the maximum value this function can handle), it sets `value` to a simple error value. Note that the return value from `factor()` is reserved for either this error value or the value 0, indicating all went well. The function returns this value on line 39.

The actual values needed by users calling the function, the square and cube of `number`, are returned not through the return mechanism, but rather by changing the values directly using the pointers that were passed into the function.

On lines 35 and 36, the pointers are assigned their return values. On line 37, `value` is assigned a success value of 0. On line 39, `value` is returned.

One improvement to this program might be to declare the following:

```
enum ERR_CODE { SUCCESS, ERROR };
```

Then, rather than returning 0 or 1, the program could return `SUCCESS` or `ERROR`. Enumerated constants are given integer values based on their order unless otherwise specified, so the first enumerated value (`SUCCESS`) is given the value 0 and the second is given the value 1.

Returning Values by Reference

Although the ReturnPointer program works, it can be made easier to read and maintain by using references rather than pointers. The ReturnReference program in Listing 12.8 shows the same program rewritten to use references and to incorporate the `ERR_CODE` enumeration.

LISTING 12.8 The Full Text of `ReturnReference.cpp`

```
#include <iostream>

enum ERR_CODE { SUCCESS, ERROR };

ERR_CODE factor(int, int&, int&);

int main()
{
    int number, squared, cubed;
    ERR_CODE result;

    std::cout << "Enter a number (0-20): ";
    std::cin >> number;

    result = factor(number, squared, cubed);
```

```
16:
17:     if (result == SUCCESS)
18:     {
19:         std::cout << "number: " << number << "\n";
20:         std::cout << "square: " << squared << "\n";
21:         std::cout << "cubed: "  << cubed   << "\n";
22:     }
23:     else
24:     {
25:         std::cout << "Error encountered!!\n";
26:     }
27:     return 0;
28: }
29:
30: ERR_CODE factor(int n, int &rSquared, int &rCubed)
31: {
32:     if (n > 20)
33:     {
34:         return ERROR;    // simple error code
35:     }
36:     else
37:     {
38:         rSquared = n * n;
39:         rCubed = n * n * n;
40:         return SUCCESS;
41:     }
42: }
```

Here's sample output for the ReturnReference program:

```
Enter a number (0-20): 15
number: 15
square: 225
cubed: 3375
```

The ReturnReference program is identical to the ReturnPointer program aside from two differences: First, the `ERR_CODE` enumeration makes the error reporting a bit more explicit on lines 34 and 40, and the error handling on line 17.

The larger change is that `factor()` is now declared to take references to `squared` and `cubed` rather than pointers. This makes the manipulation of these parameters much simpler and easier to understand.

Summary

During this hour, you worked with references, which serve a similar purpose to pointers and are sometimes mistaken for them. The difference is that pointers are variables holding the address of an object, whereas references are aliases to an object.

It's important to understand how pointers and references are distinct.

A reference is an alias to another object, which is called the target. The reference serves as an alternate name for the target. Any actions taken to the reference actually affect the target.

References provide the power of pointers with simpler syntax.

Q&A

Q. Why use references if pointers can do everything references can?

A. References are easier to use and understand. The indirection is hidden, and there is no need to repeatedly dereference the variable.

Q. Why use pointers if references are easier?

A. References cannot be `NULL` and they cannot be reassigned. Pointers offer greater flexibility but are more difficult to use.

Q. Is it true that a species went extinct at Disney World?

A. The Discovery Island nature preserve at Disney World in Orlando, Florida, was the last home of the Dusky Seaside Sparrow, a non-migratory bird whose primary habitat was Florida's Merritt Island and the St. Johns River.

The spraying of the pesticide DDT, intentional flooding to control mosquitos and highway construction all devastated the bird's habitat, reducing its population over the second half of the 20th century. By 1979, only six of the sparrows were known to exist—and all of them were males.

The last four sparrows were taken to Disney's nature preserve for a crossbreeding program with Scott's Seaside Sparrows, but it was not successful.

The species was declared extinct in 1990.

Workshop

Now that you've had the chance to see references in action, you can answer a few questions and complete a couple of exercises to check your knowledge.

Quiz

1. What is a reference?

   A. An alias

   B. A synonym

   C. Both a and b

2. What operator is used to create a reference?

   A. `->`

   B. `&`

   C. `*`

3. What is the default mechanism for passing variables to a called function in C++? What are some of the techniques to override that mechanism?

   A. Pass by value

   B. Pass by reference

   C. Pass the salad

Answers

1. C. A reference is an alias or synonym for another variable or object.

2. B. The ampersand (&) is used when declaring a reference. References must be initialized when declared. You cannot have a null reference like you can with pointers.

3. A. Pass by value, where a copy of the variable is passed to the function, not the original—which prevents the function from changing the original value. Pointers are one way to get around pass by value because the address of the original value is passed. References are another because the alias for the original variable is passed.

Activities

1. Modify the ReturnPointer program to use references rather than pointers.

2. Rewrite the ReferenceSwap program to swap three numbers.

To see solutions to these activities, visit this book's website at http://cplusplus.cadenhead.org.

HOUR 13

Developing Advanced References and Pointers

What You'll Learn in This Hour:

- How to use pass by reference to make your programs more efficient
- How to decide when to use references and when to use pointers
- How to avoid memory problems when using pointers
- How to avoid the pitfalls of using references

Passing by Reference for Efficiency

Each time you pass an object into a function by value, a copy of the object is made. Each time you return an object from a function by value, another copy is made.

With large, user-created objects, the cost of these copies is substantial. You'll use more memory than you need to and your program will run more slowly.

The size of a user-created object on the stack is the sum of each of its member variables. These, in turn, can each become user-created objects. Passing such a massive structure by copying it onto the stack can be expensive in terms of performance and memory consumption.

There is another cost, too. With the classes you create, each of these temporary copies is created when the compiler calls a special constructor: the copy constructor.

In Hour 14, "Calling Advanced Functions," you learn how copy constructors work and how you can make your own. For now, it is enough to know that the copy constructor is called each time a temporary copy of the object is put on the stack. When the temporary object is destroyed, which happens when the function returns, the object's destructor is called. If an object is returned by value, a copy of that object also must be made and destroyed.

With large objects, these constructor and destructor calls can be expensive in speed and use of memory. To illustrate this idea, the ObjectRef program in Listing 13.1 creates a stripped-down, user-created object: `SimpleCat`. A real object would be larger and more expensive, but this is sufficient to show how often the copy constructor and destructor are called.

The program creates the `SimpleCat` object and then calls two functions. The first function receives the `Cat` by value and then returns it by value. The second one takes its argument by reference, meaning it receives a pointer to the object, rather than the object itself, and returns a pointer to the object.

Passing by reference avoids creating the copy and calling the copy constructor, and is therefore generally more efficient. On the other hand, it also passes the object itself, and thus exposes that object to change in the called function.

LISTING 13.1 The Full Text of `ObjectRef.cpp`

```
#include <iostream>

class SimpleCat
{
public:
    SimpleCat();                    // constructor
    SimpleCat(SimpleCat&);          // copy constructor
    ~SimpleCat();                   // destructor
};

SimpleCat::SimpleCat()
{
    std::cout << "Simple Cat Constructor ..." << std::endl;
}

SimpleCat::SimpleCat(SimpleCat&)
{
    std::cout << "Simple Cat Copy Constructor ..." << std::endl;
}

SimpleCat::~SimpleCat()
{
    std::cout << "Simple Cat Destructor ..." << std::endl;
}

SimpleCat FunctionOne(SimpleCat theCat);
SimpleCat* FunctionTwo(SimpleCat *theCat);

int main()
{
    std::cout << "Making a cat ..." << std::endl;
    SimpleCat Frisky;
    std::cout << "Calling FunctionOne ..." << std::endl;
    FunctionOne(Frisky);
    std::cout << "Calling FunctionTwo ..." << std::endl;
    FunctionTwo(&Frisky);
```

```
37:     return 0;
38: }
39:
40: // FunctionOne, passes by value
41: SimpleCat FunctionOne(SimpleCat theCat)
42: {
43:     std::cout << "Function One. Returning ..." << std::endl;
44:     return theCat;
45: }
46:
47: // functionTwo, passes by reference
48: SimpleCat* FunctionTwo (SimpleCat *theCat)
49: {
50:     std::cout << "Function Two. Returning ..." << std::endl;
51:     return theCat;
52: }
```

The following output is displayed when the program is run:

```
 1: Making a cat ...
 2: Simple Cat Constructor ...
 3: Calling FunctionOne ...
 4: Simple Cat Copy Constructor ...
 5: Function One. Returning ...
 6: Simple Cat Copy Constructor ...
 7: Simple Cat Destructor ...
 8: Simple Cat Destructor ...
 9: Calling FunctionTwo ...
10: Function Two. Returning ...
11: Simple Cat Destructor ...
```

NOTE

The line numbers shown here do not display in the program output. They are added for the purpose of discussion in this section.

A simplified `SimpleCat` class is declared on lines 3–9. The constructor, copy constructor, and destructor all print an informative message so that you can tell when they've been called.

On line 31, `main()` prints out a message; you can see it on output line 1. On line 32, a `SimpleCat` object is instantiated. This causes the constructor to be called, and the output from the constructor is shown on line 2 of the output.

On line 33, `main()` reports that it is calling `FunctionOne()`, which creates output line 3. Because `FunctionOne()` is called passing the `SimpleCat` object by value, a copy of the `SimpleCat` object is made on the stack as an object local to the called function. This causes the copy constructor to be called, which creates output line 4.

Program execution jumps to line 43 in the called function, which prints an informative message (output line 5). The function then returns, returning the `SimpleCat` object by value. This creates yet another copy of the object, calling the copy constructor and producing line 6.

The return value from `FunctionOne()` is not assigned to any object, so the temporary object created for the return is thrown away, calling the destructor, which produces output line 7. Because `FunctionOne()` has ended, its local copy goes out of scope and is destroyed, calling the destructor and producing line 8.

Program execution returns to `main()`, and `FunctionTwo()` is called, but the parameter is passed by reference. No copy is produced, so there's no output. `FunctionTwo()` prints the message that appears as output line 10 and then returns the `SimpleCat` object, again by reference, and so again produces no calls to the constructor or destructor.

Finally, the program ends and `Frisky` goes out of scope, causing one final call to the destructor and printing output line 11.

The call to `FunctionOne()`, because it passed the cat by value, produced two calls to the copy constructor and two to the destructor, although the call to `FunctionTwo()` produced none.

Passing a `const` Pointer

Though passing a pointer to `FunctionTwo()` is more efficient, it is dangerous. `FunctionTwo()` is not supposed to change the `SimpleCat` object it is passed, yet it is given the address of the object. This exposes the object to impermissible change and defeats the protection offered in passing by value.

Passing by value is like giving a museum a photograph of your masterpiece rather than the real thing. If vandals mark it up, no harm occurs to the original. Passing by reference is like sending your home address to the museum and inviting guests to come over and look at the real thing.

If you want to provide the security of pass by value and the efficiency of pass by reference, the solution is to pass a `const` pointer to `SimpleCat`. Doing so prevents calling any non-`const` member function on `SimpleCat`, and thus protects the object from change. The ConstPasser program in Listing 13.2 demonstrates this idea.

LISTING 13.2 The Full Text of `ConstPasser.cpp`

```
#include <iostream>

class SimpleCat
{
public:
     SimpleCat();
     SimpleCat(SimpleCat&);
```

```
    ~SimpleCat();
    int GetAge() const { return itsAge; }
    void SetAge(int age) { itsAge = age; }
private:
    int itsAge;
};
SimpleCat::SimpleCat()
{
    std::cout << "Simple Cat Constructor ..." << std::endl;
    itsAge = 1;
}
SimpleCat::SimpleCat(SimpleCat&)
{
    std::cout << "Simple Cat Copy Constructor ..." << std::endl;
}
SimpleCat::~SimpleCat()
{
    std::cout << "Simple Cat Destructor ..." << std::endl;
}
const SimpleCat * const
FunctionTwo (const SimpleCat *const theCat);
int main()
{
    std::cout << "Making a cat ..." << std::endl;
    SimpleCat Frisky;
    std::cout << "Frisky is ";
    std::cout << Frisky.GetAge() << " years old" << std::endl;
    int age = 5;
    Frisky.SetAge(age);
    std::cout << "Frisky is ";
    std::cout << Frisky.GetAge() << " years old" << std::endl;
    std::cout << "Calling FunctionTwo ..." << std::endl;
    FunctionTwo(&Frisky);
    std::cout << "Frisky is ";
    std::cout << Frisky.GetAge() << " years old" << std::endl;
    return 0;
}
// functionTwo, passes a const pointer
const SimpleCat * const
FunctionTwo (const SimpleCat * const theCat)
```

```
56: {
57:     std::cout << "Function Two. Returning ..." << std::endl;
58:     std::cout << "Frisky is now " << theCat->GetAge();
59:     std::cout << " years old \n";
60:     // theCat->SetAge(8); const!
61:     return theCat;
62: }
```

Here's the output:

```
Making a cat ...
Simple Cat Constructor ...
Frisky is 1 years old
Frisky is 5 years old
Calling FunctionTwo ...
Function Two. Returning ...
Frisky is now 5 years old
Frisky is 5 years old
Simple Cat Destructor ...
```

SimpleCat has added two accessor functions: `GetAge()` on line 10, which is a `const` function; and `SetAge()` on line 11, which is not. It also has added the member variable `itsAge` on line 14.

The constructor, copy constructor, and destructor are still defined to display their messages. The copy constructor never is called, however, because the object is passed by reference and no copies are made. On line 39, an object is created, and its default age is printed on lines 40 and 41.

On line 43, `itsAge` is set using the accessor `SetAge()`, and the result is displayed on lines 43 and 44. `FunctionOne()` is not used in this program, but `FunctionTwo()` is called.

FunctionTwo() has changed slightly; the parameter and return value are now declared, on lines 33 and 34, to take a constant pointer to a constant object and to return a constant pointer to a constant object.

Because the parameter and return value are still passed by reference, no copies are made, and the copy constructor is not called. The pointer in `FunctionTwo()`, however, is now constant and, therefore, cannot call the non-`const` member function, `SetAge()`. If the call to `SetAge()` on line 60 was not commented out, the program would not compile.

Note that the object created in `main()` is not constant, and `Frisky` can call `SetAge()`. The address of this non-constant object is passed to `FunctionTwo()`, but because the `FunctionTwo()` declaration declares the pointer to be a constant pointer, the object is treated as if it were constant.

References as an Alternative to Pointers

The ConstPasser program solves the problem of making extra copies, saving the calls to the copy constructor and destructor. It uses constant pointers to constant objects, thereby solving the problem of the called function making impermissible changes to the objects passed in as parameters. The method is still somewhat cumbersome, however, because the objects passed to the function are pointers.

Because you know the parameters never will be `NULL`, it is easier to work with the function if references are passed in rather than pointers. The RefPasser program in Listing 13.3 rewrites the previous project to use references rather than pointers.

LISTING 13.3 The Full Text of `RefPasser.cpp`

```
#include <iostream>

class SimpleCat
{
public:
    SimpleCat();
    SimpleCat(SimpleCat&);
    ~SimpleCat();

    int GetAge() const { return itsAge; }
    void SetAge(int age) { itsAge = age; }

private:
    int itsAge;
};

SimpleCat::SimpleCat()
{
    std::cout << "Simple Cat Constructor ..." << std::endl;
    itsAge = 1;
}

SimpleCat::SimpleCat(SimpleCat&)
{
    std::cout << "Simple Cat Copy Constructor ..." << std::endl;
}

SimpleCat::~SimpleCat()
{
    std::cout << "Simple Cat Destructor ..." << std::endl;
}

const SimpleCat & FunctionTwo (const SimpleCat & theCat);
```

```
34:
35: int main()
36: {
37:     std::cout << "Making a cat ..." << std::endl;
38:     SimpleCat Frisky;
39:     std::cout << "Frisky is " << Frisky.GetAge()
40:               << " years old" << std::endl;
41:
42:     int age = 5;
43:     Frisky.SetAge(age);
44:     std::cout << "Frisky is " << Frisky.GetAge()
45:               << " years old" << std::endl;
46:
47:     std::cout << "Calling FunctionTwo..." << std::endl;
48:     FunctionTwo(Frisky);
49:     std::cout << "Frisky is " << Frisky.GetAge()
50:               << " years old" << std::endl;
51:     return 0;
52: }
53:
54: // functionTwo passes a ref to a const object
55: const SimpleCat & FunctionTwo (const SimpleCat & theCat)
56: {
57:     std::cout << "Function Two. Returning..." << std::endl;
58:     std::cout << "Frisky is now " << theCat.GetAge()
59:               << " years old" << std::endl;
60:     // theCat.SetAge(8);   const!
61:     return theCat;
62: }
```

This program has the following output:

```
Making a cat ...
Simple Cat Constructor ...
Frisky is 1 years old
Frisky is 5 years old
Calling FunctionTwo...
Function Two. Returning...
Frisky is now 5 years old
Frisky is 5 years old
Simple Cat Destructor ...
```

The output is identical to that produced by the previous program. The only significant change is that `FunctionTwo()` in lines 55–62 now takes and returns a reference to a constant object. Once again, working with references is somewhat simpler than working with pointers; and the same savings and efficiency, and the safety provided by using `const`, are achieved.

When to Use References and When to Use Pointers

Generally, C++ programmers strongly prefer references to pointers because they are cleaner and easier to use. References cannot be reassigned, however. If you need to point first to one object and then to another, you must use a pointer. References cannot be `NULL`, so if there is any chance that the object in question might be, you must use a pointer rather than a reference. If you want to allocate dynamic memory from the heap, you have to use pointers as discussed in previous hours.

References to Objects Not in Scope

After C++ programmers learn to pass by reference, they have a tendency to go wild. It is possible, however, to overdo it. Remember that a reference always is an alias that refers to some other object. If you pass a reference into or out of a function, be sure to ask yourself, "What is the object I'm aliasing, and will it still exist every time it's used?"

The ReturnRef program in Listing 13.4 illustrates the danger of returning a reference to an object that no longer exists.

LISTING 13.4 **The Full Text of** `ReturnRef.cpp`

```
#include <iostream>

class SimpleCat
{
public:
    SimpleCat(int age, int weight);
    ~SimpleCat() {}
    int GetAge() { return itsAge; }
    int GetWeight() { return itsWeight; }
private:
    int itsAge;
    int itsWeight;
};

SimpleCat::SimpleCat(int age, int weight):
itsAge(age), itsWeight(weight) {}

SimpleCat &TheFunction();

int main()
{
    SimpleCat &rCat = TheFunction();
```

```
23:     int age = rCat.GetAge();
24:     std::cout << "rCat is " << age << " years old!" << std::endl;
25:     return 0;
26: }
27:
28: SimpleCat &TheFunction()
29: {
30:     SimpleCat Frisky(5,9);
31:     return Frisky;
32: }
```

When you build this program, you are confronted with an error about how a reference to the local variable Frisky is being returned.

CAUTION

Some compilers are smart enough to see the reference to a null object and report a compile error. Other compilers will compile and even run. This is a bad coding practice that you should not take advantage of it when your compiler allows you to do this.

On lines 3–13, `SimpleCat` is declared. On line 22, a reference to `SimpleCat` is initialized with the results of calling `TheFunction()`, which is declared on line 18 to return a reference to a `SimpleCat`.

The body of `TheFunction()` declares a local object of type `SimpleCat` and initializes its age and weight. It then returns that local object by reference. Some compilers are smart enough to catch this error and don't let you run the program. Others let you run the program, but with unpredictable results. When `TheFunction()` returns, the local object, `Frisky`, is destroyed. The reference returned by this function is to a non-existent object, and this is a bad thing.

Returning a Reference to an Object on the Heap

You might be tempted to solve the problem in RefReturn by having `TheFunction()` create `Frisky` on the heap. That way, when you return from `TheFunction()`, `Frisky` still exists.

The problem with the approach is this: What do you do with the memory allocated for `Frisky` when you have finished with it? The Leak program in Listing 13.5 illustrates this problem.

LISTING 13.5 **The Full Text of** `Leak.cpp`

```
#include <iostream>

class SimpleCat
{
public:
    SimpleCat (int age, int weight);
    ~SimpleCat() {}
    int GetAge() { return itsAge; }
    int GetWeight() { return itsWeight; }

private:
    int itsAge;
    int itsWeight;
};

SimpleCat::SimpleCat(int age, int weight):
itsAge(age), itsWeight(weight) {}

SimpleCat & TheFunction();

int main()
{
    SimpleCat &rCat = TheFunction();
    int age = rCat.GetAge();
    std::cout << "rCat is " << age << " years old!" << std::endl;
    std::cout << "&rCat: " << &rCat << std::endl;
    // How do you get rid of that memory?
    SimpleCat *pCat = &rCat;
    delete pCat;
    // Uh oh, rCat now refers to ??
    return 0;
}

SimpleCat &TheFunction()
{
    SimpleCat *pFrisky = new SimpleCat(5,9);
    std::cout << "pFrisky: " << pFrisky << std::endl;
    return *pFrisky;
}
```

Here's the output:

```
pFrisky: 0x7918b0
rCat is 5 years old!
&rCat: 0x7918b0
```

This compiles, links, and appears to work. But it is a time bomb waiting to go off.

The function `TheFunction()` has been changed so that it no longer returns a reference to a local variable. Memory is allocated on the heap and assigned to a pointer on line 36. The address that the pointer holds is displayed, and then the pointer is dereferenced and the `SimpleCat` object is returned by reference.

On line 23, the return of `TheFunction()` is assigned to a reference to a `SimpleCat`, and that object is used to obtain the cat's age, which is displayed on line 25.

To prove that the reference declared in `main()` is referring to the object put on the heap in `TheFunction()`, the address of operator is applied to `rCat`. Sure enough, it displays the address of the object it refers to, and this matches the address of the object on the heap.

So far, so good. But how will that memory be freed? You can't call `delete` on the reference. One clever solution is to create another pointer and initialize it with the address obtained from `rCat`. This does delete the memory and plugs the memory leak. One small problem, though: What is `rCat` referring to after line 29? As stated earlier, a reference always must be an alias for an actual object. If it references a null object (as this does now), the program is invalid.

CAUTION

It cannot be overemphasized that a program with a reference to a null object might compile, but it is invalid and its performance is unpredictable.

There are actually two solutions to this problem. The first is to return a pointer to the memory created on line 36. Then the calling function can delete the pointer when it is done. To do this, change the return value of `TheFunction` to a pointer (rather than reference) and return the pointer, rather than the dereferenced pointer:

```
SimpleCat *TheFunction()
{
    SimpleCat *pFrisky = new SimpleCat(5,9);
    std::cout << "pFrisky: " << pFrisky << "\n";
    return pFrisky; // return the pointer
}
```

A better solution is to declare the object in the calling function and then pass it to `TheFunction()` by reference. The advantage of this approach is that the function that allocates the memory (the calling function) is also the function responsible for deallocating it.

Pointer, Pointer, Who Has the Pointer?

When your program allocates memory on the heap, a pointer is returned. It is imperative that you keep a pointer to that memory, because after the pointer is lost, the memory cannot be deleted and becomes a memory leak.

As you pass this block of memory between functions, one of the functions "owns" the pointer. Typically, the value in the block is passed using references, and the function that created the memory block is the one that deletes it. But this is a general rule, not an ironclad one.

It is dangerous for one function to create space in memory and another to free it, however. Ambiguity about which owns the pointer can lead to one of two problems: forgetting to delete a pointer or deleting it twice. Either one can cause serious problems in your program. It is safer to build your functions so that they delete the memory spaces they created.

If you write a function that needs to create a block of memory and then pass it back to the calling function, consider changing your interface. Have the calling function allocate the memory and then pass it into your function by reference. This moves all memory management out of your function and back to the function that is prepared to delete it.

Summary

With the completion of this hour, you now should be comfortable with how pointers and references are created in C++ and understand their strengths and weaknesses.

A pointer is a variable that holds a memory address, whereas a reference is an alias.

Both provide forms of indirection that enable functions to be more, well, functional. In many cases, however, you'll find that references are the better choice.

Q&A

Q. Why have pointers if references are easier?

A. References cannot be `NULL` and cannot be reassigned. Pointers offer greater flexibility, but are slightly more difficult to use.

Q. Why would you ever return by value from a function?

A. If the object being returned is local, you must return by value or you will be returning a reference to a non-existent object.

Q. Given the danger in returning by reference, why not always return by value?

A. There is much greater efficiency in returning by reference. Memory is saved, and the program runs faster.

Q. Where can I go to college to become a clown?

A. One place to go is the Ohio College of Clowning Arts, an institution of higher learning "dedicated to teaching students the ancient and honorable art of the clown." The school, located in Louisville, Ohio, offers 30 weeks of instruction.

Courses include Clown Characterization, Physical Clowning, and Balloons and Magic. Students progress from Associate Clown to Contributing Clown to Functional Clown to Master of Clowning. Alumni include Gumball, Bojangles, and Rufus D. Dufus.

The college is revamping its curriculum, but in the past cost from $1,295 to $1,495. Visit www.ohiocollegeofclowningarts.com for more information.

Workshop

Now that you've had the chance to learn about advanced pointer and reference topics, you can answer a few questions and complete a couple of exercises to firm up your knowledge.

Quiz

1. When dealing with large amounts of data, which approach is better?

   A. Pass by reference

   B. Pass by value

   C. Keep right except to pass

2. What keyword prevents a called function from changing the value of a pointer?

   A. `static`

   B. `enum`

   C. `const`

3. Can you create a reference to a pointer variable?

   A. Yes

   B. No

   C. None of your business

Answers

1. **A.** Pass by reference, because pass by value causes a copy to be made of the variables being passed. For a large object, this could take considerable time and memory.

2. **C.** Using the `const` keyword tells the compiler to prevent the called function from changing the value of the pointer. You get the protection of pass by value without paying the cost of making copies.

3. **A.** Yes, but you might want to be careful in doing so though because it can get to be confusing—especially considering that pointers are confusing to begin with.

Activities

1. Modify the Leak program to use pointers in the call to `TheFunction()` and use the proper deletion method to prevent memory leaks.

2. Modify the ObjectRef and RefPasser programs to display the addresses of the variables before the function calls and afterward. This will give insight into the mechanism involved.

To see solutions to these activities, visit this book's website at http://cplusplus.cadenhead.org.

HOUR 14
Calling Advanced Functions

What You'll Learn in This Hour:

- How to overload member functions
- How to support classes with dynamically allocated variables
- How to initialize objects
- How to create copy constructors

Overloaded Member Functions

In Hour 5, "Calling Functions," you learned how to implement function overloading by writing multiple functions with the same name but different parameters. Member functions also can be overloaded.

This is demonstrated by the `Rectangle` program in Listing 14.1, which implements a `Rectangle` class that has two `drawShape()` functions. One takes no parameters and draws the `Rectangle` based on the object's current values. The other takes two values, `width` and `length`, and draws a rectangle using those values, ignoring the current values.

LISTING 14.1 The Full Text of `Rectangle.cpp`

```
#include <iostream>

class Rectangle
{
public:
    Rectangle(int width, int height);
    ~Rectangle() {}

    void drawShape() const;
    void drawShape(int width, int height) const;

private:
```

```
    int width;
    int height;
};

Rectangle::Rectangle(int newWidth, int newHeight)
{
    width = newWidth;
    height = newHeight;
}

void Rectangle::drawShape() const
{
    drawShape(width, height);
}

void Rectangle::drawShape(int width, int height) const
{
    for (int i = 0; i < height; i++)
    {
        for (int j = 0; j < width; j++)
            std::cout << "*";
        std::cout << std::endl;
    }
}

int main()
{
    Rectangle box(30, 5);
    std::cout << "drawShape():" << std::endl;
    box.drawShape();
    std::cout << "\ndrawShape(40, 2):" << std::endl;
    box.drawShape(40, 2);
    return 0;
}
```

The Rectangle program displays two rectangles consisting of asterisks:

```
drawShape():
******************************
******************************
******************************
******************************
******************************

drawShape(40, 2):
****************************************
****************************************
```

On lines 9–10, the `drawShape()` function is overloaded. The implementation for these overloaded class functions is on lines 23–36.

The version of `drawShape()` that takes no parameters works by calling the version that takes two parameters, passing in the current member variables. This avoids duplicating similar code in two overloaded functions. When code is duplicated to perform the same task, a change you make later to one function could be overlooked in the other, introducing errors to your program.

The main function on lines 38–46 creates a `Rectangle` object and calls `drawShape()` twice, first with no parameters and then with two integers.

The compiler decides which function to call based on the number and type of parameters entered. A potential third overloaded function named `drawShape()` could take one dimension and use it for both width and height.

Using Default Values

Just as ordinary functions can have one or more default values, so can each function of a class. The same rules apply for declaring the default values, as illustrated by the Rectangle2 program in Listing 14.2.

LISTING 14.2 The Full Text of `Rectangle2.cpp`

```
#include <iostream>

class Rectangle
{
public:
    Rectangle(int width, int height);
     ~Rectangle(){}
     void drawShape(int aWidth, int aHeight,
         bool useCurrentValue = false) const;
private:
     int width;
     int height;
};

Rectangle::Rectangle(int aWidth, int aHeight)
{
     width = aWidth;
     height = aHeight;
}
void Rectangle::drawShape(
     int aWidth,
     int aHeight,
     bool useCurrentValue
```

```
) const
{
    int printWidth;
    int printHeight;

    if (useCurrentValue == true)
    {
        printWidth = width;
        printHeight = height;
    }
    else
    {
        printWidth = aWidth;
        printHeight = aHeight;
    }

    for (int i = 0; i < printHeight; i++)
    {
        for (int j = 0; j < printWidth; j++)
            std::cout << "*";
        std::cout << std::endl;
    }
}

int main()
{
    Rectangle box(20, 5);
    std::cout << "drawShape(0, 0, true) ..." << std::endl;
    box.drawShape(0, 0, true);
    std::cout <<"drawShape(25, 4) ..." << std::endl;
    box.drawShape(25, 4);
    return 0;
}
```

This program produces the following output:

```
drawShape(0, 0, true) ...
********************
********************
********************
********************
********************
drawShape(25, 4) ...
*************************
*************************
*************************
*************************
```

Listing 14.2 replaces the overloaded `drawShape()` function with a single function that has default parameters. The function is declared on lines 8–9 to take three parameters. The first two, `aWidth` and `aHeight`, are integers. The third, `useCurrentValue`, is a `bool` value that defaults to false.

The implementation for this function begins on lines 20–24. The third parameter, `useCurrentValue`, is evaluated. If it is true, the member variables `width` and `height` are used to set the local variables `printWidth` and `printHeight`.

If `useCurrentValue` is false, either because it defaulted to false or was set by the user to that value, the first two parameters are used to set `printWidth` and `printHeight`.

NOTE

The `Rectangle` and `Rectangle2` programs accomplish the same thing, but the overloaded functions in 14.1 are simpler to understand and more natural to use. Also, if a additional variation are needed—perhaps the user supplies either the width or the height, but not both—it is easier to extend overloaded functions. The default values approach quickly becomes too complex as new variations are added.

Initializing Objects

Constructors, like member functions, can be overloaded. The capability to overload constructors is powerful and flexible.

A rectangle object could have two constructors. One takes a length and width as parameters and makes a rectangle of that size. The second takes no parameters and makes a rectangle of a default size specified by the class. The compiler chooses the right constructor based on the number and type of the parameters.

You can overload constructors, but you can't overload destructors. Destructors always have the same signature: the name of the class prepended by a tilde (~) and no parameters.

Until now, you have set the member variables of objects in the body of the constructor.

Constructors are created in two stages: the initialization stage and the body of the constructor. A member variable can be set during the initialization or by assigning it a value in the body of the constructor. The following example shows how to initialize member variables:

```
Tricycle::Tricycle():
speed(5),
wheelSize(12)
{
    // body of constructor
}
```

To assign values in a constructor's initialization, put a colon after the closing parentheses of the constructor's parameter list. After the colon, list the name of a member variable followed by a pair of parentheses. Inside the parentheses, put an expression that initializes the member variable. If more than one variable is being set in this manner, separate each one with a comma.

The preceding example sets the `speed` member variable to 5 and the `wheelSize` variable to 12.

CAUTION

Because references and constants cannot be assigned values, they must be initialized using this technique.

To understand why it is more efficient to initialize member variables than assign to them values, you must understand the copy constructor.

The Copy Constructor

In addition to providing a default constructor and destructor, the compiler provides a default copy constructor. The copy constructor is called every time a copy of an object is made.

When you pass an object by value, either into a function or as a function's return value, a temporary copy of that object is made. If the object is a user-defined object, the class's copy constructor is called.

All copy constructors take one parameter: a reference to an object of the same class. It is a good idea to make it a constant reference, because the constructor will not have to alter the object passed in. For example:

```
Tricycle(const Tricycle &trike);
```

In this statement the `Tricycle` constructor takes a constant reference to an existing `Tricycle` object. The goal of the copy constructor is to make a copy of trike.

The default copy constructor simply copies each member variable from the object passed as a parameter to the member variables of the new object. This is called a shallow (or member-wise) copy. Though this is fine for most member variables, it does not work for member variables that are pointers to objects on the heap.

A shallow copy copies the exact values of one object's member variables into another object. Pointers in both objects end up pointing to the same memory. A deep copy, on the other hand, copies the values allocated on the heap to newly allocated memory.

An example illustrates the problem: If the `Tricycle` class includes a member variable called `durability` pointing to an integer on the heap, the default copy constructor copies the passed-in `Tricycle's` `durability` member variable to the new `Tricycle's` `durability` member variable. The two objects then point to the same memory, as illustrated in Figure 14.1.

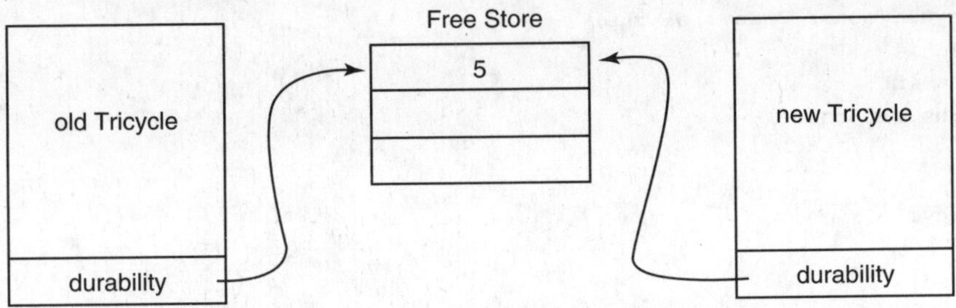

FIGURE 14.1
Using the default copy constructor.

This leads to a disaster when either `Tricycle` object goes out of scope. That object's destructor is called and attempts to clean up the allocated memory.

The other object is still pointing to that memory, however. If it tries to access that memory, the program crashes.

The solution to this problem is to define your own copy constructor and allocate memory properly in the copy. Creating a deep copy allows you to copy the existing values into new memory. The DeepCopy program in Listing 14.3 illustrates how to do this.

LISTING 14.3 The Full Text of `DeepCopy.cpp`

```
#include <iostream>

class Tricycle
{
public:
    Tricycle();                         // default constructor
    Tricycle(const Tricycle&);          // copy constructor
    ~Tricycle();                        // destructor
    int getSpeed() const { return *speed; }
    void setSpeed(int newSpeed) { *speed = newSpeed; }
    void pedal();
    void brake();

private:
    int *speed;
};

Tricycle::Tricycle()
{
```

```
    speed = new int;
    *speed = 5;
}

Tricycle::Tricycle(const Tricycle& rhs)
{
    speed = new int;
    *speed = rhs.getSpeed();
}

Tricycle::~Tricycle()
{
    delete speed;
    speed = NULL;
}

void Tricycle::pedal()
{
    setSpeed(*speed + 1);
    std::cout << "\nPedaling " << getSpeed() << " mph" << std::endl;
}
void Tricycle::brake()
{
    setSpeed(*speed - 1);
    std::cout << "\nPedaling " << getSpeed() << " mph" << std::endl;
}

int main()
{
    std::cout << "Creating trike named wichita ...";
    Tricycle wichita;
    wichita.pedal();
    std::cout << "Creating trike named dallas ..." << std::endl;
    Tricycle dallas(wichita);
    std::cout << "wichita's speed: " << wichita.getSpeed() << std::endl;
    std::cout << "dallas's speed: " << dallas.getSpeed() << std::endl;
    std::cout << "setting wichita to 10 ..." << std::endl;
    wichita.setSpeed(10);
    std::cout << "wichita's speed: " << wichita.getSpeed() << std::endl;
    std::cout << "dallas's speed: " << dallas.getSpeed() << std::endl;
    return 0;
}
```

This program creates two `Tricycle` objects and takes them for a ride:

```
Creating trike named wichita ...
Pedaling 6 mph
Creating trike named dallas ...
```

```
wichita's speed: 6
dallas's speed: 6
setting wichita to 10 ...
wichita's speed: 10
dallas's speed: 6
```

On lines 3–16, the `Tricycle` class is declared. A default constructor (line 6) and copy constructor (line 7) are declared for the class.

On line 15, the `speed` member variable is declared as a pointer to an integer. Typically, there is little reason for a class to store `int` member variables as pointers, but this helps illustrate how to manage member variables on the heap.

The default constructor on lines 24–28 allocates room on the heap for an `int` variable and assigns a value to it.

The copy constructor begins on line 24. The parameter's name is `rhs`, which stands for right-hand side and is a common naming convention for the parameter of a copy constructor.

Memory is allocated on the heap (line 26) and the value at the new memory location is assigned the value of the `speed` variable from the existing `Tricycle` (line 27).

The parameter `rhs` is a `Tricycle` passed into the copy constructor as a constant reference. The member function `rhs.getSpeed()` returns the value stored in the memory pointed to by `rhs`'s member variable `speed`. As a `Tricycle` object, `rhs` has all the member variables of any other `Tricycle`.

Figure 14.2 diagrams what is happening here. The values pointed to by the existing `Tricycle` are copied to the memory allocated for the new `Tricycle`.

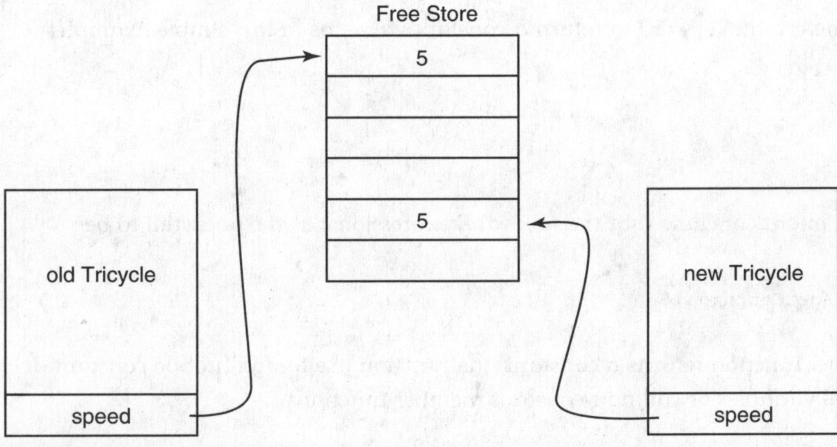

FIGURE 14.2
An illustration of deep copying.

On line 50, a Tricycle is created called wichita. The trike's pedal() function is called, which increases the speed by 1 and displays the new speed. On line 53, a new Tricycle is created called dallas using the copy constructor and passing in wichita. Had wichita been passed as a parameter to a function, this same call to the copy constructor would have been made by the compiler.

On lines 54–55, the current speed of both Tricycles is displayed. This verifies that a copy was made because dallas has the same speed as wichita, 6, not the default speed of 5. On line 57, wichita's speed is set to 10, and the speeds of both objects are displayed again. This time dallas has a speed of 10, while wichita remains 6, demonstrating that they are stored in separate areas of memory.

When the Tricycle objects fall out of scope, their destructors are automatically invoked. The implementation of the Tricycle destructor is shown on lines 30–34. delete is called on the pointer and for safety it is reassigned to NULL.

Compile-Time Constant Expressions

C++ compilers do everything they can to make programs run faster, optimizing the code that you've written wherever possible. One simple opportunity for increased efficiency is when two constants are added together, as in this sample code:

```
const int decade = 10;
int year = 2016 + decade;
```

Because both halves of the expression 2016 + decade are constants, compilers evaluate the expression and store it in compiled form as the result 2026. The compiler acts as if year was assigned the value 2026.

Functions can use the const keyword to return a constant value, as in this simple example:

```
const int getCentury()
{
    return 100;
}
```

For this reason, you might conclude that the following expression has the potential to be optimized:

```
int year = 2016 + getCentury();
```

Although the member function returns a constant, the function itself might not be constant. It might change global variables or call non-constant member functions.

Constant expressions were added to recent versions of C++ with the constexpr keyword:

```
constexpr int getCentury()
{
    return 100;
}
```

The constant expression must have a non-void return type and return an expression as its contents. The expression returned only can contain literal values, calls to other constant expressions or variables that also have been defined with constexpr.

The following statements define a constant called century and a constant expression called year using the constexpr keyword:

```
const int century = 100;
constexpr year = 2016 + century;
```

The Circle program (Listing 14.4) makes use of a constant expression to represent the value of PI, using it to calculate the area of a circle based on a radius value entered by the user.

LISTING 14.4 The Full Text of Circle.cpp

```
#include <iostream>

// get an approximate value of PI
constexpr double getPi() {
    return (double) 22 / 7;
}

int main()
{
    float radius;

    std::cout << "Enter the radius of the circle: ";
    std::cin >> radius;

    // the area equals PI * the radius squared
    double area = getPi() * (radius * radius);

    std::cout << "\nCircle's area: " << area << std::endl;

    return 0;
}
```

Here's sample output for the program for a radius of 19:

```
Enter the radius of the circle: 19

Circle's area: 1134.57
```

C++ does not have a keyword for the value PI. A reasonable approximation of its value suitable for some uses is to divide 22 by 7. When stored as a `double` in C++ it equals 3.14286, the value of PI rounded to five places.

The Circle program calculates `22/7` as a constant expression. The function can do this because it contains only one statement, `return` followed by an expression, and only includes literals, constants, or constant expressions.

Summary

During this hour, you learned how to achieve more control over the creation and destruction of objects in C++.

Constructors, like functions, can be overloaded. The number and type of parameter to the constructor enable the compiler to determine which one should be called by users of the class. A constructor may have default values just like member functions and ordinary functions.

When an object is copied, all member variables are copied by the default copy constructor. This creates problems when member variables are pointers to objects on the heap. Both the original object and the copy point to the same object. When one object goes out of scope and is destroyed, the other still has an active pointer to that object. Any attempt to use that pointer results in a crash of the program.

This problem can be fixed by writing your own copy constructor for a class. The constructor takes one parameter: the original object that will be copied. In the constructor, care can be taken so that the pointer uses new heap memory.

Q&A

Q. Why would you ever use default values when you can overload a function?

A. Because it's easier to maintain one function than two and easier to understand a function with default parameters than to study the bodies of two functions. Furthermore, updating one of the functions and neglecting to update the second is a common source of bugs.

Q. Given the problems with overloaded methods, why not always use default values instead?

A. Overloaded methods supply capabilities not available with default variables, such as varying the list of parameters by type rather than just by number.

Q. When writing a class constructor, how do you decide what to put in the initialization and what to put in the body of the constructor?

A. A simple rule of thumb is to do as much as possible in the initialization phase and initialize all member variables there. Some things such as computations and `std::cout` statements must be in the body of the constructor.

Q. Can an overloaded method have a default parameter?

A. Yes. There is no reason not to combine these powerful features. One or more of the overloaded methods can have their own default values, following the normal rules for default variables in any method.

Q. Why is horseradish hot?

A. It contains isothiocyanate.

A root native to Russia and Hungary that belongs to the mustard family, horseradish contains the mustard-like oil isothiocyanate that brings tears to your eyes, pain to your nose, and spicy flavor to your tastebuds. This only happens when the cells of the horseradish are crushed. Vinegar stops this reaction and stabilizes the flavor.

Both the fumes and the heat deteriorate rapidly upon exposure to air, so horseradish freshly diced has the maximum capability to inflict culinary suffering. As it gets older, it loses both taste and bite.

The smell of wasabi, also called Japanese horseradish, is so sharply painful that it has been used in experimental smoke detectors for the deaf.

Workshop

For the past hour, you have worked some more with member functions. You should answer a few questions and complete a couple of exercises to reinforce your knowledge of the topic.

Quiz

1. With overloaded functions, how does the compiler know which version to call?

- **A.** The function's name
- **B.** The function's number and type of parameters
- **C.** The function's return type

2. Can you use overloaded functions with defaults?

- **A.** Yes
- **B.** No
- **C.** I don't need this kind of pressure; I test poorly.

3. When destroying a pointer in a destructor, what should be assigned to the pointer for safety?

- **A.** `nullptr`
- **B.** 0
- **C.** Either a or b

Answers

1. **B.** The compiler ignores the name and return type. Only the name, number, and parameter type matter.

2. **A.** Absolutely, as long as the number and types of parameters remain unique among versions of the functions (because that's how the compiler figures out which one to call).

3. **C.** Setting it to `nullptr` or 0 has the same effect, making it a null pointer.

Activities

1. Modify the Rectangle program to create another `drawShape()` method with two integer parameters that include default values.

2. Modify the DeepCopy program to change `dallas's` speed after `wichita's` speed has been changed. Does a change to `dallas` affect `wichita`? You've already seen that changing `wichita` does not affect `dallas`.

To see solutions to these activities, visit this book's website at http://cplusplus.cadenhead.org.

HOUR 15

Using Operator Overloading

What You'll Learn in This Hour:

- ▶ How to overload operators in member functions
- ▶ How to overload the assignment operator to manage memory
- ▶ How to support classes with dynamically allocated variables

Operator Overloading

The built-in types in C++ work with operators such as addition (+) and multiplication (*), making it easy to use these types in expressions:

```
int x = 17, y = 12, z;
z = x * (y + 5);
```

The C++ compiler knows to multiply and add integers when the * and + operators appear in an expression. The preceding code adds 5 to y, then multiplies the result by x. The z integer is assigned the value 289.

A class could provide the same functionality with multiply() and add() member functions, but the syntax is a lot more complicated. Here's a snippet of code for a Number class that represents integers and performs the same work as the preceding example:

```
Number x(17);
Number y(12);
Number z, temp;
temp = y.add(5);
z = x.multiply(temp);
```

This code adds 5 to y and multiplies the result by x. The result is still 289.

As you can see, the code is longer and more complex. For a simpler approach, classes can be manipulated with operators by using a technique called operator overloading.

Operator overloading defines what happens when a specific operator is used with an object of a class. Almost all operators in C++ can be overloaded.

Expressions written using operators are easier to read and understand.

For your first exploration of operator overloading, the Counter program in Listing 15.1 creates a class of that name. A `Counter` object will be used in counting, loops, and other tasks where a number must be incremented, decremented, or monitored.

LISTING 15.1 The Full Text of `Counter.cpp`

```
 1: #include <iostream>
 2:
 3: class Counter
 4: {
 5: public:
 6:     Counter();
 7:     ~Counter(){}
 8:     int getValue() const { return value; }
 9:     void setValue(int x) { value = x; }
10:
11: private:
12:     int value;
13: };
14:
15: Counter::Counter():
16: value(0)
17: {}
18:
19: int main()
20: {
21:     Counter c;
22:     std::cout << "The value of c is " << c.getValue()
23:         << std::endl;
24:     return 0;
25: }
```

This program creates a counter and displays its current value:

```
The value of c is 0
```

As it stands, this is pretty plain-vanilla stuff. The class is defined in lines 3–13 and has only one member variable, an `int` named `value`. The default constructor, which is declared on line 6 and implemented on lines 15–17, initializes the member variable to 0.

Unlike a built-in `int`, the `Counter` object can't be incremented, decremented, added, assigned, or manipulated with operators. It can't display its value easily, either.

The following sections address these shortcomings.

Writing an Increment Method

Operator overloading provides functionality that would otherwise be missing in user-defined classes such as `Counter`. When you implement an operator for a class, you are said to be *overloading* that operator.

The most common way to overload an operator in a class is to use a member function. The function declaration takes this form:

```
returnType operatorsymbol(parameter list)
{
   // body of overloaded member function
}
```

The name of the function is `operator` followed by the operator being defined, such as + or ++. The *returnType* is the function's return type and the parameter list holds zero, one, or two parameters (depending on the operator).

The Counter2 program in Listing 15.2 illustrates how to overload the increment operator ++.

LISTING 15.2 The Full Text of `Counter2.cpp`

```
#include <iostream>

class Counter
{
public:
    Counter();
    ~Counter(){}
    int getValue() const { return value; }
    void setValue(int x) { value = x; }
    void increment() { ++value; }
    const Counter& operator++();

private:
    int value;
};

Counter::Counter():
value(0)
{}

const Counter& Counter::operator++()
{
    ++value;
    return *this;
}
```

```
26:
27: int main()
28: {
29:     Counter c;
30:     std::cout << "The value of c is " << c.getValue()
31:         << std::endl;
32:     c.increment();
33:     std::cout << "The value of c is " << c.getValue()
34:         << std::endl;
35:     ++c;
36:     std::cout << "The value of c is " << c.getValue()
37:         << std::endl;
38:     Counter a = ++c;
39:     std::cout << "The value of a: " << a.getValue();
40:     std::cout << " and c: " << c.getValue() << std::endl;
41:     return 0;
42: }
```

This program increments the `Counter` object several times and creates a second object, displaying the values as it proceeds:

```
The value of c is 0
The value of c is 1
The value of c is 2
The value of a: 3 and c: 3
```

On line 35, you can see that the increment operator is invoked on an object of the `Counter` class:

```
++c;
```

This is interpreted by the compiler as a call to the implementation of `operator++` shown on lines 21–25. This member function increments the member variable `value` and then dereferences the `this` pointer to return the current object. Because it returns the current object, it can be assigned to the variable a in line 38.

If the `Counter` object allocated memory, it would be important to override the copy constructor. In this case, the default copy constructor works fine.

Note that the value returned is a `Counter` reference, thereby avoiding the creation of an extra temporary object. It is a `const` reference because the value is not changed by the function using the object.

Overloading the Postfix Operator

The preceding project used the prefix version of the ++ increment operator, which raises the question of how the postfix operator could be overloaded. The prefix and postfix operators are both ++, so the name of the overloaded member function is not useful to distinguish between the two.

The way to handle this and overload the postfix operator is to include a `int` variable as the only parameter to the `operator++()` member function. The integer won't be used; it's just a signal that the function defines the postfix operator.

As you learned in an earlier hour, the prefix operator changes a variable's value before returning it in expressions. The postfix operator returns the value before incrementing or decrementing it.

To do this, in an overloaded member function, a temporary object must be created to hold the original value while the value of the original object is incremented. The temporary object is returned because the postfix operator requires the original value, not the incremented value.

The temporary object must be returned by value and not by reference. Otherwise, it goes out of scope as soon as the function returns.

The Counter3 program in Listing 15.3 demonstrates how to overload the prefix and the postfix operators.

LISTING 15.3 The Full Text of `Counter3.cpp`

```
#include <iostream>

class Counter
{
public:
    Counter();
    ~Counter(){}
    int getValue() const { return value; }
    void setValue(int x) { value = x; }
    const Counter& operator++();    // prefix
    const Counter operator++(int); // postfix

private:
    int value;
};

Counter::Counter():
value(0)
{}

const Counter& Counter::operator++() // prefix
```

```
22: {
23:     ++value;
24:     return *this;
25: }
26:
27: const Counter Counter::operator++(int) // postfix
28: {
29:     Counter temp(*this);
30:     ++value;
31:     return temp;
32: }
33:
34: int main()
35: {
36:     Counter c;
37:     std::cout << "The value of c is " << c.getValue()
38:         << std::endl;
39:     c++;
40:     std::cout << "The value of c is " << c.getValue()
41:         << std::endl;
42:     ++c;
43:     std::cout << "The value of c is " << c.getValue()
44:         << std::endl;
45:     Counter a = ++c;
46:     std::cout << "The value of a: " << a.getValue();
47:     std::cout << " and c: " << c.getValue() << std::endl;
48:     a = c++;
49:     std::cout << "The value of a: " << a.getValue();
50:     std::cout << " and c: " << c.getValue() << std::endl;
51:     return 0;
52: }
```

This program overloads the prefix and postfix increment operators and uses them in several statements:

```
The value of c is 0
The value of c is 1
The value of c is 2
The value of a: 3 and c: 3
The value of a: 3 and c: 4
```

The postfix operator is declared on line 11 and implemented on lines 27–32. Note that the `int` parameter in the function declaration on line 27 is not used in any fashion. It isn't even given a variable name.

Overloading the Addition Operator

The increment operator is a unary operator, which means that it takes only one operand. The addition operator (+) is a binary operator which adds two operands together, which adds a new wrinkle to how overloading works.

The next version of the `Counter` class will be able to add two `Counter` objects together using the + operator:

```
Counter var1, var2, var3;
var3 = var1 + var2;
```

Although you could write an `add()` method that takes two `Counter` objects and returns a `Counter` that contains their sum, a better technique is to overload the + operator. The Counter4 program in Listing 15.4 shows how to do this.

LISTING 15.4 The Full Text of `Counter4.cpp`

```
#include <iostream>

class Counter
{
public:
    Counter();
    Counter(int initialValue);
    ~Counter(){}
    int getValue() const { return value; }
    void setValue(int x) { value = x; }
    Counter operator+(const Counter&);

private:
    int value;
};

Counter::Counter(int initialValue):
value(initialValue)
{}

Counter::Counter():
value(0)
{}

Counter Counter::operator+(const Counter &rhs)
{
    return Counter(value + rhs.getValue());
}

int main()
```

```
31: {
32:     Counter alpha(4), beta(13), gamma;
33:     gamma = alpha + beta;
34:     std::cout << "alpha: " << alpha.getValue() << std::endl;
35:     std::cout << "beta: " << beta.getValue() << std::endl;
36:     std::cout << "gamma: " << gamma.getValue()
37:         << std::endl;
38:     return 0;
39: }
```

The program adds two `Counter` objects, storing the sum in a third:

```
alpha: 4
beta: 13
gamma: 17
```

As you can see from the output, the `gamma` object contains the sum of `alpha` plus `beta`.

The addition operator is invoked on line 33:

```
gamma = alpha + beta;
```

The compiler interprets the statement as if you had written the following code:

```
gamma = alpha.operator+(beta);
```

Line 33 invokes the `operator+` member function declared on line 11 and defined on lines 25–28.

There are two operands in an addition expression. The left operand is the object whose `operator+()` function is called. The right operand is the parameter of this method.

If you had written an `add()` method to add two objects together, it could have been called with a statement of this kind:

```
gamma = alpha.add(beta);
```

Operator overloading makes programs easier to use and understand by replacing explicit function calls.

Limitations on Operator Overloading

Although operator overloading is one of the most powerful features in the C++ language, it has limits.

Operators for built-in types such as `int` cannot be overloaded. The precedence order cannot be changed, and the *arity* of the operator—whether it is unary, binary, or trinary—cannot be altered, either. You also cannot make up new operators, so there's no way to do something such as declaring `**` to be the exponentiation (power of) operator.

Operator overloading is one of the aspects of C++ most overused and abused by new programmers. It is tempting to create new and interesting uses for some of the more obscure operators, but these often lead to code that is confusing and difficult to read.

CAUTION

Doing counterintuitive things like making the + operator subtract and the * operator add is amusing the first time you try it, but no one would do that in their code.

The real danger lies in the well-intentioned but idiosyncratic use of an operator, such as using + to concatenate a series of letters or / to split a string. There is good reason to consider these uses, but better reason to proceed with caution. The goal of overloading operators is to increase usability and understanding.

operator=

The C++ compiler provides each class with a default constructor, destructor, and copy constructor. A fourth member function supplied by the compiler, when one has not been specified in the class, defines the assignment operator.

The assignment operator's overloaded function takes the form `operator=()` and is called when you assign a value to an object, as in this code:

```
Tricycle wichita;
wichita.setSpeed(4);
Tricycle dallas;
dallas.setSpeed(13);
dallas = wichita;
```

The `Tricycle` object named `wichita` is created and its member variable `speed` given the value 4, followed by the `Tricycle` `dallas` with the value 13. The final statement uses the assignment operator =.

Because of this assignment, `dallas`'s `speed` variable is assigned the value of that variable from `wichita`. After this statement executes, `dallas.speed` will have the value 4 rather than 13.

In this case, the copy constructor is not called because `dallas` already exists, so there's no need to construct it. The compiler calls the assignment operator instead.

Hour 14, "Calling Advanced Functions," described the difference between a shallow (member-wise) copy and a deep copy. A shallow copy just copies the members, making both objects point to the same area on the heap. A deep copy allocates the necessary memory.

The same issue crops up here, with an added wrinkle. Because the object `dallas` already exists and has memory allocated, that memory must be deleted to prevent a memory leak.

For this reason, the first thing you must do when overloading the assignment operator is delete the memory assigned to its pointers with statements such as this:

```
delete speed;
```

This works, but what happens if you assign `dallas` to itself:

```
dallas = dallas;
```

No programmer is likely to do this on purpose, but the class must be able to handle this situation because it can happen by accident. References and dereferenced pointers might hide the fact that an object is being assigned to itself.

If you don't guard against this problem, the self-assignment causes `dallas` to delete its own memory allocation. After it does, when it's ready to copy the memory from the right side of the assignment, that memory is gone.

This can be prevented if the assignment operator checks to see whether the right side of the assignment operator is the object itself using the `this` pointer.

The Assignment class in Listing 15.5 uses overloading to define a custom assignment operator and avoids the same-object problem.

LISTING 15.5 The Full Text of `Assignment.cpp`

```
#include <iostream>

class Tricycle
{
public:
    Tricycle();
    // copy constructor and destructor use default
    int getSpeed() const { return *speed; }
    void setSpeed(int newSpeed) { *speed = newSpeed; }
    Tricycle operator=(const Tricycle&);

private:
    int *speed;
};

Tricycle::Tricycle()
{
    speed = new int;
    *speed = 5;
}

Tricycle Tricycle::operator=(const Tricycle& rhs)
```

```
23: {
24:     if (this == &rhs)
25:         return *this;
26:     delete speed;
27:     speed = new int;
28:     *speed = rhs.getSpeed();
29:     return *this;
30: }
31:
32: int main()
33: {
34:     Tricycle wichita;
35:     std::cout << "Wichita's speed: " << wichita.getSpeed()
36:         << std::endl;
37:     std::cout << "Setting Wichita's speed to 6 ..." << std::endl;
38:     wichita.setSpeed(6);
39:     Tricycle dallas;
40:     std::cout << "Dallas' speed: " << dallas.getSpeed()
41:         << std::endl;
42:     std::cout << "Copying Wichita to Dallas ..." << std::endl;
43:     wichita = dallas;
44:     std::cout << "Dallas' speed: " << dallas.getSpeed()
45:         << std::endl;
46:     return 0;
47: }
```

Assignment produces this output when run:

```
Wichita's speed: 5
Setting Wichita's speed to 6 ...
Dallas' speed: 5
Copying Wichita to Dallas ...
Dallas' speed: 5
```

Listing 15.5 brings back the `Tricycle` class, omitting the copy constructor and destructor to save room. On line 10, the assignment operator is declared, and on lines 22–30, it is defined.

On line 24, the current object (the `Tricycle` being assigned to) is tested to see if it is the same as the `Tricycle` being assigned. This is done by checking whether the address of `rhs` is the same as the address stored in the `this` pointer.

The equality operator (==) also can be overloaded, enabling you to determine for yourself what it means for your objects to be equal.

NOTE

On lines 26–27 of Listing 15.5, the member variable `speed` is deleted and recreated on the heap. Although this is not strictly necessary, it is good programming practice that avoids memory leaks when working with variable-length objects that do not overload their assignment operators.

Conversion Operators

What happens when you try to assign a variable of a built-in type, such as `int` or `unsigned short`, to an object of a user-defined class? Listing 15.6 brings back the `Counter` class and attempts to assign a variable of type `int` to a `Counter` object.

CAUTION

Listing 15.6 will not compile, for reasons you'll learn after preparing it.

LISTING 15.6 The Full Text of `Counter5.cpp`

```
#include <iostream>

class Counter
{
public:
    Counter();
    ~Counter() {}
    int getValue() const { return value; }
    void setValue(int newValue) { value = newValue; }
private:
    int value;
};

Counter::Counter():
value(0)
{}

int main()
{
    int beta = 5;
    Counter alpha = beta;
    std::cout << "alpha: " << alpha.getValue() << std::endl;
    return 0;
}
```

When you attempt to compile this program, it fails with an error about trying to convert an `int` to a `Counter` object in line 21.

The Counter class declared on lines 3–12 only has a default constructor. It declares no particular member function for turning an `int` into a `Counter` object, so line 21 triggers a compile error. The compiler cannot figure out, absent such a function, that an `int` should be assigned to the object's member variable `value`.

The Counter6 program (Listing 15.7) corrects this by creating a conversion operator: a constructor that takes an `int` and produces a `Counter` object.

LISTING 15.7 The Full Text of `Counter6.cpp`

```
 1: #include <iostream>
 2:
 3: class Counter
 4: {
 5: public:
 6:     Counter();
 7:     ~Counter() {}
 8:     Counter(int newValue);
 9:     int getValue() const { return value; }
10:     void setValue(int newValue) { value = newValue; }
11: private:
12:     int value;
13: };
14:
15: Counter::Counter():
16: value(0)
17: {}
18:
19: Counter::Counter(int newValue):
20: value(newValue)
21: {}
22:
23: int main()
24: {
25:     int beta = 5;
26:     Counter alpha = beta;
27:     std::cout << "alpha: " << alpha.getValue() << std::endl;
28:     return 0;
29: }
```

This code compiles successfully and produces the following line of output:

```
alpha: 5
```

The important change is on line 8, where the constructor is overloaded to take an `int`, and on lines 19–21, where the constructor is implemented. The effect of this constructor is to create a `Counter` out of an `int`.

Given this constructor, the compiler knows to call it when an integer is assigned to a `Counter` object in line 26.

The `int()` Operator

The preceding project demonstrated how to assign a built-in type to an object. It's also possible to assign an object to a built-in value, which is attempted in this code:

```
Counter gamma(18);
int delta = gamma;
cout << "delta : " << delta  << "\n";
```

If this code was added to the Counter6 program, it would not compile successfully. The class knows how to create a `Counter` from an integer, but it does not know how to accomplish the reverse and create an integer from a `Counter`.

C++ provides conversion operators that can be added to a class to specify how to do implicit conversions to built-in types. The Counter7 program in Listing 15.8 illustrates this.

LISTING 15.8 The Full Text of `Counter7.cpp`

```
#include <iostream>

class Counter
{
public:
    Counter();
    ~Counter() {}
    Counter(int newValue);
    int getValue() const { return value; }
    void setValue(int newValue) { value = newValue; }
    operator unsigned int();
private:
    int value;
};

Counter::Counter():
value(0)
{}

Counter::Counter(int newValue):
value(newValue)
{}
```

```
23:
24: Counter::operator unsigned int()
25: {
26:     return (value);
27: }
28:
29: int main()
30: {
31:     Counter epsilon(19);
32:     int zeta = epsilon;
33:     std::cout << "zeta: " << zeta << std::endl;
34:     return 0;
35: }
```

This program produces the following output:

```
zeta: 19
```

On line 11, the conversion operator is declared. Note that it has no return value. The implementation of this function is on lines 24–27. Line 26 returns the value of the object's `value` member variable. The integer returned by the function matches the type in the function declaration.

Now the compiler knows how to turn integers into `Counter` objects and vice versa, so they can be assigned to one another freely.

Note that conversion operators do not specify a return value, despite the fact that they are returning a converted value.

Summary

Operator overloading is one of the most powerful aspects of the C++ language. By defining how operators behave in the classes that you design, you make it easier to work with objects of those classes.

Almost all operators in C++ can be overloaded.

As you have seen in working with built-in types, using operators to manipulate objects is considerably easier than calling member functions. It also results in programs that are easier to comprehend.

This assumes, of course, that the behavior of overloaded operators is consistent with how they work on built-in types.

Q&A

Q. Why would you overload an operator when you can just create a member function?

A. It is easier to use overloaded operators when their behavior is well understood. Less code is required to accomplish the same task, and your classes can mimic the functionality of the built-in types.

Q. What is the difference between the copy constructor and the assignment operator?

A. The copy constructor creates a new object with the same values as an existing object. The assignment operator changes an existing object so that it has the same values as another object.

Q. What happens to the int used in the postfix operators?

A. Nothing. That `int` is never used, except as a flag to overload the postfix and prefix operators.

Q. Who was the former boyfriend that Alanis Morissette was singing about in "You Oughta Know"?

A. The incendiary breakup song from her 1995 album *Jagged Little Pill*, which reached No. 1 and has sold more than 33 million copies, was about a real person she dated. Morissette admitted that much in interviews but has never publicly identified the person.

The No. 1 suspect in the press has been the actor Dave Coulier, who played Joey in the sitcom *Full House* and its 2016 version *Fuller House*. He broke up with Morissette shortly before the release of the album.

In 2008, Coulier told the *Calgary Herald* that the song was about him. Describing what it was like when he first heard it on the radio, Coulier revealed, "I said, 'Wow, this girl is angry.' And then I said, 'Oh man, I think it's Alanis.' I listened to the song over and over again, and I said, 'I think I have really hurt this person.'"

He oughta know.

Workshop

Now that you've worked with overloaded operators, you can answer a few questions and do a couple of exercises to firm up your knowledge of the hour.

Quiz

1. Why can't you create totally new operators like `**` for exponentiation?

A. That operator isn't part of the language.

B. Because it uses an existing operator, `*`.

C. The premise of your question is questionable. You can create new operators.

2. Why is the overload syntax different for prefix and postfix increment and decrement operations?

   A. Because prefix and postfix return different values

   B. Because one uses ++ and the other uses --

   C. The syntax is not different.

3. What do conversion operators do?

   A. Convert objects to built-in types

   B. Convert built-in types to objects

   C. Both a and b

Answers

1. **A.** Adding new operators such as `**` requires a change to the compiler, because `**` is not part of the language and so the compiler would not know what to do with it.

2. **A.** The behavior differs totally depending on whether the `++` or `--` operator appears before or after a variable, so the code must follow the same behavior. Technically, it doesn't have to mimic the behavior, but users of your class will expect it to work that way.

3. **A.** They convert from the object type to a built-in type.

Activities

1. Modify the Assignment program (Listing 15.6) to overload the equality operator (==). Use that operator to compare two `Tricycle` object's speeds.

2. Modify the Counter2 program (Listing 15.5) to also overload the minus operator and use it to perform simple subtraction.

To see solutions to these activities, visit this book's website at http://cplusplus.cadenhead.org.

HOUR 16

Extending Classes with Inheritance

What You'll Learn in This Hour:

- What inheritance is
- How to derive one class from another
- How to access base member functions from derived classes
- How to override base member functions
- What protected access is and how to use it

What Is Inheritance?

It is a fundamental aspect of human intelligence to seek out, recognize, and create relationships among concepts. We build hierarchies, networks, and other interrelationships to explain and understand the ways that things interact. C++ embodies this in inheritance hierarchies, making it possible for a class to inherit from another class.

Concepts can be categorized in many different ways. When you look at your dog, what do you see? A biologist sees a network of interacting organs, a physicist sees atoms and forces at work, a taxonomist sees a representative of the species *canine domesticus*, and a child sees a companion and protector.

Each category often can be divided further into subcategories. To a taxonomist, a dog is a canine. A canine is a kind of mammal. A mammal is a kind of animal—and so forth. Taxonomists divide the world of living things into kingdom, phyla, class, order, family, genus, and species.

The taxonomist's hierarchy establishes an "is a" relationship—a dog is a canine. There are "is a" relationships everywhere. A Nissan Leaf is a kind of car, which is a kind of vehicle. A cannoli is a kind of dessert, which is a kind of food.

When something is described as a kind of something else, this means it is a specialization of that thing. That is, a car is a special kind of vehicle. Cars and buses are both vehicles. They are distinguished by their specific characteristics but share things in common with each other and other vehicles.

Inheritance and Derivation

These relationships are conveyed by inheritance. The concept of a dog inherits all the features of a mammal. Because it is a mammal, it moves and breathes air; by definition, all mammals move and breathe air. The concept of a dog adds to that definition the idea of barking, a wagging tail, and so forth. A dog has traits unique to dogs and traits common to all mammals.

Dogs can be divided further into hunting dogs and terriers; terriers can be divided into Yorkshire Terriers, Dandie Dinmont Terriers, and so forth.

A Yorkshire Terrier is a kind of terrier; therefore, it is a kind of dog; therefore, a kind of mammal; therefore, a kind of animal; and, therefore, a kind of living thing.

C++ attempts to represent these relationships by defining classes that derive from one another. Derivation is a way of expressing the "is a" relationship. You derive a new class, `Dog`, from the class `Mammal`. You don't have to state explicitly that dogs move because they inherit that from `Mammal`. Because it derives from `Mammal`, `Dog` automatically moves.

A class that adds new functionality to an existing class is said to derive from that original class. The original class is said to be the new class's base class.

If the `Dog` class derives from the `Mammal` class, `Mammal` is a base class of `Dog`. Derived classes are supersets of their base classes. Just as in the real world dogs add certain features to the idea of a mammal, the `Dog` class will add certain member functions or data to the `Mammal` class.

A base class can have more than one derived class. Just as dogs, cats, and horses are all types of mammals, their classes would all derive from the `Mammal` class.

Animals and Inheritance

To facilitate the discussion of derivation and inheritance, this section focuses on the relationships among a number of classes representing animals. Imagine that you have been asked to design a children's game—a simulation of a farm.

The game will have a whole set of farm animals, including horses, cows, dogs, cats, sheep, and so forth. You will create member functions for these classes so that they can act in the ways the child might expect, but for now you'll stub out each function with a simple `cout` statement.

Stubbing out a function means to write only enough to show that the function was called, leaving the details for later. The stub function serves as a placeholder. You do not have to fill in all the details as you work on the problem.

The Syntax of Derivation

To create a class that inherits from another class in C++, in the `class` declaration, put a colon after the class name and specify the access level of the class (`public`, `protected`, or `private`) and the class from which it derives.

Access control will be covered later. Here's an example class declaration with an access level of `public`:

```
class Dog : public Mammal
```

This statement creates a derived class called `Dog` that inherits from the base class `Mammal`. The Mammal1 program in Listing 16.1 creates a full `Dog` class derived from `Mammal`.

LISTING 16.1 The Full Text of `Mammal1.cpp`

```
#include <iostream>

enum BREED { YORKIE, CAIRN, DANDIE, SHETLAND, DOBERMAN, LAB };

class Mammal
{
public:
    // constructors
    Mammal();
    ~Mammal();

    // accessors
    int getAge() const;
    void setAge(int);
    int getWeight() const;
    void setWeight();

    // other member functions
    void speak();
    void sleep();

protected:
    int age;
    int weight;
};

class Dog : public Mammal
{
public:
    // constructors
    Dog();
    ~Dog();
```

```
33:
34:     // accessors
35:     BREED getBreed() const;
36:     void setBreed(BREED);
37:
38:     // other member functions
39:     // wagTail();
40:     // begForFood();
41:
42: protected:
43:     BREED itsBreed;
44: };
45:
46: int main()
47: {
48:     return 0;
49: }
```

This program will compile but it has no output; it is only a set of class declarations without implementations. Nonetheless, there is much to see here.

On lines 5–25, the Mammal class is declared. Because all mammals have an age and weight, these attributes are represented in this class by the member variables age and weight.

Six member functions are defined in the Mammal class: four accessor member functions, speak(), and sleep().

The Dog class inherits from Mammal, as indicated on line 27. Every Dog object has three member variables: age, weight, and breed. Note that the class declaration for Dog in lines 27–44 does not include two of these variables, age and weight. Dog objects inherit these variables from the Mammal class along with all of Mammal's member functions except for the copy operator, the constructors, and the destructor.

Private Versus Protected

A new access keyword, protected, has been introduced on lines 22 and 42 of the Mammal1 program in Listing 16.1. Previously, class data had been declared private. However, private members are not available to derived classes. You could make the age and weight member variables public, but that is not desirable. You don't want other classes accessing these data members directly.

What you want is to make the data visible to this class and its derived classes, which is accomplished by protected. Protected data members and functions are fully visible to derived classes, but are otherwise private.

There are three access specifiers: `public`, `protected`, and `private`. If a function has an instance of a class, it can access all the public member data and functions of that class. The member functions of a class, however, can access all the private data members and functions of any class from which they derive.

Therefore, the function `Dog::wagTail()` can access the private data `breed` and can access the protected data in the `Mammal` class.

Even if other classes are layered into the hierarchy between `Mammal` and `Dog` (for example, `DomesticAnimals`), the `Dog` class will still be able to access the protected members of `Mammal`, assuming that these other classes have public inheritance.

The Mammal2 program in Listing 16.2 demonstrates how to create objects of type `Dog` and access its data and member functions.

LISTING 16.2 The Full Text of `Mammal2.cpp`

```
#include <iostream>

enum BREED { YORKIE, CAIRN, DANDIE, SHETLAND, DOBERMAN, LAB };

class Mammal
{
public:
    // constructors
    Mammal(): age(2), weight(5) {}
    ~Mammal(){}

    // accessors
    int getAge() const { return age; }
    void setAge(int newAge) { age = newAge; }
    int getWeight() const { return weight; }
    void setWeight(int newWeight) { weight = newWeight; }

    // other member functions
    void speak() const { std::cout << "Mammal sound!\n"; }
    void sleep() const { std::cout << "Shhh. I'm sleeping.\n"; }

protected:
    int age;
    int weight;
};

class Dog : public Mammal
{
public:
    // constructors
```

```
31:     Dog(): breed(YORKIE) {}
32:     ~Dog() {}
33:
34:     // accessors
35:     BREED getBreed() const { return breed; }
36:     void setBreed(BREED newBreed) { breed = newBreed; }
37:
38:     // other member functions
39:     void wagTail() { std::cout << "Tail wagging ...\n"; }
40:     void begForFood() { std::cout << "Begging for food ...\n"; }
41:
42: private:
43:     BREED breed;
44: };
45:
46: int main()
47: {
48:     Dog fido;
49:     fido.speak();
50:     fido.wagTail();
51:     std::cout << "Fido is " << fido.getAge() << " years old\n";
52:     return 0;
53: }
```

When you run Mammal2, this output appears:

```
Mammal sound!
Tail wagging ...
Fido is 2 years old
```

On lines 5–25, the `Mammal` class is declared with several inline member functions. On lines 27–44, the `Dog` class is declared as a derived class of `Mammal`. These declarations give all `Dog` objects an age, weight, and breed.

On line 48, a `Dog` is declared called `fido` which inherits all the attributes of a `Mammal` and the attributes of a `Dog`. Thus, `fido` knows how to `wagTail()`, `speak()`, and `sleep()`.

Constructors and Destructors

An important aspect to understand about inheritance in C++ is that more than one constructor is called when an object of a derived class is created.

`Dog` objects are `Mammal` objects. When `fido` was created in the Mammal2 program, his base class constructor was called first, creating a `Mammal`, and then the `Dog` constructor was called, completing the construction of the `Dog` object. Because `fido` was created with no parameters, the default constructor was called in each case.

When the fido object is destroyed, the Dog destructor is called first, followed by the destructor for the Mammal part of Fido. Each destructor is given an opportunity to clean up after its own part of the object. Constructors are called in order of inheritance. Destructors are called in reverse order of inheritance.

The Mammal3 program in Listing 16.3 demonstrates how constructors and destructors are called for objects belonging to derived classes.

LISTING 16.3 The Full Text of Mammal3.cpp

```
#include <iostream>

enum BREED { YORKIE, CAIRN, DANDIE, SHETLAND, DOBERMAN, LAB };

class Mammal
{
public:
    // constructors
    Mammal();
    ~Mammal();

    // accessors
    int getAge() const { return age; }
    void setAge(int newAge) { age = newAge; }
    int getWeight() const { return weight; }
    void setWeight(int newWeight) { weight = newWeight; }

    // other member functions
    void speak() const { std::cout << "Mammal sound!\n"; }
    void sleep() const { std::cout << "shhh. I'm sleeping.\n"; }

protected:
    int age;
    int weight;
};

class Dog : public Mammal
{
public:
    // constructors
    Dog();
    ~Dog();

    // accessors
    BREED getBreed() const { return breed; }
    void setBreed(BREED newBreed) { breed = newBreed; }

```

```
    // other member functions
    void wagTail() { std::cout << "Tail wagging ...\n"; }
    void begForFood() { std::cout << "Begging for food ...\n"; }

private:
    BREED breed;
};

Mammal::Mammal():
age(3),
weight(5)
{
    std::cout << "Mammal constructor ...\n";
}

Mammal::~Mammal()
{
    std::cout << "Mammal destructor ...\n";
}

Dog::Dog():
breed(YORKIE)
{
    std::cout << "Dog constructor ...\n";
}

Dog::~Dog()
{
    std::cout << "Dog destructor ...\n";
}

int main()
{
    Dog fido; // create a dog
    fido.speak();
    fido.wagTail();
    std::cout << "Fido is " << fido.getAge() << " years old\n";
    return 0;
}
```

Here's the program's output:

```
Mammal constructor ...
Dog constructor ...
Mammal sound!
Tail wagging ...
Fido is 3 years old
Dog destructor ...
Mammal destructor ...
```

The Mammal3 program displays a line of text as constructors and destructors are called. When `fido` is created in line 71, `Mammal's` constructor is called, followed by `Dog's` constructor. At that point the `Dog` fully exists, and its member functions can be called. When `fido` goes out of scope as the `main()` function ends on line 76, `Dog`'s destructor is called, followed by a call to `Mammal`'s destructor.

Passing Arguments to Base Constructors

As you work on the classes developed during this hour, it is possible that you'll want to overload the constructor of `Mammal` to set a specific age and overload the `Dog` constructor to set a breed. How do you get the age and weight parameters passed up to the right constructor in `Mammal`? What if `Dog` needs to initialize weight but `Mammal` doesn't?

Base class initialization can be performed during class initialization by writing the base class name followed by the parameters expected by the base class, as demonstrated in the Mammal4 program (Listing 16.4).

LISTING 16.4 The Full Text of `Mammal4.cpp`

```
#include <iostream>

enum BREED { YORKIE, CAIRN, DANDIE, SHETLAND, DOBERMAN, LAB };

class Mammal
{
public:
    // constructors
    Mammal();
    Mammal(int age);
    ~Mammal();

    // accessors
    int getAge() const { return age; }
    void setAge(int newAge) { age = newAge; }
    int getWeight() const { return weight; }
    void setWeight(int newWeight) { weight = newWeight; }

    // other member functions
    void speak() const { std::cout << "Mammal sound!\n"; }
    void sleep() const { std::cout << "Shhh. I'm sleeping.\n"; }

protected:
    int age;
    int weight;
};
```

```

class Dog : public Mammal
{
public:
    // constructors
    Dog();
    Dog(int age);
    Dog(int age, int weight);
    Dog(int age, BREED breed);
    Dog(int age, int weight, BREED breed);
    ~Dog();

    // accessors
    BREED getBreed() const { return breed; }
    void setBreed(BREED newBreed) { breed = newBreed; }

    // other member functions
    void wagTail() { std::cout << "Tail wagging ...\n"; }
    void begForFood() { std::cout << "Begging for food ...\n"; }

private:
    BREED breed;
};

Mammal::Mammal():
age(1),
weight(5)
{
    std::cout << "Mammal constructor ...\n";
}

Mammal::Mammal(int age):
age(age),
weight(5)
{
    std::cout << "Mammal(int) constructor ...\n";
}

Mammal::~Mammal()
{
    std::cout << "Mammal destructor ...\n";
}

Dog::Dog():
Mammal(),
breed(YORKIE)
{
    std::cout << "Dog constructor ...\n";
```

```
}

Dog::Dog(int age):
Mammal(age),
breed(YORKIE)
{
    std::cout << "Dog(int) constructor ...\n";
}

Dog::Dog(int age, int newWeight):
Mammal(age),
breed(YORKIE)
{
    weight = newWeight;
    std::cout << "Dog(int, int) constructor ...\n";
}

Dog::Dog(int age, int newWeight, BREED breed):
Mammal(age),
breed(breed)
{
    weight = newWeight;
    std::cout << "Dog(int, int, BREED) constructor ...\n";
}

Dog::Dog(int age, BREED newBreed):
Mammal(age),
breed(newBreed)
{
    std::cout << "Dog(int, BREED) constructor ...\n";
}

Dog::~Dog()
{
    std::cout << "Dog destructor ...\n";
}

int main()
{
    Dog fido;
    Dog rover(5);
    Dog buster(6, 8);
    Dog yorkie (3, YORKIE);
    Dog dobbie (4, 20, DOBERMAN);
    fido.speak();
    rover.wagTail();
    std::cout << "Yorkie is "
        << yorkie.getAge() << " years old\n";
```

```
123:     std::cout << "Dobbie weighs "
124:         << dobbie.getWeight() << " pounds\n";
125:     return 0;
126: }
```

The Mammal4 program displays the following output, which has line numbers added so that they can be referenced in this section:

```
 1: Mammal constructor ...
 2: Dog constructor ...
 3: Mammal(int) constructor ...
 4: Dog(int) constructor ...
 5: Mammal(int) constructor ...
 6: Dog(int, int) constructor ...
 7: Mammal(int) constructor ...
 8: Dog(int, BREED) constructor ...
 9: Mammal(int) constructor ...
10: Dog(int, int, BREED) constructor ...
11: Mammal sound!
12: Tail wagging ...
13: Yorkie is 3 years old
14: Dobbie weighs 20 pounds
15: Dog destructor ...
16: Mammal destructor ...
17: Dog destructor ...
18: Mammal destructor ...
19: Dog destructor ...
20: Mammal destructor ...
21: Dog destructor ...
22: Mammal destructor ...
23: Dog destructor ...
24: Mammal destructor ...
```

In Listing 16.4, `Mammal`'s constructor has been overloaded on line 10 to take an integer, the `Mammal` object's age. The implementation on lines 58–63 initializes `age` with the value passed into the constructor and `weight` with the value 5.

`Dog` has overloaded five constructors on lines 32–36. The first is the default constructor. The second takes the age, which is the same parameter that the Mammal constructor takes. The third constructor takes both the age and the weight; the fourth takes the age and breed; and the fifth takes the age, weight, and breed.

NOTE

Note that on line 71 of Listing 16.4, `Dog`'s default constructor calls `Mammal`'s default constructor. Although it is not strictly necessary to do this, it serves to demonstrate that you intended to call the base constructor, which takes no parameters. The base constructor would be called in any case, but actually doing so makes your intentions explicit.

The implementation for the Dog constructor, which takes an integer, is on lines 77–82. In its initialization phase, Dog initializes its base class, passing in the parameter; and then it initializes its breed.

Another Dog constructor is on lines 84–90. This one takes two parameters. It initializes its base class by calling the appropriate constructor, but this time also assigns weight to its base class's variable weight. Note that you cannot assign to the base class variable in the initialization phase. So, you cannot write this code:

```
Dog::Dog(int age, int newWeight):
Mammal(age),
breed(YORKIE),
weight(newWeight) // error!
{
    std::cout << "Dog(int, int) constructor ...\n";
}
```

Why? You are not allowed to initialize a value in the base class. Similarly, you may not write the following:

```
Dog::Dog(int newAge, int newWeight):
Mammal(newAge, newWeight), // error!
breed(YORKIE)
{
    std::cout << "Dog(int, int) constructor ...\n";
}
```

Mammal does not have a constructor that takes the weight parameter. You must do this assignment within the body of the Dog constructor.

```
Dog::Dog(int newAge, int weight):
Mammal(newAge), // base constructor
breed(YORKIE) // initialization
{
    weight = weight; // assignment
}
```

Walk through the remaining constructors to make sure you are comfortable with how they work. Take note of what is initialized and what must wait for the body of the constructor.

The output has been numbered so that each line can be referred to in this analysis. Lines 1–2 of the output represent the instantiation of fido, using the default constructor.

In the output, lines 3–4 represent the creation of rover. Lines 5–6 represent buster. Note that the Mammal constructor that was called is the constructor that takes one integer, but the Dog constructor is the constructor that takes two integers.

After all the objects are created, they are used and then go out of scope. As each of the five objects is destroyed, first the Dog destructor and then the Mammal destructor is called.

This is an example of overloading base class member functions within a derived class.

Overriding Functions

A Dog object has access to all the member functions in class Mammal, as well as to any member functions, such as wagTail(), that the declaration of the Dog class might add. It also can override a base class function. Overriding a function means changing the implementation of a base class function in a derived class. When you make an object of the derived class, the correct function is called.

When a derived class creates a member function with the same return type and signature as a member function in the base class, but with a new implementation, it is said to be overriding that function.

When you override a function, it must agree in return type and in signature with the function in the base class. The signature is the function prototype other than the return type: that is, the name, the parameter list, and the keyword const, if used.

The signature of a function is its name, and the number and type of its parameters. The signature does not include the return type.

The Mammal5 program (Listing 16.5) illustrates what happens when the Dog class overrides the speak() member function in the Mammal class. To save room, the accessor functions have been left out of these classes.

LISTING 16.5 The Full Text of Mammal5.cpp

```
#include <iostream>

enum BREED { YORKIE, CAIRN, DANDIE, SHETLAND, DOBERMAN, LAB };

class Mammal
{
public:
    // constructors
    Mammal() { std::cout << "Mammal constructor ...\n"; }
    ~Mammal() { std::cout << "Mammal destructor ...\n"; }

    // other member functions
    void speak() const { std::cout << "Mammal sound!\n"; }
    void sleep() const { std::cout << "Shhh. I'm sleeping.\n"; }

protected:
```

```
17:     int age;
18:     int weight;
19: };
20:
21: class Dog : public Mammal
22: {
23: public:
24:     // constructors
25:     Dog() { std::cout << "Dog constructor ...\n"; }
26:     ~Dog() { std::cout << "Dog destructor ...\n"; }
27:
28:     // other member functions
29:     void wagTail() { std::cout << "Tail wagging ...\n"; }
30:     void begForFood() { std::cout << "Begging for food ...\n"; }
31:     void speak() const { std::cout << "Woof!\n"; }
32:
33: private:
34:     BREED breed;
35: };
36:
37: int main()
38: {
39:     Mammal bigAnimal;
40:     Dog fido;
41:     bigAnimal.speak();
42:     fido.speak();
43:     return 0;
44: }
```

Here's the output of Mammal5:

```
Mammal constructor ...
Mammal constructor ...
Dog constructor ...
Mammal sound!
Woof!
Dog destructor ...
Mammal destructor ...
Mammal destructor ...
```

On line 31, the `Dog` class overrides the `speak()` member function of the Mammal class, causing `Dog` objects to say "Woof!" when the function is called. On line 39, a `Mammal` object is created, causing the first line of output to be displayed when the `Mammal` constructor is called. On line 40, a `Dog` object is created, causing the next two lines of output, where the `Mammal` constructor and then the `Dog` constructor are called.

On line 41, the `Mammal` object calls its `speak()` function. On line 42, the `Dog` object calls its `speak()` function. The output reflects that the correct functions were called. Finally, the two objects go out of scope and their destructors are called.

Overloading Versus Overriding

The terms *overloading* and *overriding* sound similar and do similar things in C++. When you overload a member function, you create more than one function with the same name but with different signatures. When you override a member function, you create a function in a derived class with the same name as a function in the base class and with the same signature.

Hiding the Base Class Member Function

In the Mammal5 program you just created, the `Dog` class's member function `speak()` hides the base class's function. This is just what is wanted, but it can have unexpected results. If `Mammal` has a `move()` member function that is overloaded, and `Dog` overrides that function, the `Dog` function hides all the `Mammal` functions with that name.

If Mammal overloads `move()` as three functions—one that takes no parameters, one that takes an integer, and one that takes an integer and a direction—and `Dog` overrides just the `move()` function which takes no parameters, it will not be easy to access the other two functions using a `Dog` object. The Mammal6 program in Listing 16.6 illustrates this problem.

LISTING 16.6 The Full Text of `Mammal6.cpp`

```
#include <iostream>

class Mammal
{
public:
    void move() const { std::cout << "Mammal moves one step\n"; }
    void move(int distance) const
        { std::cout << "Mammal moves " << distance <<" steps\n"; }
protected:
    int age;
    int weight;
};

class Dog : public Mammal
{
public:
    void move() const { std::cout << "Dog moves 5 steps\n"; }
}; // you may receive a warning that you are hiding a function!

int main()
{
```

```
22:     Mammal bigAnimal;
23:     Dog fido;
24:     bigAnimal.move();
25:     bigAnimal.move(2);
26:     fido.move();
27:     // fido.move(10);
28:     return 0;
29: }
```

The Mammal6 program produces this output when run:

```
Mammal moves one step
Mammal moves 2 steps
Dog moves 5 steps
```

All the extra member functions and data have been removed from these classes. On lines 6–8, the `Mammal` class declares the two overloaded `move()` functions. On line 17, `Dog` overrides the version of `move()` with no parameters. These are invoked on lines 24–26, and the output reflects this as executed.

Line 27, however, is commented out because it would causes a compiler error. Although the `Dog` class could have called the `move(int)` function if it had not overridden the version of `move()` without parameters, now that it has done so it must override both to use both. This is reminiscent of the rule that if you supply any constructor the compiler will no longer supply a default constructor.

It is a common mistake to hide a base class member function, when you intend to override it, by forgetting to include the keyword `const`. That keyword is part of the signature, and leaving it off changes the signature and thus hides the member function instead of overriding it.

Some compilers will give you a warning as you write the Mammal6 program somewhere around lines 14–18. Although you are allowed to hide base class member functions from derived classes, it often is done by mistake, prompting some compilers to issue a warning.

Calling the Base Member Function

If you have overridden a base member function, it is still possible to call it by fully qualifying the name of the function. You do this by writing the base name, followed by two colons, and then the function name. For example:

```
Mammal::move()
```

It would have been possible to rewrite line 27 in Listing 16.6 so that it would compile:

```
27:     fido.Mammal::move(10);
```

This calls the `Mammal` member function explicitly. This hour's final project, the Mammal7 program in Listing 16.7, illustrates this idea.

LISTING 16.7 The Full Text of `Mammal7.cpp`

```
 1: #include <iostream>
 2:
 3: class Mammal
 4: {
 5: public:
 6:     void move() const { std::cout << "Mammal moves one step\n"; }
 7:     void move(int distance) const
 8:         { std::cout << "Mammal moves " << distance << " steps\n"; }
 9: protected:
10:     int age;
11:     int weight;
12: };
13:
14: class Dog : public Mammal
15: {
16: public:
17:     void move() const;
18: };
19:
20: void Dog::move() const
21: {
22:     std::cout << "Dog moves ...\n";
23:     Mammal::move(3);
24: }
25:
26: int main()
27: {
28:     Mammal bigAnimal;
29:     Dog fido;
30:     bigAnimal.move(2);
31:     fido.Mammal::move(6);
32:     return 0;
33: }
```

Mammal7 produces this output when run:

```
Mammal moves 2 steps
Mammal moves 6 steps
```

On line 28, a `Mammal` object is created; and on line 29, a `Dog` object is created. The member function call on line 30 invokes the `move()` function of `Mammal`, which takes an integer.

If you wanted to invoke `move(int)` on the `Dog` object, there's a problem. `Dog` overrides the `move()` function but doesn't overload it and does not provide a version that takes an `int`. This is solved by the explicit call to the base class `move(int)` function on line 31.

Summary

If this is your first introduction to class inheritance, you might find yourself wondering if the work of creating base classes and derived classes is worth the effort. Deciding where to put member variables and functions among a set of related classes can take some time and planning.

The reason to do the work is that it makes your classes more powerful and reusable.

When you've designed a set of related classes well, you can extend a base class and design a new derived class much more easily. You only have to focus on the things that make the new class different from its parent.

Q&A

Q. Are inherited members and functions passed along to subsequent generations? If `Dog` derives from `Mammal` and `Mammal` derives from `Animal`, does `Dog` inherit `Animal`'s functions and data?

A. Yes. As derivation continues, derived classes inherit the sum of all the functions and data in all their base classes.

Q. Can a derived class make a public base function private?

A. Yes, and it will then remain private for all subsequent derivations.

Q. When did Constantinople become Istanbul?

A. The city of Istanbul, Turkey, became known as Constantinople during the reign of the East Roman emperor Theodosius II from 408 to 450. The name honored the emperor Constantine the Great, who had made the city the eastern capital of the Roman empire.

Some centuries later, the name Istanbul began to be used as well, which roughly translates to mean "The City."

After the creation of the Republic of Turkey, a law was passed in 1930 that asked the rest of the world to start calling the city Istanbul. To put some teeth in the request, the Turkish postal service began rejecting packages addressed to Constantinople.

The name change inspired the 1953 song "Istanbul (Not Constantinople)," performed by the Four Lads, and a 1990 remake by They Might Be Giants.

"Why did Constantinople get the works?" the song asks. "That's nobody's business but the Turks."

Workshop

Now that you've had the chance to work with inheritance, you can answer a few questions and do a couple of exercises to firm up your knowledge.

Quiz

1. What access keyword limits a member variable to an object and its derived classes?

   A. `public`

   B. `private`

   C. `protected`

2 In what order are constructors called in a derived class?

   A. In order of inheritance downward

   B. In order of inheritance upward

   C. In order the classes are defined in the source code

3. Why would you want to hide a base class member function in a derived class?

   A. To prevent it from being used

   B. To call that function

   C. There's no reason to do this

Answers

1. **C.** The `protected` keyword limits access to member variables and member functions so that derived classes can use them but no other classes can.
2. **A.** The base class constructor is called first, followed by the derived class constructor.
3. **A.** Sometimes the behavior of the derived class is different enough from the base that some of the base member functions are inappropriate. Because it is not always possible to modify the base class (if you do not have the source for it, for example), this is the mechanism to use.

Activities

1. In the Mammal6 program (Listing 16.6), uncomment line 27. What happens? What do you have to do to make it work?
2. Modify the Mammal2 program (Listing 16.2) to use a text string rather than an enumerated data type as the breed.

To see solutions to these activities, visit this book's website at http://cplusplus.cadenhead.org.

HOUR 17

Using Polymorphism and Derived Classes

What You'll Learn in This Hour:

- What virtual member functions are
- How to use virtual destructors and copy constructors
- How virtual member functions enable you to use your base classes polymorphically
- The costs and dangers in using virtual member functions

Polymorphism Implemented with Virtual Member Functions

The previous hour emphasized the fact that a `Dog` object is a `Mammal` object. This meant that the `Dog` object inherited the attributes (data) and capabilities (member functions) of its base class. The relationship between a base class and derived class runs deeper than that in C++.

Polymorphism allows derived objects to be treated as if they were base objects. For example, suppose you create specialized `Mammal` types such as `Dog`, `Cat`, `Horse`, and so forth. All these derive from `Mammal`, and `Mammal` has a number of member functions factored out of the derived classes. One such function is `speak()`, which implements the capability of all mammals to make noise.

You'd like to teach each of the derived types to specialize how they speak. A dog says "woof," a cat says "meow," and so forth. Each class must be able to override how it implements the `speak()` member function.

At the same time, when you have a collection of `Mammal` objects such as a `Farm` with `Dog`, `Cat`, `Horse`, and `Cow` objects, you want the farm to be able to tell each of these objects to `speak()` without knowing or caring about the details of how they implement the `speak()` function. When you treat these objects as if they are all mammals by calling the `Mammal.speak()` function, you are treating them polymorphically.

NOTE

Polymorphism is an unusual word that means the ability to take many forms. It comes from the roots *poly*, which means many, and *morph*, which means form. You are dealing with `Mammal` in its many forms.

You can use polymorphism to declare a pointer to `Mammal` and assign to it the address of a `Dog` object you create on the heap. Because a `Dog` "is a" `Mammal`, the following is perfectly legal:

```
Mammal* pMammal = new Dog;
```

You then can use this pointer to invoke any member function on `Mammal`. What you would like is for those functions that are overridden in `Dog` to call the correct function.

Virtual member functions let you do that. When you treat these objects polymorphically, you call the member function on the `Mammal` pointer and don't know or care what the actual object is or how it implements its function.

A virtual member function is declared with the `virtual` keyword. Here's an example from this hour's first project:

```
virtual void speak() const { std::cout << "Mammal speak!\n"; }
```

The Mammal8 program in Listing 17.1 illustrates how virtual functions implement polymorphism.

LISTING 17.1 The Full Text of `Mammal8.cpp`

```
#include <iostream>

class Mammal
{
public:
    Mammal():age(1) { std::cout << "Mammal constructor ...\n"; }
    ~Mammal() { std::cout << "Mammal destructor ...\n"; }
    void move() const { std::cout << "Mammal, move one step\n"; }
    virtual void speak() const { std::cout << "Mammal speak!\n"; }

protected:
    int age;
};

class Dog : public Mammal
{
public:
    Dog() { std::cout << "Dog constructor ...\n"; }
    ~Dog() { std::cout << "Dog destructor ..\n"; }
    void wagTail() { std::cout << "Wagging tail ...\n"; }
```

```
21:     void speak() const { std::cout << "Woof!\n"; }
22:     void move() const { std::cout << "Dog moves 5 steps ...\n"; }
23: };
24:
25: int main()
26: {
27:     Mammal *pDog = new Dog;
28:     pDog->move();
29:     pDog->speak();
30:     return 0;
31: }
```

Mammal8 displays this output:

```
Mammal constructor...
Dog constructor ...
Mammal, move one step
Woof!
```

On line 9, `Mammal` is provided a virtual member function called `speak()`. The designer of the class thereby signals that she expects this class to eventually be another class's base type. The derived class will probably want to override this function.

On line 27, a pointer to `Mammal` is created, `pDog`, but it is assigned the address of a new `Dog` object. Because a `Dog` is a `Mammal`, this is a legal assignment. The pointer then is used to call the `move()` function. Because the compiler knows `pDog` only to be a `Mammal`, it looks to the `Mammal` object to find the `move()` function.

Next, the pointer calls the `speak()` function. Because `speak()` is virtual, the `speak()` function overridden in `Dog` is invoked.

As far as the calling function knew, it had a `Mammal` pointer, but a function of `Dog` was called. In fact, if you have an array of pointers to `Mammal`, each of which points to a subclass of `Mammal`, you can call each in turn and the correct function is called. The Mammal9 program (Listing 17.2) illustrates this idea.

LISTING 17.2 The Full Text of `Mammal9.cpp`

```
#include <iostream>

class Mammal
{
public:
    Mammal():age(1) {  }
    ~Mammal() { }
    virtual void speak() const { std::cout << "Mammal speak!\n"; }
protected:
```

```
    int age;
};

class Dog : public Mammal
{
public:
    void speak() const { std::cout << "Woof!\n"; }
};

class Cat : public Mammal
{
public:
    void speak() const { std::cout << "Meow!\n"; }
};

class Horse : public Mammal
{
public:
    void speak() const { std::cout << "Whinny!\n"; }
};

class Pig : public Mammal
{
public:
    void speak() const { std::cout << "Oink!\n"; }
};

int main()
{
    Mammal* array[5];
    Mammal* ptr;
    int choice, i;
    for (i = 0; i < 5; i++)
    {
        std::cout << "(1) dog (2) cat (3) horse (4) pig: ";
        std::cin >> choice;
        switch (choice)
        {
        case 1:
            ptr = new Dog;
            break;
        case 2:
            ptr = new Cat;
            break;
        case 3:
            ptr = new Horse;
            break;
```

```
57:         case 4:
58:             ptr = new Pig;
59:             break;
60:         default:
61:             ptr = new Mammal;
62:             break;
63:         }
64:         array[i] = ptr;
65:     }
66:     for (i=0; i < 5; i++)
67:     {
68:         array[i]->speak();
69:     }
70:     return 0;
71: }
```

Here's a sample run of the Mammal9 program:

```
(1) dog (2) cat (3) horse (4) pig: 1
(1) dog (2) cat (3) horse (4) pig: 3
(1) dog (2) cat (3) horse (4) pig: 4
(1) dog (2) cat (3) horse (4) pig: 2
(1) dog (2) cat (3) horse (4) pig: 5
Woof!
Whinny!
Oink!
Meow!
Mammal speak!
```

This stripped-down program, which provides only the barest functionality to each class, illustrates virtual member functions in their purest form. Four classes are declared (`Dog`, `Cat`, `Horse`, and `Pig`), all derived from `Mammal`.

On line 8, `Mammal`'s `speak()` function is declared to be virtual. On lines 16, 22, 28, and 34, the four derived classes override the implementation of `speak()`.

The user is prompted to pick which objects to create, and the pointers are added to the array in the `for` loop that begins on line 42.

NOTE

Note that at compile time it is impossible to know which objects will be created, and therefore, which `speak()` member functions will be invoked. The pointer `ptr` is bound to its object at runtime. This is called *late binding* or *runtime binding*, as opposed to static binding or compile-time binding.

How Virtual Member Functions Work

When a derived object, such as a `Dog` object, is created, first the constructor for the base class is called, and then the constructor for the derived class is called. Figure 17.1 shows what the `Dog` object looks like after it is created. Note that the `Mammal` part of the object is contiguous in memory with the `Dog` part.

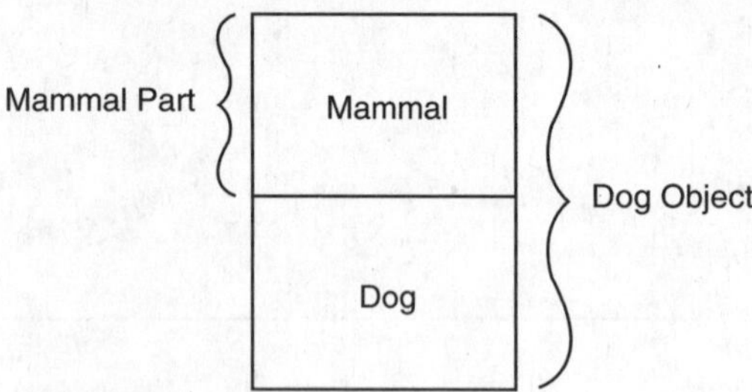

FIGURE 17.1
The `Dog` object after it is created.

When a virtual function is created in an object, the object must keep track of that function. Many compilers build a virtual function table, called a *v-table*. One of these is kept for each type, and each object of that type keeps a virtual table pointer (called a *v-pointer* or `vptr`), which points to that table.

Each object's v-pointer points to the v-table that, in turn, has a pointer to each of the virtual member functions. When the `Mammal` part of the `Dog` is created, the v-pointer is initialized to point to the virtual member functions for `Mammal`, as shown in Figure 17.2.

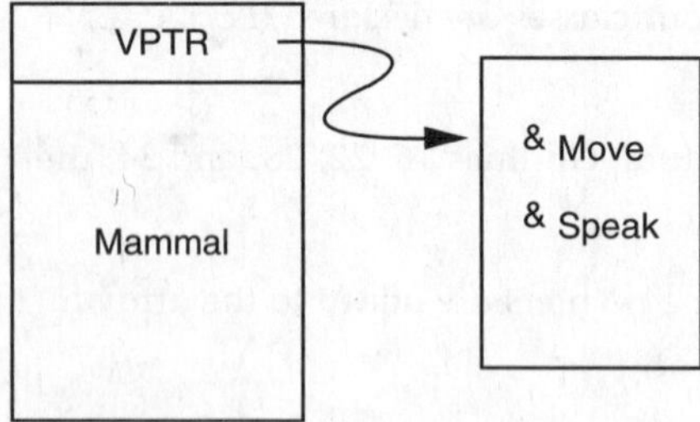

FIGURE 17.2
The v-table of a `Mammal`.

When the Dog constructor is called and the Dog part of this object is added, the v-pointer is adjusted to point to the virtual function overrides (if any) in the Dog object, as illustrated in Figure 17.3.

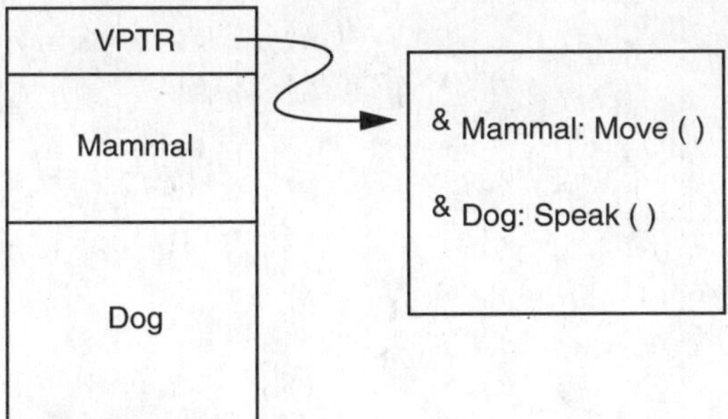

FIGURE 17.3
The v-table of a Dog.

When a pointer to a Mammal is used, the v-pointer continues to point to the correct function, depending on the real type of the object. Thus, when speak() is invoked, the correct function is invoked.

You Can't Get There from Here

If the Dog object had a member function called wagTail() that was not in the Mammal class, you couldn't use the pointer to Mammal to access that function (unless you cast it to be a pointer to Dog). Because wagTail() is not a virtual function and is not in a Mammal object, you can't get there without either a Dog object or a Dog pointer.

Although you can transform the Mammal pointer into a Dog pointer, there usually are better and safer ways to call the wagTail() member function. C++ frowns on explicit casts because they are error-prone. This subject is addressed in depth when multiple-inheritance is covered in Hour 18, "Making Use of Advanced Polymorphism," and again when templates are covered in Hour 24, "Dealing with Exceptions and Error Handling."

Slicing

Note that the virtual function magic only operates on pointers and references. Passing an object by value will not enable the virtual member functions to be invoked. The Mammal10 program in Listing 17.3 illustrates this problem.

LISTING 17.3 The Full Text of Mammal10.cpp

```
#include <iostream>

class Mammal
{
```

```
public:
    Mammal():age(1) { }
     ~Mammal() { }
     virtual void speak() const { std::cout << "Mammal speak!\n"; }
protected:
     int age;
};

class Dog : public Mammal
{
public:
     void speak() const { std::cout << "Woof!\n"; }
};

class Cat : public Mammal
{
public:
     void speak()const { std::cout << "Meow!\n"; }
};

void valueFunction(Mammal);
void ptrFunction(Mammal*);
void refFunction(Mammal&);

int main()
{
     Mammal* ptr=0;
     int choice;
     while (1)
     {
         bool fQuit = false;
         std::cout << "(1) dog (2) cat (0) quit: ";
         std::cin >> choice;
         switch (choice)
         {
         case 0:
             fQuit = true;
             break;
         case 1:
             ptr = new Dog;
             break;
         case 2:
             ptr = new Cat;
             break;
         default:
             ptr = new Mammal;
             break;
         }
```

```
53:         if (fQuit)
54:         {
55:             break;
56:         }
57:         ptrFunction(ptr);
58:         refFunction(*ptr);
59:         valueFunction(*ptr);
60:     }
61:     return 0;
62: }
63:
64: void valueFunction(Mammal mammalValue)  // This function is called last
65: {
66:     mammalValue.speak();
67: }
68:
69: void ptrFunction (Mammal *pMammal)
70: {
71:     pMammal->speak();
72: }
73:
74: void refFunction (Mammal &rMammal)
75: {
76:     rMammal.speak();
77: }
```

Here's a sample run and the corresponding output:

```
(1) dog (2) cat (0) quit: 2
Meow!
Meow!
Mammal speak!
(1) dog (2) cat (0) quit: 1
Woof!
Woof!
Mammal speak!
(1) dog (2) cat (0) quit: 0
```

On lines 3–23, stripped-down versions of the `Mammal`, `Dog`, and `Cat` classes are declared. Three functions are declared: `ptrFunction()`, `refFunction()`, and `valueFunction()`. They take a pointer to a `Mammal`, a `Mammal` reference, and a `Mammal` object, respectively. All three functions then do the same thing: They call the `speak()` member function.

The user is prompted to choose a `Dog` or `Cat`; based on the choice he makes, a pointer to the correct type is created in the `switch` statement in lines 38–52.

In the first line of the output, the user chooses Dog. The Dog object is created on the heap in line 44. The Dog then is passed as a pointer, as a reference, and by value to the three functions. The pointer and references all invoke the virtual member functions, and the Dog->speak() member function is invoked. This is shown on the first two lines of output after the user's choice.

The dereferenced pointer is passed by value, however. The function expects a Mammal object, so the compiler slices down the Dog object to just the Mammal part. At that point, the Mammal speak() function is called, as reflected in the third line of output after the user's choice.

This experiment then is repeated for the Cat object, with similar results.

Virtual Destructors

It is permitted and even common in C++ to pass a pointer to a derived object when a pointer to a base object is expected. What happens when that pointer to a derived object is deleted? If the destructor is virtual, as it should be, the right thing happens—the derived class's destructor is called. Because the derived class's destructor will automatically invoke the base class's destructor, the entire object will be properly destroyed.

The rule of thumb is this: If any of the functions in your class are virtual, the destructor also should be virtual.

Virtual Copy Constructors

As previously stated, no constructor can be virtual. Nonetheless, there are times when your program desperately needs to pass in a pointer to a base object and have a copy of the correct derived object that is created. A common solution to this problem is to create a clone member function in the base class and to make it virtual. A clone function creates a new copy of the current object and returns that object.

Because each derived class overrides the clone function, a copy of the derived class is created. The Mammal11 program (Listing 17.4) shows how this is used.

LISTING 17.4 The Full Text of Mammal11.cpp

```
#include <iostream>

class Mammal
{
public:
    Mammal():age(1) { std::cout << "Mammal constructor ...\n"; }
    virtual ~Mammal() { std::cout << "Mammal destructor ...\n"; }
    Mammal (const Mammal &rhs);
    virtual void speak() const { std::cout << "Mammal speak!\n"; }
    virtual Mammal* clone() { return new Mammal(*this); }
    int getAge() const { return age; }

```

```
protected:
    int age;
};
Mammal::Mammal (const Mammal &rhs):age(rhs.getAge())
{
    std::cout << "Mammal copy constructor ...\n";
}
class Dog : public Mammal
{
public:
    Dog() { std::cout << "Dog constructor ...\n"; }
    virtual ~Dog() { std::cout << "Dog destructor ...\n"; }
    Dog (const Dog &rhs);
    void speak() const { std::cout << "Woof!\n"; }
    virtual Mammal* clone() { return new Dog(*this); }
};
Dog::Dog(const Dog &rhs):
Mammal(rhs)
{
    std::cout << "Dog copy constructor ...\n";
}
class Cat : public Mammal
{
public:
    Cat() { std::cout << "Cat constructor ...\n"; }
    virtual ~Cat() { std::cout << "Cat destructor ...\n"; }
    Cat (const Cat&);
    void speak() const { std::cout << "Meow!\n"; }
    virtual Mammal* Clone() { return new Cat(*this); }
};
Cat::Cat(const Cat &rhs):
Mammal(rhs)
{
    std::cout << "Cat copy constructor ...\n";
}
enum ANIMALS { MAMMAL, DOG, CAT};
const int numAnimalTypes = 3;
int main()
{
    Mammal *array[numAnimalTypes];
    Mammal *ptr;
```

```
    int choice, i;
    for (i = 0; i < numAnimalTypes; i++)
    {
        std::cout << "(1) dog (2) cat (3) mammal: ";
        std::cin >> choice;
        switch (choice)
        {
        case DOG:
            ptr = new Dog;
            break;
        case CAT:
            ptr = new Cat;
            break;
        default:
            ptr = new Mammal;
            break;
        }
        array[i] = ptr;
    }
    Mammal *otherArray[numAnimalTypes];
    for (i=0; i < numAnimalTypes; i++)
    {
        array[i]->speak();
        otherArray[i] = array[i]->clone();
    }
    for (i=0; i < numAnimalTypes; i++)
    {
        otherArray[i]->speak();
    }
    return 0;
}
```

The following output demonstrates one run of the program:

```
(1) dog (2) cat (3) mammal: 3
Mammal constructor ...
(1) dog (2) cat (3) mammal: 1
Mammal constructor ...
Dog constructor ...
(1) dog (2) cat (3) mammal: 2
Mammal constructor ...
Cat constructor ...
Mammal speak!
Mammal copy constructor ...
Woof!
Mammal copy constructor ...
Dog copy constructor ...
Meow!
```

```
15: Mammal copy constructor ...
16: Mammal speak!
17: Woof!
18: Mammal speak!
```

Listing 17.4 is similar to the previous two listings, except that a new virtual function has been added to the `Mammal` class: `clone()`. This function returns a pointer to a new `Mammal` object by calling the copy constructor, passing in itself (`*this`) as a `const` reference.

`Dog` and `Cat` both override the `clone()` function, initializing their data and passing in copies of themselves to their own copy constructors. Because `clone()` is virtual, this effectively creates a virtual copy constructor, as shown in line 83.

The user is prompted to choose dogs, cats, or mammals, and these are created in lines 65–76. A pointer to each choice is stored in an array on line 77.

As the program iterates over the array, each object has its `speak()` and `clone()` functions called, in turn, in lines 82–83. The result of the `clone()` call is a pointer to a copy of the object, which then is stored in a second array in line 83.

On line 1 of the output, the user is prompted and responds with 3, choosing to create a mammal. The `Mammal` constructor is called. On line 3, the user chooses 1 and a dog is created. The `Mammal` and `Dog` constructors are invoked. Finally, on line 6, the user chooses 2 for a cat. The `Mammal` and `Cat` constructors are called.

Line 9 of the output represents the call to `speak()` on the first object, the Mammal from line 82 (within the first `for` loop). The virtual `speak()` function is called, and the correct version of `speak()` is invoked. The `clone()` function then is called, and as this is also virtual, `Mammal`'s `clone()` function is invoked, causing the `Mammal` constructor to be called.

The same is repeated for `Dog` in lines 11–13 of the output, and then for `Cat` in lines 14–16. Finally, the new array is iterated (output lines 14–18, code lines 85–88), and each of the new objects has `speak()` invoked.

The difference between this approach and the use of a copy constructor is that you, as the programmer, must explicitly call the `clone()` function. The copy constructor is called automatically when an object is copied. Remember that you always can override the copy function in a derived class. But that approach reduces the flexibility you have.

The Cost of Virtual Member Functions

Because objects with virtual member functions must maintain a v-table, some overhead is required to employ them. If you have a small class from which you do not expect to derive other classes, there might be no reason to have any virtual functions at all.

After you declare any functions virtual, you've paid most of the price of the v-table (although each entry does add a small memory overhead). At that point, you want the destructor to be virtual, and the assumption will be that all other functions probably will also be virtual. Take a long hard look at any non-virtual functions, and be certain you understand why they are not virtual.

Summary

Polymorphism enables the same interface to be implemented with different member functions in a set of classes related by inheritance.

This makes it possible for related objects to be used in the same manner, even if each object implements the behavior differently.

Polymorphism achieves an important goal in object-oriented programming by letting similar objects handle related functionality by reusing an interface.

Q&A

Q. Why not make all class functions virtual?

A. There is overhead with the first virtual function in the creation of a v-table. After that, the overhead is trivial. Many C++ programmers feel that if one function is virtual, all others should be. Other programmers disagree, believing that there should always be an explicit reason for what you do in a program.

Q. If a function `someFunc()` is virtual in a base class and also is overloaded so as to take either an integer or two integers, and the derived class overrides the function taking one integer, what is called when a pointer to a derived object calls the two-integer function?

A. This causes the compiler to balk with an error. The overriding of the one-integer form of the function hides the entire base class function. The compiler fails with a message stating that the function requires only one integer.

Q. What is the origin of "Rudolph the Red-Nosed Reindeer"?

A. "Rudolph the Red-Nosed Reindeer" began as a 1939 poem by Robert May, a 34-year-old copywriter for the Montgomery Ward department store in Chicago. May's boss wanted something to give children in the store, and it became so popular that five million copies were distributed in the '30s and '40s.

The poem was written when May's wife was seriously ill. Like Rudolph, May's four-year-old daughter felt left out—her mother couldn't do things with her like other mothers could.

In 1949, Johnny Marks and singer Gene Autry recorded the song based on the `poem`, and it became one of the top-selling singles of all time.

The reindeer almost wasn't named Rudolph. Two other names May proposed were Rollo and Reginald.

Workshop

You spent the past hour learning about polymorphism and derived classes. Now you should answer a few questions and do a couple of exercises to firm up that knowledge.

Quiz

1. How does a C++ program know which virtual function to call when the objects are stored in a variable of the base class type?

  A. The function has a `virtual` keyword.

  B. A v-table is used.

  C. That's not possible.

2. What type of member function cannot be virtual?

  A. Constructor

  B. Destructor

  C. Clone

3. What is it called when a pointer is bound to an object at runtime, as in polymorphism?

  A. Late binding

  B. Static binding

  C. Dereferencing

Answers

1. B. The v-table keeps track of this information for you. It is the overhead associated with this table that makes virtual functions slightly more expensive to use than regular functions.

2. A. The constructor (including the copy constructor).

3. A. Late binding is when it occurs at runtime. Static binding is when it occurs during compilation.

Activities

1. Modify the `Mammal8` program by commenting out line 21: the `speak()` member function within `dog`. Can you think of examples where it makes sense to do this?
2. Modify the `Mammal10` program to remove the `virtual` on line 8 (definition of `speak()` in the base class)? Can you see why the override functions are never called?

To see solutions to these activities, visit the book's website at http://cplusplus.cadenhead.org.

HOUR 18
Making Use of Advanced Polymorphism

What You'll Learn in This Hour:

- What casting down is and why you might want to do it
- What abstract data types are
- What pure virtual functions are

Problems with Single Inheritance

In previous hours, derived objects were treated polymorphically with their base classes. You saw that if the base class has a member function `speak()` that is overridden in the derived class, a pointer to a base object that is assigned to a derived object will do the right thing. The Mammal12 program in Listing 18.1 illustrates this idea.

LISTING 18.1 The Full Text of `Mammal12.cpp`

```
#include <iostream>

class Mammal
{
public:
    Mammal():age(1) { std::cout << "Mammal constructor ...\n"; }
    virtual ~Mammal() { std::cout << "Mammal destructor ...\n"; }
    virtual void speak() const { std::cout << "Mammal speak!\n"; }
protected:
    int age;
};

class Cat : public Mammal
{
public:
    Cat() { std::cout << "Cat constructor ...\n"; }
    ~Cat() { std::cout << "Cat destructor ...\n"; }
    void speak() const { std::cout << "Meow!\n"; }
```

```
19: };
20:
21: int main()
22: {
23:     Mammal *pCat = new Cat;
24:     pCat->speak();
25:     return 0;
26: }
```

When you run the Mammal12 program, the following output displays:

```
Mammal constructor ...
Cat constructor ...
Meow!
```

On line 8, `speak()` is declared to be a virtual member function, then it is overridden on line 18 and invoked on line 24. Note again that `pCat` is declared to be a pointer to `Mammal`, but the address of a `Cat` is assigned to it. As discussed in Hour 17, "Using Polymorphism and Derived Classes," this is the essence of polymorphism.

What happens, however, if you want to add a member function to `Cat` that is inappropriate for `Mammal`? Suppose you want to add a function called `purr()`. Cats purr, but other mammals do not. You would declare your class like this:

```
class Cat: public Mammal
{
public:
    Cat() { std::cout << "Cat constructor ...\n"; }
    ~Cat() { std::cout << "Cat destructor ...\n"; }
    void speak() const { std::cout << "Meow!\n"; }
    void purr() const { std::cout << "Rrrrrrrr!\n"; }
};
```

The problem is this: If you now call `purr()` using your pointer to `Mammal`, you get a compiler error stating that "'Purr' is not a member of Mammal."

When your compiler tries to resolve `purr()` in its `Mammal` virtual table, there is no entry. You can move this function up to the base class, but that is a bad idea. Although it works as an expedient, populating your base class with functions that are specific to derived classes is poor programming practice and a recipe for difficult-to-maintain code.

In fact, this entire problem is a reflection of bad design. Generally, if you have a pointer to a base class that is assigned to a derived class object, it is because you *intend* to use that object polymorphically, and in this case, you ought not even try to access functions that are specific to the derived class.

The problem is not that you have such specific functions; it is that you are trying to get at them with the base class pointer. In an ideal world, when you have such a pointer you would not try to get at those functions.

But this is not an ideal world, and at times, you find yourself with a collection of base objects—for example, a zoo full of mammals. At one point or another, you might realize you have a `Cat` object and you want the darn thing to purr. In this case, there might be only one thing to do: cheat.

To cheat, cast your base class pointer to your derived type. You say to the compiler, "I know this is really a cat, so go and do what I tell you."

To make this work, you'll use the `dynamic_cast` operator. This operator ensures that when you cast, you cast safely.

Here's how it works: If you have a pointer to a base class, such as `Mammal`, and you assign to it a pointer to a derived class, such as `Cat`, you can use the `Mammal` pointer polymorphically to access virtual functions. Then, if you need to get at the `Cat` object to call the `purr()` member function, you create a `Cat` pointer using the `dynamic_cast` operator to do so. At runtime, the base pointer is examined. If the conversion is proper, your new `Cat` pointer is fine. If the conversion is improper—you didn't really have a `Cat` object after all—your new pointer will be `null`. The Mammal13 program in Listing 18.2 illustrates this.

LISTING 18.2 **The Full Text of** `Mammal13.cpp`

```
#include <iostream>

class Mammal
{
public:
    Mammal():age(1) { std::cout << "Mammal constructor ...\n"; }
    virtual ~Mammal() { std::cout << "Mammal destructor ...\n"; }
    virtual void speak() const { std::cout << "Mammal speak!\n"; }
protected:
    int age;
};

class Cat: public Mammal
{
public:
    Cat() { std::cout << "Cat constructor ...\n"; }
    ~Cat() { std::cout << "Cat destructor ...\n"; }
    void speak() const { std::cout << "Meow!\n"; }
    void purr() const { std::cout << "Rrrrrrrrrr!\n"; }
};

class Dog: public Mammal
```

```
{
public:
    Dog() { std::cout << "Dog constructor ...\n"; }
    ~Dog() { std::cout << "Dog destructor ...\n"; }
    void speak() const { std::cout << "Woof!\n"; }
};

int main()
{
    const int numberMammals = 3;
    Mammal* zoo[numberMammals];
    Mammal* pMammal;
    int choice, i;
    for (i = 0; i < numberMammals; i++)
    {
        std::cout << "(1) Dog (2) Cat: ";
        std::cin >> choice;
        if (choice == 1)
            pMammal = new Dog;
        else
            pMammal = new Cat;

        zoo[i] = pMammal;
    }

    std::cout << "\n";

    for (i = 0; i < numberMammals; i++)
    {
        zoo[i]->speak();

        Cat *pRealCat =  dynamic_cast<Cat *> (zoo[i]);

        if (pRealCat)
            pRealCat->purr();
        else
            std::cout << "Uh oh, not a cat!\n";

        delete zoo[i];
        std::cout << "\n";
    }

    return 0;
}
```

When you run Mammal13, you're asked three times to create either a `Dog` object or `Cat` object. After the third response, each object is tested by calling either `speak()` or `speak()` and `purr()`. Here's sample output:

```
(1) Dog (2) Cat: 1
Mammal constructor ...
Dog constructor ...
(1) Dog (2) Cat: 2
Mammal constructor ...
Cat constructor ...
(1) Dog (2) Cat: 1
Mammal constructor ...
Dog constructor ...

Woof!
Uh oh, not a cat!
Dog destructor ...
Mammal destructor ...

Meow!
Rrrrrrrrrr!
Cat destructor ...
Mammal destructor ...

Woof!
Uh oh, not a cat!
Dog destructor ...
Mammal destructor ...
```

On lines 38–45, the user is asked to choose to add either a `Cat` or a `Dog` object to the array of `Mammal` pointers. The `for` loop that begins in line 50 walks through the array and on line 52, each object's virtual `speak()` member function is called. These functions respond polymorphically: Cats meow, and dogs say woof!

`Cat` objects should purr, but the `purr()` function must not be called on `Dog` objects. The `dynamic_cast` operator in line 54 ensures that the object is a `Cat`. When it is, the pointer will not equal `null` and passes the conditional test on line 56.

Abstract Data Types

Often, you will create a hierarchy of classes together. For example, you might create a `Shape` class as a base class to derive a `Rectangle` and a `Circle`. From `Rectangle`, you might derive `Square` as a special case of `Rectangle`.

Each of the derived classes overrides the `draw()` member function, the `getArea()` function, and so forth. Listing 18.3 illustrates a bare-bones implementation of the `Shape` class and its derived `Circle` and `Rectangle` classes.

LISTING 18.3 The Full Text of `Shape.cpp`

```
#include <iostream>

class Shape
{
public:
    Shape() {}
    virtual ~Shape() {}
    virtual long getArea() { return -1; } // error
    virtual long getPerim() { return -1; }
    virtual void draw() {}
};

class Circle : public Shape
{
public:
    Circle(int newRadius):radius(newRadius) {}
    ~Circle() {}
    long getArea() { return 3 * radius * radius; }
    long getPerim() { return 9 * radius; }
    void draw();
private:
    int radius;
    int circumference;
};

void Circle::draw()
{
    std::cout << "Circle drawing routine here!\n";
}

class Rectangle : public Shape
{
public:
    Rectangle(int newLen, int newWidth):
        length(newLen), width(newWidth) {}
    virtual ~Rectangle() {}
    virtual long getArea() { return length * width; }
    virtual long getPerim() { return 2 * length + 2 * width; }
    virtual int getLength() { return length; }
    virtual int getWidth() { return width; }
    virtual void draw();
private:
    int width;
    int length;
};

```

```
void Rectangle::draw()
{
    for (int i = 0; i < length; i++)
    {
        for (int j = 0; j < width; j++)
            std::cout << "x ";

        std::cout << "\n";
    }
}

class Square : public Rectangle
{
public:
    Square(int len);
    Square(int len, int width);
    ~Square() {}
    long getPerim() { return 4 * getLength(); }
};

Square::Square(int newLen):
    Rectangle(newLen, newLen)
{}

Square::Square(int newLen, int newWidth):
    Rectangle(newLen, newWidth)
{
    if (getLength() != getWidth())
        std::cout << "Error, not a square ... a rectangle?\n";
}

int main()
{
    int choice;
    bool fQuit = false;
    Shape * sp;

    while (1)
    {
        std::cout << "(1) Circle (2) Rectangle (3) Square (0) Quit: ";
        std::cin >> choice;

        switch (choice)
        {
        case 1:
            sp = new Circle(5);
            break;
        case 2:
```

```
 95:              sp = new Rectangle(4, 6);
 96:              break;
 97:          case 3:
 98:              sp = new Square(5);
 99:              break;
100:          default:
101:              fQuit = true;
102:              break;
103:          }
104:          if (fQuit)
105:              break;
106:
107:          sp->draw();
108:          std::cout << "\n";
109:      }
110:      return 0;
111: }
```

When run, this program asks the user one or more times to choose between creating a circle, rectangle, or square. When 0 is chosen rather than a shape, it exits. Here's a look at the output for a run:

```
(1) Circle (2) Rectangle (3) Square (0) Quit: 3
x x x x x
x x x x x
x x x x x
x x x x x
x x x x x

(1) Circle (2) Rectangle (3) Square (0) Quit: 2
x x x x x x
x x x x x x
x x x x x x
x x x x x x

(1) Circle (2) Rectangle (3) Square (0) Quit: 0
```

On lines 3–11, the `Shape` class is declared. The `getArea()` and `getPerim()` member functions return an error value, and `draw()` takes no action. Only specific types of shapes such as circles and rectangle can be drawn; shapes as an abstraction cannot be drawn.

`Circle` derives from `Shape` and overrides the three virtual member functions. Note that there is no reason to add the word `virtual`, because that is part of their inheritance. But there is no harm in doing so either, as shown in the `Rectangle` class on lines 36–41.

`Square` derives from `Rectangle`, and it too overrides the `getPerim()` member function, inheriting the rest of the functions defined in `Rectangle`.

It is troubling, though, that it is possible to instantiate a `Shape` object, and it might be desirable to make that impossible. The `Shape` class exists only to provide an interface for the classes derived from it. It is an *abstract data type*, or ADT.

An abstract data type represents a concept (like a shape) rather than an object (like a circle). In C++, an ADT is always the base class to other classes, and it is not valid to make an instance of an ADT. Therefore, if you make `Shape` an ADT, it is not possible to make an instance of a `Shape` object.

Pure Virtual Functions

C++ supports the creation of abstract data types with pure virtual functions. A pure virtual function is a virtual function that *must* be overridden in the derived class. A virtual function is made pure by initializing it with 0, as in the following statement:

```
virtual void draw() = 0;
```

Any class with one or more pure virtual functions is an ADT, and it is illegal to instantiate an object of a class that is an ADT. Trying to do so causes a compile-time error. Putting a pure virtual function in your class signals two things to clients of your class:

- Don't make an object of this class; derive from it.
- Make sure to override the pure virtual function.

Any class that derives from an ADT inherits the pure virtual function as pure, so it must override every pure virtual function if it wants to instantiate objects. Therefore, if `Rectangle` inherits from `Shape`, and `Shape` has three pure virtual functions, `Rectangle` must override all three or it, too, will be an ADT.

A virtual function is declared to be abstract by writing `= 0` after the function declaration, as in this statement:

```
virtual long getArea() = 0;
```

Here's a rewrite of the `Shape` class to be an abstract data type:

```
class Shape
{
public:
    Shape() {}
    virtual ~Shape() {}
    virtual long getArea() = 0;
    virtual long getPerim() = 0;
    virtual void draw() = 0;
private:
};
```

If this definition of Shape were substituted in lines 3–11 of Listing 18.3, it would become impossible to make an object of class Shape.

Implementing Pure Virtual Functions

Typically, the pure virtual functions in an abstract base class are never implemented. Because no objects of that type are ever created, there is no reason to provide implementations, and the ADT works purely as the definition of an interface to objects that derive from it.

It is possible, however, to provide an implementation to a pure virtual function. The function then can be called by objects derived from the ADT, perhaps to provide common functionality to all the overridden functions.

The Shape2 program in Listing 18.4 defines Shape as an ADT and includes an implementation for the pure virtual function draw(). The Circle class overrides draw(), as it must, and then chains up to the base class function for additional functionality.

In this example, the additional functionality is simply an additional message displayed. A more robust graphical class could set up a shared drawing mechanism, perhaps setting up a window that all derived classes will use.

LISTING 18.4 The Full Text of Shape2.cpp

```
#include <iostream>

class Shape
{
public:
    Shape() {}
    virtual ~Shape() {}
    virtual long getArea() = 0;
    virtual long getPerim()= 0;
    virtual void draw() = 0;
private:
};

void Shape::draw()
{
    std::cout << "Abstract drawing mechanism!\n";
}

class Circle : public Shape
{
public:
    Circle(int newRadius):radius(newRadius) {}
    ~Circle() {}
    long getArea() { return 3 * radius * radius; }
```

```
    long getPerim() { return 9 * radius; }
    void draw();
private:
    int radius;
    int circumference;
};

void Circle::draw()
{
    std::cout << "Circle drawing routine here!\n";
    Shape::draw();
}

class Rectangle : public Shape
{
public:
    Rectangle(int newLen, int newWidth):
        length(newLen), width(newWidth) {}
    virtual ~Rectangle() {}
    long getArea() { return length * width; }
    long getPerim() { return 2 * length + 2 * width; }
    virtual int getLength() { return length; }
    virtual int getWidth() { return width; }
    void draw();
private:
    int width;
    int length;
};

void Rectangle::draw()
{
    for (int i = 0; i < length; i++)
    {
        for (int j = 0; j < width; j++)
            std::cout << "x ";

        std::cout << "\n";
    }
    Shape::draw();
}

class Square : public Rectangle
{
public:
    Square(int len);
    Square(int len, int width);
    ~Square() {}
    long getPerim() {return 4 * getLength();}
};
```

```

Square::Square(int newLen):
    Rectangle(newLen, newLen)
{}

Square::Square(int newLen, int newWidth):
    Rectangle(newLen, newWidth)
{
    if (getLength() != getWidth())
        std::cout << "Error, not a square ... a rectangle?\n";
}

int main()
{
    int choice;
    bool fQuit = false;
    Shape * sp;

    while (1)
    {
        std::cout << "(1) Circle (2) Rectangle (3) Square (0) Quit: ";
        std::cin >> choice;

        switch (choice)
        {
        case 1:
            sp = new Circle(5);
            break;
        case 2:
            sp = new Rectangle(4, 6);
            break;
        case 3:
            sp = new Square(5);
            break;
        default:
            fQuit = true;
            break;
        }
        if (fQuit)
            break;
        sp->draw();
        std::cout << "\n";
    }
    return 0;
}
```

Again, the user is asked which shapes to create. Here's sample output:

```
(1) Circle (2) Rectangle (3) Square (0) Quit: 3
x x x x x
x x x x x
x x x x x
x x x x x
x x x x x
Abstract drawing mechanism!

(1) Circle (2) Rectangle (3) Square (0) Quit: 2
x x x x x x
x x x x x x
x x x x x x
x x x x x x
Abstract drawing mechanism!

(1) Circle (2) Rectangle (3) Square (0) Quit: 0
```

On lines 3–12, the abstract data type `Shape` is declared, with all three of its accessors declared to be pure virtual. Note that this is not necessary. If any one were declared pure virtual, the class would have been an ADT. But it's good programming practice not to count on this: Declare all functions in an ADT virtual that are virtual.

The `getArea()` and `getPerim()` member functions are not implemented, but `draw()` is. `Circle` and `Rectangle` both override `draw()` and both chain up to the base member function, taking advantage of shared functionality in the base class.

Complex Hierarchies of Abstraction

At times, you will derive ADTs from other ADTs. It might be that you want to make some of the derived pure virtual functions non-pure and leave others pure.

If you create the `Animal` class, you can make `eat()`, `sleep()`, `move()`, and `reproduce()` pure virtual functions. Perhaps you derive `Mammal` and `Fish` from `Animal`.

On examination, you could decide that every `Mammal` will reproduce in the same way, and so you make `Mammal::reproduce()` non-pure but leave `eat()`, `sleep()`, and `move()` as pure virtual functions.

From `Mammal` you derive `Dog`, and `Dog` must override and implement the three remaining pure virtual functions so that you can make objects of type `Dog`.

What you say, as class designer, is that no `Animal` or `Mammal` objects can be instantiated, but that all `Mammal` objects can inherit the provided `reproduce()` member function without overriding it.

The Animal class in Listing 18.5 illustrates this technique with a bare-bones implementation of these classes.

LISTING 18.5 The Full Text of Animal.cpp

```
#include <iostream>

enum COLOR { Red, Green, Blue, Yellow, White, Black, Brown } ;

class Animal // common base to both horse and bird
{
public:
    Animal(int);
    virtual ~Animal() { std::cout << "Animal destructor ...\n"; }
    virtual int getAge() const { return age; }
    virtual void setAge(int newAge) { age = newAge; }
    virtual void sleep() const = 0;
    virtual void eat() const = 0;
    virtual void reproduce() const = 0;
    virtual void move() const = 0;
    virtual void speak() const = 0;
private:
    int age;
};

Animal::Animal(int newAge):
age(newAge)
{
    std::cout << "Animal constructor ...\n";
}

class Mammal : public Animal
{
public:
    Mammal(int newAge):Animal(newAge)
        { std::cout << "Mammal constructor ...\n";}
    virtual ~Mammal() { std::cout << "Mammal destructor ...\n";}
    virtual void reproduce() const
        { std::cout << "Mammal reproduction depicted ...\n"; }
};

class Fish : public Animal
{
public:
    Fish(int newAge):Animal(newAge)
        { std::cout << "Fish constructor ...\n";}
```

```
    virtual ~Fish()
        { std::cout << "Fish destructor ...\n"; }
    virtual void sleep() const
        { std::cout << "Fish snoring ...\n"; }
    virtual void eat() const
        { std::cout << "Fish feeding ...\n"; }
    virtual void reproduce() const
        { std::cout << "Fish laying eggs ...\n"; }
    virtual void move() const
        { std::cout << "Fish swimming ...\n";  }
    virtual void speak() const { }
};

class Horse : public Mammal
{
public:
    Horse(int newAge, COLOR newColor):
        Mammal(newAge), color(newColor)
        { std::cout << "Horse constructor ...\n"; }
    virtual ~Horse()
        { std::cout << "Horse destructor ...\n"; }
    virtual void speak() const
        { std::cout << "Whinny!\n"; }
    virtual COLOR getcolor() const
        { return color; }
    virtual void sleep() const
        { std::cout << "Horse snoring ...\n"; }
    virtual void eat() const
        { std::cout << "Horse feeding ...\n"; }
    virtual void move() const
        { std::cout << "Horse running ...\n";}

protected:
    COLOR color;
};

class Dog : public Mammal
{
public:
    Dog(int newAge, COLOR newColor ):
        Mammal(newAge), color(newColor)
        { std::cout << "Dog constructor ...\n"; }
    virtual ~Dog()
        { std::cout << "Dog destructor ...\n"; }
    virtual void speak() const
        { std::cout << "Whoof!\n"; }
```

```
    virtual void sleep() const
        { std::cout << "Dog snoring ...\n"; }
    virtual void eat() const
        { std::cout << "Dog eating ...\n"; }
    virtual void move() const
        { std::cout << "Dog running...\n"; }
    virtual void reproduce() const
        { std::cout << "Dogs reproducing ...\n"; }

protected:
    COLOR color;
};

int main()
{
    Animal *pAnimal = 0;
    int choice;
    bool fQuit = false;

    while (1)
    {
        std::cout << "(1) Dog (2) Horse (3) Fish (0) Quit: ";
        std::cin >> choice;

        switch (choice)
        {
        case 1:
            pAnimal = new Dog(5, Brown);
            break;
        case 2:
            pAnimal = new Horse(4, Black);
            break;
        case 3:
            pAnimal = new Fish(5);
            break;
        default:
            fQuit = true;
            break;
        }
        if (fQuit)
            break;

        pAnimal->speak();
        pAnimal->eat();
        pAnimal->reproduce();
        pAnimal->move();
        pAnimal->sleep();
```

```
135:          delete pAnimal;
136:          std::cout << "\n";
137:      }
138:      return 0;
139: }
```

Here's sample output from a run of the program:

```
(1) Dog (2) Horse (3) Fish (0) Quit: 1
Animal constructor ...
Mammal constructor ...
Dog constructor ...
Whoof!
Dog eating ...
Dogs reproducing ...
Dog running...
Dog snoring ...
Dog destructor ...
Mammal destructor ...
Animal destructor ...

(1) Dog (2) Horse (3) Fish (0) Quit: 0
```

On lines 5–19, the abstract data type `Animal` is declared. `Animal` has non-pure virtual accessors for age, which are shared by all `Animal` objects. It has five pure virtual functions: `sleep()`, `eat()`, `reproduce()`, `move()`, and `speak()`.

Mammal derives from `Animal` and is declared on lines 27–35. It adds no data. It overrides `reproduce()`, however, providing a common form of reproduction for all `Mammal` objects. `Fish` must override `reproduce()` because `Fish` derives directly from Animal and cannot take advantage of `Mammal` reproduction.

`Mammal` classes no longer have to override the `reproduce()` function, but they are free to do so if they choose (as `Dog` does on lines 94–95). `Fish`, `Horse`, and `Dog` all override the remaining pure virtual functions so that objects of their type can be instantiated.

In the body of the program, an `Animal` pointer is used to point to the various derived objects in turn. The virtual member functions are invoked and the correct function is called in the derived class, based on the runtime binding of the pointer.

It would cause a compile-time error to try to instantiate an `Animal` or a `Mammal`, because both are abstract data types.

Which Types Are Abstract?

In one program, the class `Animal` is abstract; in another it is not. What determines whether to make a class abstract?

The answer to this question is decided not by any real-world, intrinsic factor, but by what makes sense in the design of your program. If you are writing a program that depicts a farm or a zoo, you might want `Animal` to be an abstract data type but `Dog` to be a class from which you can instantiate objects.

On the other hand, if you are making an animated kennel, you might want to keep `Dog` as an abstract data type and only instantiate types of dogs: retrievers, terriers, and so forth. The level of abstraction is a function of how finely you need to distinguish your types.

Summary

During this hour, you learned about abstract data types and pure virtual functions, two aspects of the C++ language that make its support for object-oriented programming more robust.

An abstract data type is a class that cannot be implemented as an object. Instead, it defines common member variables and functions for its derived classes.

A function becomes a pure virtual function by adding `= 0` to the end of its declaration. If a class contains at least one pure function, the class is an abstract data type.

The compiler will not allow objects of an abstract data type to be instantiated.

Q&A

Q. Why is dynamic casting bad?

A. The point of virtual functions is to let the virtual table, rather than the programmer, determine the runtime type of the object.

Q. Why bother making an abstract data type? Why not just make it non-abstract and avoid creating any objects of that type?

A. The purpose of many of the conventions in C++ is to enlist the compiler in finding bugs to avoid runtime bugs in completed code. Making a class abstract by giving it pure virtual functions causes the compiler to flag any objects created of that abstract type as errors. It also means that you can share the abstract data types with other applications or programmers.

Q. Has anyone ever studied Silbo, the whistling language used on Gomera in the Canary Islands?

A. The best reference on the topic of Silbo Gomero and similar forms of speech is Whistled Languages, a 1976 book by R. G. Busnel and A. Classe that's available at many public libraries.

Silbo allows shepherds to communicate over deep ravines and narrow valleys at distances of 3 miles or more. The language has fallen into disuse on the island of 21,000.

The disappearance of rural society and the introduction of the phone reduced the Gomeran whistle to being used primarily in demonstrations (although these days schoolchildren are being taught it).

A speaker of Silbo Gomero is referred to in Spanish as a silbador.

Workshop

After learning more about polymorphism, answer a few questions and do a couple of exercises to firm up your knowledge.

Quiz

1. Is there a difference between a virtual member function and an overridden member function in the base class?
   - **A.** Yes
   - **B.** No
   - **C.** Reply hazy, try again
2. What makes an abstract data type abstract?
   - **A.** The `abstract` keyword
   - **B.** It has at least one pure virtual function
   - **C.** It has all pure virtual functions
3. Is it OK to supply base class member functions that apply only to specific derived classes?
   - **A.** Yes
   - **B.** No
   - **C.** It varies

Answers

1. **A.** A virtual function expects to be overridden in the derived classes. An overridden function does not have to be in derived classes.
2. **B.** The class is abstract because it has at least one pure virtual function that cannot be called directly. Because of that function, you cannot create a concrete example of that class and must derive a class from the abstract with the proper member functions and instantiate from the derived class.
3. **B.** Base class member functions that apply only to some classes make it much harder to use derived objects. The function only can be called after checking the data type of each object.

Activities

1. Modify the Animal program in Listing 18.5 to instantiate an object of `Animal` or `Mammal` type. What does the compiler tell you and why?
2. Modify the Mammal13 program in Listing 18.2 to see what happens if you remove the `if` test in lines 56–59 and call the `purr()` member function in all cases. Which objects work properly and which fail?

To see solutions to these activities, visit this book's website at http://cplusplus.cadenhead.org.

HOUR 19

Storing Information in Linked Lists

What You'll Learn in This Hour:

- What a linked list is
- How to create a linked list
- How to encapsulate functionality through inheritance

Linked Lists and Other Structures

Arrays are like boxes for mailing items. They are useful containers, but are each a fixed size. If you pick a container that is too large, you waste space and may even be charged more. If you pick one that is too small, there's not enough room to hold what you need to ship.

In programming, it's useful to have a container that's exactly the right size for the data it contains. One way to accomplish this is with a linked list.

A *linked list* is a data structure that consists of small containers that connect together. Containers, in this context, are classes that contain the objects to be held in the list. The idea is to write a class that holds one object of your data—such as one `Cat` or one `Rectangle`—and knows how to point to the next container in the list. You create one container for each object and chain them together.

These linked containers are called *nodes*. The first node in the list is called the *head*, and the last node in the list is called the *tail*.

Lists come in three fundamental forms. From simplest to most complex, they are:

- Singly linked
- Doubly linked
- Trees

In a *singly linked list*, each node points to the next one forward, but not backward. To find a particular node, you start at the top and go from node to node in sequence. A *doubly linked list* enables you to move backward and forward to the next node and previous node. A *tree* is a complex structure built from nodes, each of which can point in two or three directions. Figure 19.1 shows these three fundamental structures.

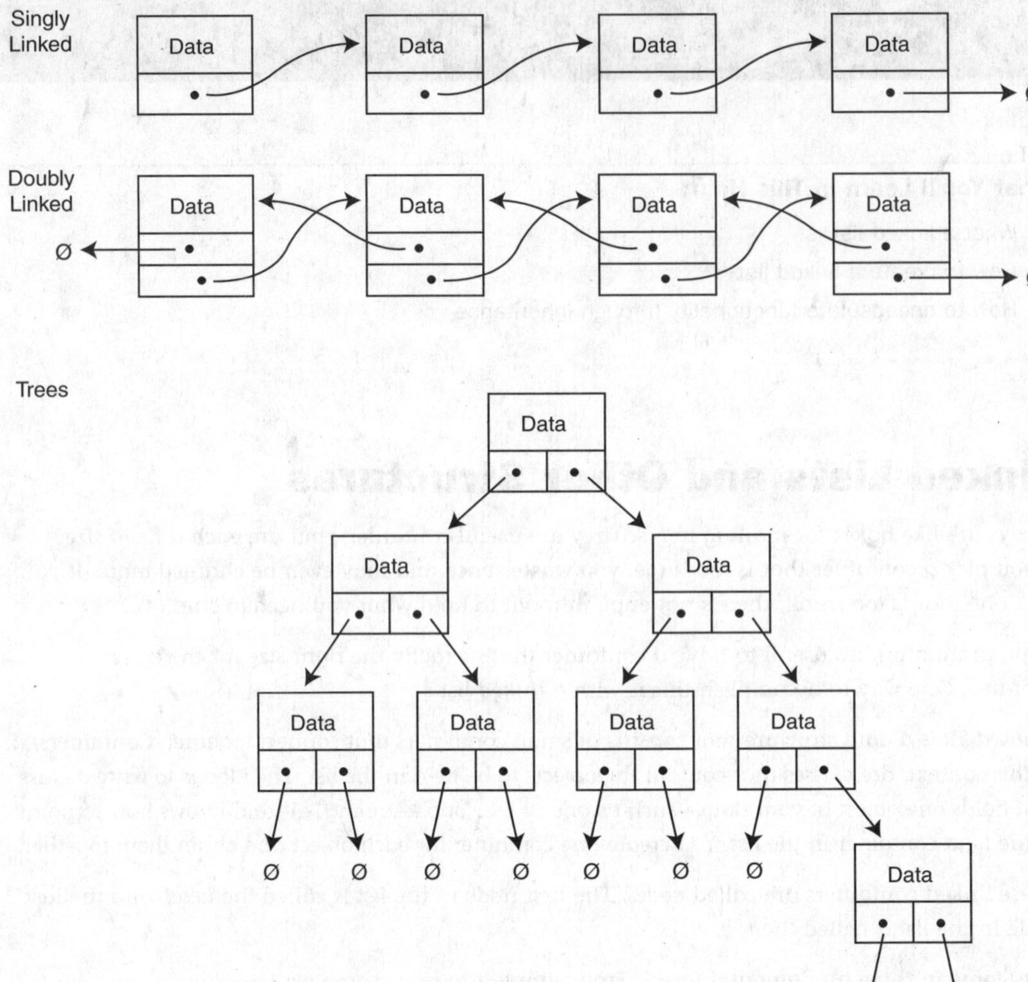

FIGURE 19.1
Linked lists.

Computer scientists have created even more complex and clever data structures, most of which rely on interconnecting nodes.

Linked List Case Study

In this section, we examine a linked list in detail as a case study into how to use inheritance, polymorphism, and encapsulation to manage large projects. It's also a chance to explore how to create complex structures in C++.

Delegation of Responsibility

A fundamental premise of object-oriented programming is that each object does one thing very well and delegates to other objects anything that is not part of its mission.

A car is a demonstration of this idea. The engine's job is to produce the power. Distribution of that power is not the engine's job; that is up to the transmission. Turning is not the job of the engine or the transmission; that is delegated to the wheels.

A well-designed machine has lots of small, well-understood parts, each doing its own job and working together to accomplish a greater good. A well-designed program is much the same: Each class sticks to its own assignment, but together they create a functioning program.

Component Parts

The linked list will consist of nodes. The node class itself will be abstract; we'll use three subtypes to accomplish the work. There will be a head and tail node to manage those parts of the list and zero or more internal nodes. The internal nodes will keep track of the actual data to be held in the list.

Note that the data and the list are quite distinct. You can save any type of data you like in a list. It isn't the data that is linked together; it is the node that *holds* the data that is linked.

A program doesn't actually know about the nodes; it only works with the list. The list does little work, simply delegating to the nodes.

This hour's first project, the LinkedList program, demonstrates an object-oriented approach to linked lists. The program has three primary classes: `Data`, `Node`, and `LinkedList`. When it is run, the program asks the user for a series of integers, storing each in an object of the `Data` class. These objects are stored in a `LinkedList` object and displayed in numerical order, even if they weren't entered in that order.

The `LinkedList` class uses a `HeadNode` class that's one of three implementations of the abstract class `Node`. The other two are `TailNode` and `InternalNode`. Only the `InternalNode` objects hold data.

The full program is in Listing 19.1. The source code is heavily commented to better explain how each part works. To develop an understanding of how it works, read it beginning where the `main()` function starts in line 170 and hop to each constructor and member function. The comments should give you a good idea of what is taking place even before you enter the code yourself.

LISTING 19.1 The Full Text of `LinkedList.cpp`

```
#include <iostream>

enum { kIsSmaller, kIsLarger, kIsSame };

// Any class in this linked list must support two
// functions: show (displays the value) and compare
// (returns relative position).
class Data
{
public:
    Data(int newVal):value(newVal) {}
    ~Data() {}
    int compare(const Data&);
    void show() { std::cout << value << "\n"; }
private:
    int value;
};

// A function that decides where in the list a
// particular object belongs.
int Data::compare(const Data& otherData)
{
    if (value < otherData.value)
        return kIsSmaller;
    if (value > otherData.value)
        return kIsLarger;
    else
        return kIsSame;
}

// forward class declarations
class Node;
class HeadNode;
class TailNode;
class InternalNode;

// An ADT representing the node object in the list.
// Every derived class must override insert() and show().
class Node
{
public:
    Node() {}
    virtual ~Node() {}
    virtual Node* insert(Data* data) = 0;
    virtual void show() = 0;
private:
};
```

```
// A node to hold objects of type Data.
class InternalNode : public Node
{
public:
    InternalNode(Data* data, Node* next);
    virtual ~InternalNode() { delete next; delete data; }
    virtual Node* insert(Data* data);
    virtual void show()
        { data->show(); next->show(); } // delegate!

private:
    Data* data;  // the data itself
    Node* next;  // points to next node in the linked list
};

// a simple constructor
InternalNode::InternalNode(Data* newData, Node* newNext):
data(newData), next(newNext)
{
}

// A function to store a new object in the list.
// The object is passed to the node which figures out
// where it goes and inserts it into the list.
Node* InternalNode::insert(Data* otherData)
{
    // is the new object bigger or smaller than me?
    int result = data->compare(*otherData);

    switch (result)
    {
    // if it is the same as me it goes first
    case kIsSame:       // fall through
    case kIsLarger:     // new data comes before me
        {
            InternalNode* dataNode =
                new InternalNode(otherData, this);
            return dataNode;
        }

    // it is bigger, so pass it on to the next
    // node and let it handle it.
    case kIsSmaller:
        next = next->insert(otherData);
        return this;
    }
```

```
    return this; // appease the compiler
}

// The last node in the list
class TailNode : public Node
{
public:
    TailNode() {}
    virtual ~TailNode() {}
    virtual Node* insert(Data* data);
    virtual void show() {}
private:
};

// If data comes to me, it must be inserted before me
// since nothing goes after the tail
Node* TailNode::insert(Data* data)
{
    InternalNode* dataNode = new InternalNode(data, this);
    return dataNode;
}

// The head node, which holds no data but instead points
// to the beginning of the list.
class HeadNode : public Node
{
public:
    HeadNode();
    virtual ~HeadNode() { delete next; }
    virtual Node* insert(Data* data);
    virtual void show() { next->show(); }
private:
    Node* next;
};

// The first node in the list, which creates the tail
HeadNode::HeadNode()
{
    next = new TailNode;
}

// Since nothing comes before the head, just pass
// the data on to the next node
Node* HeadNode::insert(Data* data)
{
    next = next->insert(data);
    return this;
}
```

```

// I get all the credit and do none of the work
class LinkedList
{
public:
    LinkedList();
    ~LinkedList() { delete head; }
    void insert(Data* data);
    void showAll() { head->show(); }
private:
    HeadNode* head;
};

// At birth, I create the head node, which creates
// the tail node.
LinkedList::LinkedList()
{
    head = new HeadNode;
}

// Delegate to a head node
void LinkedList::insert(Data* pData)
{
    head->insert(pData);
}

// put all these classes to the test
int main()
{
    Data* pData;
    int val;
    LinkedList ll;

    // store user values in a linked list
    while (true)
    {
        std::cout << "What value (0 to stop)? ";
        std::cin >> val;
        if (!val)
            break;
        pData = new Data(val);
        ll.insert(pData);
    }

    // display the list
    ll.showAll();
    return 0;
}
```

When you run the LinkedList program, enter a series of numeric values one at a time. These values are used as the data stored in each linked list node. After you have entered as many values as you want, choose 0 to finish input. The nodes in the linked list will be displayed in ascending numeric order, as in this example:

```
What value (0 to stop)? 7
What value (0 to stop)? 4
What value (0 to stop)? 13
What value (0 to stop)? 8
What value (0 to stop)? 5
What value (0 to stop)? 0
4
5
7
8
13
```

The first thing to note is the enumerated constant (line 3), which provides three constant values: `kIsSmaller`, `kIsLarger`, and `kIsSame`. Every object that might be held in this linked list must support a `compare()` member function. These constants are the result value returned by this function.

The `Data` class is declared on lines 8–17, and the `compare()` function is implemented on lines 21–29. A `Data` object holds a value and can compare itself with other `Data` objects. It also supports a `show()` member function to display the value of the `Data` object.

The easiest way to understand the workings of the linked list is to step through an example of using one. On line 170, the main program is declared; on line 172, a pointer to a `Data` object is declared; and on line 174, a linked list is defined.

When the linked list is created, the constructor that begins on line 158 is called. The only work done in the constructor is to allocate a `HeadNode` object and to assign that object's address to the pointer held in the linked list (line 160).

This allocation of a `HeadNode` invokes the `HeadNode` constructor shown on line 131. This in turn allocates a `TailNode` and assigns its address to the head node's `next` pointer. The creation of the `TailNode` calls the `TailNode` constructor shown on line 102, an inline function that does nothing.

Thus, by the simple act of allocating a linked list on the stack, the list is created, a head and a tail node are created and their relationship is established, as illustrated in Figure 19.2.

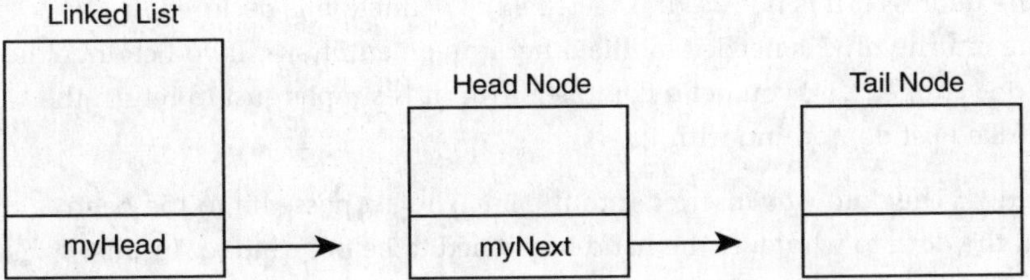

FIGURE 19.2
The linked list after its creation.

Continuing in the `main()` function, line 177 uses `while(true)` for an infinite loop. The user is prompted for values to add to the linked list. The code on line 181 evaluates the value entered. If the value is 0, execution of the program breaks out of the loop.

If the value is not 0, a new `Data` object is created and inserted into the list (lines 183–184).

For illustration purposes, assume the user runs the program and enters the value 15 as the first number. This invokes the `insert()` member function on line 184.

The linked list immediately delegates responsibility for inserting the object to its head node in line 166. This invokes the function `insert()` on line 138. The head node immediately passes the responsibility to whatever node its `next` variable points to. In this first case, it is pointing to the tail node. (When the head node was born, it created a link to a tail node.) This invokes the `insert()` function on line 111.

TailNode`::insert()` knows that the object it has been handed must be inserted immediately before itself, so the new object will be placed in the list right before the tail node. Therefore, on line 113 it creates a new `InternalNode` object, passing in the data and a pointer to itself. This invokes the constructor for the `InternalNode` object, shown on line 65.

The `InternalNode` constructor does nothing more than initialize its `Data` pointer with the address of the `Data` object it was passed and its `next` pointer with the node's address it was passed. In this case, the node it points to is the tail node. (The tail node passed in its own `this` pointer.)

Now that the `InternalNode` has been created, the address of that internal node is assigned to the pointer `dataNode` on line 113, and that address is in turn returned from the `TailNode::insert()` member function.

This returns us to `HeadNode::insert()`, where the address of the `InternalNode` is assigned to the `HeadNode`'s `next` pointer (on line 140). Finally, the `HeadNode`'s address is returned to the linked list on line 166, although this value is not stored in a variable. Nothing is done with it because the linked list already knows the address of the head node.

Why bother returning the address if it is not used? The `insert()` function is declared in the base class, `Node`. The return value is needed by the other implementations. If you change the return value of `HeadNode::insert()`, you get a compiler error; it is simpler just to return the `HeadNode` and let the linked list do nothing with it.

Let's review what happened: The data was inserted into the list. The list passed it to the head. The head blindly passed the data to whatever the head happened to be pointing to. In this first case, the head was pointing to the tail. The tail immediately created a new internal node, initializing the new node to point to the tail. The tail then returned the address of the new node to the head, which reassigned its `next` pointer to point to the new node.

Presto! The data is in the list in the right place, as illustrated in Figure 19.3.

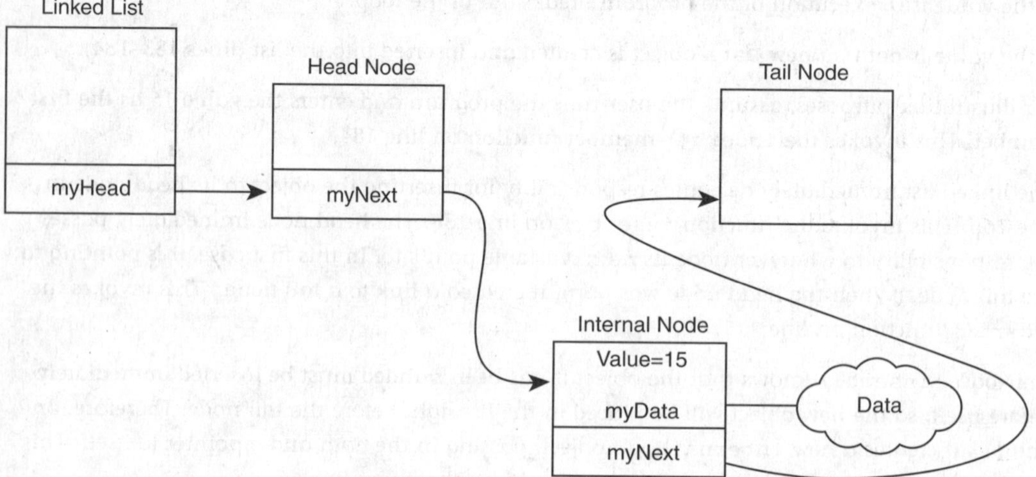

FIGURE 19.3
The linked list after the first node is inserted.

After inserting the first node, program control resumes at line 179. Once again, the value is evaluated. For illustration purposes, assume that the value 3 is entered. This causes a new `Data` object to be created on line 183 and inserted into the list on line 184.

Once again, on line 164 the list passes the data to its `HeadNode`. The HeadNode`::insert()` function in turn passes the new value to whatever its `next` happens to be pointing to. As you know, it is now pointing to the node that contains the `Data` object whose value is 15. This invokes the InternalNode`::insert()` function on line 73.

On line 76, the `InternalNode` uses its `data` pointer to tell its `Data` object (the one whose value is 15) to call its `compare()` member function, passing in the new `Data` object (whose value is 3). This invokes the `compare()` function shown on line 21.

The two values are compared; and, because `value` is 15 and `otherData.value` is 3, the returned value is `kIsLarger`. This causes program flow to jump to lines 84–85.

A new `InternalNode` is created for the new `Data` object. The new node points to the current `InternalNode` object, and the new `InternalNode`'s address is returned from the `InternalNode::insert()` function to the `HeadNode`. Thus, the new node, whose object's value is smaller than the current node's object's value, is inserted into the list, and the list now looks like Figure 19.4.

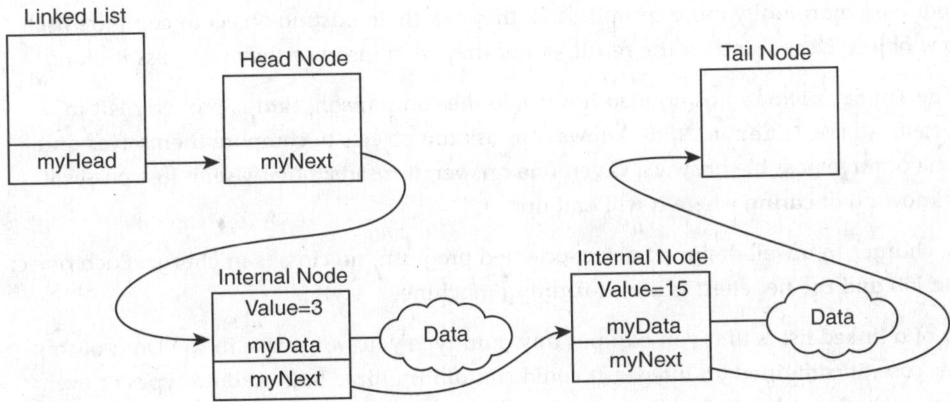

FIGURE 19.4
The linked list after the second node is inserted.

In the third invocation of the loop, the customer adds the value 8. This is larger than 3 but smaller than 15, and so should be inserted between the two existing nodes. Progress is exactly like the previous example except that when the node whose object's value is 3 does the compare, rather than returning `kIsLarger`, it returns `kIsSmaller` (meaning that the object whose value is 3 is smaller than the new object, whose value is 8).

This causes the `InternalNode::insert()` function to branch to line 92. Instead of creating a new node and inserting it, the `InternalNode` passes the new data on to the `Insert` function of whatever its `next` pointer happens to be pointing to. In this case, it invokes `InsertNode` on the `InternalNode` whose `Data` object's value is 15.

The comparison is done again, and now a new `InternalNode` is created. This new InternalNode points to the `InternalNode` whose `Data` object's value is 15, and its address is passed back to the `InternalNode` whose `Data` object's value is 3, as shown on line 93.

The net effect is that the new node is inserted into the list at the right location.

The end result of all of this is that you have a sorted list of data items—no matter the order in which you enter the data.

Linked Lists as Objects

In object-oriented programming, each individual object is given a narrow and well-defined set of responsibilities. The linked list is responsible for maintaining the head node. The `HeadNode` immediately passes any new data on to whatever it currently points to, without regard for what that might be.

The TailNode, whenever it is handed data, creates a new node and inserts it. It knows only one thing: If this came to me, it gets inserted right before me.

Internal nodes are marginally more complicated; they ask their existing object to compare itself with the new object. Depending on the result, either they then insert or they just pass it along.

Note that the `InternalNode` has no idea how to do the comparison; that is properly left to the object itself. All the `InternalNode` knows is to ask the objects to compare themselves and to expect one of three possible answers. Given one answer, it inserts; otherwise, it just passes it along, not knowing or caring where it will end up.

So who's in charge? In a well-designed object-oriented program, no class is in charge. Each object does its own job and the net effect is a well-running machine.

The beauty of a linked list is that you can put any data type you would like in the Data of this class. In this case, it contained an integer. It could contain multiple built-in data types or even other objects (including other linked lists).

The use of dynamic memory allows linked lists to use very little memory when small, and lots of memory if they grow large. The important thing is that they only use enough to hold the data they now contain. Arrays, on the other hand, are allocated to a specific size, which is both wasteful and limiting.

NOTE

Because linked lists are more useful than arrays, you might be wondering why not use them all the time? The power comes at a cost. Linked lists are sequential in nature, which means that you have to start at one end and work your way to the other end to find the item you want. That access can be relatively slow.

Summary

Because there's so much to learn in C++, the projects undertaken in this book have often been short and illustrative. That makes it easier to focus on their functionality.

As you begin your own programming projects, you will find that the classes you create are never quite so simple.

The linked list case study during this hour consisted of five classes: `Data`, `HeadNode`, `TailNode`, `InternalNode`, and `LinkedList`. True to object-oriented programming methodology, each class took care of its own work and relied on the other objects to do theirs.

By understanding how these objects work together, you can develop a better sense of how to manage the relationships between objects.

Q&A

Q. Why should you create a linked list if an array will work?

A. An array must have a fixed size, whereas a linked list can be sized `dynamically` at runtime, making a more efficient use of memory.

Q. Why do you separate the data object from the node?

A. This programming practice fosters reuse. After you get your node objects working properly, you can reuse that code for any number of objects that might want to live in a list.

Q. If you want to add other objects to the list, do you have to create a new list type and a new node type?

A. For now, yes. But it's possible to implement a linked list in a more generic way where the objects it holds are concerned. We'll solve that when we get to Hour 23, "Creating Templates."

Q. What was the name of the Greek who carried a lantern and was looking for an honest man?

A. That was Diogenes, a philosopher who died around 320 B.C. Diogenes stressed self-sufficiency and the rejection of luxury, and his teachings caused him to be sent into exile away from his birthplace of Sinope, Paphlygonia. (I guess he didn't have tenure.)

In addition to his search for an honest man, which Diogenes conducted with a lit lantern in broad daylight, there are other apocryphal stories associated with him.

He slept in public buildings, lived in poverty, begged for food and was strongly antifamily. Diogenes believed that men and women should be promiscuous and that any resulting children should be raised by the community instead of individual families.

Workshop

Now that you've learned how to implement a complex data structure, answer a few questions and perform a couple of exercises to link it all together.

Quiz

1. What's the first node in a linked list called?

   A. The origin

   B. The head

   C. The top

2. What two things does a linked list node contain?

   A. Behavior and data

   B. Functions and variables

   C. Data and a node pointer

3. How many pointers are needed for a doubly linked list?

   A. 2

   B. 1

   C. Either a or b

Answers

1. **B.** As the name implies, it contains the head of the linked list. It is very important to know where the list starts so it can be accessed.
2. **C.** The data can be any type of object. The pointer indicates the next member of the linked list.
3. **A.** Each node in a doubly linked list has two pointers, one for `next` and one for `previous`, so that you can start at either end and work your way toward the opposite end.

Activities

1. Rewrite the LinkedList program (Listing 19.1) to hold `Tricycle` objects rather than integers.
2. Add a function to the `LinkedList` class (Listing 19.1) that displays a count of the number of nodes the list contains.

To see solutions to these activities, visit this book's website at http://cplusplus.cadenhead.org.

HOUR 20

Using Special Classes, Functions, and Pointers

What You'll Learn in This Hour:

- What static member variables and static member functions are
- How to use static member variables and static member functions
- What friend functions and friend classes are
- How to use friend functions to solve special problems
- How to use pointers to member functions

Static Member Data

Until now, you have probably thought of the data in each object as unique to that object and not shared among objects in a class. For example, if you have five `Robot` objects, each has its own age, weight, and other data. The age of one does not affect the age of another.

Sometimes you'll want to keep track of information shared among the many objects of a class. For example, you might want to know how many `Robot` objects have been created and how many are still in existence.

Unlike other member variables, *static* member variables are shared among all instances of a class. They occupy the middle ground between global data, which is available to all parts of your program, and member data, which usually is available only to each object.

You can think of a static member as belonging to the class rather than to the object. Normal member data is one per object, but static members are one per class.

The StaticRobot program in Listing 20.1 declares a `Robot` object with a static data member, `howManyRobots`. This variable keeps track of how many `Robot` objects have been created by incrementing a static variable. The variable increases with each construction and decreases with each destruction.

LISTING 20.1 The Full Text of `StaticRobot.cpp`

```
#include <iostream>

class Robot
{
public:
    Robot(int newAge = 1):age(newAge){ howManyRobots++; }
    virtual ~Robot() { howManyRobots--; }
    virtual int getAge() { return age; }
    virtual void setAge(int newAge) { age = newAge; }
    static int howManyRobots;

private:
    int age;
};

int Robot::howManyRobots = 0;

int main()
{
    const int maxRobots = 5;
    Robot *gestalt[maxRobots];
    int i;
    for (i = 0; i < maxRobots; i++)
        gestalt[i] = new Robot(i);

    for (i = 0; i < maxRobots; i++)
    {
        std::cout << "There are ";
        std::cout << Robot::howManyRobots;
        std::cout << " robots left!\n";
        std::cout << "Deleting the one which is ";
        std::cout << gestalt[i]->getAge();
        std::cout << " years old\n";
        delete gestalt[i];
        gestalt[i] = 0;
    }
    return 0;
}
```

Run the program to see it create five robots and then delete the objects:

```
There are 5 robots left!
Deleting the one which is 0 years old
There are 4 robots left!
Deleting the one which is 1 years old
```

```
There are 3 robots left!
Deleting the one which is 2 years old
There are 2 robots left!
Deleting the one which is 3 years old
There are 1 robots left!
Deleting the one which is 4 years old
```

On lines 3–14, the simplified class `Robot` is declared. On line 10, `howManyRobots` is declared to be a static member variable of type `int`.

The declaration of `howManyRobots` does not define an integer; no storage space is set aside. Unlike the non-static member variables, no storage space is set aside for static members as a result of instantiating a `Robot` object, because the `howManyRobots` member variable is not in the object. Therefore, on line 16 the variable is defined and initialized.

It is a common mistake to forget to define the static member variables of classes. You don't need to do this for `age` on line 13 because it is a non-static member variable and is defined each time you make a `Robot` object, which is done here on line 24.

The constructor for `Robot` increments the static member variable on line 6. The destructor decrements it on line 7. Therefore, at any moment, `howManyRobots` has an accurate count of how many `Robot` objects were created but not yet destroyed.

The main function that begins on line 18 instantiates five `Robot` objects and puts them in an array. This calls five `Robot` constructors; thus `howManyRobots` is incremented from 0 to 5.

The program then loops through each of the five positions in the array and displays the value of `howManyRobots` before deleting the current `Robot` pointer. The output reflects that the starting value is 5 (after all, five are constructed), and that each time the loop is run, one fewer `Robot` remains.

Note that `howManyRobots` is public and is accessed directly by `main()`. It is preferable to make it private along with the other member variables and provide a public accessor, as long as you always will access the data through an instance of `Robot`. If you'd like to access this data directly without necessarily having a `Robot` object available, you have two options: Keep it public or provide a static member function.

Static Member Functions

Static member functions are like static member variables: They exist not in an object but in the scope of the class. Therefore, they can be called without having an object of that class, as illustrated in Listing 20.2.

LISTING 20.2 The Full Text of `StaticFunction.cpp`

```
#include <iostream>

class Robot
{
public:
    Robot(int newAge = 1):age(newAge){ howManyRobots++; }
    virtual ~Robot() { howManyRobots--; }
    virtual int gGetAge() { return age; }
    virtual void setAge(int newAge) { age = newAge; }
    static int getHowMany() { return howManyRobots; }
private:
    int age;
    static int howManyRobots;
};

int Robot::howManyRobots = 0;

void countRobots();

int main()
{
    const int maxRobots = 5;
    Robot *gestalt[maxRobots];
    int i;
    for (i = 0; i < maxRobots; i++)
    {
        gestalt[i] = new Robot(i);
        countRobots();
    }

    for (i = 0; i < maxRobots; i++)
    {
        delete gestalt[i];
        countRobots();
    }
    return 0;
}

void countRobots()
{
    std::cout << "There are " << Robot::getHowMany()
        << " robots.\n";
}
```

The StaticFunction program creates five robots, calling the `countRobots()` static function each time to see how many robots exist, as the output demonstrates:

```
There are 1 robots.
There are 2 robots.
There are 3 robots.
There are 4 robots.
There are 5 robots.
There are 4 robots.
There are 3 robots.
There are 2 robots.
There are 1 robots.
There are 0 robots.
```

The static member variable `howManyRobots` is declared to have private access on line 13 of the `Robot` declaration. The public accessor `getHowMany()` is declared to be both public and static on line 10.

Because `getHowMany()` is public, it can be accessed by any function. Because it is static, there is no need to have an object of type `Robot` on which to call it. Therefore, on line 41, the function `countRobots()` is able to access the public static accessor even though it has no access to a `Robot` object. Of course, you could have called `getHowMany()` on any `Robot` objects available in `main()`, as with any other accessor function.

NOTE

Static member functions do not have a `this` pointer, so they cannot be declared `const`. Also, because member data variables are accessed in member functions using the `this` pointer, static member functions cannot access any non-static member variables.

Containment of Classes

As you have seen previously, it is possible for the member data of a class to include objects of another class. This establishes a "contains" relationship between the enclosing class (outer class) and a class used as its member data (inner class). C++ programmers say that the outer class contains the inner class. An `Employee` class might contain `String` objects for the name of the employee as well as integers for the employee's salary and so forth.

The String class in Listing 20.3 defines a stripped-down but useful class. The file should be saved as `String.hpp` and is used in another program later in this section.

LISTING 20.3 The Full Text of `String.hpp`

```
#include <iostream>
#include <string.h>

class String
{
public:
    // constructors
    String();
    String(const char *const);
    String(const String&);
    ~String();

    // overloaded operators
    char& operator[](int offset);
    char operator[](int offset) const;
    String operator+(const String&);
    void operator+=(const String&);
    String& operator= (const String &);

    // general accessors
    int getLen() const { return len; }
    const char* getString() const { return value; }
    // static int constructorCount;

private:
    String(int); // private constructor
    char* value;
    int len;
};

// default constructor creates string of 0 bytes
String::String()
{
    value = new char[1];
    value[0] = '\0';
    len = 0;
    // std::cout << "\tDefault string constructor\n";
    // constructorCount++;
}

// private (helper) constructor, used only by
// class functions for creating a new string of
// required size. Null filled.
String::String(int len)
{
    value = new char[len + 1];
    int i;
```

```
    for (i = 0; i < len; i++)
        value[i] = '\0';
    len = len;
    // std::cout << "\tString(int) constructor\n";
    // constructorCount++;
}

String::String(const char* const cString)
{
    len = strlen(cString);
    value = new char[len + 1];
    int i;
    for (i = 0; i < len; i++)
        value[i] = cString[i];
    value[len] = '\0';
    // std::cout << "\tString(char*) constructor\n";
    // constructorCount++;
}

String::String(const String& rhs)
{
    len = rhs.getLen();
    value = new char[len + 1];
    int i;
    for (i = 0; i < len; i++)
        value[i] = rhs[i];
    value[len] = '\0';
    // std::cout << "\tString(String&) constructor\n";
    // constructorCount++;
}

String::~String()
{
    delete [] value;
    len = 0;
    // std::cout << "\tString destructor\n";
}

// operator equals, frees existing memory
// then copies string and size
String& String::operator=(const String &rhs)
{
    if (this == &rhs)
        return *this;
    delete [] value;
    len = rhs.getLen();
    value = new char[len + 1];
    int i;
```

```
    for (i = 0; i < len; i++)
        value[i] = rhs[i];
    value[len] = '\0';
    return *this;
    // std::cout << "\tString operator=\n";
}

// non-constant offset operator, returns
// reference to character so it can be
// changed!
char& String::operator[](int offset)
{
    if (offset > len)
        return value[len - 1];
    else
        return value[offset];
}

// constant offset operator for use
// on const objects (see copy constructor!)
char String::operator[](int offset) const
{
    if (offset > len)
        return value[len-1];
    else
        return value[offset];
}

// creates a new string by adding current
// string to rhs
String String::operator+(const String& rhs)
{
    int totalLen = len + rhs.getLen();
    int i, j;
    String temp(totalLen);
    for (i = 0; i < len; i++)
        temp[i] = value[i];
    for (j = 0; j < rhs.getLen(); j++, i++)
        temp[i] = rhs[j];
    temp[totalLen] = '\0';
    return temp;
}

// changes current string, returns nothing
void String::operator+=(const String& rhs)
{
    int rhsLen = rhs.getLen();
    int totalLen = len + rhsLen;
```

```
144:     int i, j;
145:     String temp(totalLen);
146:     for (i = 0; i < len; i++)
147:         temp[i] = value[i];
148:     for (j = 0; j < rhs.getLen(); j++, i++)
149:         temp[i] = rhs[i - len];
150:     temp[totalLen] = '\0';
151:     *this = temp;
152: }
153:
154: // int String::constructorCount = 0;
```

There's no `main()` function in this listing, so it can't be run as a program.

Any time you need the `String` class, you can include this code with an `#include` preprocessor directive. For example, at the top of the Employee program in Listing 20.4, `#include "string.hpp"` appears. This adds the `String` class to the program.

Note that a number of statements in Listing 20.3 are commented out; they are used later this hour in the exercises. On line 23, the static member variable `constructorCount` is declared, and on line 154 it is initialized. This variable is incremented in each `String` constructor. (While these statements are comments, these things don't happen, of course.)

The Employee program (Listing 20.4) contains an `Employee` class that makes use of three `String` objects.

LISTING 20.4 **The Full Text of** `Employee.cpp`

```
#include "String.hpp"

class Employee
{
public:
    Employee();
    Employee(const char*, const char*, const char*, long);
    ~Employee();
    Employee(const Employee&);
    Employee& operator=(const Employee&);

    const String& getFirstName() const { return firstName; }
    const String& getLastName() const { return lastName; }
    const String& getAddress() const { return address; }
    long getSalary() const { return salary; }

    void setFirstName(const String& fName)
        { firstName = fName; }
    void setLastName(const String& lName)
```

```
        { lastName = lName; }
    void setAddress(const String& newAddress)
        { address = newAddress; }
    void setSalary(long newSalary) { salary = newSalary; }
private:
    String firstName;
    String lastName;
    String address;
    long salary;
};

Employee::Employee():
    firstName(""),
    lastName(""),
    address(""),
    salary(0)
{}

Employee::Employee(const char* newFirstName, const char* newLastName,
    const char* newAddress, long newSalary):
    firstName(newFirstName),
    lastName(newLastName),
    address(newAddress),
    salary(newSalary)
{}

Employee::Employee(const Employee& rhs):
    firstName(rhs.getFirstName()),
    lastName(rhs.getLastName()),
    address(rhs.getAddress()),
    salary(rhs.getSalary())
{}

Employee::~Employee() {}

Employee& Employee::operator=(const Employee& rhs)
{
    if (this == &rhs)
        return *this;

    firstName = rhs.getFirstName();
    lastName = rhs.getLastName();
    address = rhs.getAddress();
    salary = rhs.getSalary();

    return *this;
}

int main()
```

```
69: {
70:     Employee snett("Silver", "Burdett", "800 East 96th St.", 20000);
71:     snett.setSalary(50000);
72:     String lastName("Snett");
73:     snett.setLastName(lastName);
74:     snett.setFirstName("Sam");
75:
76:     std::cout << "Name: ";
77:     std::cout << snett.getFirstName().getString();
78:     std::cout << " " << snett.getLastName().getString();
79:     std::cout << ".\nAddress: ";
80:     std::cout << snett.getAddress().getString();
81:     std::cout << ".\nSalary: " ;
82:     std::cout << snett.getSalary() << "\n";
83:     return 0;
84: }
```

The following output is displayed when the Employee program runs:

```
Name: Sam Snett.
Address: 800 East 96th St..
Salary: 50000
```

Listing 20.4 shows the `Employee` class, which contains three `String` objects: `firstName`, `lastName`, and `address`.

On line 70, an `Employee` object is created and four values are passed in to initialize it. On line 71, the `Employee` access function `setSalary()` is called, with the literal 50000.

On line 72, a string is created and initialized using a C++ string constant. This string object then is used as an argument to `setLastName()` on line 73.

On line 74, the `Employee` function `setFirstName()` is called with another string constant. `Employee` does not have a function `setFirstName()` that takes a character string as its argument; `setFirstName()` requires a constant string reference.

The compiler resolves this because it knows how to make a `String` object from a constant character string. It knows this because you told it how to do so on line 9 of Listing 20.3.

Accessing Members of the Contained Class

`Employee` objects do not have special access to the member variables of `String`. If the Employee object `snett` tries to access the member variable `len` of its own `firstName` member variable, this causes a compile-time error. This lack of access is not much of a burden, however. The accessor functions provide an interface for the `String` class. The `Employee` class need not worry about the implementation details any more than it worries about how the integer variable, `salary`, stores its information.

Filtering Access to Contained Members

Note that the String class provides operator+. The designer of the Employee class has blocked access to operator+ being called on Employee objects by declaring that all the String accessors, such as getFirstName(), return a constant reference. operator+ can't be a const function because it changes the object it is called on, so attempting to write the following causes a compile-time error:

```
String buffer = snett.getFirstName() + snett.getLastName();
```

The getFirstName() function returns a constant String; you can't call operator+ on a constant object.

To fix this, overload getFirstName() to be non-const:

```
const String& getFirstName() const { return firstName; }
String& getFirstName() { return firstName; }
```

Note that the return value is no longer const and that the member function itself is no longer const. Changing the return value is not sufficient to overload the function name; you must change the constancy of the function itself. Because both a const and a non-const version are provided, the compiler invokes the const version wherever possible (for example, when a client calls getFirstName) and the non-const version as needed (for example, when invoked with operator+).

Copying by Value Versus by Reference

When you pass Employee objects by value, all their contained strings are copied as well, so copy constructors are called. This is very expensive; it takes up memory and it takes time.

When you pass Employee objects by reference using pointers or references, all this is saved. This is why C++ programmers work hard never to pass anything larger than a few bytes by value.

Friend Classes and Functions

Sometimes you will create classes together, as a set. These paired classes might need access to one another's private members, but you might not want to make that information public.

If you want to expose your private member data or functions to another class, you must declare that class to be a *friend*. This extends the interface of your class to include the friend class.

This friendship cannot be transferred and is not inherited. It also is not commutative. Assigning Class1 to be a friend of Class2 does not make Class2 a friend of Class1. (That's kind of a jerk move by Class2, in my opinion.)

Declarations of friend classes should be used with extreme caution. If two classes are inextricably entwined, and one must frequently access data in the other, there might be good reason to use this declaration. It is often just as easy to use public accessors instead. Doing so allows you to change one class without having to recompile the other.

At times, you will want to grant the friend level of access not to an entire class, but only to one or two functions of that class. You can do this by declaring the member functions of the other class to be friends, instead of declaring the entire class to be a friend. In fact, you can declare any function, whether or not it is a member function of another class, to be a friend function.

Pointers to Functions

Just as an array name is a constant pointer to the first element of the array, a function name is a constant pointer to the function. It is possible to declare a pointer variable that points to a function and to invoke the function by using that pointer. This can prove very useful; it allows you to create programs that decide which functions to invoke based on user input.

The only tricky part about function pointers is understanding the type of the object being pointed to. A pointer to `int` points to an integer variable, and a pointer to a function must point to a function of the appropriate return type and signature.

Consider this declaration:

```
long (*funcPtr)(int);
```

The `funcPtr` variable is declared to be a pointer that points to a function which takes an integer parameter and returns a `long`. The parentheses around `*funcPtr` are necessary because the parentheses around `int` have higher precedence than the indirection operator (`*`). Without the first parenthesis, this would declare a function that takes an integer and returns a pointer to a `long`.

Examine these two declarations:

```
long* func(int);
long (*funcPtr)(int);
```

The first, `func()`, is a *function* taking an integer and returning a pointer to a variable of type `long`. The second, `funcPtr`, is a *pointer* to a function taking an integer and returning a variable of type `long`.

The declaration of a function pointer always includes the return type and parentheses indicating the type of the parameters, if any. The FunctionPointer program in Listing 20.5 illustrates the declaration and use of function pointers.

LISTING 20.5 The Full Text of `FunctionPointer.cpp`

```
#include <iostream>

void square(int&, int&);
void cube(int&, int&);
void swap(int&, int&);
void getVals(int&, int&);
void printVals(int, int);

int main()
{
    void (*pFunc)(int&, int&);
    bool fQuit = false;

    int valOne = 1, valTwo = 2;
    int choice;
    while (fQuit == false)
    {
        std::cout << "(0) Quit (1) Change Values "
            << "(2) Square (3) Cube (4) Swap: ";
        std::cin >> choice;
        switch (choice)
        {
        case 1:
            pFunc = getVals;
            break;
        case 2:
            pFunc = square;
            break;
        case 3:
            pFunc = cube;
            break;
        case 4:
            pFunc = swap;
            break;
        default :
            fQuit = true;
            break;
        }

        if (fQuit)
            break;

        printVals(valOne, valTwo);
        pFunc(valOne, valTwo);
        printVals(valOne, valTwo);
    }
```

```
    return 0;
}

void printVals(int x, int y)
{
    std::cout << "x: " << x << " y: " << y << "\n";
}

void square(int &rX, int &rY)
{
    rX *= rX;
    rY *= rY;
}

void cube(int &rX, int &rY)
{
    int tmp;

    tmp = rX;
    rX *= rX;
    rX = rX * tmp;

    tmp = rY;
    rY *= rY;
    rY = rY * tmp;
}

void swap(int &rX, int &rY)
{
    int temp;
    temp = rX;
    rX = rY;
    rY = temp;
}

void getVals(int &rValOne, int &rValTwo)
{
    std::cout << "New value for valOne: ";
    std::cin >> rValOne;
    std::cout << "New value for valTwo: ";
    std::cin >> rValTwo;
}
```

Here's the output of FunctionPointer:

```
(0) Quit (1) Change Values (2) Square (3) Cube (4) Swap: 1
x: 1 y: 2
New value for valOne: 12
New value for valTwo: 9
```

```
x: 12 y: 9
(0) Quit (1) Change Values (2) Square (3) Cube (4) Swap: 4
x: 12 y: 9
x: 9 y: 12
(0) Quit (1) Change Values (2) Square (3) Cube (4) Swap: 0
```

On lines 3–6, four functions are declared, each with the same return type and signature, returning `void` and taking two references to integers.

On line 11, `pFunc` is declared to be a pointer to a function that returns `void` and takes two integer reference parameters. Any of the previous functions can be pointed to by `pFunc`. The user is repeatedly offered the choice of which functions to invoke, and `pFunc` is assigned accordingly. On lines 43–45, the current values of the two integers are displayed, the currently assigned function is invoked, and then the values are printed again.

The pointer to a function does not need to be dereferenced, although you are free to do so. Therefore, if `pFunc` is a pointer to a function taking an integer and returning a variable of type `long`, and you assign `pFunc` to a matching function, you can invoke that function with either of these:

```
pFunc(x);
(*pFunc)(x);
```

The two forms are identical. The former is just a shorthand version of the latter.

Arrays of Pointers to Functions

Just as you can declare an array of pointers to integers, you can declare an array of pointers to functions returning a specific value type and with a specific signature. The ArrayFunction program in Listing 20.6 demonstrates this.

LISTING 20.6 The Full Text of `ArrayFunction.cpp`

```
#include <iostream>

void square(int&, int&);
void cube(int&, int&);
void swap(int&, int&);
void getVals(int&, int&);
void printVals(int, int);

int main()
{
    int valOne=1, valTwo=2;
    int choice, i;
```

```
    const int maxArray = 5;
    void (*pFuncArray[maxArray])(int&, int&);

    for (i=0;i < maxArray; i++)
    {
        std::cout << "(1) Change Values "
            << "(2) Square (3) Cube (4) Swap: ";
        std::cin >> choice;
        switch (choice)
        {
        case 1:
            pFuncArray[i] = getVals;
            break;
        case 2:
            pFuncArray[i] = square;
            break;
        case 3:
            pFuncArray[i] = cube;
            break;
        case 4:
            pFuncArray[i] = swap;
            break;
        default:
            pFuncArray[i] = 0;
        }
    }

    for (i = 0; i < maxArray; i++)
    {
        pFuncArray[i](valOne, valTwo);
        printVals(valOne, valTwo);
    }
    return 0;
}

void printVals(int x, int y)
{
    std::cout << "x: " << x << " y: " << y << "\n";
}

void square(int &rX, int &rY)
{
    rX *= rX;
    rY *= rY;
}

void cube(int &rX, int &rY)
```

```
60: {
61:     int tmp;
62:
63:     tmp = rX;
64:     rX *= rX;
65:     rX = rX * tmp;
66:
67:     tmp = rY;
68:     rY *= rY;
69:     rY = rY * tmp;
70: }
71:
72: void swap(int &rX, int &rY)
73: {
74:     int temp;
75:     temp = rX;
76:     rX = rY;
77:     rY = temp;
78: }
79:
80: void getVals(int &rValOne, int &rValTwo)
81: {
82:     std::cout << "New value for valOne: ";
83:     std::cin >> rValOne;
84:     std::cout << "New value for valTwo: ";
85:     std::cin >> rValTwo;
86: }
```

Here's sample output using five user-selected options:

```
(1) Change Values (2) Square (3) Cube (4) Swap: 1
(1) Change Values (2) Square (3) Cube (4) Swap: 2
(1) Change Values (2) Square (3) Cube (4) Swap: 3
(1) Change Values (2) Square (3) Cube (4) Swap: 4
(1) Change Values (2) Square (3) Cube (4) Swap: 2
New value for valOne: 2
New value for valTwo: 3
x: 2 y: 3
x: 4 y: 9
x: 64 y: 729
x: 729 y: 64
x: 531441 y: 4096
```

In the `for` loop beginning on line 16, the user is asked to pick the functions to invoke. Each member of the array is assigned the address of the appropriate function. In the loop on lines 40–44, each function is invoked in turn. Line 42 executes the function whose address is stored in the `pFuncArray` array. The result is displayed after each invocation.

CAUTION

As mentioned at the beginning of the book. these projects do not guard against invalid user input. If a value other than 1, 2, 3, or 4 is selected in the ArrayFunction program, it tries to call an undefined function on line 42 and fails with an error.

Passing Pointers to Functions to Other Functions

The pointers to functions (and arrays of pointers to functions, for that matter) can be passed to other functions that may take action and then call the right function using the pointer.

For example, you might improve the ArrayFunction program by passing the chosen function pointer to another function (outside of `main()`) that will display the values, invoke the function, and then show them again. The FunctionPasser program (Listing 20.7) shows how this is done.

LISTING 20.7 The Full Text of `FunctionPasser.cpp`

```
#include <iostream>

void square(int&,int&);
void cube(int&, int&);
void swap(int&, int&);
void getVals(int&, int&);
void printVals(void (*)(int&, int&),int&, int&);

int main()
{
    int valOne=1, valTwo=2;
    int choice;
    bool fQuit = false;

    void (*pFunc)(int&, int&);

    while (fQuit == false)
    {
        std::cout << "(0) Quit (1) Change Values "
            << "(2) Square (3) Cube (4) Swap: ";
        std::cin >> choice;
        switch (choice)
        {
        case 1:
            pFunc = getVals;
            break;
        case 2:
            pFunc = square;
            break;
```

```
        case 3:
            pFunc = cube;
            break;
        case 4:
            pFunc = swap;
            break;
        default:
            fQuit = true;
            break;
        }
        if (fQuit == true)
            break;
        printVals(pFunc, valOne, valTwo);
    }

    return 0;
}

void printVals(void (*pFunc)(int&, int&),int& x, int& y)
{
    std::cout << "x: " << x << " y: " << y << "\n";
    pFunc(x, y);
    std::cout << "x: " << x << " y: " << y << "\n";
}

void square(int &rX, int &rY)
{
    rX *= rX;
    rY *= rY;
}

void cube(int &rX, int &rY)
{
    int tmp;

    tmp = rX;
    rX *= rX;
    rX = rX * tmp;

    tmp = rY;
    rY *= rY;
    rY = rY * tmp;
}

void swap(int &rX, int &rY)
{
    int temp;
```

```
77:      temp = rX;
78:      rX = rY;
79:      rY = temp;
80: }
81:
82: void getVals(int &rValOne, int &rValTwo)
83: {
84:      std::cout << "New value for valOne: ";
85:      std::cin >> rValOne;
86:      std::cout << "New value for valTwo: ";
87:      std::cin >> rValTwo;
88: }
```

Here's a sample run of the program:

```
(0) Quit (1) Change Values (2) Square (3) Cube (4) Swap: 1
x: 1 y: 2
New value for valOne: 7
New value for valTwo: 9
x: 7 y: 9
(0) Quit (1) Change Values (2) Square (3) Cube (4) Swap: 3
x: 7 y: 9
x: 343 y: 729
(0) Quit (1) Change Values (2) Square (3) Cube (4) Swap: 2
x: 343 y: 729
x: 117649 y: 531441
(0) Quit (1) Change Values (2) Square (3) Cube (4) Swap: 4
x: 117649 y: 531441
x: 531441 y: 117649
(0) Quit (1) Change Values (2) Square (3) Cube (4) Swap: 0
```

On line 15, `pFunc` is declared to be a pointer to a function returning `void` and taking two parameters, both of which are integer references. On line 7, `printVals` is declared to be a function taking three parameters. The first is a pointer to a function that returns `void` but takes two integer reference parameters, and the second and third arguments to `printVals` are integer references. The user again is prompted which functions to call, then on line 42 `printVals()` is called.

There is a more readable way of writing this with `typedef`.

Using `typedef` with Pointers to Functions

The construct `void (*)(int&, int&)` in the FunctionPasser program is cumbersome. You can use `typedef` to simplify this, by declaring a type `VPF` as a pointer to a function returning `void` and taking two integer references:

```
typedef  void (*VPF) (int&, int&);
```

The pFunc variable is declared to be of type VPF:

```
VPF pFunc;
```

The member function printVals() is declared to take three parameters, a VPF and two integer references:

```
void printVals(VPF pFunc,int& x, int& y)
```

Remember that typedef creates a synonym; the only difference is readability.

Pointers to Member Functions

Up to this point, all of the function pointers you've created have been for general, non-class functions. It also is possible to create pointers to functions that are members of classes.

To create a pointer to member function, use the same syntax as with a pointer to a function, but include the class name and the scoping operator (::). Therefore, if pFunc points to a member function of the class Shape, which takes two integers and returns void, the declaration for pFunc is the following:

```
void (Shape::*pFunc)(int, int);
```

Pointers to member functions are used in exactly the same way as pointers to functions, except that they require an object of the correct class on which to invoke them. The MemberPointer program in Listing 20.8 illustrates the use of pointers to member functions.

LISTING 20.8 The Full Text of MemberPointer.cpp

```
#include <iostream>

enum BOOL { FALSE, TRUE };

class Mammal
{
public:
    Mammal():age(1) {  }
    virtual ~Mammal() { }
    virtual void speak() const = 0;
    virtual void move() const = 0;
protected:
    int age;
};

class Dog : public Mammal
{
public:
```

```
    void speak() const { std::cout << "Woof!\n"; }
    void move() const { std::cout << "Walking to heel ...\n"; }
};

class Cat : public Mammal
{
public:
    void speak() const { std::cout << "Meow!\n"; }
    void move() const { std::cout << "Slinking ...\n"; }
};

class Horse : public Mammal
{
public:
    void speak() const { std::cout << "Winnie!\n"; }
    void move() const { std::cout << "Galloping ...\n"; }
};

int main()
{
    void (Mammal::*pFunc)() const = 0;
    Mammal* ptr = 0;
    int animal;
    int method;
    bool fQuit = false;

    while (fQuit == false)
    {
        std::cout << "(0) Quit (1) Dog (2) Cat (3) Horse: ";
        std::cin >> animal;
        switch (animal)
        {
        case 1:
            ptr = new Dog;
            break;
        case 2:
            ptr = new Cat;
            break;
        case 3:
            ptr = new Horse;
            break;
        default:
            fQuit = true;
            break;
        }
        if (fQuit)
            break;
```

```
66:
67:             std::cout << "(1) Speak (2) Move: ";
68:             std::cin >> method;
69:             switch (method)
70:             {
71:             case 1:
72:                 pFunc = &Mammal::speak;
73:                 break;
74:             default:
75:                 pFunc = &Mammal::move;
76:                 break;
77:             }
78:
79:             (ptr->*pFunc)();
80:             delete ptr;
81:         }
82:         return 0;
83: }
```

The program asks users to choose a type of object and then the behavior (function) to call on that object. Here's one run:

```
(0) Quit (1) Dog (2) Cat (3) Horse: 1
(1) Speak (2) Move: 1
Woof!
(0) Quit (1) Dog (2) Cat (3) Horse: 2
(1) Speak (2) Move: 1
Meow!
(0) Quit (1) Dog (2) Cat (3) Horse: 3
(1) Speak (2) Move: 2
Galloping ...
(0) Quit (1) Dog (2) Cat (3) Horse: 0
```

On lines 5–14, the abstract data type `Mammal` is declared with two pure virtual member functions, `speak()` and `move()`. `Mammal` is subclassed into `Dog`, `Cat`, and `Horse`, each of which overrides `speak()` and `move()`.

The `main()` function asks the user to choose which type of animal to create, and then a new subclass of `Animal` is created and assigned to `ptr` in the `switch` block on lines 49–63.

The user then is prompted for which function to invoke and that function is assigned to the pointer `pFunc`. On line 79, the function chosen is invoked by the object created, by using the pointer `ptr` to access the object and `pFunc` to access the function.

Finally, on line 80, `delete` is called on the pointer `ptr` to return the memory set aside for the object to the heap.

NOTE

There is no reason to call `delete` on `pFunc` because this is a pointer to code, not to an object on the heap. In fact, attempting to do so generates a compile-time error.

Arrays of Pointers to Member Functions

As with pointers to functions, pointers to member functions can be stored in an array. The array can be initialized with the addresses of various member functions, and those can be invoked by offsets into the array. Listing 20.9 illustrates this technique.

LISTING 20.9 The Full Text of `MPFunction.cpp`

```
#include <iostream>

class Dog
{
public:
    void speak() const { std::cout << "Woof!\n"; }
    void move() const { std::cout << "Walking to heel ...\n"; }
    void eat() const { std::cout << "Gobbling food ...\n"; }
    void growl() const { std::cout << "Grrrrr\n"; }
    void whimper() const { std::cout << "Whining noises ...\n"; }
    void rollOver() const { std::cout << "Rolling over ...\n"; }
    void playDead() const
        { std::cout << "Is this the end of Little Caesar?\n"; }
};

typedef void (Dog::*PDF)() const;

int main()
{
    const int maxFuncs = 7;
    PDF dogFunctions[maxFuncs] =
        {   &Dog::speak,
            &Dog::move,
            &Dog::eat,
            &Dog::growl,
            &Dog::whimper,
            &Dog::rollOver,
            &Dog::playDead
        };

    Dog* pDog =0;
    int method;
    bool fQuit = false;

```

```
35:     while (!fQuit)
36:     {
37:         std::cout << "(0) Quit (1) Speak (2) Move (3) Eat (4) Growl\n";
38:         std::cout << "(5) Whimper (6) Roll Over (7) Play Dead: ";
39:         std::cin >> method;
40:         if (method == 0)
41:         {
42:             fQuit = true;
43:             break;
44:         }
45:         else
46:         {
47:             pDog = new Dog;
48:             (pDog->*dogFunctions[method - 1])();
49:             delete pDog;
50:         }
51:         std::cout << std::endl;
52:     }
53:     return 0;
54: }
```

This program produces the following output:

```
(0) Quit (1) Speak (2) Move (3) Eat (4) Growl
(5) Whimper (6) Roll Over (7) Play Dead: 3
Gobbling food ...

(0) Quit (1) Speak (2) Move (3) Eat (4) Growl
(5) Whimper (6) Roll Over (7) Play Dead: 5
Whining noises ...

(0) Quit (1) Speak (2) Move (3) Eat (4) Growl
(5) Whimper (6) Roll Over (7) Play Dead: 6
Rolling over ...

(0) Quit (1) Speak (2) Move (3) Eat (4) Growl
(5) Whimper (6) Roll Over (7) Play Dead: 1
Woof!

(0) Quit (1) Speak (2) Move (3) Eat (4) Growl
(5) Whimper (6) Roll Over (7) Play Dead: 0
```

On lines 3–14, the class `Dog` is created with seven member functions all sharing the same return type and signature. On line 16, a `typedef` declares `PDF` to be a pointer to a member function of `Dog` that takes no arguments, returns no values, and is `const`. This is the signature of the seven member functions of `Dog`.

On lines 21–29, the array `dogFunctions` is declared to hold seven such member functions, and it is initialized with the addresses of these functions.

On lines 37–39, the user is prompted to pick a function. Unless the user enters 0 to quit, a new `Dog` is created on the heap and the correct function is invoked on the array on line 48.

Summary

This hour covered several ways to make your functions more powerful.

Static member variables serve as a way to store information about an entire class of objects. They're also useful as a technique in which objects of the same class can exchange information with each other.

Static member functions provide a place for behavior that fits a class but does not require a specific object of that class to operate on.

Friend functions make it possible for one class to expose its private member variables and functions to another class that would not otherwise have access. Although normally these things are handled via inheritance between a base class and derived class, using friend functions gives special access to a class outside of its inheritance hierarchy.

Q&A

Q. Why use static data when you can use global data?

A. Static data is scoped to the class. It therefore is available only through an object of the class—through an explicit and full call using the class name if the data is public, or by using a static member function. Static data is typed to the class type, however, and the restricted access and strong typing makes static data safer than global data.

Q. Why use static member functions when you can use global functions?

A. Static member functions are scoped to the class and can be called only by using an object of the class or an explicit full specification (such as *`ClassName::FunctionName()`*).

Q. Why not make all classes friends of all the classes they use?

A. Making one class a friend of another exposes the implementation details and reduces encapsulation. The ideal in object-oriented programming is to keep as many of the details of each class as possible hidden from all other classes.

Q. Why did Ohio State football coach Woody Hayes punch a player on an opposing team back in the '70s?

A. Hayes, the fiery coach who led the Buckeyes to three national championships, punched a Clemson Tigers player because he was a notorious bad loser. The player had just intercepted a pass late in a bowl game.

In the 1978 Gator Bowl in Jacksonville, Florida, the Buckeyes had the ball and were trailing Clemson 17-15 with a little over two minutes left. Charlie Bauman intercepted an Art Schlichter pass and was knocked out of bounds on the Ohio State sideline.

Hayes punched him in the neck and also hit one of his own players who was trying to restrain him. The coach was fired one day later and died in 1987.

The coach once explained his competitiveness this way: "Nobody despises losing more than I do. That's what got me into trouble over the years, but it also made a man with mediocre ability into a pretty good coach."

Workshop

Now that you've had the chance to learn about static functions and friend functions, you can answer a few questions to see how well your brain is functioning.

Quiz

1. How many copies of a static member variable exist for a class?

   A. None

   B. One

   C. One for each object of the class

2. What keyword makes a member function static?

   A. `static`

   B. `friend`

   C. `const`

3. When should you call `delete` after you're done using a function pointer?

   A. Always

   B. Never

   C. Sometimes

Answers

1. **B.** Only one version is instantiated for all objects of that class.

2. **A.** The `static` keyword makes both member variables and functions static for the entire class.

3. **B.** Unlike a pointer that holds an address in memory, which should be deleted when no longer needed, a function pointer points to code and cannot be freed with `delete`.

Activities

1. Take the comments out of the String class in Listing 20.3. Rerun the Employee program in Listing 20.4 to reveal how often these functions are called.
2. Modify the ArrayFunction program in Listing 20.6 to reject inappropriate input.

To see solutions to these activities, visit this book's website at http://cplusplus.cadenhead.org.

HOUR 21
Using New Features of C++14

What You'll Learn in This Hour:

- ▶ How to create safer null pointers
- ▶ How to make constant expressions
- ▶ How to assign auto-typed variables
- ▶ How to use the new range-based `for` loop

The Newest Version of C++

Since the C++ programming language was created by Bjarne Stroustrop in 1979, it has undergone several significant revisions.

In 1983, its name was changed from C for Classes to C++, and numerous features such as virtual functions, operator overloading, and references were added. Two years later, the first edition of Stroustrop's book *The C++ Programming Language* was published, offering a full reference to a language that had not yet become an official standard.

In 1989, version 2.0 of C++ came out and included such features as multiple inheritance, static member functions, and abstract classes.

Nine years later, the C++ standards committee published the standardized version of the language, a version described informally as C++98.

In 2011, C++11 was released after several years in which its sliding schedule led it to be dubbed C++0x. (The 0x were a placeholder for the final two numbers in the year.)

The latest and greatest version of the language is C++14. Most current C++ tools fully support this version, so you can begin taking advantage of the newest improvements to the language.

Using auto in Function Return Types

C++ is a type-safe language, providing an important assurance that all data will remain in the form it takes when its variable is declared. The burden has been on the programmer to use each variable according to type. But with each new version of the language, more type safety has been ensured by the compiler.

In C++11, the auto keyword could be used in a variable declaration to let the compiler infer the data type. This made it possible to do things like this:

```
auto length = 50;
auto width = 30;
auto height = 3;
auto area = length * width * height;

std::cout << "Area: " << area << std::endl;
```

The variables all are integers, which the compiler knows. The length, width, and height variables are integers because they are assigned integer literals as values when they are declared. The area variable is an integer because it is the result of an expression multiplying three integers.

C++ extends this type inference capability by making it possible to use auto as the return type of a function.

As the compiler does with variable declarations, the auto keyword causes the function's return type to be determined by the context. This function has auto as the return type:

```
auto getSalaryMultiple(int years)
{
    if (years < 10)
    {
        return 1.1;
    }
    return 1.25;
}
```

The function takes the years an employee has worked as a parameter, returning a multiplier of 1.1 for less than 10 years and 1.25 otherwise. This would be multiplied by the employee's current salary to calculate the new salary.

The compiler determines that the function returns a double value because both return statements return literals of that type.

In order for auto to be used as a function's return type, every return statement in that function must return the same type. If the preceding code was changed so that the final statement returned 2 instead of 1.25, compilation fails with this error message:

```
error: inconsistent deduction for 'auto': 'double' and then 'int'
```

This hour's first project is the AutoArea program in Listing 21.1, which determines the area of a 3-D rectangle by its length, width, and height.

LISTING 21.1 The Full Text of AutoArea.cpp

```
 1: #include <iostream>
 2:
 3: auto findArea(auto length, auto width, auto height) {
 4:   return length * width * height;
 5: }
 6:
 7: int main()
 8: {
 9:     auto length = 50.0;
10:     auto width = 30.0;
11:     auto height = 3.5;
12:
13:     auto area = findArea(length, width, height);
14:
15:     std::cout << "Area: " << area << std::endl;
16:     return 0;
17: }
```

Like all programs in this hour, AutoArea must be compiled with the command-line option `--std=c++14` because it uses a new feature of C++14.

When run, it produces a single line of output:

```
Area: 5250;
```

This program defines a `findArea()` function, specifying the function's return type as `auto` in line 3 in Listing 21.1. It also uses auto as the type of all three parameters to the function.

The compiler figures out the actual type of the parameters and return value in lines 9–11. Those statements declare the variables `length`, `width`, and `height` and initialize them with double floating-point numbers.

The type of those literals is deduced as `double`. So when the `findArea()` function multiplies three doubles in line 4 and returns that value, that's determined to be `double` as well.

The AutoArea program works with double values without ever explicitly defining a variable to be such using the `double` keyword. This enables the program to be revised in an interesting and unusual way.

Return to your editor and change the values in lines 9–11 so that the statements become the following:

```
auto length = 50;
auto width = 30;
auto height = 3;
```

All three of the literals are now integers, making the data type deduced by the compiler `int` instead of `double`.

The program will compile and run successfully:

```
Area: 4500;
```

Because of type deduction, the entire program changed its behavior, shifting to employ integer values and a multiplication expression that produces an integer. The compiler did this work for you.

In a recursive function that calls itself, the recursive call must be preceded by another `return` statement whose type can be determined by the compiler.

In a simple demonstration program like AutoArea the benefit of this flexibility may not seem like much to crow about. But in a large C++ program, changing the data type of something can cascade to other variables, parameters, and return types, requiring modifications to each that account for the new type.

The more your programs use auto-deduction, the more flexible they become as you refactor them.

CAUTION

The `auto` keyword can be used in a forward declaration of a function, but there's a catch: The function must be defined before any code that calls the function. Otherwise, the compiler will fail with an error.

Improved Numeric Literals

Two small changes introduced with the C++14 release are of arguably lesser significance than other improvements but are useful nonetheless. Integer literals now can be expressed as binary values and can contain digit separators.

To express an integer in binary, precede it with the characters "0b" or "0B", as in this statement:

```
int role = 0b11111111;
```

This gives `role` the decimal value 255 (a byte with all eight bits set).

Here's another example that sets role to decimal 15:

```
int role = 0b00001111;
```

Binary literals can be used in expressions as well, such as this statement:

```
int role = 0b00001111 - 0b00001101;
```

The result of the expression is decimal 2 (the binary literal 0b00000010).

A digit separator is a character placed in large numbers to make them more readable. One of the most common usages is in money, where the number 10000000 is tougher to comprehend at a glance than $10,000,000.

In that figure of currency, a comma (,) is the digit separator. One appears every three digits for purpose of readability. The separator has no effect on the actual value.

The new digit separator in C++ is the single quote character (').

Here's a statement that uses it:

```
long long ouch = 19'241'686'248'628;
```

The variable ouch is the U.S. national debt in whole dollars at the moment this was written (around $19.24 trillion and counting). The separator character (') is ignored by the C++ compiler. If you displayed this variable, the output would be the following:

```
19241686248628;
```

At the time of this writing a vigorous campaign is underway to select a new president. One of the candidates may even be president by the time you read this. If that's the case, based on the ironclad promises all of them have made on the campaign trail, the above number should be much lower.

To check whether that happened, pause this hour for a moment and visit the National Debt Clock website at www.brillig.com/debt_clock to compare our 14-digit figure to the current one. We'll wait for you to get back.

[Dramatic pause]

Welcome back. Yes, that is a staggeringly large increase in a short amount of time.

The constexpr Keyword

A constant expression function is a function whose value can be determined by the compiler, enabling that constant value to be substituted in place of the function.

The function must be preceded by the keyword `constexpr` and meet three criteria:

- The function must return a value (not `void`)
- The entire body of the function must be a single `return` statement that returns an expression
- The expression must evaluate to a constant after substitution.

The constant expression cannot be called before it is defined.

Here's a snippet of code that is a valid constant expression:

```
constexpr double expand(int original)
{
    return original * 1.5;
}
```

The use of `constexpr` improves C++ by enabling a programmer for the first time to signal the intent that the code be used as a constant expression.

The keyword says to the compiler that this function is a constant when the parameters to the function all are constants. If any of the parameters is not a constant, it should be evaluated dynamically.

One of the most common situations where `constexpr` comes in handy is in the declaration of arrays.

When an array is initialized in C++, the size of that array must be a constant. There often are times where it would be convenient to set the size of an array by calling a function. Here's an approach that could be attempted:

```
const int getArraySize(int hours)
{
    return 60 * 60 * hours;
}

int ticks[getArraySize(24)];
```

Because the array size set between the [and] brackets must be a constant, an older C++ compiler will fail with an error "array bound is not an integer constant before ']' token."

By changing the `const` keyword in the function declaration to `constexpr` and compiling the program to the C++14 standard, you can solve this problem.

The ArrayMaxer program in Listing 21.2 demonstrates this approach. The program creates an array of integers, stores a value in each of the array elements, then displays a value of one element.

LISTING 21.2 The Full Text of `ArrayMaxer.cpp`

```
 1: #include <iostream>
 2:
 3: constexpr int getArraySize()
 4: {
 5:  return 1024;
 6: }
 7:
 8: int main()
 9: {
10:
11:     int bolts[getArraySize()];
12:     int boltsSize = sizeof(bolts) / sizeof(bolts[0]);
13:
14:     for (int i = 0; i < boltsSize; i++)
15:     {
16:            bolts[i] = i * boltsSize;
17:     }
18:
19:     std::cout << "Value of bolts[10]: " << bolts[10] << std::endl;
20:
21:     return 0;
22: }
```

Compile the program with the `-std=c++14` option and run it to produce the following output:

```
Value of bolts[10]: 10240;
```

The constant expression function is defined in lines 3–6 of Listing 21.2. The `constexpr` keyword precedes the function's return type, name, and parameters.

This function meets the criteria for a constant expression function by returning a value (an integer), consisting of a single `return` statement, and evaluating to a constant when executed. Also, the function is defined before it is called on line 11.

The program iterates through all elements of the `bolts` array, giving each one a value. The `for` loop in lines 14–17 makes use of the `boltSize` variable to know when the end of the array has been reached.

This variable is declared on line 12 and makes use of the C++ built-in `sizeof()` function in a way you may not have encountered before. As you may recall from Hour 3, "Creating Variables and Constants," `sizeof()` returns the number of bytes a variable's data type occupies. It can be used on simple data types such as `int` or `long` and on entire arrays.

Looping through every element in an array requires some way of knowing when the end of the array has been reached. Calling `sizeof()` on an array returns the total number of bytes that array holds. By dividing this by the `sizeof()` for a single array element, the result is the number of elements.

The addition of `constexpr` is a compiler optimization that replaces a lot of approaches that were cumbersome and much more complicated.

Lambda Expressions

The most asked-for feature to be added to C++ in recent years is lambda expressions, which enable the creation of inline anonymous functions. The syntax can seem a bit confusing at first, but as you master their use, you will find they provide powerful functionality that can make your source code easier to understand.

A lambda expression resembles a statement and can be defined in a single line of code. The expression is stored in a variable and called like a function.

Here's an example:

```
auto aarhus = [](){ std::cout << "Solidum petit in profundis!" << std::endl; };
aarhus();
```

This code produces the following output:

```
Solidum petit in profundis!
```

The anonymous function executes the code between the { and } braces. Note that there's a semi-colon at the end of the line following the } brace.

The function is stored in the variable `aarhus` and run using the same syntax as calling a function.

The lambda expression can have one or more arguments, which are specified within the parenthesis marks after the [] square brackets.

This example has two arguments:

```
auto multiply = [](int x, int y){ std::cout << "Total: " << x * y << std::endl; };
multiply(7, 17);
```

Here's the output:

```
Total: 117
```

When a lambda expression has no arguments, the parentheses can be left out of the expression. The first example didn't have any, so here's another version of that expression:

```
auto aarhus = []{ std::cout << "Solidum petit in profundis!" << std::endl; };
```

The expression can return a value by specifying its return type (or `auto`) after a `->` operator.

Here's a rewrite of the previous example that returns the sum of multiplying `x` and `y`.

```
auto multiply = [] (int x, int y) -> int { return x * y; };
int sum = multiply(7, 17);
std::cout << "Total: " << sum << std::endl;
```

A lambda expression normally does not have access to the variables defined in the scope that encloses the expression.

You can change this with the last part of the expression to be put to work: the [] square brackets, which are called the capture block.

To make one or more variables from the enclosing scope available in the lambda expression, list them inside the [and] brackets separated by commas.

This code puts the capture block to use:

```
int x = 7;
auto multiply = [x] (int y) -> int { return x * y; };
int sum = multiply(17);
std::cout << "Total: " << sum << std::endl;
```

The output remains the same.

Summary

Many programmers have begun to use the term Modern C++ to refer to C++14 and its predecessor C++11. With new versions coming out at a much speedier pace than in the past, C++ creator Bjarne Stroustrop has expressed enormous excitement about the current state of the language. He wrote on his website, "The pieces just fit together better than they used to and I find a higher-level style of programming more natural than before and as efficient as ever."

For more of his thoughts, visit his site at www.stroustrup.com.

Q&A

Q. Are there any risks to using the `auto` keyword?

A. One of the biggest is when you're mistaken about what data type is being assigned by the statement. A common blunder in C++ is to assume that the literal 3.5 is a `float` literal. It's actually a `double`. So if you've created an `auto`-typed variable using a value like that and you don't realize it's a double, you could make assumptions about how you can use the variable in a program.

Q. With C++11 and C++14 coming just three years apart, when is the next version of C++ expected to come out?

A. The current plan is to produce the next version during the year 2017 as C++17, keeping the streak of three-year intervals that is dramatically faster than how the language used to be improved.

The version has not yet been declared "feature complete" at the time of this writing, so it's not yet clear this schedule will be hit.

The working name C++1z has been adopted during development as an indicator it may slide to 2018 or 2019 if there are unexpected delays or obstacles to implementation.

For the current status of this version, visit the C++ standardization website at https://isocpp.org/std/status.

Q. Who invented the crossword puzzle?

A. The crossword puzzle was devised by Arthur Wynne in 1913 for the New York World newspaper. The first one was published on December 21, 1913, and described as a "Word-Cross."

Wynne created new puzzles each week for the newspaper. His puzzles had the same rules as current crossword puzzles but an unusual shape. Words crisscrossed each other on a diamond shaped grid with black squares in the middle.

Wynne quickly settled on a rectangular shape and the name "Cross-Word." Eleven years later in 1924, fledgling book publishers Dick Simon and Lincoln Schuster introduced crosswords to an international audience by issuing a collection of New York World puzzles that became a bestseller.

The first crossword puzzle is available online at www.fun-with-words.com/worlds_first_crossword.html. If you can figure out a seven-letter word for "a written acknowledgment" that starts with R, I'd appreciate the help.

Workshop

Now that you've spent an hour on the future of C++, answer a few questions and undertake exercises to see how much knowledge you brought back to the present.

Quiz

1. Which of the following is not an acceptable place to use the `auto` keyword?

   A. Initializing a variable with a literal

   B. Returning a value from a function

   C. Both A. and B. are acceptable

2. What types can a `nullptr` be converted to using casting?

   A. int

   B. bool

   C. none

3. What can the `constexpr` keyword be used to define?

   A. Functions

   B. Variables

   C. Functions and variables

Answers

1. **C.** The `auto` keyword can be used as the type of a variable when it is initialized and the type of a function parameter.

2. **B.** The `nullptr` has the `bool` value of `false` after being cast, which C++ supports because of existing code that relies on the behavior.

3. **C.** Any variable or function declared with `constexpr` is implicitly treated as a `const`.

Activities

1. Write a program that takes the U.S. national debt, adds $2.35 billion a day for 10 days and displays the result with a lambda expression.

2. Write a program with a `square()` function that multiplies a number by itself and has two auto-typed variables as parameters. Call the function multiple times with an `int`, `long`, `float`, and `double`. Store the result of the function in an `auto`-typed variable and display it.

To see solutions to these activities, visit this book's website at http://cplusplus.cadenhead.org.

HOUR 22

Employing Object-Oriented Analysis and Design

What You'll Learn in This Hour:

- How to analyze problems from an object-oriented perspective
- How to design your program from an object-oriented perspective
- How to apply the syntax of C++ to implement design objectives
- How to design for reusability and extensibility

The Development Cycle

Many books and articles have been written about the development cycle. Some propose a *waterfall* technique, in which designers determine what the program should do. Architects determine how the program will be built, what classes will be used, and so forth. Programmers implement the design and architecture. By the time the design and architecture are given to the programmer, they are complete; all the programmer needs to do is implement the required functionality.

Even if the waterfall technique worked, it would be a poor technique for writing good programs. As the programmer proceeds, there is a necessary and natural feedback cycle between what has been written so far and what remains to be done. While it is true that good C++ programs are designed in great detail before a line of code is written, it is not true that that design remains unchanged throughout the cycle.

The amount of design that must be finished up front, before programming begins, is a function of the size of the program. A highly complex effort, involving dozens of programmers working for many months, will require a more fully articulated architecture than a quick-and-dirty application written in one day by a single programmer.

This hour focuses on the design of large, complex programs that will be expanded and enhanced over many years. Many programmers enjoy working at the bleeding edge of technology; they tend to write programs whose complexity pushes at the limits of their tools and understanding. In many ways, C++ was designed to extend the complexity that a programmer can manage.

Simulating an Alarm System

A *simulation* is a computer model of a real-world system. There are many reasons to build a simulation, but a good design must start with an understanding of what questions you hope the simulation will answer.

As a starting point, examine this problem: You have been asked to simulate the alarm system for a house. The house has four bedrooms, a finished basement, and an under-the-house garage.

The downstairs has the following windows: three in the kitchen, four in the dining room, one in the half-bathroom, two each in the living room and the family room, and two small windows next to the front door. All four bedrooms are upstairs; each bedroom has two windows except for the master bedroom, which has four. There are two baths, each with one window. Finally, there are four half-windows in the basement and one window in the garage.

Normal access to the house is through the front door. In addition, the kitchen has a sliding glass door, and the garage has two doors for the cars and one door for easy access to the basement. There also is a cellar door in the backyard.

All the windows and doors have alarms, and there is a panic button on each phone and one next to the bed in the master bedroom. The grounds have alarms, as well, although these alarms are carefully calibrated so that they are not set off by small animals or birds.

A central alarm system in the basement sounds a warning chirp when the alarm has been tripped. If the alarm is not disabled within a set amount of time, the police are called. If a panic button is pushed, the police are called immediately.

The alarm also is wired into the fire and smoke detectors and the sprinkler system. The alarm system itself is fault tolerant, has its own internal backup power supply, and is encased in a fireproof box.

Conceptualization

In the *conceptualization* phase, you try to understand what the customer hopes to gain from the program: What is this program for? What questions might this simulation answer? For example, you might be able to use the simulation to answer these questions: How long might a sensor be broken before anyone notices? Is there a way to defeat the window alarms without the police being notified?

The conceptualization phase is a good time to think about what is inside the program and what is outside. Are the police represented in the simulation? Is control of the actual house alarm in the system itself?

Analysis and Requirements

The conceptualization phase gives way to the analysis phase. During analysis, your job as object-oriented programming analyst is to help the customer understand what she requires from the program. Exactly what behavior will the program exhibit? What kinds of interactions can the customer expect?

These requirements are typically captured in a series of documents, which might include use cases. A *use case* is a description of how the system will be used. It describes interactions and use patterns, helping the programmer capture the design goals of the system.

NOTE

Unified Modeling Language (UML) is one way of representing your requirements and analysis. The advantage of using UML to represent your information is twofold: It's graphical and it follows a standard form, so many people will be able to understand it. Although it is beyond the scope of this book to teach UML (there are many good books on that topic alone), you should know that it includes ways of representing use cases. It is particularly suited for object-oriented development, because it supports abstract and other types of classes directly.

A good book for learning UML is *Sams Teach Yourself UML in 24 Hours, Third Edition* (ISBN: 0-672-32640-X), by Joseph Schmuller.

High-Level and Low-Level Design

After the product is fully understood and the requirements have been captured in the appropriate documentation, it is time to move on to the high-level design. During this phase of the design the programmer doesn't worry about the platform, operating system, or programming language issues. He concentrates, instead, on how the system will work: What are the major components? How do they interact with one another?

One way to approach this problem is to set aside issues relating to the user interface, focusing only on the components of the problem space.

The problem *space* is the set of problems and issues your program is trying to solve. The *solution space* is the set of possible solutions to the problems.

As your high-level design evolves you'll want to begin thinking about the responsibilities of the objects you identify—what they do and what information they hold. You also want to think about their collaborations—what objects they interact with.

For example, clearly you have sensors of various types, a central alarm system, buttons, wires, and telephones. Further thought persuades that you also must simulate rooms, perhaps floors, and possibly groups of people such as owners and police.

The sensors can be divided into motion detectors, trip wires, sound detectors, smoke detectors, and so forth. All these are types of sensors, although there is no such thing as a sensor *per se*. This is a good indication that sensor is an abstract data type (ADT).

As an ADT, the class `Sensor` would provide the complete interface for all types of sensors, and each derived type would provide the implementation. Clients of the various sensors would use them without regard to which type of sensor they are, and they would each "do the right thing" based on their real type.

To create a good ADT, you need to have a complete understanding of what sensors do, rather than how they work. For example, are sensors passive devices or are they active? Do they wait for some element to heat up, a wire to break, or a piece of caulk to melt, or do they probe their environment? Perhaps some sensors have only a binary state (triggered or untriggered), but others have a more analog state (what is the current temperature?). The interface to the abstract data type should be sufficiently complete to handle all the anticipated needs of the myriad derived classes.

Other Objects

The design continues in this way, teasing out the other classes that are required to meet the specification. For example, if a log is to be kept, probably a timer is needed; should the timer poll each sensor, or should each sensor file its own report periodically?

The user is going to need to be able to set up, disarm, and program the system, so a terminal of some sort is required. You might want a separate object in your simulation for the alarm program itself.

Designing the Classes

As you solve these problems, you will begin to design your classes. For example, you already have an indication that `HeatSensor` will derive from `Sensor`. If the sensor is to make periodic reports, it might also derive via multiple inheritance from `Timer`, or it might have a timer as a member variable.

The `HeatSensor` will probably have member functions, such as `currentTemp()` and `setTempLimit()`, and probably will inherit functions such as `soundAlarm()` from its base class, `Sensor`.

A frequent issue in object-oriented design is that of encapsulation. You can imagine a design in which the alarm system has a setting for `maxTemp`. The alarm system asks the heat sensor what the current temperature is, compares it to the maximum temperature, and sounds the alarm if it is too hot. One could argue that this violates the principle of encapsulation. Perhaps it would be better if the alarm system didn't know or care about the details of temperature analysis—arguably that should be in the `HeatSensor`.

Whether or not you agree with that argument, it is the kind of decision you want to focus on during the analysis of the design. To continue this analysis, one could argue that only the sensor and the `Log` object should know any details of how sensor activity is logged; the `Alarm` object shouldn't know or care.

Good encapsulation is marked by each class having a coherent and complete set of responsibilities, and no other class having the same responsibilities. If the `Sensor` is responsible for noting the current temperature, no other class should have that responsibility.

On the other hand, other classes might help deliver the necessary functionality. For example, although it might be the responsibility of the `Sensor` class to note and log the current temperature, it might implement that responsibility by delegating to a `Log` object the job of actually recording the data.

Maintaining a firm division of responsibilities makes your program easier to extend and maintain. When you decide to change the alarm system for an enhanced module, its interface to the log and sensors will be narrow and well defined. Changes to the alarm system should not affect the `Sensor` classes, and vice versa.

Should the `HeatSensor` have a `reportAlarm()` function? All sensors will need the capability to report an alarm. This is a good indication that `reportAlarm()` should be a virtual member function of `Sensor`, and that `Sensor` might be an abstract base class. It is possible that `HeatSensor` will chain up to `Sensor`'s more general `reportAlarm()` member function; the overridden function will just fill in the details it is uniquely qualified to supply.

NOTE

For additional information about object-oriented concepts, consider the Addison-Wesley book *The Object-Oriented Thought Process, Fourth Edition* (ISBN: 0-321-86127-2), by Matt Weisfeld.

Adding More Classes

When your sensors report an alarm condition, they want to provide a lot of information to the object that phones the police and to the log. It might well be that you want to create a `Condition` class, whose constructor takes a number of measurements. Depending on the complexity of the measurements, these too might be objects, or they might be simple scalar values such as integers.

It is possible that `Condition` objects are passed to the central alarm object, or that `Condition` objects are subclassed into `Alarm` objects, which themselves know how to take emergency action. Perhaps there is no central object; instead, there might be sensors that know how to create `Condition` objects. Some `Condition` objects would know how to log themselves; others might know how to contact the police.

A well-designed, event-driven system need not have a central coordinator. One can imagine the sensors all independently receiving and sending message objects to one another, setting parameters, taking readings, and monitoring the house. When a fault is detected, an `Alarm` object is created that logs the problem—such as by sending a message to the `Log` object—and takes the appropriate action.

Event Loops

To simulate such an event-driven system, your program needs to create an event loop. An event loop is typically an infinite loop such as `while(true)` that gets messages from the operating system (mouse clicks, keyboard presses, and so on) and dispatches them one at a time, returning to the loop until an exit condition is satisfied. The SimpleEvent program in Listing 22.1 implements a rudimentary event loop.

LISTING 22.1 The Full Text of `SimpleEvent.cpp`

```
#include <iostream>

class Condition
{
public:
    Condition() { }
    virtual ~Condition() {}
    virtual void log() = 0;
};

class Normal : public Condition
{
public:
    Normal() { log(); }
    virtual ~Normal() {}
    virtual void log()
        { std::cout << "Logging normal conditions ...\n"; }
};

class Error : public Condition
{
public:
    Error() { log(); }
    virtual ~Error() {}
    virtual void log() { std::cout << "Logging error!\n"; }
};

class Alarm : public Condition
{
```

```
public:
    Alarm();
    virtual ~Alarm() {}
    virtual void warn() { std::cout << "Warning!\n"; }
    virtual void log() { std::cout << "General alarm log\n"; }
    virtual void call() = 0;
};

Alarm::Alarm()
{
    log();
    warn();
}

class FireAlarm : public Alarm
{
public:
    FireAlarm() { log();};
    virtual ~FireAlarm() {}
    virtual void call() { std::cout<< "Calling fire department!\n"; }
    virtual void log() { std::cout << "Logging fire call\n"; }
};

int main()
{
    int input;
    int okay = 1;
    Condition *pCondition;
    while (okay)
    {
        std::cout << "(0) Quit (1) Normal (2) Fire: ";
        std::cin >> input;
        okay = input;
        switch (input)
        {
        case 0:
            break;
        case 1:
            pCondition = new Normal;
            delete pCondition;
            break;
        case 2:
            pCondition = new FireAlarm;
            delete pCondition;
            break;
        default:
```

```
76:                pCondition = new Error;
77:                delete pCondition;
78:                okay = 0;
79:                break;
80:            }
81:        }
82:        return 0;
83: }
```

The SimpleEvent program takes one of three options as input. Here's one run of the program:

```
(0) Quit (1) Normal (2) Fire: 1
Logging normal conditions ...
(0) Quit (1) Normal (2) Fire: 2
General alarm log
Warning!
Logging fire call
(0) Quit (1) Normal (2) Fire: 0
```

The simple loop on lines 58–81 enables the user to enter input simulating a normal report from a sensor and a report of a fire. Note that the effect of this report is to spawn a `Condition` object whose constructor calls various member functions.

Calling virtual member functions from a constructor can cause confusing results if you are not mindful of the order of the construction of objects. For example, when the `FireAlarm` object is created on line 72, the order of construction is `Condition`, `Alarm`, `FireAlarm`.

The `Alarm` constructor calls `Log`, but it is `Alarm`'s `Log()` constructor that is invoked, not `FireAlarm`'s, despite `Log()` being declared virtual.

This is because at the time `Alarm`'s constructor runs, there is no `FireAlarm` object. Later, when `FireAlarm` itself is constructed, its constructor calls `Log()` again, and this time `FireAlarm::Log()` is called.

PostMaster: A Case Study

Here's another problem on which to practice your object-oriented analytical skills: You have been hired by Defective Software to start a new software project and to hire a team of C++ programmers to implement your program. Sam Snett, vice-president of New Product Development, is your new boss. He wants you to design and build PostMaster, a utility to read email from various providers. The potential customer is a business person who uses more than one email product (for example, Gmail, Yahoo Mail, and Microsoft Outlook).

The customer will be able to configure PostMaster to connect to each of the email providers. PostMaster will get the mail and present it in a uniform manner, enabling the customer to organize the mail, reply, forward letters among services, and so forth.

PostMaster Professional, to be developed as version two of PostMaster, already is anticipated. It will add an administrative assistant mode that will enable the user to designate another person to read some or all of the mail, handle routine correspondence, and so forth. There also is speculation in the marketing department that an artificial-intelligence component might add the capability for PostMaster to pre-sort and prioritize the mail based on subject and content keywords and associations.

Other enhancements have been talked about, including the capability to handle not only mail but discussion groups, such as Internet message boards and mail lists. It is obvious that Defective has great hopes for PostMaster, and you are under severe time constraints to bring it to market, although you seem to have a nearly unlimited budget.

Measure Twice, Cut Once

You set up your office and order your equipment; your first order of business is to get a good specification for the product. After examining the market, you decide to recommend that development be focused on a single platform, and you set out to decide among Linux, Mac OS, and Windows.

You have many painful meetings with Vice President Snett. It becomes clear that there is no right choice, so you decide to separate the front end—that is, the user interface (or UI)—from the back end—the communications and database part. To get things going quickly, you decide to write for Windows, followed later by Mac OS and perhaps Linux.

This simple decision has enormous ramifications for your project. It quickly becomes obvious that you need a class library or a series of libraries to handle memory management, the various user interfaces, and perhaps also the communications and database components.

Snett believes strongly that projects live or die by having one person with a clear vision, so he asks that you do the initial architectural analysis and design before hiring any programmers. You set out to analyze the problem.

Divide and Conquer

It quickly becomes obvious that you have more than one problem to solve. You divide the project into these significant subprojects:

- **Communications**: The capability for the software to dial into the email provider over a network.
- **Database**: The capability to store data and to retrieve it from disk.

- **Email: The** capability to read various email formats and to write new messages to each system.
- **Editing**: State-of-the-art editors for the creation and manipulation of messages.
- **Platform issues**: The various user interface issues presented by each platform.
- **Extensibility**: Planning for growth and enhancements.
- **Organization and scheduling**: Managing the programmers and their code interdependencies. Each group must devise and publish schedules, then be able to plan accordingly. Senior management and marketing need to know when the product will be ready.

You decide to hire a manager to handle one of these items: organization and scheduling. You hire senior developers to help you analyze and design, and then to manage the implementation of the remaining areas. These senior developers will create the following teams:

- **Communications**: Responsible for network communications. They deal with packets, streams, and bits rather than with email messages per se.
- **Message format**: Responsible for converting messages from each email provider to a canonical form (PostMaster standard), and back. It also is this team's job to write these messages to files and to get them back from files as needed.
- **Message editors**: This group is responsible for the entire UI of the product on each platform. It is the editors' job to ensure that the interface between the back end and the front end of the product is sufficiently narrow so that extending the product to other platforms does not require duplication of code.

Message Format

You decide to focus on the message format first, setting aside the issues relating to communications and user interface. These will follow after you understand more fully what it is you are dealing with. There is little sense in worrying about how to present the information to the user until you understand what kind of information it is.

An examination of the email formats reveals that they have many things in common, despite their differences. Each email message has a point of origination, a destination, and a creation date. Nearly all such messages have a title or subject line, and a body that might consist of simple text, rich text (text with formatting), graphics, and perhaps even sound or other fancy additions. Most email services also support attachments so that users can send programs and other files.

You confirm your early decision that you will read each mail message in its original format and transform it into PostMaster format. This way you only will have to store one record format, and writing to and reading from the disk will be simplified. You also decide to separate the header information (sender, recipient, date, title, and so on) from the body of the message. Often the user will want to scan the headers without necessarily reading the contents of all the messages. You anticipate that a time might come when users will want to download only the headers from the message provider, without getting the text at all, but for now you intend that version one of PostMaster always will get the full message, although it might not display it to the user.

Initial Class Design

This analysis of the messages leads you to design the `Message` class. In anticipation of extending the program to non-email messages, you derive `EmailMessage` from the abstract base `Message`. From `EmailMessage` you derive `PostMasterMessage`, `InterchangeMessage`, `OutlookMessage`, `GmailMessage`, and so on.

Messages are a natural choice for objects in a program handling mail messages, but finding all the right objects in a complex system is the greatest challenge of object-oriented programming. In some cases, such as with messages, the primary objects seem to fall out of your understanding of the problem. More often, however, you have to think long and hard about what you are trying to accomplish to find the right objects.

Don't despair. Most designs are not perfect the first time. A good starting point is to describe the problem out loud. Make a list of all the nouns and verbs you use when describing the project. The nouns are good candidates for objects. The verbs might be the functions of those objects (or they might be objects in their own right). This is not a foolproof technique, but it is a good technique to use when getting started on your design.

Now the question arises, "Should the message header be a separate class from the body?" If so, do you need parallel hierarchies—`ForumBody` and `ForumHeader` as well as `EmailBody` and `EmailHeader`?

Parallel hierarchies often are a warning sign of a bad design. It is a common error in object-oriented design to have a set of objects in one hierarchy and a matching set of manager objects in another. The burden of keeping these hierarchies up-to-date and in sync with each other soon becomes overwhelming: a classic maintenance nightmare.

There are no hard-and-fast rules to designing a class hierarchy, of course, and at times parallel hierarchies are the most efficient way to solve a particular problem. Nonetheless, if you see your design moving in this direction, you should rethink the problem because a more elegant solution might be available.

When the messages arrive from the email provider, they will not necessarily be separated into header and body; many will be one large stream of data that your program will have to disentangle. Perhaps your hierarchy should reflect that idea directly.

Further reflection on the tasks at hand leads youto list the properties of these messages, with an eye toward introducing capabilities and data storage at the right level of abstraction. Listing properties of your objects is a good way to find the data members, as well as to shake out other objects you might need.

Mail messages will need to be stored, as will the user's preferences, phone numbers, and so forth. Storage clearly needs to be high up the hierarchy. Should the mail messages necessarily share a base class with the preferences?

Rooted Hierarchies Versus Non-Rooted

There are two overall approaches to inheritance hierarchies: You can have all, or nearly all, of your classes descend from a common root class, or you can have more than one inheritance hierarchy. An advantage of a common root class is that you often can avoid multiple inheritance; a disadvantage is that many times implementation will climb up into the base class.

A set of classes is rooted if all share a common ancestor. Non-rooted hierarchies do not all share a common base class.

Because you know that your product will be developed on many platforms, and because multiple inheritance is complex and not necessarily well supported by all compilers on all platforms, your first decision is to use a rooted hierarchy and single inheritance. You decide to identify those places where multiple inheritance might be used in the future. You then can design so that breaking apart the hierarchy and adding multiple inheritance at a later time need not be traumatic to your entire design.

You decide to prefix the name of all your internal classes with the letter `p`, so that you can easily and quickly tell which classes are yours and which are from other libraries.

Your root class will be `pObject`. Nearly every class you create will descend from this object. `pObject` itself will be kept fairly simple; only the data that absolutely every item shares will appear in this class.

If you want a rooted hierarchy, you should give the root class a fairly generic name (like `pObject`) and few capabilities. The point of a root object is to be able to create collections of all its descendants and refer to them as instances of `pObject`. The trade-off is that rooted hierarchies often push the interface up into the root class.

The next likely candidates for top-of-the-hierarchy status are `pStored` and `pWired`. `pStored` objects are saved to a file at various times (for example, when the program is not in use), and pWired objects are sent over the network. Because nearly all your objects will need to be stored to files, it makes sense to push this functionality high up in the hierarchy. All the objects that are sent over the network must be stored, but not all stored objects must be sent over the network, so it makes sense to derive pWired from pStored.

Each derived class acquires all the knowledge (data) and functionality (member functions) of its base class, and each should have at least one discrete additional capability. Thus, pWired might add various functions, but all these functions are designed to facilitate transfer of data over a modem.

It is possible that all wired objects are stored, or that all stored objects are wired, or that neither of those statements is true. If only some wired objects are stored, and only some stored objects are wired, you will be forced either to use multiple inheritance or to design around the problem. A potential hack for such a situation would be to inherit Wired from Stored, then make the stored functions do nothing or return an error for those objects that are sent over a network but never stored.

In fact, you realize that some stored objects clearly are not wired (for example, user preferences). All wired objects, however, are stored, so your inheritance hierarchy so far is as reflected in Figure 22.1.

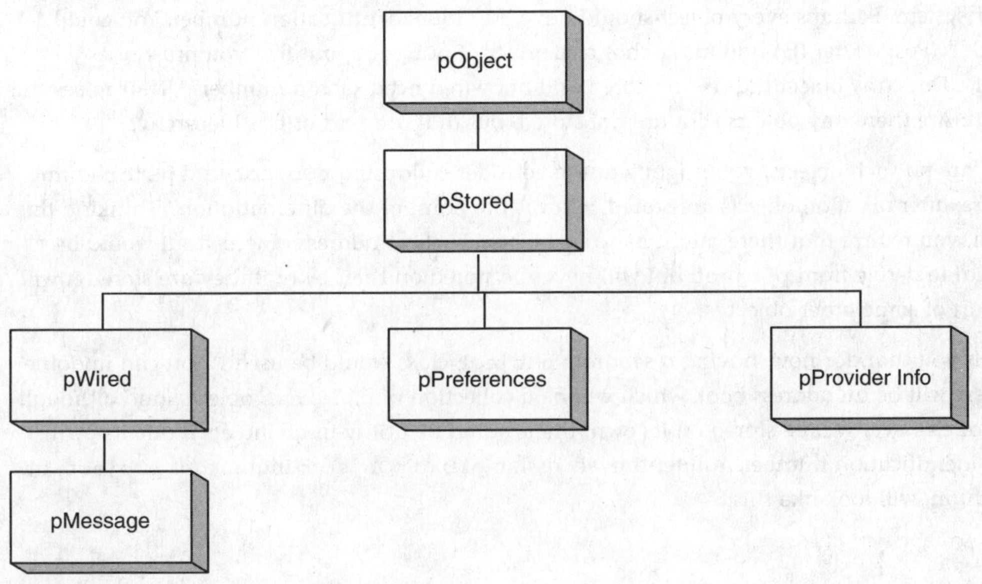

FIGURE 22.1
Initial inheritance hierarchy.

NOTE

One question you will confront throughout the design phase of your program is which routines you might buy and which you must write yourself. It is entirely possible that you can take advantage of existing commercial libraries to solve some or all of your communications issues. Licensing fees and other non-technical concerns must also be resolved.

It often is advantageous to purchase such a third-party library, and to focus your energies on your specific program rather than to reinvent the wheel about secondary technical issues. You might even want to consider purchasing libraries that were not necessarily intended for use with C++, if they can provide fundamental functionality you'd otherwise have to engineer yourself. This can be instrumental in helping you hit your deadlines.

Designing the Interfaces

It is important, at this stage of designing your product, to avoid being concerned with implementation. You want to focus all your energies on designing a clean interface among the classes, then delineating what data and member functions each class will need.

It often is a good idea to have a solid understanding of the base classes before trying to design the more derived classes, so you decide to focus first on `pObject`, `pStored`, and `pWired`.

The root class, `pObject`, only will have those data and functions that are common to everything on your system. Perhaps every object should have a unique identification number. You could create `pID` (PostMaster ID) and make that a member of `pObject`; but first you must ask yourself, "Does any object that is not stored and not wired need such a number?" That raises this question: Are there any objects that are not stored, but that are part of this hierarchy?

If there are no such objects, you might want to consider collapsing `pObject` and `pStored` into one class; after all, if all objects are stored, what is the point of the differentiation? Thinking this through, you realize that there might be some objects, such as address objects, that would be beneficial to derive from `pObject` but will never be stored on their own; if they are stored it will be as part of some other object.

This tells you that, for now, having a separate `pObject` class would be useful. You can imagine that there will be an address book which will be a collection of `pAddress` objects, and although no `pAddress` ever will be stored on its own, there would be utility in giving each one its own unique identification number. You tentatively assign `pID` to `pObject`; that means `pObject`, at a minimum, will look like this:

```
class pOjbect
{
public:
   pObject();
   ~pObject();
```

```
    pID GetID() const;
    void SetID();
private:
    pID itsID;
}
```

Take note of a number of things about this class declaration. First, this class is not declared to derive from any other; this is your root class. Second, there is no attempt to show implementation, even for member functions such as `GetID()` that are likely to have inline implementation when you are done.

Third, `const` member functions already are identified; this is part of the interface, not the implementation. Finally, a new data type is implied: `pID`. Defining `pID` as a type rather than using something such as an `unsigned long` makes your design more flexible.

Perhaps `pID` will use an `unsigned long` internally to represent the PostMaster ID. This is still a better approach than making the ID an `unsigned long` integer in the class `pObject`. If it turns out that you don't need an `unsigned long`, or that an `unsigned long` is not sufficiently large, you can modify `pID`. That modification will affect every place `pID` is used, and you won't have to track down and edit every file with a `pID` in it.

For now, you use `typedef` to declare `pID` to be `ULONG` which, in turn, you declare to be `unsigned long`. This raises the question: Where do these declarations go?

When programming a large project, an overall design of the files is needed. A standard approach, one that you are following on this project, is that each class appears in its own header file and the implementation for the class member functions appears in an associated `.cpp` file. Therefore, you will have a file called `Object.hpp` and another called `Object.cpp`. You anticipate having other files such as `Message.hpp` and `Message.cpp` with the declaration of `pMessage` and the implementation of its functions, respectively.

Building a Prototype

For a project as large as PostMaster, it is unlikely that your initial design will be complete and perfect. It would be easy to become overwhelmed by the sheer scale of the problem, and trying to create all of the classes and to complete their interface before writing a line of working code is a recipe for disaster.

There are a number of good reasons to try out your design on a prototype—a quick-and-dirty working example of your core ideas. There are a number of different types of prototypes, each meeting different needs.

An interface design prototype provides the chance to test the look and feel of your product with potential users.

A functionality prototype does not have the final user interface, but enables users to try out various features, such as forwarding messages or attaching files.

Finally, an architecture prototype might be designed to give you a chance to develop a smaller version of the program and to assess how easily your design decisions will scale up as the program is fleshed out.

It is imperative to keep your prototyping goals clear. Are you examining the user interface, experimenting with functionality, or building a scale model of your final product? A good architecture prototype makes a poor user interface prototype, and vice versa.

It also is important to keep an eye on overengineering the prototype, or becoming so concerned with the investment you've made in the prototype that you are reluctant to tear down the code and redesign as you progress.

The 80/80 Rule

A good design rule of thumb at this stage is to design for those things that 80% of the people want to do 80% of the time, and to set aside your concerns about the remaining 20%. The boundary conditions will need to be addressed sooner or later, but the core of your design should focus on the 80/80.

Accordingly, you might decide to start by designing the principal classes, setting aside the need for the secondary classes. Further, when you identify multiple classes that will have similar designs with only minor refinements, you might choose to pick one representative class and focus on that, leaving until later the design and implementation of its close cousins.

NOTE

There is another rule, the 80/20 rule, that states this: The first 20 percent of your program will take 80 percent of your time to code; the remaining 80 percent of your program will take the other 80 percent of your time!

The real rule is that 80 percent of the time is required to do 20 percent of the work—or that 80 percent of a company's profit will come from 20 percent of the customers. This rule has wide application.

Designing the `PostMasterMessage` Class

In keeping with these considerations, you decide to focus on `PostMasterMessage`, the class most directly under your control.

As part of its interface, `PostMasterMessage` needs to talk with other types of messages, of course. You hope to be able to work closely with the other message providers, and to get their message format specifications, but for now you can make some smart guesses just by observing what is sent to your computer as you use their services.

In any case, you know that every PostMasterMessage will have a sender, a recipient, a date, and a subject, as well as the body of the message and perhaps attached files. This tells you that you'll need accessors for each of these attributes, as well as member functions to report on the size of the attached files, the size of the messages, and so forth.

Some of the services to which you will connect use rich text—text with formatting instructions to set the font, character size, and attributes such as bold and italic. Other services do not support these attributes, and those that do might use their own proprietary scheme for managing rich text. Your class needs conversion functions for turning rich text into plain ASCII, and perhaps for turning other formats into PostMaster formats.

The Application Programming Interface

An application programming interface (API) is a set of documentation and functions for using a service. Many of the mail providers will give you an API so that PostMaster mail can take advantage of their more advanced features, such as rich text and embedding files. You also want to publish an API for PostMaster so that other providers can plan for working with PostMaster in the future.

Your PostMasterMessage class needs to have a well-designed public interface, and the conversion functions will be a principal component of PostMaster's API. Listing 22.2 illustrates what PostMasterMessage's interface looks like so far.

CAUTION

Because this listing does not define the base class (MailMessage), it will not compile.

LISTING 22.2 The Full Text of PostMasterMessage.cpp

```
class PostMasterMessage : public MailMessage
{
public:
      PostMasterMessage();
      PostMasterMessage(
            pAddress sender,
            pAddress recipient,
            pString subject,
            pDate creationDate);

      // other constructors here
      // remember to include copy constructor
      // as well as constructor from storage
      // and constructor from wire format
      // Also include constructors from other formats
      ~PostMasterMessage();
```

```
    pAddress& getSender() const;
    void setSender(pAddress&);
    // other member accessors
    // operator functions here, including operator equals
    // and conversion routines to turn PostMaster messages
    // into messages of other formats.

private:
    pAddress sender;
    pAddress recipient;
    pString  subject;
    pDate creationDate;
    pDate lastModDate;
    pDate receiptDate;
    pDate firstReadDate;
    pDate lastReadDate;
};
```

Class `PostMasterMessage` is declared to derive from `MailMessage`. A number of constructors will be provided, facilitating the creation of `PostMasterMessage` objects from other types of mail messages.

A number of accessors are anticipated for reading and setting the various member data, as well as operators for turning all or part of a message into other message formats. You anticipate storing these messages to files and reading them from the wire, so accessors are needed for those purposes as well.

Programming in Large Groups

Even this preliminary architecture is enough to indicate how your development groups ought to proceed. The Communications group can go ahead and start work on the communications back end, negotiating a narrow interface with the Message Format group.

The Message Format group will probably lay out the general interface to the `Message` classes, a process you already began, and then will turn its attention to the question of how to write data to a file and read it back. After this file interface is well understood, the team will be in a good position to negotiate the interface to the communications layer.

The message editors will be tempted to create editors with an intimate knowledge of the internals of the message class, but this would be a bad design mistake. They too must negotiate a very narrow interface to the message class; message editor objects should know very little about the internal structure of messages.

Ongoing Design Considerations

As the project continues, you will repeatedly confront this basic design issue: In which class should you put a given set of functionality (or information)? Should the message class have this function, or should the address class? Should the editor store this information, or should the message store it itself?

Your classes should operate on a need-to-know basis, much like international super spies. They shouldn't share any more knowledge than absolutely necessary.

As you progress with your program, you will face hundreds of design issues. They will range from the more global questions, "What do we want this to do?" to the more specific, "How do we make this work?"

Although the details of your implementation won't be finalized until you ship the code, and some of the interfaces will continue to shift and change as you work, you must ensure that your design is well understood early in the process. It is imperative that you know what you are trying to build before you write the code. The single most frequent cause of software projects dying on the vine must be that there is not sufficient agreement, early enough in the process, about what is being built.

To get a feel for what the design process is like, examine this question: What will be on the menu? For PostMaster, the first choice is probably New Mail Message, and this raises another design issue: When the user selects New Mail Message, what happens? Does an editor get created, which in turn creates a mail message, or does a new mail message get created, which then creates the editor?

The command you are working with is New Mail Message, so creating a new mail message seems like the obvious thing to do. But what happens if the user clicks Cancel after starting to write the message? Perhaps it would be cleaner to first create the editor and have it create (and own) the new message.

The problem with this approach is that the editor will need to act differently if it is creating a message than if it is editing the message. If the message is created first, then handed to the editor, only one set of code needs to exist because everything is an edit of an existing message.

If a message is created first, who creates it? Is it created by the menu command code? If so, does the menu also tell the message to edit itself, or is this part of the constructor of the message?

It makes sense for the constructor to do this at first glance; after all, every time you create a message you'll probably want to edit it. Nonetheless, this is not a good design idea. First, it is possible that the premise is wrong; you might create "canned" messages (for instance, automatic error messages mailed to the system operator) that are not put into an editor. Second, and more importantly, a constructor's job is to create an object; it should do no more and no less than that. After a mail message is created, the constructor's job is done. Adding a call to the edit function just confuses the role of the constructor and makes the mail message vulnerable to failures in the editor.

Worse yet, the edit function will call another class—the editor—causing its constructor to be called. But the editor is not a base class of the message, nor is it contained within the message. It would be unfortunate if the construction of the message depended on successful construction of the editor.

Finally, you won't want to call the editor at all if the message can't be successfully created; yet successful creation would, in this scenario, depend on calling the editor! Clearly, the best approach is to fully return from message's constructor before calling `Message::Edit()`.

This is the kind of design decision you'll need to make repeatedly, and the designs you make will play a major role in whether the software is reliable, error-free, and maintainable.

Working with Driver Programs

One approach to bringing design issues to the surface quickly is to create a driver program early in the process. A driver program is one that exists only to test other objects and their member functions. For example, the driver program for PostMaster might offer a simple menu that will create `PostMasterMessage` objects, manipulate them, and otherwise exercise some of the design. Another term for this is a *test harness.*

Listing 22.3 illustrates a somewhat more robust definition of the `PostMasterMessage` class and a simple driver program. Because the program is so long, it contains a lot of comments to help explain what the code is doing.

LISTING 22.3 The Full Text of `Driver.cpp`

```
#include <iostream>
#include <string.h>

typedef unsigned long pDate;

enum SERVICE { PostMaster, Interchange,
     Gmail, Hotmail, AOL, Internet };

class String
{
public:
     // constructors
     String();
     String(const char *const);
     String(const String&);
```

```
    ~String();

    // overloaded operators
    char& operator[](int offset);
    char operator[](int offset) const;
    String operator+(const String&);
    void operator+=(const String&);
    String& operator=(const String&);
    friend std::ostream& operator<<
        (std::ostream& stream, String& newString);
    // General accessors
    int getLen() const { return len; }
    const char* getString() const { return string; }
    // static int constructorCount;

private:
    String(int); // private constructor
    char* string;
    int len;
};

// default constructor creates string of 0 bytes
String::String()
{
    string = new char[1];
    string[0] = '\0';
    len = 0;
    // std::cout << "\tDefault string constructor\n";
    // constructorCount++;
}

// private (helper) constructor, used only by
// class functions for creating a new string of
// required size.  Null filled.
String::String(int newLen)
{
    string = new char[newLen + 1];
    int i;
    for (i = 0; i <= newLen; i++)
        string[1] = '\0';
    len = newLen;
    // std::cout << "\tString(int) constructor\n";
    // constructorCount++;
}

// Converts a character array to a String
String::String(const char* const cString)
{
```

```
    len = strlen(cString);
    string = new char[len + 1];
    int i;
    for (i = 0; i < len; i++)
        string[i] = cString[i];
    string[len]='\0';
    // std::cout << "\tString(char*) constructor\n";
    // constructorCount++;
}

// copy constructor
String::String(const String &rhs)
{
    len = rhs.getLen();
    string = new char[len + 1];
    int i;
    for (i = 0; i < len; i++)
        string[i] = rhs[i];
    string[len] = '\0';
    // std::cout << "\tString(String&) constructor\n";
    // constructorCount++;
}

// destructor, frees allocated memory
String::~String ()
{
    delete [] string;
    len = 0;
    // std::cout << "\tString destructor\n";
}

String& String::operator=(const String &rhs)
{
    if (this == &rhs)
        return *this;
    delete [] string;
    len = rhs.getLen();
    string = new char[len + 1];
    int i;
    for (i = 0; i < len; i++)
        string[i] = rhs[i];
    string[len] = '\0';
    return *this;
    // std::cout << "\tString operator=\n";
}

//non constant offset operator, returns
// reference to character so it can be changed
```

```
char &String::operator[](int offset)
{
    if (offset > len)
        return string[len - 1];
    else
        return string[offset];
}

// constant offset operator for use
// on const objects (see copy constructor!)
char String::operator[](int offset) const
{
    if (offset > len)
        return string[len - 1];
    else
        return string[offset];
}

// creates a new string by adding current
// string to rhs
String String::operator+(const String& rhs)
{
    int  totalLen = len + rhs.getLen();
    String temp(totalLen);
    int i, j;
    for (i = 0; i < len; i++)
        temp[i] = string[i];
    for (j = 0; j < rhs.getLen(); j++, i++)
        temp[i] = rhs[j];
    temp[totalLen]='\0';
    return temp;
}

// changes current string, returns nothing
void String::operator+=(const String& rhs)
{
    int rhsLen = rhs.getLen();
    int totalLen = len + rhsLen;
    String  temp(totalLen);
    int i, j;
    for (i = 0; i < len; i++)
        temp[i] = string[i];
    for ( j = 0; j < rhs.getLen(); j++, i++)
        temp[i] = rhs[i - len];
    temp[totalLen]='\0';
    *this = temp;
}

```

```
// int String::ConstructorCount = 0;

std::ostream& operator<<(std::ostream& stream,
                         String& newString)
{
    stream << newString.getString();
    return stream;
}

class pAddress
{
public:
    pAddress(SERVICE newService,
            const String& newAddress,
            const String& newDisplay):
        service(newService),
        addressString(newAddress),
        displayString(newDisplay)
    {}
    // pAddress(String, String);
    // pAddress();
    // pAddress(const pAddress&);
    ~pAddress(){}
    friend std::ostream& operator<<(
      std::ostream& stream, pAddress& address);
    String& getDisplayString()
    { return displayString; }
private:
    SERVICE service;
    String addressString;
    String displayString;
};

std::ostream& operator<<
  ( std::ostream& stream, pAddress& address)
{
    stream << address.getDisplayString();
    return stream;
}

class PostMasterMessage
{
public:
//  PostMasterMessage();

    PostMasterMessage(const pAddress& newSender,
                      const pAddress& newRecipient,
                      const String& newSubject,
```

```
                    const pDate& newCreationDate);

      ~PostMasterMessage(){}

    void Edit(); // invokes editor on this message

    pAddress& getSender()  { return sender; }
    pAddress& getRecipient()  { return recipient; }
    String& getSubject()  { return subject; }
    //  void setSender(pAddress& );
    // other member accessors

    // operator functions here, including operator equals
    // and conversion routines to turn PostMaster messages
    // into messages of other formats.

private:
    pAddress sender;
    pAddress recipient;
    String  subject;
    pDate creationDate;
    pDate lastModDate;
    pDate receiptDate;
    pDate firstReadDate;
    pDate lastReadDate;
};

PostMasterMessage::PostMasterMessage(
    const pAddress& newSender,
    const pAddress& newRecipient,
    const String& newSubject,
    const pDate& newCreationDate):
    sender(newSender),
    recipient(newRecipient),
    subject(newSubject),
    creationDate(newCreationDate),
    lastModDate(newCreationDate),
    firstReadDate(0),
    lastReadDate(0)
{
    std::cout << "Postmaster message created. \n";
}

void PostMasterMessage::Edit()
{
    std::cout << "Postmaster message edit function called\n";
}
```

```
256:
257: int main()
258: {
259:     pAddress sender(
260:         PostMaster, "james@ekzemplo.com", "James");
261:     pAddress recipient(
262:         PostMaster, "sharon@ekzemplo.com","Sharon");
263:     PostMasterMessage postMasterMessage(
264:         sender, recipient, "Greetings", 0);
265:     std::cout << "Message review... \n";
266:     std::cout << "From:\t\t"
267:         << postMasterMessage.getSender() << "\n";
268:     std::cout << "To:\t\t"
269:         << postMasterMessage.getRecipient() << "\n";
270:     std::cout << "Subject:\t"
271:         << postMasterMessage.getSubject() << "\n";
272:     return 0;
273: }
```

Here's the output:

```
Postmaster message created.
Message review...
From:           James
To:             Sharon
Subject:        Greetings
```

On line 4, `pDate` is type-defined to be an `unsigned long`. It is somewhat uncommon for dates to be stored as a long integer, typically as the number of seconds since an arbitrary starting date, such as January 1, 1900. In this program, the `long` integer used as a date is a placeholder; you expect to eventually turn `pDate` into a real class.

On lines 6–7, an enumerated constant, `SERVICE`, is defined to enable the address objects to keep track of what type of address they are, including PostMaster, Gmail, and so forth.

Lines 9–167 represent the interface to and implementation of `String`, which is close to what you have seen for this functionality in previous chapters. The `String` class is used for a number of member variables in all the message classes and in other classes used by messages, and as such, it is pivotal in your program. A full and robust `String` class will be essential to making your message classes complete.

On lines 169–191, the `pAddress` class is declared. This represents only the fundamental functionality of this class, and you would expect to flesh this out after your program is better understood. These objects represent essential components in every message: both the sender's address and that of the recipient. A fully functional `pAddress` object will be able to handle forwarding messages, replies, and so forth.

It is the pAddress object's job to keep track of both the display string and the internal routing string for its service. One unresolved question for your design is whether there should be one pAddress object, or whether it should be subclassed for each service type. For now, the service is tracked as an enumerated constant that is a member variable of each pAddress object.

Lines 200–233 represent the interface to the PostMasterMessage class. In this particular listing, this class stands on its own, but soon you'll want to make this part of its inheritance hierarchy. When you do redesign this to inherit from Message, some of the member variables might move into the base classes, and some of the member functions might override base class member functions.

Other constructors, accessors, and member functions will be required to make this class fully functional. This program shows that your class does not have to be 100% complete before you can write a simple driver program to test some of your assumptions.

On lines 251–254, the Edit() function is stubbed out in just enough detail to indicate where the editing functionality will be put after this class is fully operational.

Lines 257–273 represent the driver program. Currently, this program does nothing more than exercise a few of the accessor functions and the operator<< overload. Nonetheless, this gives you the starting point for experimenting with PostMasterMessages and a framework within which you can modify these classes and examine the impact.

Summary

Prior to the development of these object-oriented techniques, analysts and programmers tended to think of programs as functions that acted on data.

Object-oriented programming focuses on the integrated data and functionality as discrete units that have both knowledge (data) and capabilities (functions).

A thorough grounding in the methodology of object-oriented programming, coupled with time devoted to the design process for a program before a single line of code is written, is necessary to develop robust and efficient C++ software.

Q&A

Q. Is object-oriented programming finally the silver bullet that will solve all programming problems?

A. Yes! All of the toughest challenges of programming can be met. Let there be great rejoicing in the streets, and in the pubs, and in the computer labs. The glorious age of OOP is upon us and shall last a thousand and thousand years.

Excuse me. I got a bit carried away there.

No methodology in programming will solve all problems, of course. But for large, complex problems, however, object-oriented analysis, design, and programming can provide the programmer with tools to manage enormous complexity in ways that were previously impossible.

Q. What is the systematic IUPAC name for a carboxylic acid with a potassium ion in place of the acid hydrogen?

A. Potassium octanoate, according to professor Henri Favre, the chairman of the Commission on Nomenclature of Organic Chemistry for IUPAC, the International Union of Pure and Applied Chemistry.

"There is no specific use for this corrosive acid," Favre told me.

IUPAC is a scientific council that recommends names for chemicals, atomic weights, and related areas of study. In 2004, the group participated in the decision to name atomic element 111 roentgenium after German physicist Wilhelm Conrad Röntgen.

Workshop

You spent the past hour learning about object-oriented analysis and design. You can now answer a few questions and undertake exercises to lock in what you have learned.

Quiz

1. What is it called when you determine what end users want a not-yet-developed program to do?

A. Precoding

B. Requirement gathering

C. Analysis

2. What does API stand for?

A. Automated programming input

B. Application programming interface

C. Awesome Programmers International

3. What function name overrides the insertion operator?

A. `operator<<`

B. `operator>>`

C. It cannot be overridden.

Answers

1. **B.** A lot needs to be done before coding starts: requirement gathering (what does the end user want?), analysis (what is needed to fulfill those requirements), and design (how will we meet those requirements?).
2. **B.** An API is the set of documentation and functions for using a service. You don't get to know how the code is working, just how to use it. The implementation details are hidden from you.
3. **A.** The insertion operator `<<` inserts data into an output stream.

Activities

1. In the SimpleEvent program in Listing 22.1, add a `std::cout` message to each destructor to find out when the destructors are called.
2. Create a class hierarchy of chess pieces with a base class for each type of move possible and derived classes for each type of piece.

To see solutions to these activities, visit this book's website at http://cplusplus.cadenhead.org.

HOUR 23

Creating Templates

What You'll Learn in This Hour:

- What templates are and how to use them
- Why templates are a better alternative to macros
- How to create class templates

What Are Templates?

In Hour 19, "Storing Information in Linked Lists," you learned how to make a linked list. Your linked list was encapsulated: The list knew only about its head pointer; the head pointer delegated its work to internal pointers, and so forth.

One design weakness of the linked list was that it only knew how to handle the data types it was created to work with. If you wanted to put anything else into your linked list, you couldn't do it. You couldn't, for example, make a linked list of `Car` objects, or of `Robot` objects, or any other object that wasn't of the same type as those in the original list.

The old way of solving this problem was to create new versions of the object for each new data type. A more object-oriented way is to create a `List` base class and derive from it the `CarList` and `RobotList` classes. You then can cut and paste much of the `LinkedList` class into the new `RobotList` declaration. In the future, however, when you want to make a list of `Car` objects, you have to make a new class and repeat most of the same code.

Neither of these are satisfactory solutions. Over time, the `List` class and its derived classes will have to be extended. Making sure that all the changes are propagated to all the related classes will be a nightmare.

Templates, a relatively new addition to C++, offer a solution to this problem. Unlike old-fashioned macros, templates are an integrated part of the language, are type-safe, and very flexible.

Templates enable you to create a general class and pass types as parameters to the template to build specific instances of the parameterized type.

Instances of the Template

Templates enable you to teach the compiler how to make a list of any type of thing, instead of creating a set of type-specific lists. A `PartsList` is a list of parts; a `RobotList` is a list of robots. The only way in which they differ is the type of the thing on the list. With templates, the type of the thing on the list becomes a parameter to the definition of the class.

The act of creating an object from a class or a specific type from a template is called instantiation, and the individual classes are called instances of the template.

Template Definition

You declare a parameterized `List` object (a template for a list) with the `template` keyword, as in this code:

```
template <class T> // declare the template and the parameter
class List         // the class being parameterized
{
public:
   List();
   // full class declaration here
};
```

The keyword `template` is used at the beginning of every declaration and definition of a template class. The template's parameters follow the keyword `template`; they are the items that will change with each instance. For example, in the list template shown in this code, the type of the objects stored in the list will change. One instance might store a list of `Integer` objects, another a list of `Animal` objects.

In this code, the keyword `class` is used, followed by the identifier `T`. The keyword `class` indicates that this parameter is a type. The identifier `T` is used throughout the rest of the template definition to refer to the parameterized type. One instance of this class will substitute `int` everywhere `T` appears, and another will substitute `Robot`.

To declare an `int` and a `Robot` instance of the parameterized list class, you would write the following:

```
List<int> intList;
List<Robot> robotList;
```

The object `intList` is of the type list of integers; the object `robotList` is a list of `Robot` objects. You now can use the type `List<int>` anywhere you would normally use a type—as the return value from a function, as a parameter to a function, and so forth.

The ParamList program (Listing 23.1) parameterizes the `List` object. This is an excellent technique for building templates: Get your object working on a single type, as we did in Hour 19. Then by parameterizing, generalize your object to handle any type.

LISTING 23.1 The Full Text of `ParamList.cpp`

```
#include <iostream>

enum { kIsSmaller, kIsLarger, kIsSame};

// Any class in this linked list must support two
// functions: show (displays the value) and compare
// (returns relative position).
class Data
{
public:
    Data(int newVal):value(newVal) {}
    ~Data()
    {
        std::cout << "Deleting Data object with value: ";
        std::cout << value << "\n";
    }
    int compare(const Data&);
    void show() { std::cout << value << "\n"; }
private:
    int value;
};

// A function that decides where in the list a
// particular object belongs.
int Data::compare(const Data& otherObject)
{
    if (value < otherObject.value)
        return kIsSmaller;
    if (value > otherObject.value)
        return kIsLarger;
    else
        return kIsSame;
}

// Another class to put into the linked list.
class Robot
{
public:
    Robot(int newAge): age(newAge) {}
    ~Robot()
    {
```

```
        std::cout << "Deleting ";
        std::cout << age << "-year-old robot.\n";
    }
    int compare(const Robot&);
    void show()
    {
        std::cout << "This robot is ";
        std::cout << age << " years old\n";
    }
private:
    int age;
};

// This class compares a different value than Data.
int Robot::compare(const Robot& otherRobot)
{
    if (age < otherRobot.age)
        return kIsSmaller;
    if (age > otherRobot.age)
        return kIsLarger;
    else
        return kIsSame;
}

// An ADT representing the node object in the list.
// Every derived class must override insert() and show().
template <class T>
class Node
{
public:
    Node(){}
    virtual ~Node() {}
    virtual Node* insert(T* object) = 0;
    virtual void show() = 0;
private:
};

template <class T>
class InternalNode: public Node<T>
{
public:
    InternalNode(T* object, Node<T>* next);
    ~InternalNode(){ delete next; delete object; }
    virtual Node<T> * insert(T * object);
    virtual void show()
    {
        object->show();
        next->show();
```

```
    } // delegate!
private:
    T* object;        // the object itself
    Node<T>* next; // points to next node in the linked list
};

// a simple constructor
template <class T>
InternalNode<T>::InternalNode(T* newObject, Node<T>* newNext):
object(newObject),next(newNext)
{
}

// A function to store a new object in the list.
// The object is passed to the node which figures out
// where it goes and inserts it into the list.
template <class T>
Node<T>* InternalNode<T>::insert(T* newObject)
{
    // is the new object bigger or smaller than me?
    int result = object->compare(*newObject);

    switch(result)
    {
    // if it is the same as me it goes first
    case kIsSame:   // fall through
    case kIsLarger: // new object comes before me
        {
            InternalNode<T>* objectNode =
                new InternalNode<T>(newObject, this);
            return objectNode;
        }
    // it is bigger, so pass it on to the next
    // node and let it handle it.
    case kIsSmaller:
        next = next->insert(newObject);
        return this;
    }
    return this;  // appease the compiler
}

// The last node in the list
template <class T>
class TailNode : public Node<T>
{
public:
    TailNode() {}
    virtual ~TailNode() {}
```

```
    virtual Node<T>* insert(T * object);
    virtual void show() { }
private:
};

// If object comes to me, it must be inserted before me
// since nothing goes after the tail
template <class T>
Node<T>* TailNode<T>::insert(T * object)
{
    InternalNode<T>* objectNode =
    new InternalNode<T>(object, this);
    return objectNode;
}

// The head node, which holds no data but instead points
// to the beginning of the list.
template <class T>
class HeadNode : public Node<T>
{
public:
    HeadNode();
    virtual ~HeadNode() { delete next; }
    virtual Node<T>* insert(T * object);
    virtual void show() { next->show(); }
private:
    Node<T> * next;
};

// The first node in the list, which creates the tail
template <class T>
HeadNode<T>::HeadNode()
{
    next = new TailNode<T>;
}

// Since nothing comes before the head, just pass
// the object on to the next node
template <class T>
Node<T> * HeadNode<T>::insert(T* object)
{
    next = next->insert(object);
    return this;
}

// I get all the credit and do none of the work.
template <class T>
class LinkedList
```

```
{
public:
    LinkedList();
    ~LinkedList() { delete head; }
    void insert(T* object);
    void showAll() { head->show(); }
private:
    HeadNode<T> * head;
};

// At birth, I create the head node, which creates
// the tail node.
template <class T>
LinkedList<T>::LinkedList()
{
    head = new HeadNode<T>;
}

// Delegate to a head node
template <class T>
void LinkedList<T>::insert(T* pObject)
{
    head->insert(pObject);
}

// put all these classes to the test
int main()
{
    Robot* pRobot;
    Data* pData;
    int val;
    LinkedList<Robot> listOfRobots;
    LinkedList<Data> listOfData;

    // store user values in a linked list
    while (true)
    {
        std::cout << "What value (0 to stop)? ";
        std::cin >> val;
        if (!val)
            break;
        pRobot = new Robot(val);
        pData = new Data(val);
        listOfRobots.insert(pRobot);
        listOfData.insert(pData);
    }

    // display the list
```

```
    std::cout << "\n";
    listOfRobots.showAll();
    std::cout << "\n";
    listOfData.showAll();
    std::cout << "\n ************ \n\n";
    return 0;
}
```

The ParamList program asks for a series of values that will be used to set the ages of `Robot` objects. It then uses the same values to create `Data` objects. The objects are sorted by the integer value they hold in ascending order. Here's the output for a run where 9, 15, and 7 were the values entered:

```
What value (0 to stop)? 9
What value (0 to stop)? 15
What value (0 to stop)? 7
What value (0 to stop)? 0

This robot is 7 years old
This robot is 9 years old
This robot is 15 years old

7
9
15

 ************

Deleting Data object with value: 15
Deleting Data object with value: 9
Deleting Data object with value: 7
Deleting 15-year-old robot.
Deleting 9-year-old robot.
Deleting 7-year-old robot.
```

The program contains a lot of the same code as the LinkedList program in Hour 19.

The biggest change is that each of the class declarations and member functions is now preceded by

```
template class <T>
```

This tells the compiler that you are parameterizing this list on a type that you will define later, when you instantiate the list. For example, the declaration of the `Node` class now becomes

```
template <class T>
class Node
```

This indicates that `Node` will not exist as a class in itself, but rather that you will instantiate `Node`s of `Robot`s and `Node`s of `Data` objects. The actual type you'll pass in is represented by `T`.

Thus, `InternalNode` now becomes `InternalNode<T>` (read that as "`InternalNode` of `T`"). And `InternalNode<T>` points not to a `Data` object and another `Node`; rather, it points to a `T` (whatever type of object) and a `Node<T>`. You can see this on lines 118–119.

Look carefully at the `insert()` function defined on lines 107–129. The logic is just the same, but where we used to have a specific type (`Data`) we now have `T`. Thus, on line 107 the parameter is a pointer to a `T`. Later, when we instantiate the specific lists, the `T` will be replaced by the compiler with the right type (`Data` or `Robot`).

The important thing is that the `InternalNode` can continue working, indifferent to the actual type. It knows to ask the objects to compare themselves. It doesn't care whether `Robot` objects compare themselves in the same way `Data` objects do. In fact, we can rewrite this so that `Robot` objects don't keep their age. We can have them keep their birth date and compute their relative age on-the-fly, and the `InternalNode` won't care a bit.

Using Template Items

You can treat template items as you would any other type. You can pass them as parameters, either by reference or by value, and you can return them as the return values of functions, also by value or by reference.

The TemplateList program in Listing 23.2 demonstrates how to pass `Template` objects. Compare the following listing with the code in Listing 23.1.

LISTING 23.2 The Full Text of `TemplateList.cpp`

```
#include <iostream>

enum { kIsSmaller, kIsLarger, kIsSame};

class Data
{
public:
    Data(int newVal):value(newVal) {}
    ~Data()
    {
        std::cout << "Deleting Data object with value: ";
        std::cout << value << "\n";
    }
    int compare(const Data&);
    void show() { std::cout << value << "\n"; }
private:
```

```
    int value;
};

int Data::compare(const Data& otherObject)
{
    if (value < otherObject.value)
        return kIsSmaller;
    if (value > otherObject.value)
        return kIsLarger;
    else
        return kIsSame;
}

class Robot
{
public:
    Robot(int newAge): age(newAge) {}
    ~Robot()
    {
        std::cout << "Deleting " << age
            << "-year-old robot.\n";
    }
    int compare(const Robot&);
    void show()
    {
        std::cout << "This robot is " << age
            << " years old\n";
    }
private:
    int age;
};

int Robot::compare(const Robot& otherRobot)
{
    if (age < otherRobot.age)
        return kIsSmaller;
    if (age > otherRobot.age)
        return kIsLarger;
    else
        return kIsSame;
}

template <class T>
class Node
{
public:
    Node() {}
    virtual ~Node() {}
```

```
    virtual Node* insert(T* object) = 0;
    virtual void show() = 0;
private:
};

template <class T>
class InternalNode: public Node<T>
{
public:
    InternalNode(T* theObject, Node<T>* next);
    virtual ~InternalNode(){ delete next; delete object; }
    virtual Node<T>* insert(T* object);
    virtual void show()
    {
        object->show();
        next->show();
    }
private:
    T* object;
    Node<T>* next;
};

template <class T>
InternalNode<T>::InternalNode(T* newObject, Node<T>* newNext):
object(newObject), next(newNext)
{
}

template <class T>
Node<T>* InternalNode<T>::insert(T* newObject)
{
    int result = object->compare(*newObject);

    switch(result)
    {
    case kIsSame:
    case kIsLarger:
        {
            InternalNode<T> * objectNode =
            new InternalNode<T>(newObject, this);
            return objectNode;
        }
    case kIsSmaller:
        next = next->insert(newObject);
        return this;
    }
    return this;
}
```

```

template <class T>
class TailNode : public Node<T>
{
public:
    TailNode() {}
    virtual ~TailNode() {}
    virtual Node<T>* insert(T* object);
    virtual void show() {}
private:
};

template <class T>
Node<T>* TailNode<T>::insert(T* object)
{
    InternalNode<T>* objectNode =
        new InternalNode<T>(object, this);
    return objectNode;
}

template <class T>
class HeadNode : public Node<T>
{
public:
    HeadNode();
    virtual ~HeadNode() { delete next; }
    virtual Node<T>* insert(T* object);
    virtual void show() { next->show(); }
private:
    Node<T>* next;
};

template <class T>
HeadNode<T>::HeadNode()
{
    next = new TailNode<T>;
}

template <class T>
Node<T>* HeadNode<T>::insert(T* object)
{
    next = next->insert(object);
    return this;
}

template <class T>
```

```
class LinkedList
{
public:
    LinkedList();
    ~LinkedList() { delete head; }
    void insert(T* object);
    void showAll() { head->show(); }
private:
    HeadNode<T>* head;
};

template <class T>
LinkedList<T>::LinkedList()
{
    head = new HeadNode<T>;
}

template <class T>
void LinkedList<T>::insert(T* pObject)
{
    head->insert(pObject);
}

void myFunction(LinkedList<Robot>& listOfRobots);
void myOtherFunction(LinkedList<Data>& listOfData);

int main()
{
    LinkedList<Robot> listOfRobots;
    LinkedList<Data> listOfData;

    myFunction(listOfRobots);
    myOtherFunction(listOfData);

    std::cout << "\n";
    listOfRobots.showAll();
    std::cout << "\n";
    listOfData.showAll();
    std::cout << "\n ************ \n\n";
    return 0;
}

void myFunction(LinkedList<Robot>& listOfRobots)
{
    Robot* pRobot;
    int val;
```

```

    while (true)
    {
        std::cout << "\nHow old is your robot (0 to stop)? ";
        std::cin >> val;
        if (!val)
            break;
        pRobot = new Robot(val);
        listOfRobots.insert(pRobot);
    }
}

void myOtherFunction(LinkedList<Data>& listOfData)
{
    Data* pData;
    int val;

    while (true)
    {
        std::cout << "\nWhat value (0 to stop)? ";
        std::cin >> val;
        if (!val)
            break;
        pData = new Data(val);
        listOfData.insert(pData);
    }
}
```

This is the output of the program:

```
How old is your robot (0 to stop)? 12
How old is your robot (0 to stop)? 2
How old is your robot (0 to stop)? 6
How old is your robot (0 to stop)? 0
What value (0 to stop)? 3
What value (0 to stop)? 9
What value (0 to stop)? 5
What value (0 to stop)? 0
This robot is 2 years old
This robot is 6 years old
This robot is 12 years old

3
5
9

************
```

```
Deleting Data object with value: 9
Deleting Data object with value: 5
Deleting Data object with value: 3
Deleting 12-year-old robot.
Deleting 6-year-old robot.
Deleting 2-year-old robot.
```

This code is much like the previous example, but this time we pass the `LinkedList` objects by reference to their respective functions for processing.

A pointer to a `Robot` object is created on line 203. After the robot's age is input by the user on line 208, a new `Robot` object is created and its address is assigned to the pointer.

The linked list's `insert()` member function is called with the `Robot` pointer, causing the object referenced by that pointer to be inserted in the list.

The same process is followed in lines 219–229, but this time to add a `Data` object to the list.

This is a powerful feature of the C++ language. After the lists are instantiated, they can be treated as fully defined types, passed into functions, and returned as values.

Summary

C++ is a popular language to use when creating programming languages. As you are introduced to features such as templates, the reason becomes clear. C++ exposes the building blocks of the language to modification.

Templates enable the functionality of a class to be adapted to more than one data type without repeating code for each type.

With templates, code can be written in the abstract that applies to multiple types of data.

Q&A

Q. Why use templates when macros will do?

A. Templates are type-safe and built in to the language. The compiler can do a lot more with templates to ensure they are used correctly, making the resulting program less likely to contain errors.

Q. What is the difference between the parameterized type of a template function and the parameters to a normal function?

A. A regular function (non-template) takes parameters on which it may take action. A template function allows you to parameterize the type of a particular parameter to the function.

Q. When do you use templates and when do you use inheritance?

A. Use templates when all the behavior or nearly all the behavior is unchanged, but the type of the item on which your class acts is different. If you find yourself copying a class and changing only the type of one or more of its members, it might be time to consider using a template.

Q Is there any place in the United States you can pan for gold?

A The Florida company Big Ten has published maps you can use to pan for gold in eight states. It sells six gold maps of California and the West Coast and five more for Alabama, Georgia, Michigan, North Carolina, South Carolina, and Virginia.

Individual maps sell for around $29, and sets sell for more. Shipping and handling is $5.

To order, write to Big Ten, Box 321231-W, Cocoa Beach, FL 32932-1231, or visit http://www.goldmaps.com.

"Usually people will find specks, but sometimes you don't find anything the first time you're out," map creator Charles Overbey said. "It's a fun outing."

Workshop

Now that you've had the chance to learn about templates, you can answer a few questions and do a couple of exercises to firm up your knowledge of the topic.

Quiz

1. How does the compiler know you are defining a template rather than a regular class?

   A. The preprocessor determines it.

   B. The `template` keyword is used.

   C. The `T` type is used in a statement.

2. In the code `template <class T>`, what is the `T`?

   A. The parameterized type

   B. A member variable

   C. A class identifier

3. In the ParamList program (Listing 23.1), how does the compiler know when to destruct the objects contained within the linked list?

   A. It occurs automatically.

   B. The linked lists fall out of scope.

   C. The linked list must delete them.

Answers

1. **B.** The compiler knows because the prefix `template <class T>` is used.
2. **A.** The `T` will appear in the class wherever a specific data type would have appeared in a normal class.
3. **C.** When the main function exits, the linked lists fall out of scope, and the destructor for that class is called. Because the individual (contained) objects are dynamically allocated, it is up to the linked list to delete them also.

Activities

1. Compare the ParamList program in Listing 23.1 to the LinkedList program in Listing 19.1 and note all the differences.
2. Extend the ParamList program by adding a Cyborg class. Store it in a linked list and treat it just like `Robot` objects in the `main()` function.

To see solutions to these activities, visit this book's website at http://cplusplus.cadenhead.org.

HOUR 24
Dealing with Exceptions and Error Handling

What You'll Learn in This Hour:

- What exceptions are
- How exceptions are used and what issues they raise
- How to create bug-free code
- Where to go from here

Bugs, Errors, Mistakes, and Code Rot

The code in this book was created for illustrative purposes. It has purposely not dealt with errors to keep the focus on the central issues being presented. Real-world programs, on the other hand, must take error conditions into consideration. In fact, anticipating and handling errors can account for the largest part of the code!

The computer scientist Gerald Weinberg once said, "If builders built houses the way programmers built programs, the first woodpecker to come along would destroy civilization." Too many commercial programs from some of the biggest vendors in the business have bugs. Too many open source programs that are used on millions of Internet computers and other devices have bugs. Serious bugs.

Writing robust, bug-free programs should be the number-one priority of anyone serious about programming. The biggest expense in major programming efforts often is testing, finding, and fixing bugs.

There are a number of discrete kinds of bugs that can trouble a program. The first is poor logic: The program does just what you asked, but you haven't thought through the algorithms properly. The second is syntactic: You used the wrong idiom, function, or structure. These two are the most common, and they are the ones most programmers are on the lookout for. Far harder to find are subtle bugs that pop up only when the user does something unexpected. These little logic bombs can lurk until they're finally encountered and the program blows up.

Research and real-world experience have consistently shown that the later in the development process you find a problem, the more it costs to fix. The least expensive problems to fix are the ones you avoid creating. The next cheapest are those that the compiler spots. The C++ language standard forces compilers to put a lot of energy into reporting a growing list of errors at compile time.

Bugs that are compiled but caught at the first test—those that crash every time—are less expensive to find and fix than those that only crash once in a while.

A bigger problem than logic or syntactic bugs is unnecessary fragility: Your program works just fine if the user enters a number when you ask for one, but it crashes if the user enters letters. Other programs crash if they run out of memory, or if the hard disk is full, or if the Internet connection drops.

To combat this fragility, programmers strive to make their programs bulletproof. A bulletproof program is one that can handle anything that comes up at runtime, from bizarre user input to running out of memory. If you watch out and prepare for these things, you can avoid a crash.

Handling the Unexpected

Programmers use design reviews and exhaustive testing to find logic errors.

A different kind of error that may arise is called an *exception*.

Exceptions take their name from exceptional circumstances. Some things that may occur in a program can't be eliminated. Instead, you only can prepare for them. For example, computers will run out of memory from time to time. That's not something a programmer can prevent. Programs only can respond when it occurs, using one of these approaches:

- Crash the program.
- Inform the user and exit gracefully.
- Inform the user and allow the user to try to recover and continue.
- Take corrective action and continue without alerting the user.

Although it is not necessary or even desirable for every program you write to automatically and silently recover from all exceptional circumstances, it is clear that you must do better than crashing.

C++ exception handling provides a type-safe, integrated technique for coping with the predictable but unusual conditions that arise while running a program.

Exceptions

In C++, an *exception* is an object that is passed from the area of code where a problem occurs to the part of the code that is going to handle the problem. When an exception occurs it is said to be *thrown*. When an exception is handled, it is said to be *caught*.

The type of the exception determines which area of code will handle the problem. The contents of the object thrown as an exception may be used to provide feedback on the problem to the user.

The basic idea behind exceptions is fairly straightforward:

- The actual allocation of resources (for example, the allocation of memory or the locking of a file) is usually done at a very low level in the program.
- The logic of what to do when an operation fails, memory cannot be allocated, or a file cannot be locked is usually high in the program, with the code for interacting with the user.
- Exceptions provide an express path from the code that allocates resources to the code that can handle the error condition. If there are intervening layers of functions, they are given an opportunity to clean up memory allocations, but are not required to include code whose only purpose is to pass along the error condition.

How Exceptions are Used

A `try` block is created to surround areas of code that might have a problem and throw an exception. For example:

```
try
{
   someDangerousFunction();
}
```

A `catch` block is the block immediately following a `try` block in which exceptions are handled. For example:

```
try
{
   someDangerousFunction();
}
catch (outOfMemory)
{
   // take action to recover from low memory condition
}
catch (fileNotFound)
{
   // take action when a file is not found
}
```

The basic steps in using exceptions are these:

1. Identify those areas of the program in which you begin an operation that might raise an exception, and put them in `try` blocks.

2. Create `catch` blocks to catch the exceptions if they are thrown, to clean up allocated memory, and to inform the user as appropriate. The Exception program in Listing 24.1 illustrates the use of both `try` blocks and `catch` blocks.

NOTE

When an exception is thrown (or raised), control transfers to the `catch` block immediately following the current `try` block.

LISTING 24.1 The Full Text of `Exception.cpp`

```
#include <iostream>

const int defaultSize = 10;

// define the exception class
class XBoundary
{
public:
    XBoundary() {}
    ~XBoundary() {}
private:
};

class Array
{
public:
    // constructors
    Array(int size = defaultSize);
    Array(const Array &rhs);
    ~Array() { delete [] pType; }

    // operators
    Array& operator=(const Array&);
    int& operator[](int offSet);
    const int& operator[](int offSet) const;

    // accessors
    int getSize() const { return size; }

    // friend function
    friend std::ostream& operator<<(std::ostream&, const Array&);
```

```

private:
    int *pType;
    int size;
};

Array::Array(int newSize):
size(newSize)
{
    pType = new int[size];
    for (int i = 0; i < size; i++)
        pType[i] = 0;
}

Array& Array::operator=(const Array &rhs)
{
    if (this == &rhs)
        return *this;
    delete [] pType;
    size = rhs.getSize();
    pType = new int[size];
    for (int i = 0; i < size; i++)
        pType[i] = rhs[i];
    return *this;
}

Array::Array(const Array &rhs)
{
    size = rhs.getSize();
    pType = new int[size];
    for (int i = 0; i < size; i++)
        pType[i] = rhs[i];
}

int& Array::operator[](int offSet)
{
    int size = getSize();
    if (offSet >= 0 && offSet < size)
        return pType[offSet];
    throw XBoundary();
    return pType[offSet];
}

const int& Array::operator[](int offSet) const
{
    int size = getSize();
    if (offSet >= 0 && offSet < size)
        return pType[offSet];
```

```
        throw XBoundary();
    return pType[offSet];
}

std::ostream& operator<<(std::ostream& output,
                         const Array& array)
{
    for (int i = 0; i < array.getSize(); i++)
        output << "[" << i << "] " << array[i] << "\n";
    return output;
}

int main()
{
    Array intArray(20);
    try
    {
        for (int j = 0; j < 100; j++)
        {
            intArray[j] = j;
            std::cout << "intArray[" << j
                << "] OK ..." << "\n";
        }
    }
    catch (XBoundary)
    {
        std::cout << "Unable to process your input\n";
    }
    std::cout << "Done\n";
    return 0;
}
```

Running the program produces this output:

```
intArray[0] OK ...
intArray[1] OK ...
intArray[2] OK ...
intArray[3] OK ...
intArray[4] OK ...
intArray[5] OK ...
intArray[6] OK ...
intArray[7] OK ...
intArray[8] OK ...
intArray[9] OK ...
intArray[10] OK ...
intArray[11] OK ...
intArray[12] OK ...
intArray[13] OK ...
```

```
intArray[14] OK ...
intArray[15] OK ...
intArray[16] OK ...
intArray[17] OK ...
intArray[18] OK ...
intArray[19] OK ...
Unable to process your input
Done
```

Listing 24.1 presents a somewhat stripped-down `Array` class, created just to illustrate a simple use of exceptions. On lines 6–12, an exception class is declared called `XBoundary`.

The most important thing to notice about this class is that there is absolutely nothing that makes it an exception class. Any class will do just fine to handle exceptions. What makes this an exception is that it is thrown, as shown on line 71, and that it is caught, as shown on line 104.

The offset operators throw `XBoundary` when the client of the class attempts to access data outside the array (lines 71 and 80). This is superior to the way normal arrays handle such a request; they just return whatever garbage happens to be in memory at that location, a surefire way to crash the program.

On line 95, a `try` block begins that ends on line 103. Within that `try` block, 100 integers are added to the array that was declared on line 94.

On line 104, the `catch` block to catch `XBoundary` exceptions is declared.

Using `try` and `catch` Blocks

Figuring out where to put `try` blocks is the hardest part of using exceptions; it is not always obvious which actions might raise an exception. The next question is where to catch the exception. You might want to throw all memory exceptions where the memory is allocated, but to catch the exceptions high in the program where you deal with the user interface.

When trying to determine `try` block locations, look for where you allocate memory or use resources. Other things to look for are out-of-bounds errors and illegal input.

Catching Exceptions

Catching exceptions works as follows: When an exception is thrown, the call stack is examined. The call stack is the list of function calls created when one part of the program invokes another function.

The call stack tracks the execution path. If `main()` calls the function `Animal::getFavoriteFood()`, and `getFavoriteFood()` calls

`Animal::lookupPreferences()`, which in turn calls `fstream::operator>>()`, all these are on the call stack. A recursive function might be on the call stack many times.

The exception is passed up the call stack to each enclosing block. As the stack is unwound, the destructors for local objects on the stack are invoked and the objects are destroyed.

After each `try` block are one or more `catch` statements. If the exception matches one of the `catch` statements, it is considered to be handled by having that statement execute. If it doesn't match any, the unwinding of the stack continues.

If the exception reaches all the way to the beginning of the program (the `main()` method) and still is not caught, the function `terminate()` is called, which in turn calls `abort()` to abort the program.

It is important to note that the exception unwinding of the stack is a one-way street. As it progresses, the stack is unwound, and objects on the stack are destroyed. There is no going back: After the exception is handled, the program continues after the `try` block of the `catch` statement that handled the exception.

In the Exception program, execution continues on line 104, the first line after the `try` block of the `catch` statement that handled the `XBoundary` exception. When an exception is raised, program flow continues after the `catch` block, not after the point where the exception was thrown.

More Than One Catch

It is possible for more than one condition to cause an exception. In this case, `catch` statements can be lined up one after another, much like the conditions in a `switch` statement. The equivalent to the `default` statement is the "catch everything" statement, indicated by `catch()`.

CAUTION

Be careful about putting in two `catch` statements where one `catch` is a base class and the other `catch` is a derived class that is more specific. The code will actually do the steps of both `catch` statements; sometimes you want that behavior and sometimes you don't, but you should be aware that this will happen.

Catching by Reference and Polymorphism

You can take advantage of the fact that exceptions are just classes to use them polymorphically. By passing the exception by reference, you can use the inheritance hierarchy to take the appropriate action based on the runtime type of the exception.

The PolyException program in Listing 24.2 illustrates using exceptions polymorphically.

LISTING 24.2 The Full Text of PolyException.cpp

```
#include <iostream>

const int defaultSize = 10;

// define the exception classes
class XBoundary {};

class XSize
{
public:
    XSize(int newSize):size(newSize) {}
    ~XSize(){}
    virtual int getSize() { return size; }
    virtual void printError()
    { std::cout << "Size error. Received: "
        << size << "\n"; }
protected:
    int size;
};

class XTooBig : public XSize
{
public:
    XTooBig(int size):XSize(size) {}
    virtual void printError()
    {
        std::cout << "Too big! Received: ";
        std::cout << XSize::size << "\n";
    }
};

class XTooSmall : public XSize
{
public:
    XTooSmall(int size):XSize(size) {}
    virtual void printError()
    {
        std::cout << "Too small! Received: ";
        std::cout << XSize::size << "\n";
    }
};

class XZero : public XTooSmall
{
public:
    XZero(int newSize):XTooSmall(newSize){}
    virtual void printError()
```

```
    {
        std::cout << "Zero Received: ";
        std::cout << XSize::size << "\n";
    }
};

class XNegative : public XSize
{
public:
    XNegative(int size):XSize(size){}
    virtual void printError()
    {
        std::cout << "Negative! Received: ";
        std::cout << XSize::size << "\n";
    }
};

class Array
{
public:
    // constructors
    Array(int size = defaultSize);
    Array(const Array &rhs);
    ~Array() { delete [] pType; }

    // operators
    Array& operator=(const Array&);
    int& operator[](int offSet);
    const int& operator[](int offSet) const;

    // accessors
    int getSize() const { return size; }

    // friend function
    friend std::ostream& operator<< (std::ostream&, const Array&);


private:
    int *pType;
    int  size;
};

Array::Array(int newSize):
size(newSize)
{
    if (newSize == 0)
        throw XZero(size);

    if (newSize < 0)
```

```
        throw XNegative(size);

    if (newSize < 10)
        throw XTooSmall(size);

    if (newSize > 30000)
        throw XTooBig(size);

    pType = new int[newSize];
    for (int i = 0; i < newSize; i++)
        pType[i] = 0;
}

int& Array::operator[] (int offset)
{
    int size = getSize();
    if (offset >= 0 && offset < size)
        return pType[offset];
    throw XBoundary();
    return pType[offset];
}

const int& Array::operator[] (int offset) const
{
    int size = getSize();
    if (offset >= 0 && offset < size)
        return pType[offset];
    throw XBoundary();
    return pType[offset];
}

int main()
{
    try
    {
        int choice;
        std::cout << "Enter the array size: ";
        std::cin >> choice;
        Array intArray(choice);
        for (int j = 0; j < 100; j++)
        {
            intArray[j] = j;
            std::cout << "intArray[" << j << "] OK ..."
                << "\n";
        }
    }
    catch (XBoundary)
    {
        std::cout << "Unable to process your input\n";
```

```
146:     }
147:     catch (XSize& exception)
148:     {
149:         exception.printError();
150:     }
151:     catch (...)
152:     {
153:         std::cout << "Something went wrong,"
154:             << "but I've no idea what!" << "\n";
155:     }
156:     std::cout << "Done\n";
157:     return 0;
158: }
```

The output reflects running the program three times, first passing in an array size of 5, then 50,000, and finally 12:

```
Enter the array size: 5

Too small! Received: 5
Done

Enter the array size: 50000
Too big! Received: 50000
Done

Enter the array size: 12
intArray[0] OK ...
intArray[1] OK ...
intArray[2] OK ...
intArray[3] OK ...
intArray[4] OK ...
intArray[5] OK ...
intArray[6] OK ...
intArray[7] OK ...
intArray[8] OK ...
intArray[9] OK ...
intArray[10] OK ...
intArray[11] OK ...
Unable to process your input
Done
```

Listing 24.2 declares a `printError()` virtual function in the `XSize` class that displays an error message and the actual size of the class. This is overridden in each of the derived classes.

On line 147, the exception object is declared to be a reference. When `printError()` is called with a reference to an object, polymorphism causes the correct version of `printError()` to be invoked.

The first time through the user asks for an array of size 5. This causes the `XTooSmall` exception to be thrown; that is the `xSize` exception caught on line 147.

The second time through the user asks for an array of 50,000, and that causes the `XTooBig` exception to be thrown. This also is caught on line 147, but polymorphism causes the right error string to print. When the user finally asks for an array of size 12, the array is populated until the `XBoundary` exception is thrown and caught on line 143.

Writing Professional-Quality Code

With templates and exceptions under your belt, you are prepared to handle the more advanced aspects of C++. Before this 24-hour journey ends, it's worthwhile to take some time to discuss writing professional-quality code. When you go beyond hobbyist interest and work as part of a development team, you must write code that not only works but can be understood by others. Your code also must be maintained and supported by you, as the customer's demands change, and also by others after you leave the project.

Although it doesn't matter which style you adopt, it is important to adopt a consistent coding style. An adherence to style makes it easier to guess what you meant by a particular part of the code, and you avoid having to look up whether you spelled the function with an initial cap the last time you invoked it.

The following guidelines just one way of doing things, but they've been tested by personal experience. You can just as easily devise your own, but these will get you started.

Though Ralph Waldo Emerson said, "Foolish consistency is the hobgoblin of small minds," Emerson never had to deliver a 100,000-line C++ web application on deadline. Having some consistency in your code is a good thing. It makes your life, and the life of your co-workers, easier if you follow the style of your group. That doesn't mean the style has to be permanently fixed (improvements and new ideas come along all the time), but the consistency makes it easier for everyone to work together.

Understand that there are many different styles, and you can run into serious disagreements on the following topics. Remember that these are guidelines, not absolutes.

Braces

How to align braces can be the most controversial topic between C and C++ programmers. Here are the tips I suggest:

- Matching braces should be aligned vertically.
- The outermost set of braces in a definition or declaration should be at the left margin. Statements within should be indented. All other sets of braces should be in line with their leading statement.

- For really long blocks, you should put a comment after the close brace identifying the purpose of the block. When you look at the close brace and are not sure where the open brace is, that is a "really long block." For example:

```
if (condition == true)
{
   // many lines of code including other blocks

   // more lines of code including other blocks

   // even more lines of code including other blocks

} // if (condition == true)
```

- No code should appear on the same line as a brace. For example:

```
if (condition == true)
{
   j = k;
   someFunction();
}
m++;
```

Long Lines

Keep lines to the width that can be displayed on a single screen. Code that is off to the right is easily overlooked, and scrolling horizontally is annoying. When a line is broken, indent the following lines. Try to break the line at a reasonable place, and try to leave the intervening operator at the end of the previous line (as opposed to the beginning of the following line) so that it is clear that the line does not stand alone and that there is more coming.

Try to keep your functions short enough to show the entire function on one page.

Tab size should be three or four spaces. Make sure your editor converts each tab to that size.

`switch` Statements

Indent `switch` statements as follows to conserve horizontal space:

```
switch(variable)
{
case ValueOne:
    actionOne();
    break;
case ValueTwo:
    actionTwo();
    break;
```

```
default:
    // bad action!
    break;
}
```

Program Text

You can follow several tips to create easy-to-read code. Code that is easy to read is easy to maintain:

- Use whitespace to help readability.
- Objects and arrays are really referring to one thing. Don't use spaces within object references (., ->, []).
- Unary operators are associated with their operand, so don't put a space between them. Do put a space on the side away from the operand. Unary operators include !, ~, ++, --, -, * (for pointers), & (casts), and sizeof.
- Binary operators should have spaces on both sides: +, =, *, /, %, >>, <<, <, >, ==, !=, &, |, &&, ||, ?:, =, +=, and so on.
- Don't use lack of spaces to indicate precedence (4+ 3*2).
- Put a space after commas and semicolons, not before.
- Parentheses should not have spaces on either side.
- Keywords, such as if, should be set off by a space: if (a == b).
- The body of a comment should be set off from the // with a space.
- Place the pointer or reference indicator next to the type name, not the variable name. Do this:

  ```
  char* foo;
  int& theInt;
  ```

  rather than this:

  ```
  char *foo;
  int &theInt;
  ```
- Do not declare more than one variable on the same line unless they are related.

Identifier Names

Here are some guidelines for working with identifiers:

- Identifier names should be long enough to be descriptive.
- Avoid cryptic abbreviations.
- Take the time and energy to spell things out.

- Short names (i, p, x, and so on) only should be used where their brevity makes the code more readable and where the usage is so obvious that a descriptive name is not needed.
- The length of a variable's name should be proportional to its scope.
- Make sure identifiers look and sound different from one another to minimize confusion.
- Function (or method) names usually are verbs or verb-noun phrases: `search()`, `reset()`, `findParagraph()`, `showCursor()`. Variable names are usually abstract nouns, possibly with an additional noun: `count`, `state`, `windSpeed`, `windowHeight`. Boolean variables should be named appropriately: `windowIconized`, `fileIsOpen`.

Spelling and Capitalization of Names

Spelling and capitalization should not be overlooked when creating your own style. Some tips for these areas include the following:

- Identifiers should be consistent—use mixed case where appropriate. Function names, class, `typedef`, `struct` names, data members and locals should begin with a lowercase letter with each subsequent word in the identifier capitalized (as in `myVariable` or `closeAllFiles()`). This style is called *camel case*.
- Enumerated constants should begin with a few lowercase letters as an abbreviation for the `enum`. For example:

```
enum TextStyle
{
    tsPlain,
    tsBold,
    tsItalic,
    tsUnderscore,
};
```

Comments

Comments can make it much easier to understand a program. Often, you will not work on a program for weeks, months, or even years while you turn your attention to higher-priority projects. In this time, you can forget what certain code does or why it has been included. Problems in understanding code also can occur when someone else reads your code. Comments that are applied in a consistent, well thought-out style can be well worth the effort. There are several tips to remember concerning comments:

- Wherever possible, use C++ `//` comments rather than the `/*  */` style.
- Higher-level comments are infinitely more important than process details. Add value; do not merely restate the code. For example:

```
n++; // n is incremented by one
```

- This comment isn't worth the time it takes to type it in. Concentrate on the semantics of functions and blocks of code. Say what a function does. Indicate side effects, types of parameters, and return values. Describe all assumptions that are made (or not made), such as "assumes *n* is non-negative" or "will return –1 if *x* is invalid." Within complex logic, use comments to indicate the conditions that exist at that point in the code.
- Use complete English sentences with appropriate punctuation and capitalization. The extra typing is worth it. Don't be overly cryptic, and don't abbreviate. What seems exceedingly clear to you as you write code can be amazingly obtuse in a few months.
- Include comments at the top of your program, functions, and header source modules to define the purpose of that module, inputs, outputs, parameters, initial author, and any changes (including date and author).
- Use blank lines freely to help the reader understand what is going on. Separate statements into logical groups.

Access

The way you access portions of your program also should be consistent. Some tips for access are these:

- Always use `public:`, `private:`, and `protected:` labels; don't rely on the defaults.
- List the public members first, then protected, then private. List the data members in a group after the member functions.
- Put the constructors first in the appropriate section; followed by the destructor. List overloaded member functions with the same name adjacent to each other. Group accessors together when possible.
- Consider alphabetizing the member function names within each group and alphabetizing the member variables. Be sure to alphabetize the filenames in `include` statements.
- Even though the use of the `virtual` keyword is optional when overriding, use it anyway; it helps to remind you that it is virtual, and also keeps the declaration consistent.

Class Definitions

Try to keep the definitions of member functions in the same order as the declarations. It makes things easier to find.

When defining a function, place the return type and all other modifiers on a previous line so that the class name and function name begin on the left margin. This makes it much easier to find functions.

`include` Files

Try as hard as you can to keep from including files in header files. The ideal minimum is the header file for the class from which the current class. Other mandatory includes will be those for objects that are members of the class being declared. Classes that are merely pointed to or referenced only need forward references of the form.

Don't leave out an `include` file in a header just because you assume that whatever `.cpp` file includes this one also will have the needed `include`.

`const`

Use `const` wherever appropriate: for parameters, variables, and member functions. Often there is a need for both a `const` and a non-`const` version of a function; don't leave one out if both are needed. Be careful when explicitly casting from `const` to non-`const` and vice versa—sometimes this is the only way to do something—but be certain that it makes sense, and include a comment.

Summary

After 24 hours, you're ready to start tackling your own programming projects with the C++ language.

The complexity of the language might still seem daunting—Bjarne Stroustrop created a language so powerful that it remains in vogue over 37 years after its creation.

There's a lot more to be learned about C++, and you could immediately dive into more advanced books, courses, and websites.

Don't do that yet.

The best way to grow your knowledge of C++ is to apply what you've learned to your own code. Many of the features of the language require familiarity to master, such as operator overloading, templates, and object-oriented class hierarchies.

Even a lifetime C++ coder discovers new techniques and capabilities of the language.

Q&A

Q. Why use `try` blocks when you can use general exception handling?

A. The `try` block allows specific exception handling within that section of code. You get to have general handling for all code and specific handing for the code within the `try` block.

Q. Why do the Alabama Crimson Tide have an elephant as their mascot?

A. A fan called them elephants during a 1930 game against Ole Miss and the name stuck.

"At the end of the quarter, the earth started to tremble," sportswriter Everett Strupper wrote in the October 8, 1930, Atlanta Journal. "Some excited fan in the stands bellowed, 'Hold your horses, the elephants are coming,' and out stamped this Alabama varsity." Sportswriters dubbed the team's linemen the "Red Elephants."

That 1930 team had a 10-0 record, outscored its opponents 217-13, defeated Washington State in the Rose Bowl, and was declared national champions.

Q. What should I do now that I've reached the end of the book?

A. Keep learning! You can try examples, write code, and read other resources available online and in print.

Workshop

Now that you've finished all 24 hours, you can answer a few final questions on exceptions and continue with an exercise to firm up your knowledge of C++.

Quiz

1. What is the purpose of a `try` block?

  A. To run code that might cause an exception

  B. To throw exceptions

  C. To ignore errors

2. What is the difference between a `throw` and a `try`?

  A. `try` might not cause an exception.

  B. There's no difference.

  C. `try` always causes an exception.

3. How do you declare a default `catch` block?

  A. `catch (everything)`

  B. `catch (default)`

  C. `catch (...)`

Answers

1. **A.** The `try` block contains a set of statements in which the exceptions for those statements will be handled in the attached `catch` block.
2. **A.** The `try` block contains code that might cause an exception to be thrown. The `throw` statement automatically throws an exception.
3. **C.** To define a `catch` block that will catch anything not already listed in another `catch` block (much like the default label in a `switch` statement), you include three periods inside the argument list instead of listing an exception name: `catch (...)`.

Activities

1. There is only one exercise for this hour: Go forth and program! Make sure you try the programs in this book and any samples that might have come with your C++ development tool.

To see solutions to these activities, visit this book's website at http://cplusplus.cadenhead.org.

APPENDIX A

Binary and Hexadecimal

Binary and hexadecimal numbering systems are extremely useful for C++ programmers.

When you look at the number 145, you instantly see "one hundred forty-five" without much reflection. In order to understand binary and hexadecimal numbering, you must reexamine the number 145 and see it not as a number but as a code for a number.

Consider the relationship between the number three and 3. The numeral 3 is a symbol on a piece of paper; the number three is an idea. The numeral is used to represent the number.

The distinction can be made clear by realizing that three, 3, |||, and *** all can be used to represent the same idea of three.

In base 10 math, also called *decimal math*, you use combinations of the numerals 0, 1, 2, 3, 4, 5, 6, 7, 8, and 9 to represent all numbers. How is the number ten represented?

We could have evolved a strategy of using the letter A to represent ten; or we might have used IIIIIIIIII to represent that idea. The Romans used X. The Arabic system, which we use, makes use of position in conjunction with numerals to represent values. The first (rightmost) column is used for ones, and the next column (to the left) is used for tens. Thus, the number fifteen is represented as 15 (one, five). It is 1 ten and 5 ones.

Certain rules emerge from which generalizations can be made:

1. Base 10 uses the digits 0–9.
2. The columns are powers of ten: 1s, 10s, 100s, and so on.
3. If the third column is 100, the largest number you can make with two columns is 99. More generally, with *n* columns you can represent 0 to (10^n–1). So with three columns, you can represent 0 to (10^3–1), or 0–999.

Other Bases

It is not an arbitrary choice that we use base 10; after all, our species has 10 fingers. One can imagine a different base, however. Using the rules found in base 10, here's how you can describe base 8:

1. The digits in base 8 are 0–7.
2. The columns are powers of 8: 1s, 8s, 64s, and so on.
3. With *n* columns, you can represent 0 to 8^n–1.

To distinguish numbers written in each base, write the base as a subscript next to the number. The number fifteen in base 10 would be written as 15_{10} and read as "one, five, base ten."

Therefore, to represent the number 15_{10} in base 8, you would write 17_8. This is read "one, seven, base eight." Note that it also can be read "fifteen," because that is the number it continues to represent.

Why 17? The 1 means 1 eight, and the 7 means 7 ones. One eight plus seven ones equals fifteen. Consider fifteen asterisks:

```
*****     *****
*****
```

The natural tendency is to make two groups, a group of ten asterisks and another of five. This would be represented in decimal as 15 (1 ten and 5 ones). You also can group the asterisks as follows:

```
****        *******
****
```

That is, eight asterisks and seven. That would be represented in base eight as 17_8. That is, 1 eight and 7 ones.

Around the Bases

You can represent the number fifteen in base 10 as 15, or 15_{10}, in base 9 as 16_9, in base 8 as 17_8, in base 7 as 21_7. Why 21_7? In base 7, there is no numeral 8. To represent fifteen, you need two 7s and one 1.

How do you generalize the process? To convert a base 10 number to base 7, think about the columns: In base 7, they are ones, sevens, forty-nines, three-hundred forty-threes, and so on. Why these columns? They represent 7^0, 7^1, 7^2, 7^3, and so forth. Create a table for yourself:

4	3	2	1
7^3	7^2	7^1	7^0
343	49	7	1

NOTE

One of the rules of mathematics is that any value raised to the zero power has a result of one. $7^0 = 1$, $10^0 = 1$, $217,549,343^0 = 1$.

The first row represents the column number. The second row represents the power of 7. The third row represents the decimal value of each number in that row.

To convert from a decimal value to base 7, here is the procedure: Examine the number and decide which column to use first. If the number is 200, for example, you know that column 4 (343) is 0, and you don't have to worry about it.

To find out how many 49s there are, divide 200 by 49. The answer is 4, so put 4 in column 3 and examine the remainder: 4. There are no 7s in 4, so put a 0 in the sevens column. There are 4 ones in 4, so put a 4 in the 1s column. The answer is 404_7.

To convert the number 968_{10} to base 6:

5	4	3	2	1
6^4	6^3	6^2	6^1	6^0
1296	216	36	6	1

There are no 1296s in 968, so column 5 has 0. Dividing 968 by 216 yields 4 with a remainder of 104. Column 4 is 4. Dividing 104 by 36 yields 2 with a remainder of 32. Column 3 is 2. Dividing 32 by 6 yields 5 with a remainder of 2. The answer, therefore, is 4252_6.

5	4	3	2	1
6^4	6^3	6^2	6^1	6^0
1296	216	36	6	1
0	4	2	5	2

There is a shortcut when converting from a value of one base to a value of another base (such as 6) to base 10. You can multiply:

4 * 216	=	864
2 * 36	=	72
5 * 6	=	30
2 * 1	=	2
968		

Binary

Base 2 is the ultimate extension of this idea. There are only two digits: 0 and 1. The columns are as follows:

Col:	8	7	6	5	4	3	2	1
Power:	2^7	2^6	2^5	2^4	2^3	2^2	2^1	2^0
Value:	128	64	32	16	8	4	2	1

To convert the number 88_{10} to base 2, you follow the same procedure. There are no 128s, so column 8 is 0.

There is one 64 in 88, so column 7 is 1, and 24 is the remainder. There are no 32s in 24, so column 6 is 0.

There is one 16 in 24, so column 5 is 1. The remainder is 8. There is one 8 in 8, and so column 4 is 1. There is no remainder, so the rest of the columns are 0:

0 1 0 1 1 0 0 0

To test this answer, convert it back:

```
1 * 64 =  64
0 * 32 =   0
1 * 16 =  16
1 *  8 =   8
0 *  4 =   0
0 *  2 =   0
0 *  1 =   0
          88
```

Why Base 2?

The power of base 2 is that it corresponds cleanly to what a computer needs to represent. Computers do not know anything at all about letters, numerals, instructions, or programs. At their core, they are just circuitry, and at a given juncture, there either is a lot of power or there is very little.

To keep the logic clean, engineers do not treat this as a relative scale (a little power, some power, more power, or lots of power), but rather as a binary scale (enough power or not enough power). This is simplified to "yes" or "no." Yes or no can be represented as 1 or 0. By convention, 1 means true or yes.

After you make this great leap of intuition, the power of binary becomes clear: With 1s and 0s, you can represent the fundamental truth of every circuit. (There is power or there isn't.) All a computer ever knows is, "Is it on, or is it off?" On equals 1, off equals 0.

Bits, Bytes, and Nybbles

After the decision is made to represent truth and falsehood with 1s and 0s, binary digits (or bits) become very important. Because early computers could send 8 bits at a time, it was natural to start writing code using 8-bit numbers (called *bytes*).

NOTE

Half a byte (4 bits) is called a *nybble*! You also may see this spelled as nibble.

With 8 binary digits, you can represent up to 256 different values. Why? Examine the columns: If all 8 bits are set (1), the value is 255. If none is set (all the bits are clear or zero), the value is 0. So 0–255 is 256 possible states.

What's a KB?

It turns out that 2^{10} (1,024) is roughly equal to 10^3 (1,000). This coincidence was too good to miss, so computer scientists started referring to 2^{10} bytes as 1KB or 1 kilobyte, based on the scientific prefix of kilo for thousand.

Similarly, 1,024 * 1,024 (1,048,576) is close enough to one million to receive the designation 1MB or 1 megabyte, and 1,024 megabytes is called 1 gigabyte (*giga* implies thousand-million or billion).

Binary Numbers

Computers use patterns of 1s and 0s to encode everything they do. Machine instructions are encoded as a series of 1s and 0s and interpreted by the fundamental circuitry. Arbitrary sets of 1s and 0s can be translated back into numbers by computer scientists, but it would be a mistake to think that these numbers have intrinsic meaning.

For example, the Intel x86 chip set interprets the bit pattern 1001 0101 as an instruction. You certainly can translate this into decimal 149, but that number has no special meaning.

Sometimes the numbers are instructions, sometimes they are values, and sometimes they are codes. One important standardized code set is ASCII. In ASCII, every letter and punctuation is given a seven-digit binary representation. For example, the lowercase letter *a* is represented by 110 0001. This is not a number, although you can translate it to the number 97_{10} (64 + 32 + 1). It is in this sense that people say that the letter *a* is represented by 97_{10} in ASCII; but the truth is that the binary representation of 97_{10}, 1100001, is the encoding of the letter *a*, and the decimal value 97 is a human convenience.

Hexadecimal

Because binary numbers are difficult to read, a simpler way to represent the same values is sought. Translating from binary to base 10 involves a fair bit of manipulation of numbers; but it turns out that translating from base 2 to base 16 is simple, because there is a very good shortcut.

To understand this, you must first understand base 16, which is known as hexadecimal. In base 16, there are 16 numerals: 0, 1, 2, 3, 4, 5, 6, 7, 8, 9, A, B, C, D, E, and F. The last six are arbitrary; the letters A–F were chosen because they are easy to represent on a keyboard. The columns in hexadecimal are as follows:

4	3	2	1
16^3	16^2	16^1	16^0
4096	256	16	1

To translate from hexadecimal to decimal, you can multiply. Thus, the number $F8C_{16}$ represents the following:

```
F * 256 = 15 * 256 =    3840
8 * 16 =                128
C * 1 = 12 * 1 =        12
                        3980
```

Translating the number FC_{16} to binary is best done by translating first to base 10, and then to binary:

```
F * 16 = 15 * 16 =      240
C * 1 = 12 * 1 =        12
                        252
```

Converting 252_{10} to binary requires the chart:

Col:	9	8	7	6	5	4	3	2	1
Power:	2^8	2^7	2^6	2^5	2^4	2^3	2^2	2^1	2^0
Value:	256	128	64	32	16	8	4	2	1

```
There are no 256s.
1 128 leaves 124
1 64 leaves 60
1 32 leaves 28
1 16 leaves 12
1 8 leaves 4
1 4 leaves 0
0
0
1    1    1    1    1    1    0    0
```

Thus, the answer in binary is 1111 1100.

Now, it turns out that if you treat this binary number as two sets of four digits, you can do a magical transformation.

The right set is 1100. In decimal, that is 12, or in hexadecimal it is C.

The left set is 1111, which in base 10 is 15, or in hex is F.

Thus, you have the following:

```
1111    1100
F       C
```

Putting the two hex numbers together is FC, which is the real value of $1111\ 1100_2$. This shortcut always works. You can take any binary number of any length and reduce it to sets of four, translate each set of four to hex, and put the hex numbers together to get the result in hex.

You can shortcut the hexadecimal to binary conversion by using the reverse process. Split the hexadecimal number into individual digits and convert each of them into four binary digits (bits). If you remember that the values of the first four bits are 8, 4, 2, and 1, you can easily convert from hexadecimal to binary—because each hex digit can be treated as an individual four bits.

Here's a much larger number:

```
1011 0001 1101 0111
```

The columns are 1, 2, 4, 8, 16, 32, 64, 128, 256, 512, 1024, 2048, 4096, 8192, 16384, and 32768:

```
1 x 1 =         1
1 x 2 =         2
1 x 4 =         4
0 x 8 =         0

1 x 16 =         16
0 x 32 =         0
1 x 64 =         64
1 x 128 =        128

1 x 256 =          256
0 x 512 =          0
0 x 1024 =         0
0 x 2048 =         0

1 x 4096 =     4,096
1 x 8192 =     8,192
0 x 16384 =    0
1 x 32768 =    32,768
Total:          45,527
```

Converting this to hexadecimal requires a chart with the hexadecimal values:

```
65536    4096    256    16    1
```

There are no 65,536s in 45,527, so the first column is 4096. There are 11 4096s (45,056), with a remainder of 471. There is one 256 in 471 with a remainder of 215. There are 13 16s (208) in 215 with a remainder of 7. Thus, the hexadecimal number is B1D7.

Checking the math:

```
B (11) * 4096 =      45,056
1 * 256 =            256
D (13) * 16 =        208
7 * 1 =              7
Total               45,527
```

The shortcut version is to take the original binary number, 1011000111010111, and break it into groups of four: 1011 0001 1101 0111. Each of the four is then evaluated as a hexadecimal number:

```
1011 =
1 x 1 =  1
1 x 2 =  2
0 x 4 =  0
1 x 8 =  8
Total    11
Hex:     B

0001 =
1 x 1 =   1
0 x 2 =   0
0 x 4 =   0
0 * 8 =   0
Total     1
Hex:      1

1101 =
1 x 1 =   1
0 x 2 =   0
1 x 4 =   4
1 x 8 =   8
Total     13
Hex =     D

0111 =
1 x 1 =   1
1 x 2 =   2
1 x 4 =   4
0 x 8 =   0
Total     7
Hex:      7

Total Hex:  B1D7
```

APPENDIX B

Glossary

This appendix contains definitions for the key terms you will see throughout the book in alphabetical order. As you read each hour and see a term you do not recognize, you should be able to turn to this appendix and find out more.

A

Abstract data type (ADT): This represents a concept (like shape) rather than an object (like circle). As the name implies, it is an abstract form.

Accessor methods: Methods used to access private member variables.

ANSI: The American National Standards Institute is a nonprofit that acts as the guardian of standards within the United States. Most countries and many regions (for example, the European Union) have similar organizations. In some cases, those organizations are part of the government, but ANSI is not a governmental agency. Go to www.ansi.org for more information.

Arity: How many terms an operator takes. The possible values for a C++ operator's arity are unary, binary, and ternary.

Array: A collection of objects all of the same type.

ASCII (American Standard Code for Information Interchange): A system for encoding the characters, numerals, and punctuation used by many computers.

Assignment operator (=): Causes the operand on the left side of the assignment operator to have its value changed to the value on the right side of the assignment operator.

B

Binary operator: An operator that takes two terms, such as `a+b`.

C

C++14: The most recent release of the C++ language, which was published on December 15, 2014, after 19 months of development.

Case sensitive: When uppercase and lowercase letters are considered to be different. (`playerScore` is not the same as `PlayerScore`.)

Class: The definition of a new type. A class is implemented as data and related functions.

Clients: Other classes or functions that make use of your class.

Comment: Text that does not affect the operation of your program, but which is added to instruct or inform the programmer.

Compiler: Software that can translate a program from human-readable form to machine code, producing an object file that will later be linked (see linker) and run.

Compiling: The first step in transforming code from a compiler into what is called object code in an object file (`.obj`).

Compound statement: Replaces a single statement with a series of statements between an opening brace and a closing brace.

Conceptualization: The core idea of the software project.

Constant: Data storage locations whose value will not change while the program is running.

Constant member function: A constant member function promises that it won't change the value of any of the members of the class.

D

Data members: See **member variables.**

Data hiding: Hiding the state of a class in private member variables.

Decrementing: Decreasing a value by 1 (when applied to the `--` operator).

Deep copy: Copies the values of member variables, and creates copies of objects pointed to by member pointers.

Default constructor: A constructor with no parameters.

#define: A command that defines a string substitution.

Doubly linked list: A linked list in which nodes point both to the next node in the list and also the previous node in the list.

Driver program: A test program.

E

Efficiency: A topic where major changes to program code are made to save minute amounts of time. Although you want to keep this in mind as you write programs, unless you are writing real-time systems (controlling medical equipment or missiles), in many situations you should let the compiler worry about the details of efficient code.

Encapsulation: Creating self-contained objects so that other objects cannot modify their internal state.

Enumerated constants: A named set of constants.

Exception: An object that is passed from the area of code where a problem occurs to the part of the code that is going to handle the problem.

Executable program: A program that runs on your operating system.

Expression: Any statement that returns a value.

F

Friend: Keyword to provide another class with access to the current class's private member variables and methods.

Function: A block of code that performs a service, such as adding two numbers or printing to the screen.

Function declaration: Tells the compiler the name, return type, and parameters of the function.

Function definition: Tells the compiler how the function works; it is the body of the function.

Function parameter list: The list of all the parameters and their types, separated by commas.

G

Global variables: Variables accessible from anywhere within the program.

H

Heap: The area of memory left over after the code space, global name space, and stack are allocated. This also is known as the "free store" and is the source of memory dynamically allocated using `new` or `malloc`.

I

Implementation (also called class *implementation*): The code and declarations of data within a class. This is the code that is accessed using the **interface**. This information is typically stored in a .cpp file and compiled into object or library form. In many cases, the interface (in the form of a header file) and the compiled code (object or library file) is provided and not the actual class code—which prevents it from being modified.

Incrementing: Increasing a value by 1 (when applied to the ++ operator).

Indirection: Accessing the value at an address held by a pointer.

Infinite loop: A loop that has a condition which causes it to loop forever, instead of ending after looping a finite number of times. This can be a logic error or an intentional design by a programmer. When it's intentional, there must be something that causes the loop to end.

Inheritance: Creating a new type that can extend the characteristics of an existing type.

Instantiation: Creating an object from a class, or a type from a template.

Interface (also called class *interface*): The definition of data and methods that can be accessed by other classes and code. The interface tells how the code is used. This information often is stored in a header file and included into the using module.

Interpreter: An interpreter translates a program from human-readable form to machine code while the program is running.

ISO: International Organization for Standardization. An international standards body similar to ANSI. ISO is not a governmental agency. Go to www.iso.org for more information.

Iteration: Doing the same thing again and again.

L

L-value: An l-value is an operand that can be on the left side of an operator.

Library: A collection of linkable files that were supplied with your compiler, you purchased separately, or created yourself.

Linked list: A data structure that consists of nodes linked to one another.

Linker: A program that builds an executable (runnable) file from the object code files produced by the compiler.

Linking: The second step in creating an executable file; links together the object files produced by a compiler into an executable program.

Literal constant: A value typed directly into the program, such as 35.

Local variables: Variables that exist only within a function.

M

Member functions (also called member methods): The functions of your class.

Member methods: See member functions.

Member variables (also known as data members): The variables in your class.

Method definition: A definition that begins with the name of the class followed by two colons, the name of the function, and its parameters.

O

Object: An instance of a class.

Object oriented: A programming approach that takes the next step beyond procedural and structural programming. As the name implies, it takes advantage of the behavior of objects (defined in classes).

OO: See object oriented.

Operand: A mathematical term referring to the part of an expression operated upon by an operator.

Operator: A symbol that causes the compiler to take an action.

Overriding: When a derived class creates a member function that changes the implementation of a function in the base class. The overridden method must have the same return type and signature as the base method.

P

Pointer: A variable that holds a memory address.

Problem space: The set of problems and issues your program will try to solve.

Procedural programming: A series of actions performed on a set of data.

Polymorphism: The ability to treat many subtypes as if they were of the same base type.

Postfix operator: The postfix operator (zombies++) increments after evaluation in an expression.

Precedence value: The precedence value tells the compiler the order in which to evaluate operators.

Prefix operator: The prefix operator (--zombies) increments before evaluation in an expression.

Preprocessor: A program that runs before your compiler and handles lines that begin with a pound (#) symbol.

Prototype: Declaration of a function.

Private access: Access available only to the methods of the class itself or to methods of classes derived from the class.

Public access: Access available to methods of all classes.

Pure virtual function: A virtual function that must be overridden in the derived class because it has no code behind it. It is purely abstract with no implementation in the base class.

R

R-value: An r-value is an operand that can be on the right side of an operator.

RAM: Random access memory.

Reference: An alias to an object.

Relational operators: Determine whether two numbers are equal or if one is greater or less than the other.

S

Scope: Where a variable is visible and can be accessed.

Shallow copy: Copies the exact values of one object's member variables to another object. Also called a member-wise copy.

Signature: The name of a function and its arguments.

Signed: A variable type that can hold negative and positive values.

Simulation: A computer model of part of a real-world system.

Singly linked list: A linked list in which nodes point to the next node in the list, but not back to the previous.

Solution space: The set of possible solutions to the problem.

Spaghetti code: Programs written in a convoluted and difficult-to-read format with limited structure, which gets its name because program flow looks like a plate of spaghetti that is difficult to follow.

Stack: A special area of memory allocated for your program to hold the data required by each of the functions in your program. Another term for stack is LIFO (last in, first out) queue. The last (most recent) item placed in the LIFO is the first one pulled out.

Statement: A way to control the sequence of execution, evaluate an expression, or do nothing (the `null` statement).

Static member data: Unlike most member data elements within a class, this does not get replicated for each object created. Only one copy of these elements exists and can be accessed by all the objects of that class. It is typically used to keep track of the number of objects or anything else that applies to all member objects.

Static member functions: Like **static member data**, these exist in the scope of the class, not individual objects and can be invoked without referencing a specific object.

Stray pointer (also called a *dangling pointer*): The name for a pointer that is created when you perform `delete` on it and then try to access the memory that has been freed. This is a common bug that is difficult to debug because the fault (accessing the memory improperly) typically takes place long after the `delete`.

String: An array of characters ending with a null character.

Structured programming: A systematic approach to breaking programs down into procedures.

Symbolic constant: A typed and named value marked as constant, such as BoilingPoint.

Stubbing out: Writing only enough of a function to compile, leaving the details for later.

Subscript: Offsets into an array. The fourth element of `myArray` would be accessed as `myArray[3]`.

T

Template: Provides the ability to create a general class or method and pass types as parameters.

Ternary operator: An operator that takes three terms. In C++, there is only one ternary operator, the `?` operator, used as

```
a < b ? true : false;
```

which will return true if `a` is less than `b`, and otherwise will return false.

Token: A string of characters.

Tree: A complex data structure built from nodes, each of which points to one or more child nodes.

Type: The size and characteristics of an object.

Typedef: A data type definition, which acts as a synonym for a built-in data type.

U

UML: Unified Modeling Language. A standard, graphical means of representing requirements and design.

Unary operator: An operator that takes only one term, such as `a++`, as opposed to a binary operator, which takes two terms, such as `a + b`.

Unsigned: A variable type that only can hold positive values.

Use case: A description of how a program will be used.

V

Variable: A named memory location in which you can store a value.

Virtual method: One of the means by which C++ implements **polymorphism**. This allows you to treat derived objects as if they were base objects.

v-table: The internal mechanism that keeps track of the virtual functions created within individual objects.

W

Waterfall: A method in which each stage is completed before the product is passed on to the next stage. Each stage is discrete and self-contained. This can be applied to software development or any project (including building a house or car or so forth).

Whitespace: Spaces, tabs, and new lines.

APPENDIX C
This Book's Website

This book has a website with source code files, answers to reader questions, and more assistance.

If you're unclear about any of the topics covered in the book, visit the book's website at http://cplusplus.cadenhead.org for assistance.

The book's website offers the following:

- Error corrections and clarifications: When errors are brought to my attention, they are described on the site with the corrected text and any other material that could help.
- Answers to reader questions: If readers have questions that aren't covered in this book's Q&A sections, many are presented on the site.
- The source code, class files, and resources required for all programs you create during the 24 hours of this book.
- Sample C++ programs: Working versions of some programs featured in this book are available on the site.
- Solutions, including source code, for activities suggested at the end of each hour.
- Updated links to the sites mentioned in this book: If sites mentioned in the book have changed addresses and I know about the new link, I'll offer it here.

You can also send me email by visiting the book's website. Click the Feedback link on any page.

—Rogers Cadenhead

APPENDIX D
Using the MinGW C++ Compiler on Windows

This book works with any programming tool or integrated development environment (IDE) that supports C++14, the current version of the C++ programming language. If you already have an IDE such as Microsoft Visual Studio or C++ Builder and you know it supports C++14, you can use it and stop reading this appendix right now.

A popular and free option for Windows users who want to learn C++ is the GCC compiler, part of an open source programming toolkit for the language. GCC, which is available for Windows, Mac OS, and Linux, is a set of programs that are used in a command window instead of a graphical user interface. You edit programs in any text editor you like, then type commands to make the C++ compiler and linker create a program's executable code.

GCC is included in MinGW, a set of programs called Minimalist GNU for Windows. In this appendix you learn how to download, install, and set up MinGW to work on a Windows computer.

Downloading MinGW-w64

The most up-to-date version of MinGW for Windows is MinGW-64, which can be downloaded from the project's SourceForge repository at http://sourceforge.net/projects/mingw-w64. This site holds a lot of files, including the source code for advanced programmers to examine and modify, but all you need is the program's main installation file for Windows.

Click the Files link in the navigation bar (which also includes links such as Summary, Support, and Wiki).

A page opens listing the project's folders and files. Near the top, there should be a line that reads "Looking for the latest version?" followed by a link with the text **Download Official MinGW-w64 installer**. Click this link. The MinGW-64 download should begin automatically after a few seconds.

(If you can't find this link, try http://sourceforge.net/projects/mingw-w64/files/latest/download?source=files.)

This download is an installation wizard. Run it to begin installing the software.

The wizard presents you with setup settings such as Version, Architecture, and Build Revision. As a new user of MinGW-w64, you can click Next to accept the default values for these settings.

You are asked for a destination folder in which to store the software. Instead of using the default value, here's a better choice: In the Destination Folder text field, type **C:\MinGW**, as shown in Figure D.1. (This assumes that `C:\` is your main drive, as it is for most Windows users.)

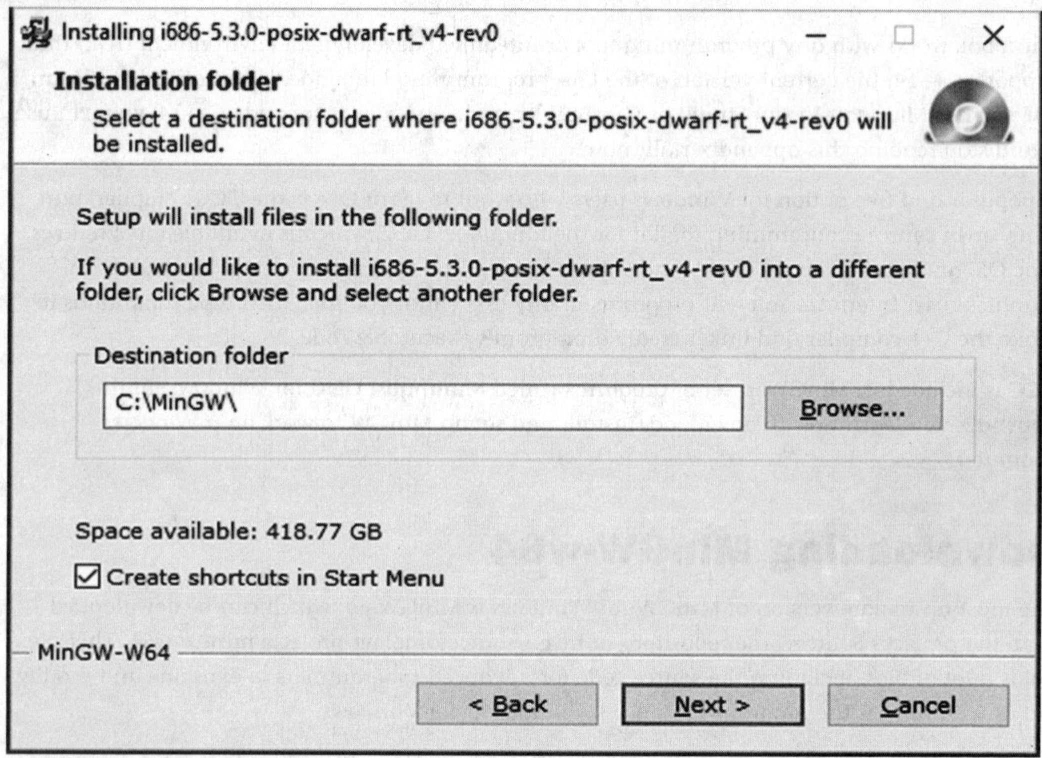

FIGURE D.1
Choosing a folder for MinGW.

Click Next to install the software in the chosen folder. This process is tracked by a progress bar, and when it's complete, click Finish to close the wizard.

After the software has been installed, you must manually configure Path, a Windows environment variable.

Setting the Path Environment Variable

The MinGW tools are used in a command window. For these commands to work, Windows must know where the GCC compiler and the other tools can be found.

These tools are in the `bin` subfolder inside the project's main folder.

If you chose `C:\MinGW` as the main folder, the tools are in `C:\MinGW\mingw32\bin`.

This folder must be included in Path, an environment variable that contains a list of folders. Windows uses Path to locate programs when you type a command.

There's an Environment Variables dialog in the Control Panel.

On Windows 10, set the Path variable with these steps:

1. In the Search box on the task bar, enter **environment**. A list of search results appears above the box.
2. One of the top search results is **Enter environment variables for your account**. Click this result. The System Properties dialog opens.
3. Click the Environment Variables button. A dialog with that title opens.
4. In the System Variables pane, scroll down and choose **Path**, then click the Edit button below the System Variables pane. The Edit Environment Variables dialog appears.
5. The Edit Environment Variables dialog lists all the folders in the Path. To add a new folder, click the New button. An entry opens up at the bottom of the list, as shown in Figure D.2.

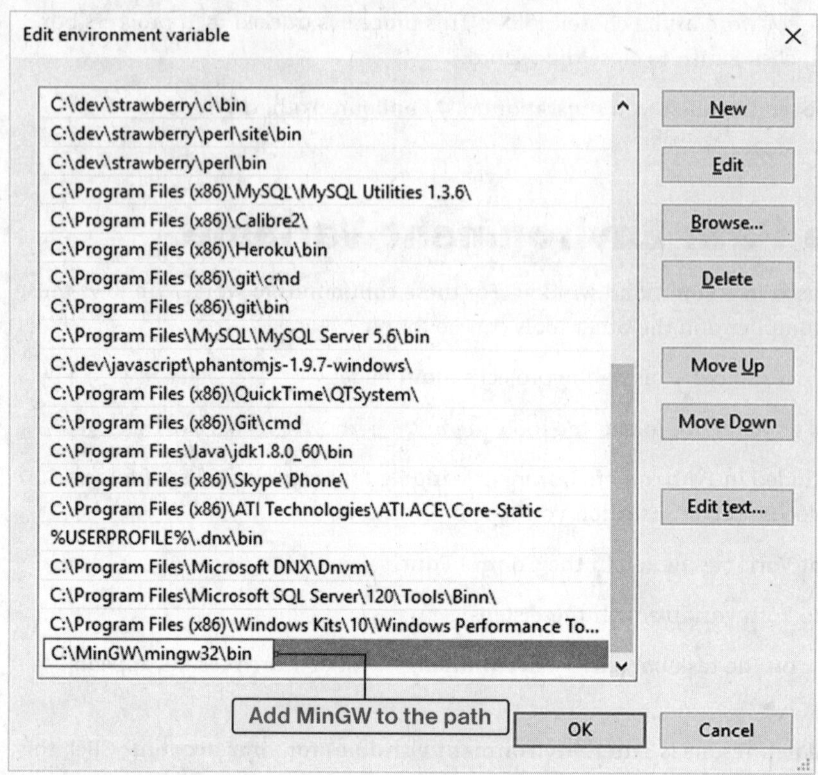

FIGURE D.2
Editing the Path system variable.

Add MinGW to the Path

6. Enter the location of the MinGW tools, **C:\MinGW\mingw32\bin**, and hit Enter. This folder is added to the list at the bottom.
7. Because there might be an older version of GCC on your computer, it's a good idea to move it to the top. Select **C:\MinGW\mingw32\bin** and click the Move Up button repeatedly until it is the first item in the list.
8. Click OK to close the dialog, OK to close the Environment Variables dialog, and OK to close the System Variables dialog.

The location of MinGW has been added to your path. Proceed to the section "Testing Your Installation."

On earlier versions of Windows, set the Path variable with these steps:

1. On the Start menu, right-click Computer or My Computer, then choose Properties from the pop-up menu that appears.
2. Click the **Advanced system settings** link. The System Properties dialog opens.
3. Click the Environment Variables button. The Environment Variables dialog opens.
4. In the System Variables pane, scroll down until you see the Path item.
5. Choose Path, then click the Edit button under the System Variables pane.
6. The Edit System Variable dialog opens (Figure D.3).

FIGURE D.3
Editing the Path system variable.

7. In the Variable Value field, move the cursor all the way to the left.
8. At that cursor position, enter the location of the MinGW tools, **C:\MinGW\mingw32\bin**, and click OK.

This adds MinGW to your path.

After changing the path, close any command windows you currently have open and then open a new window.

Testing Your Installation

MinGW requires the use of a command window to compile C++ programs, run them, and handle other tasks.

A command window is a way to operate a computer by typing commands using the keyboard, rather than using the mouse. Few programs designed for Windows users require the command window today.

To get to a command window in Windows, do one of the following:

- On Windows 10, enter Command Prompt in the search box, then click the Command Prompt icon.
- On Windows 8, choose Start, click the Search magnifying glass icon at upper-right, enter Command Prompt in the search box, and click the Command Prompt icon.
- On Windows 7, Vista, XP, or Server 2003, choose Start, All Programs, Accessories, Command Prompt.
- On Windows 98 or Me, choose Start, Programs, MS-DOS Prompt.
- On Windows NT or 2000, choose Start, Programs, Accessories, Command Prompt.

When you open a command window, it displays a line where you can type commands, as seen in Figure D.4.

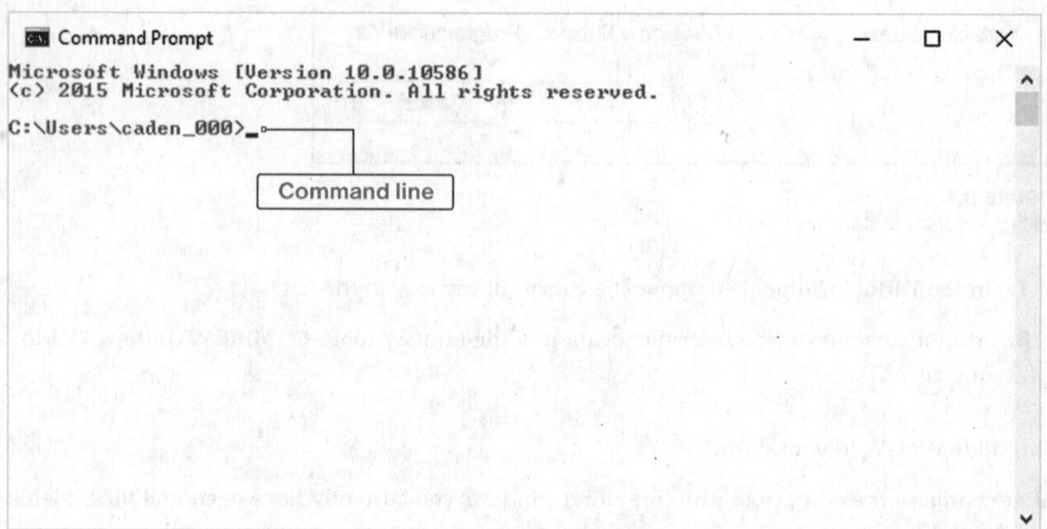

FIGURE D.4
Using a newly opened command-line window.

Command line

The command window uses commands adopted from MS-DOS, the Microsoft operating system that preceded Windows. MS-DOS supports the same functions as Windows—copying, moving, and deleting files and folders; running programs; scanning and repairing a hard drive; formatting a floppy disk; and so on.

In the window, a cursor blinks on the command line whenever you can type in a new command. In Figure D.4, `C:\Users\caden_000>` is the command line.

Because MS-DOS can be used to delete files and even format your hard drive, you should learn something about the operating system before experimenting with its commands.

However, you need to know only a few things about MS-DOS to use MinGW: how to create a folder, how to open a folder, and how to run a program.

Opening Folders in MS-DOS

When you are using MS-DOS on a Windows system, you have access to all the folders you normally use in Windows. For example, if you have a Windows folder on your C: hard drive, the same folder is accessible as `C:\Windows` from a command line.

To open a folder in MS-DOS, type the command `CD`, followed by the name of the folder, and press Enter. Here's an example:

```
CD C:\Temp
```

When you enter this command, the Temp folder on your system's C: drive is opened, if it exists. After you open a folder, the command line is updated with the name of that folder, as shown in Figure D.5.

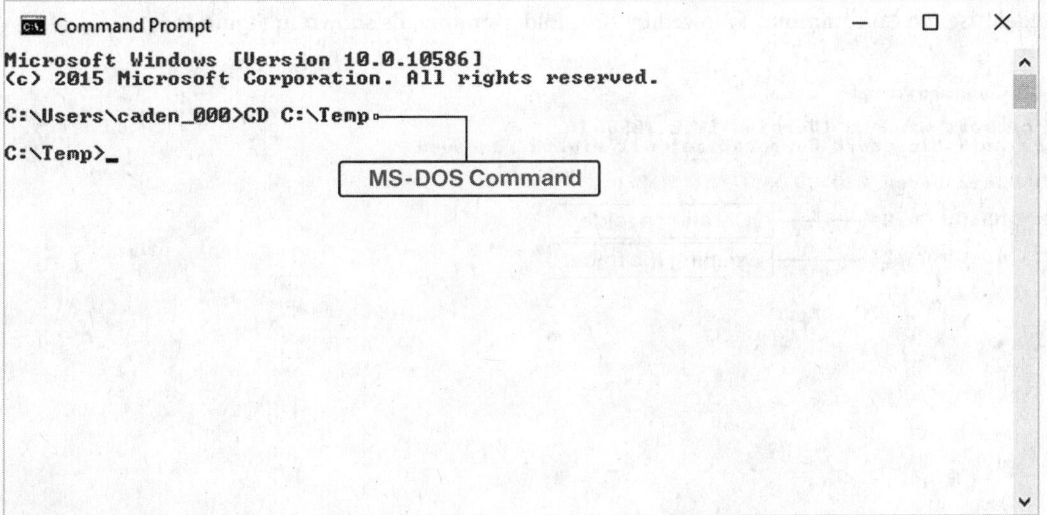

FIGURE D.5
Opening a folder in a command-line window.

MS-DOS command

You also can use the `CD` command in other ways:

- Type `CD \` to open the root folder on the current hard drive.
- Type `CD` *foldername* to open a subfolder matching the name you've used in place of *foldername*, if that subfolder exists.
- Type `CD ..` to open the folder that contains the current folder. For example, if you are in `C:\Windows\Fonts` and you use the `CD ..` command, `C:\Windows` is opened.
- It's helpful to create a folder for the programs you create in this book, such as one named `Cpp24`. If you already have done this, you can switch to that folder by using the following commands:

```
CD \

CD Cpp24
```

If you haven't created that folder yet, you can do so using an MS-DOS command.

Creating Folders in MS-DOS

To create a folder from a command line, type the command `MD` followed by the folder's name, and press Enter, as in the following example:

```
MD C:\Stuff
```

The Stuff folder is created in the root folder of the system's C: drive. To open a newly created folder, use the `CD` command followed by that folder's name, as shown in Figure D.6.

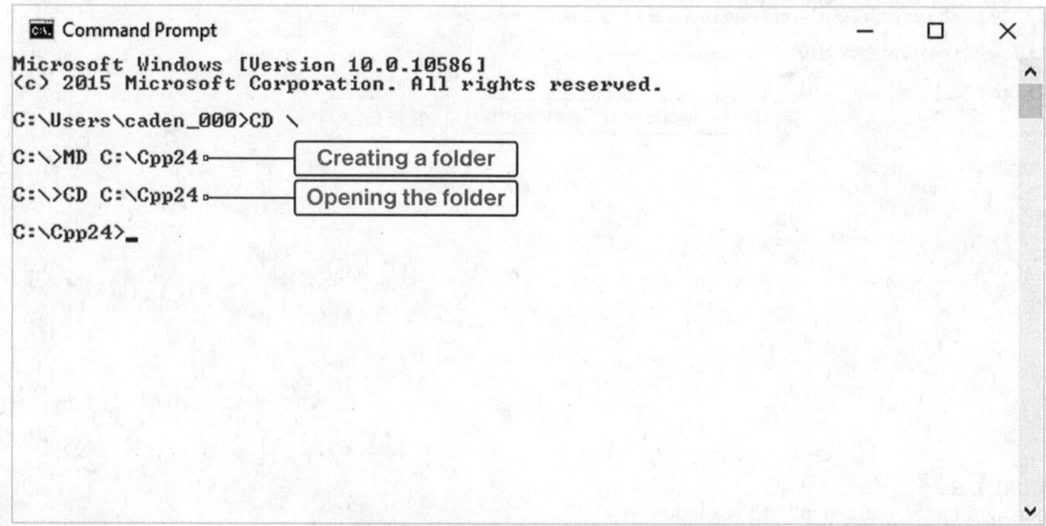

FIGURE D.6
Creating a new folder in a command-line window.

Creating a folder

Opening the folder

If you haven't already created a `Cpp24` folder, you can do so from a command line:

1. Change to the root folder (using the `CD \` command).
2. Type the command `MD C:\Cpp24` and press Enter.

After `C:\Cpp24` has been created, you can go to it at any time from a command line by using this command:

```
CD \Cpp24
```

The last thing you need to learn about MS-DOS to use MinGW is how to run programs.

Running Programs in MS-DOS

The simplest way to run a program at the command line is to type its name and press Enter. For example, type `DIR` and press Enter to see a list of files and subfolders in the current folder.

You also can run a program by typing its name followed by a space and some options that control how the program runs. These options are called *arguments*.

To see an example of this, change to the root folder (using `CD \`) and type `DIR Cpp24`. You'll see a list of files and subfolders contained in the Cpp24 folder, if it contains any.

After you have installed MinGW, run the GCC compiler to see that it works. Type the following command at a command line:

```
g++ --version
```

`g++` is the name of the GCC compiler, and `--version` is an argument that tells it to display its version number.

You can see an example of this in Figure D.7, but your version number might be different, depending on what version of the kit you have installed.

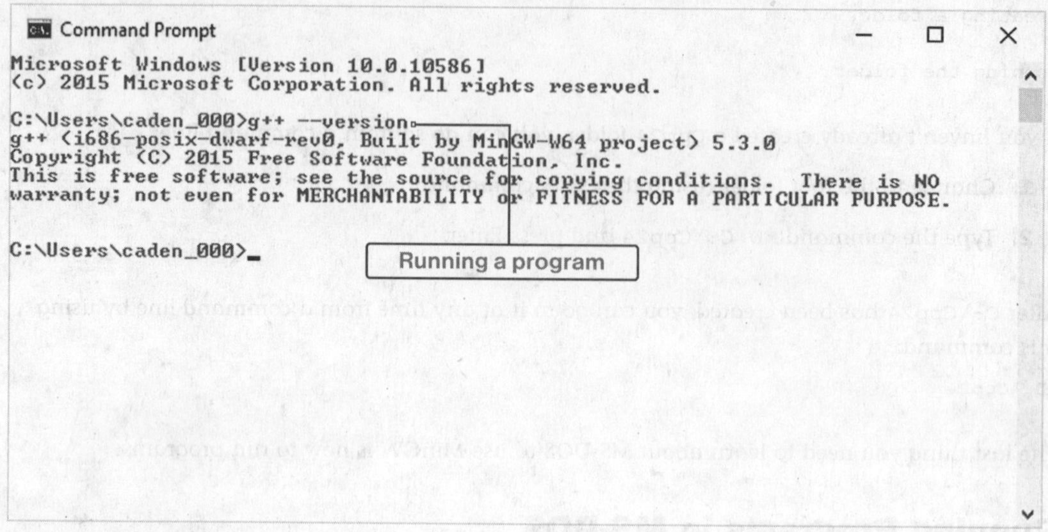

FIGURE D.7
Running GCC in a command window.

`Running a program`

If you see an incorrect version number or a "Bad command or filename" error after running `g++ --version`, you need to check that the folder you added to Path for MinGW exists and contains the program g++.exe.